Sweet Chariot

THE FRED W. MORRISON SERIES

IN SOUTHERN STUDIES

The University of

North Carolina Press

Chapel Hill & London

ANN PATTON MALONE

Sweet Chariot

Slave Family and Household Structure in Nineteenth-Century Louisiana

© 1992 The University of North Carolina Press

Manufactured in the United States of America

96   95   94   93   92

5   4   3   2   1

Library of Congress Cataloging-in-Publication Data

Malone, Ann Patton.

Sweet chariot : slave family and household structure in nineteenth-century Louisiana / Ann Patton Malone.

   p.   cm. — (The Fred W. Morrison series in Southern studies)

Includes bibliographical references (p.   ) and index.

ISBN 0-8078-2026-1 (cloth : alk. paper)

1. Slaves—Louisiana—Family relationships. 2. Louisiana—Population—History—19th century. 3. Afro-Americans—Louisiana—History—19th century.   I. Title.   II. Series

E445.L8M35   1992

305.5′67′09763—dc20   91-50787

CIP

Portions of chapters 1 and 2 appeared in somewhat different form in Ann Patton Malone, "Searching for the Family and Household Structure of Rural Louisiana Slaves, 1810–1864," *Louisiana History* 28 (Fall 1987): 357–79. Reprinted as "The Family and Household Structure of Rural Louisiana Slaves, 1810–1864," in *Women and the Family in a Slave Society*, edited by Paul Finkelman, © by Garland Publishing Company. Reprinted with permission of the publishers.

IN MEMORY OF

ODESSA ANDERSON AND

NEIL SHIPMAN

◆ CONTENTS ◆

A section of illustrations follows page 202.

TABLES, FIGURES, & MAPS

TABLES

FIGURES

MAPS

This study of family and household composition among slaves of rural Louisiana benefited greatly from the aid and support of several individuals and institutions. In the research phase, invaluable assistance was rendered by the staffs of the Southern Historical Collection at the University of North Carolina, the Archives Division of the Louisiana State University, and the Morgan City Library and Archives, Morgan City, Louisiana. Equally important in the expeditious use of my limited time and funds were the clerks of court and their assistants in parishes throughout rural Louisiana and counties in Kentucky and New Jersey. Three individuals should be mentioned by name for leading me to important sources that might otherwise have been overlooked. They are the late Dudley A. Sisk of Lexington, Kentucky; Mrs. Lela King Kehman, Archivist, Morgan City Archives; and Mrs. Elizabeth Dart, St. Francisville, Louisiana.

A large personal and intellectual debt is owed to several professors with whom I studied at Tulane University. The first is Bennett H. Wall, who taught a fellow southerner to view our sectional history in a more comprehensive manner, required me to keep my feet on the ground, and provided unstinting encouragement and inspiration. The second is the late Professor Peter Cominos, who first introduced me to the social history perspective, both in concept and methodology. The third is the late Professor Hugh F. Rankin, whose scholarly example and ability to tell a good tale without sacrificing analytical content inspired me.

The true motivators behind this work, and any of my work on working folk of the South and the institutions they devised to keep pride intact and hope alive, are the numerous men and women of quiet courage whom I have met in Texas, Louisiana, and Georgia during four decades of residence there. Among these are two, both now deceased, to whom this work is dedicated—Odessa Anderson, an African-American woman of indomitable spirit of Darst Creek, Texas, and a Georgian, Neil Shipman, grandson and namesake of a remarkable freedman turpentine worker whose refusal to accept anything less than full citizenship led to his murder.

Jerry W. DeVine and Michael Erdman of Tifton and Albany, Georgia, provided technical assistance and advice on the quantification aspects of the study. Sharon Hagan was as patient as she was efficient in typing a long, involved manuscript. Glenn Conrad, Orville Vernon Burton, Bennett H. Wall, and John B. Boles made many valuable and warmly appreciated suggestions. A special thanks must go to my skillful and understanding copyeditor, Trudie Calvert.

Finally, I must gratefully acknowledge the support and encouragement of friends who lifted my flagging spirits on many occasions—Rose Koppel, Neva Wall, Jerry and Becky DeVine, Eloise Hester, Bobbie Walker, Beth Lange, Terri Ryburn-Lamonte, Carl and Gloria Ekberg, Marie Gordon, Enoch Williams, and my family—Gail and Charley Batey, Bart Baenziger, Tori Farr and Cody Farr-Baenziger, Julie Baenziger, Yvette Robinson, and Jeff Baenziger.

Sweet Chariot

The slave community of the old Hercules O'Connor plantation in West Feliciana Parish had been evolving since the 1790s. It was strong and stable by the 1820s, almost all of its people descendants of the original workers. Late in that decade, under pressure from creditors and relations, the long-widowed owner, Rachel O'Connor, now old and ailing, transferred titles for seventeen of her slaves to her half-brother and heir David Weeks, who lived in the bayou-laced sugar country a hundred miles away.[1] Weeks and his wife, owners of the elegant Shadows in St. Mary Parish, had many slaves; therefore, the widow consoled herself that—during her lifetime at least—the paper transfer would not seriously affect her "black family."

But almost immediately, labor shortages and other economic exigencies connected with the start-up of another sugar operation convinced Weeks to request the "loan" of his O'Connor slaves. The dismemberment of the old community began. One of the first to go was a middle-aged slave the people called Sam Rock, a widower with several grown or half-grown children and a host of close kin. Sam Rock was a man whom white people described as a pillar of his community but slaves often called the root; he evoked a comforting image of one who not only provided his family and community with guidance and strength in their daily lives but who also helped anchor them to their cultural values and historical identity. We can imagine Sam Rock assuring the bewildered group congregated in the quarters before his departure that he would be gone for just a little while—a few months—that he only had to help Master David get his new place going, then he would come back home. Meanwhile, his son Leven would take care of things. The people of the O'Connor plantation did not see Sam Rock for ten years. He returned for a short visit in 1841 but was soon sent back to the Weeks's island plantation, Grand Cote, and eventually died there.[2]

After Sam Rock left, many of strong young sons from the old families were also called away, a few at a time. In their late teens, most of the young men had never been away from the plantation on which they were born. In response to the series of transfers, the O'Connor slave community—like a wooden top receiving a glancing blow that interrupted its steady whir—

wobbled and tottered on its fragile axis, uncertain about its absent members' return and fearful as to who might leave next. The elderly slaves, former allies of the mistress with whom they had shared a lifetime, now avoided her or served her in stony silence. Friends and relatives of the transfers mourned, and each new departure reopened the wounds of severance. On Grand Cote, several of the O'Connor young men made a risky effort to find their way back to their home plantation though they were woefully ignorant of the geography involved. They reached their destination but were recovered, sent back, and punished for absconding.[3]

Leven, left in charge by his father, did indeed provide responsible and reassuring leadership in the traumatic decade after Sam Rock left. He served as his old mistress's overseer and was trusted and loved by the people. But in August 1840, he was stricken with fever and died. The next day the people buried him cradling in his arms an infant daughter who died the same night. Reeling from ten years of uncertainty and painful separation, the community reacted severely to this and other losses occasioned by natural causes. Sam Rock's mistress observed that "Sam's children keep asking about their father more than usual since they lost their elder brother Leven."[4] Each additional death magnified the O'Connor slaves' near-desperate desire for family reunification and a return to community solidarity. Perhaps the unrest and the persistent pleading for contact with those sent away led to Sam Rock's one visit, in 1841, which his old mistress again recorded: "Old Sam Rock arrived safe. The poor old man mourns the death of his son Leven and his daughter that died last year. Otherwise his joy would have no bounds. I felt much overcome at seeing him and his children meet."[5]

David Weeks died in 1834, and Rachel O'Connor followed by June 1846. Estate documents show that only one or two of the O'Connor slaves sent to Grand Cote ever returned home to Feliciana and that Weeks's heirs sold several men in St. Mary as "bad subjects."[6]

The story of the O'Connor slave community provides an example of the natural tendency among enslaved folk to form stable families, households, and communities; the extreme vulnerability of even the most stable slave communities; the great value slaves placed on family ties and community cohesion; a sometimes reluctant but obvious recognition by owners of their slaves' intense familial attachments; and a persistent urge within a fragmented slave community to reunite or rebuild despite the pain associated with such efforts and adjustments. These tendencies will be explored in this book, although from a more analytical perspective.

Recent historians of slavery in the United States have added greatly to our understanding of the characteristics, forms, and functions associated with the slave family and the plantation community. Indeed, the slave family of the nineteenth-century South has been the focus of a lively historical debate for more than three decades, much of it over the relative stability and longevity of the slave family and the degree to which it was matrifocal.[7] Despite these revisionist works and their sometimes biased but often solidly researched predecessors, much remains unknown about the structure of slave families, households, and communities.

Perhaps the reason for this neglect is that the history of household organization is still a relatively new field for United States historians. Early historians of slavery and the South were little concerned with the slaves' internal society. The pioneering works of Kenneth Stampp, Stanley Elkins, and David Brion Davis in the 1950s and 1960s changed the focus of the debate, and in the 1970s a spate of major works reinterpreted slavery from the perspective of slaves as well as owners. These studies did not, however, delve into slave household organization in any depth. No broad syntheses and few monographs have analyzed United States slave community structures using the analytical procedures popularized by the Cambridge Group for the History of Population and Social Structure in England and employed by demographic historians throughout the industrialized world.[8] Robert Fogel and Stanley Engerman's provocative attempt to interpret American slavery through the use of statistical analysis in *Time on the Cross* (1974) promoted a healthy reevaluation. But in that wide-ranging and significant work, the authors did not analyze slave family and household composition in their brief chapter on the slave family. Eugene Genovese, in his monumental qualitative study of American slavery, *Roll, Jordan, Roll,* also published in 1974, adroitly discussed the roles, values, and relative stability of the slave family, but he did not deeply investigate how slaves were structured into families, households, and residential units. Herbert Gutman went beyond description of slave family roles and adaptive devices and sought analytical models for slave family development in *The Black Family in Slavery and Freedom* (1976). He analyzed a few slave communities in Mississippi, Alabama, and Louisiana, but his most detailed household analysis was of postbellum African Americans. His structural analysis of slave communities, though informative, dealt more directly with kinship than household composition. John Blassingame's way-pointing book *The Slave Community*, appearing in 1972, did not directly consider structural aspects. The few historians who have analyzed the domestic arrangements of slave communities have generally studied only one or two communities in the eighteenth-century Chesapeake region or in the Caribbean.[9]

These general works and a large number of monographs, articles, and dissertations on slave demographic topics have told us much about the roles and functions of slave families and communities.[10] A gap still remains, however, in our knowledge of how slaves of the southern United States organized into domestic units and how that organization developed or changed over time. *Sweet Chariot* seeks to address that omission.

First, the book tests recent studies of slavery with regard to one major aspect of slave life in a particular region—how bondspeople organized into families, households, and communities and how that organization was influenced over time by internal and external factors. Second, it describes patterns in Louisiana slave family household organization and distinguishes those family household types that were most significant and representative, as well as those that consistently acted as indicators of change. Third, it projects a simple statistical model of Louisiana slave household organization that can be used for comparison with other populations. Fourth, it demonstrates how slave structures might vary from the model according to time intervals, size of slaveholding, or the type of agriculture in which the slaves worked. And fifth, it argues that though models may be constructed, they must be developmental, always evolving and adapting—although in fairly rational and predictable ways.

Perhaps equally useful to the reader will be a review of what is not attempted in this volume. It does not substantially explore African or Caribbean influences on familial patterns or roles in slave society. Nor does it address in detail the influence of religion or white domestic arrangements on the slave family. These subjects are of immense importance and have been at least partially explored by Genovese, Gutman, and John B. Boles in reference to the South as a whole and by C. Peter Ripley, Joe Gray Taylor, and others in regard to Louisiana.[11] This book seeks to contribute to and complement more generalized social and cultural studies by providing, for one slave state, a framework of slave domestic organization upon which other historians can reconstruct the complex, multidimensional organism of slave domestic life. I am confident that the models and patterns of slave family and household organization presented here are representative of nineteenth-century Louisiana. Evidence that I have analyzed thus far suggests that they will hold for other lower South, expansive, nineteenth-century slave states. But whether they will represent upper South slave communities or eighteenth-century slave societies remains to be determined. I have begun such a comparison, but for now, I make no such claim.

Two persistent themes in this book may, on the surface, appear contradictory—the mutability and yet the constancy of Louisiana slave household organization. The slave family (and its extensions, the slave household and community) was far more diverse and adaptable than previously believed. In nineteenth-century Louisiana, its forms were plastic, not fixed; its structure was organic, not static. Slave domestic organization molded to fit the changing requirements and circumstances of the community. In spite of the viability and diversity of their domestic arrangements, Louisiana slaves exhibited constants both in their preferred household forms and in the general developmental patterns that they displayed in their unending search for stable social organizations and sustained familial relationships.

Although always under alteration, slave communities of Louisiana, and probably everywhere in the South, had an unenunciated collective vision of the structure that would provide the desirable framework of their internal social order. Their society was to be a closely knit and interrelated collection of simple families, built around couples and parents (or a parent) and their children and often grandchildren as well. These families would form the heart of the preferred society, but singles would be well integrated into the larger tribal community, whether they were young and unattached, old and widowed, or individuals who had never married. Essential to this vision was generational depth—requiring the presence of both children and elders in abundance. This profile was observed in the most mature and stable Louisiana slave communities. The vision is similar to that of the Western, European-derived ideal except that it is more tolerant of solitaires and more accepting of single-parent family households and multiple family households as normal and contributing to the community.

The themes of mutability and constancy will be found in every chapter and on almost every page of *Sweet Chariot*. They emerged from both the measurable and the impressionistic evidence. Indeed, the title of the book, derived from the words of a slave spiritual, was chosen because it suggested the dual themes. Religious faith often provided a "sweet chariot" for people living under a degrading, dehumanizing system of forced and permanent servitude. That same imagery could be applied to their family, household, and community structure. That chariot was constructed from human materials—individuals, families, and kin welded into a cohesive unit or community. These domestic groups provided slaves with a protective structure, a defensive building, a fluid, adaptive fortress on wheels—a chariot. This invisible chariot was not impenetrable, but it was strong and mobile, often enabling its occupants to elude or survive attacks. Just as many slaves had faith that God's love would be sufficient to carry his people home to a heavenly reward, they depended upon the affection and support they received in their domestic organizations to enable them to survive the dangers and humiliations of slavery with a semblance of dignity and belonging.

Two models emerged from my study of Louisiana slave households. One of these is a very simple statistical model derived from a quantitative study of more than one hundred Louisiana slave communities studied over time. The second is a developmental model that demonstrates persistent patterns in the evolution of slave families, households, and communities.

To gauge patterns in household composition, I conducted a search in plantation and parish records for documents showing slave family relationships and household designations. The result was a sample of 155 slave communities representing 26 parishes located in all of the major slaveholding regions of the state over a period of fifty-four years. The data were drawn from a variety of sources but primarily from probate court records such as inventories and appraisements, estate partitions, and estate sales bills, as well as conveyances of plantations with the entire slave community attached, plantation records, private papers, and correspondence. In short, inventories of communities were drawn from any reliable source yielding a full listing of slaves belonging to a definable, recognized unit and also indicating familial or household relationships.[12] Hundreds more inventories did not list slaves so that relationships could not be determined; more often than not, enumerators listed slaves by gender groups without noting full familial relationships. Unless relationships could be reliably determined through linkage with other records, such communities were not included in the sample. The resulting data were analyzed according to total numbers, total numbers of males and females, and sums, means, and percentages in all standard family household types and categories according to an adaptation of the typology employed first by the Cambridge Group.[13] The first section of this book will present and analyze the findings from this study. The entire book will attempt to explain what the statistical model means for Louisiana slaves' attempts to achieve stability and sustenance in their primary groups. But before proceeding, a few definitions are in order.

The simple family—Peter Laslett uses the term *simple family* to "cover what is variously described as the nuclear family, the elementary family or (not very logically, since spouses are not physiologically connected), the biological family." A conjugal link (husband-wife or parent-child) must be present in all cases. Additionally, as Laslett explains, "for a simple family to appear . . . it is necessary for at least two individuals connected by that link or arising from it to be coresident."[14] In the Louisiana sample, simple families are those made up of married couples without children present, married couples with offspring, or single persons with offspring.[15] Historians and laypeople alike often misuse the term *nuclear family* to refer only to the form of the simple family consisting of both parents and their child or children. In fact, all simple families are nuclear in form. To avoid further confusion, I will use the term *standard nuclear family* when referring to full nuclear units—those composed of fathers, mothers, and their offspring. The term *nuclear* will also include the so-called truncated nuclear families, those composed of married couples without children in their households and single-parent households.[16]

The solitaire household—According to Laslett, "no solitary can form a conjugal family unit."[17] Therefore, the solitary unit cannot be considered a family, but it is a household. Solitaires can be single, widowed, or of unknown marital status. They can be part of a kinship group, but to be considered part of a family or another household, they must share residence with it. Otherwise, no matter how many brothers, sisters, aunts, uncles, grown children, or parents are part of the solitaire's community, the solitaire constitutes a household.[18]

Non-nuclear family households—Laslett refers to this as a "no family" category, but others describe the classification as "non-nuclear," which seems more appropriate because some of the members are related although they do not form the conjugal unit of husband-wife or parent-child.[19] In the Louisiana sample, non-nuclear households could be of three kinds: co-resident siblings (brothers and/or sisters forming a household together without spouses or children present), other co-resident relatives (again, without spouses or children), and co-residents who were not related but resided together and perceived themselves as a unit.

Extended family households—The complex forms found on Louisiana plantations were extended family households and multiple family households. Laslett defines extended family households as those consisting of a "conjugal family unit with the addition of one or more relatives other than offspring."[20] Households exhibiting upward extension are those in which an older-generation relative resides in a household headed by a younger-generation relative. An example would be that of a husband and wife absorbing one of their parents into their household. Downward-extended households were more common in the sample. An illustration would be a couple with a grandchild whose parents were absent. In a laterally extended household a same-generation relative lived with a simple nuclear family. An example would be a couple with a sibling of one spouse living in the household.

Multiple family households—A more significant complex form among the sampled slaves was the multiple family household. The secondary unit (second "family") could be extended upward, downward, or laterally. The form encountered most frequently was that of downward disposition, which commonly consisted of a nuclear family unit plus an unmarried daughter and grandchild, the latter two forming the second "family" or conjugal unit. Laslett defined multiple family households as those that "comprise all forms of domestic groups which include two or more conjugal units connected by kinship or marriage."[21]

The methods used and the subjects explored in this volume might be unfamiliar to some readers and require a rather complicated organization. The book is divided into three parts. The three chapters in Part I present the findings from the broad quantitative study. These chapters are statistical in nature and serve as a necessary backdrop for the increasingly personalized chapters that follow.

Part II seeks in three chapters to communicate the evolutionary nature of individual slave communities by examining the changing organizations of three Louisiana slave communities, those of Oakland, Petite Anse, and Tiger Island plantations. Collective studies can effectively demonstrate how slaves were generally organized into households and can be used to suggest how and why that organization responded to demographic and economic trends. The statistical data explained in Part I will acquaint readers with such patterns. These numbers alone, however, reveal little about the individual slaves and masters who resided on the sampled plantations. Comprehension of causation through collective statistics is necessarily limited to the general rather than the specific, and questions still remain. Specifically, how were the family, household, and community organizations of Louisiana slaves affected by their owners' choices or financial situation? How much could slaves influence their own household structure? Did owners' deaths or migration decisions directly affect slave kinship development or community cohesion? Precisely what was the impact on slave communities of such external events as the Panics of 1819 or 1837 or the Civil War? These questions can be adequately dealt with only through microcosmic study of individual slave communities as they evolved and adapted over time. Therefore, Part II examines in detail three slave communities over several generations.

In Part III, two chapters put the quantitative study and the case studies in the larger context of slavery in Louisiana and the United States.

If the organization seems less than uniform, the reader should bear in mind that the book proceeds from the presentation of quantitative findings to those that are increasingly qualitative, usually combining the two. It proceeds from a general, statistical approach to one that is far more specific and localized and only partly statistical to (in the last part) one that is again general but primarily nonstatistical and qualitative. And it proceeds from an analytical approach in Part I to a combination of analytical and descriptive approaches in Part II, to an almost entirely descriptive and narrative approach in Part III.

In all sections, however, the book addresses the same simple question: How might the ways his or her community was organized into families and households affect the quality of life for a slave of nineteenth-century Louisiana?

PART I
The Collective Experience and Louisiana Slave Household Organization

CHAPTER ONE

Family and Household Organization

Sweet Chariot focuses on a single aspect of the experience of slavery in rural Louisiana—the ways slaves were constituted into families and households within a community. Recent scholarship has contributed a rich storehouse of information, slave biographies and the oral histories of former slaves have provided a personal perspective, and collections of planters' papers have proved invaluable. But even with all of these resources to draw upon, historians have found slave family, household, and community structure very difficult to describe with certitude. One is reminded of Peter Laslett's now-famous question that in the late 1960s helped launch a new area of social history in Britain—did our ancestors have enough to eat?[1] Just as bookshelves were filled with volumes detailing the lives and activities of kings and Parliament in seventeenth-century England, and yet very little was known about life among the common folk, so too we have little reliable information concerning one of the most basic elements of slave society: how slaves were organized into fundamental units of affection and support. To gain some insight into this problem, a basic framework of slave domestic organization was constructed through statistical analysis of slave communities in Louisiana. The major purpose of the statistical study was to arrive at a profile of slave household composition in rural Louisiana, 1810–64, the latter year being the last in which enough slave inventories were available to constitute a reliable set. The statistical profile that evolved is illustrated in table 1.1 and figure 1.1. One important clarification must be made before proceeding. Most historians of the family are primarily interested in the numbers and percentages of units belonging to each family household type in a sampled society because they are tracing the development of household forms. Although that information was generated, its analysis was not among the objectives of this study. I am more interested in the social reality—determining how many slaves were part of the various household types. I am only incidentally concerned with the evolution and variations of household types.

Explaining the meaning of the statistical model in terms of Louisiana slaves' attempts to achieve stability and sustenance in their primary groups will engage the whole of this book, but the statistical findings can be quickly summarized. As can be seen in figure 1.1, nearly three-fourths of the sampled slaves were members of simple families, 6 percent lived in multiple family households, 2 percent were in extended family households, 1 percent formed non-nuclear households, and 18.3 percent were solitaires. For these broad categories, the data yielded few surprises or significant variations from conclusions arrived at by other historians. The most significant household types for Louisiana slaves were—in order—simple family, solitaire, and multiple family households; extended and non-nuclear forms had no numerical significance.

The simple family was the dominant household type among both slave and free populations of the nineteenth-century United States. Indeed, it has been called the prevailing household type for the whole of Western society for several centuries. It is not surprising, therefore, that nearly three-fourths of Louisiana slaves were organized into various classifications of the type (see figure 1.2). How slaves were grouped *within* this broad designation is of considerable significance. How many of the slaves formed part of families with both parents present? How many were part of households headed by only one parent, and how often was this single parent an unmarried mother? The debate around these questions will be discussed in the concluding chapter.

In the Louisiana sample, slightly fewer than one-half of the sampled slaves of all ages were members of standard nuclear family households,

TABLE 1.1.

Household Composition among Rural Louisiana Slaves, 1810–1864

Household type	Total slaves	Number of units	Percent of total units in type	Mean n slaves	Mean size of unit	Percent of total slaves in type
Solitaire						
Females	553.0	553.0	13.9	3.5	1	5.4
Males	1,328.0	1,328.0	33.3	8.5	1	12.9
Non-nuclear						
Co-resident siblings	90.0	33.0	0.8	0.5	2.7	0.9
Co-resident relatives	–	–	–	–	–	–
Unrelated co-residents	33.0	9.0	0.2	0.2	3.6	0.3
Simple family						
Married couple alone	836.0	418.0	10.5	5.3	2.0	8.1
Married couple with children	5,034.0	1,023.0	25.6	32.4	4.9	48.7
Single female with children	1,493.0	439.0	11.0	9.6	3.4	14.5
Single male with children	183.0	57.0	1.4	1.1	3.2	1.8
Extended family						
Extended up	28.0	5.0	0.1	0.1	5.6	0.3
Extended down	55.0	14.0	0.4	0.3	3.9	0.5
Extended laterally	113.0	23.0	0.6	0.7	4.9	1.0
Multiple family						
Secondary unit up	34.0	7.0	0.2	0.2	4.8	0.3
Secondary unit down	510.0	72.0	1.8	3.2	7.0	4.9
Secondary unit lateral	39.0	8.0	0.2	0.2	4.8	0.3
Total	10,329.0	3,989.0	100.0	65.8		100.0

Source: Louisiana Slave Households Data Base.

FIGURE 1.1.

Louisiana Slaves in Major Family Household Types, 1810–1864, by Percentage

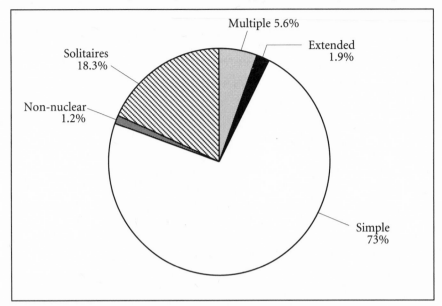

Source: Louisiana Slave Households Data Base.

either as parents or as children, but this does not necessarily mean that slave families were hopelessly unstable. Residence in a standard nuclear family for 50 percent (or more) of the members in a slave community usually indicated that the community was relatively stable and mature. Signs of instability generally appeared in Louisiana communities only when the percentage of individuals in standard nuclear families dropped below about 40 percent.

Does the fact that about half of the slaves in the sample did not form households containing both parents and children mean that the traditionalists were right—that a large percentage of slaves resided in mother-headed households? The prevalence of families headed by single mothers was widely exaggerated in the old literature of slavery. In fact, it was the "myth of the matriarchy" that prompted many of the new studies of the slave family.[2] This topic too will be extensively treated in the concluding chapter. As figure 1.2 shows, female-headed single-parent households did not predominate on most Louisiana holdings at any time, but the category encompassed 14.5 percent of the population. And in certain phases of slave

FIGURE 1.2.

Louisiana Slaves in Major Family Household Types, 1810–1864, with Simple Family Categories, by Percentage

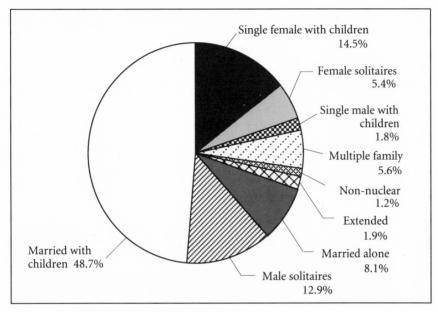

Single female with children
14.5%

Female solitaires
5.4%

Single male with children
1.8%

Multiple family
5.6%

Non-nuclear
1.2%

Extended
1.9%

Married alone
8.1%

Male solitaires
12.9%

Married with children 48.7%

Source: Louisiana Slave Households Data Base.

community development, the numbers and percentages of slaves living in matrifocal households were much higher. Male-headed single parent households were extremely rare, almost never as much as 2 percent of the slave population. To complete the profile of the simple family categories, about 8 percent of the sampled slaves lived in households consisting of childless couples or couples whose children had departed the household.

Although the simple family household (and its subtypes) is perhaps the most informative category in the makeup of slave communities of Louisiana, the structure of slave society cannot be fully understood without taking all categories into account. The second largest number of slaves belonged to a household type that was not technically a family at all, the solitaires. Slaves were as likely to be part of this no-family group as they were to be a part of a single-parent household. The solitaires in Louisiana were always a force to be reckoned with, and, as in the case of the female-headed households, they often made up a much larger percentage than the 18 percent indicated in the overall sample. This was particularly true in the early, expansive, and unstable stages of community development. Solitaires also tended to be male rather than female, revealing a gender imbalance that is not reflected in the slave population as a whole.

Non-nuclear, extended, and multiple family households embraced smaller percentages of slaves than the simple family and solitaire household types. The non-nuclear category was by far the least significant household type, containing only about 1 percent of the slaves sampled. Most of the small number of non-nuclear family households were made up of co-resident siblings. Extended family households encompassed only 2 percent of the slaves, with small percentages in each of the forms of extension. Slaves in the multiple family classification totaled about 6 percent of the sample. The only form encountered frequently was that of downward disposition; it involved 5 percent of the sampled slaves and was quite common in the later stages of community development because it involved three generations. Most commonly, it consisted of a nuclear family unit plus an unmarried daughter and grandchild, the latter two forming the second "family" or conjugal unit.

What does this composite profile mean for the experience of an "average" slave? First, it suggests that in nineteenth-century rural Louisiana a slave had less than a fifty-fifty chance of being part of a family consisting of children and both parents. This grim reality reflects the vulnerability of slave families to forced separations, but it also reflects a greater openness among slave families to alternative forms, a flexibility that slowly evolved from necessity. The odds are also influenced by a variable that has nothing to do with slavery—the high mortality rates in Louisiana that frequently separated mates and robbed children of at least one parent.

A second and more positive conclusion that can be drawn from the profile is that nearly three-quarters of the sampled slaves lived in households of blood relatives, in families that might consist of both parents and their children, or childless married couples, or single parents and their children, or some extended or multiple family unit, or even a household consisting of cousins or siblings. In some form, a family made up of very close kin residing together and identifying with each other met the psychological needs of a majority of Louisiana slaves and afforded as much protection as the system of slavery would allow.

It is true that roughly one-fifth of the sampled slaves had no discernible close relations, but solitaires were in no way excluded from a general sense of community. The multifaceted slave community indeed functioned as an extension of the conjugal family, as suggested by Blassingame, Genovese, Gutman, and others. United by shared circumstances, intimate working and living conditions, and a common set of cultural values, a slave residential and working unit generally developed into a supportive community within a few years, especially if even remote kinship was initially present. Though families predominated in the slave communities studied, no evidence was found to suggest that solitary members were shunned or stigmatized.

My statistical study supplemented by traditional research suggests that in their domestic organizations, as well as their cultural forms, Louisiana slaves found ways to take care of their own and to mitigate some of the harshness of life in slavery's shadow. Because slaves lacked the autonomy to form separate formalized institutions, informal education, socialization, religious activity, occupational training, courtship, and even internal governance often took place within the framework of their domestic organizations—the family, household, kinship group, and community. Domestic organizations provided slaves with a safe house where masks could be dropped. Perhaps the aspect of slaves' existence least recognized by their owners was the well-guarded richness and surprising strength of their family life and community structure.

The construction or model described in the foregoing pages was the composite household organization found among 10,329 slaves who lived in Louisiana from 1810 to 1864. It provides a profile, a useful "norm." But it represents a large and static time span and does not take into consideration variations in slave household structure within segments of that time span. Therefore, statistics were generated concerning household organization by decennial intervals, as well as by the size of the slaveholding and the geographic area and type of agriculture associated with the community. The first of these factors turned out to be of signal importance. The patterns that emerged when household development was related to decades contributed greatly to the development of a second model, which takes into account cyclical variations in slave household composition.

CHAPTER TWO

The Effects of
Periodization

The statistical model explained in Chapter 1 provides a profile of domestic organization found among more than ten
thousand slaves who lived in Louisiana during the course of
half a century. But much might depend upon when the slave
lived during that broad time span. To gauge whether slave
household composition varied significantly by time period,
the sampled communities were analyzed by decades.

LOUISIANA SLAVE HOUSEHOLD
COMPOSITION, 1810–1819

Among the broad external forces that shaped and influenced
the family and household composition of slaves in the 1810–
19 period the most compelling factor was demographic.
Masters and slaves poured into the shallow cup of the lower
Mississippi valley in a steady stream. The population of
Louisiana expanded more than 100 percent, a higher rate of
increase than in any subsequent decade.[1] People were lured
to Louisiana by cheap land, high cotton prices, and the
expectation of handsome profits for those who got to the
fresh land first, with sufficient labor to supply the ravenous

British market for cotton. Cotton was no newcomer to Louisiana; it had been grown as a staple since the 1740s, and French planters had employed a cotton gin fifty years before Eli Whitney's invention. But Whitney's more efficient, cheaper, and simpler gin of 1793 provided the impetus for highly profitable cotton production. The cotton boom began to gain momentum about 1795, and following the Louisiana Purchase, it contributed to a major agricultural and demographic expansion into the Southwest.[2]

Cotton was not the only profitable staple of early Louisiana. Indigo was another, but—portentous for the expansion of slavery—a few planters produced sugarcane as a staple in the 1790s. In 1803, at least eighty-one sugar plantations were in operation in Louisiana. By 1815, Louisiana sugar estates were producing 10 million pounds of sugar annually, and that amount doubled by 1818.[3] The temperate climate and fertile soil of the Mississippi River delta were ideal for the cultivation of sugarcane, but even after the introduction in 1817 of a variety that matured in a shorter growing season, Louisiana could compete with foreign production only with the assistance of a protective tariff.[4] When cotton prices were low, Louisiana planters experimented with cane in geographically feasible areas, but a wide-scale conversion was still some time in the future.

Despite wide fluctuations, cotton prices were generally high from 1800 to 1819. In 1801, when prices for slaves and land in Louisiana were relatively low, cotton prices ranged from 22 to 44 cents per pound. Prices declined considerably during the uncertain years before the outbreak of war with England in 1812, ranging from 8.9 to 10.7 cents per pound in 1811 and dropping even further after war was declared.[5] When the war ended in 1815, cotton prices climbed to 29.4 cents per pound and by 1817 peaked at an enticing 33.9 cents. These favorable conditions resulted in notable population increases after 1815. Despite some planters' flirtations with sugar production, the high cotton prices "strengthened the tendency of migrating planters to stay within the cotton latitudes," at least for the rest of the decade.[6]

Although many of the migrants were small farmers who tilled modest cotton acreages with the labor of their sons and perhaps a few slaves, the fortunes to be made in the boom years between 1815 to 1819 were dependent upon large-scale production using gang labor. Ambitious Louisiana cotton planters hungered for more slaves, and slaveholders of the northeastern and southeastern states quickly responded to the voracious lower South

FIGURE 2.1.

Louisiana Slaves in Major Family Household Types, 1810–1819, by Percentage

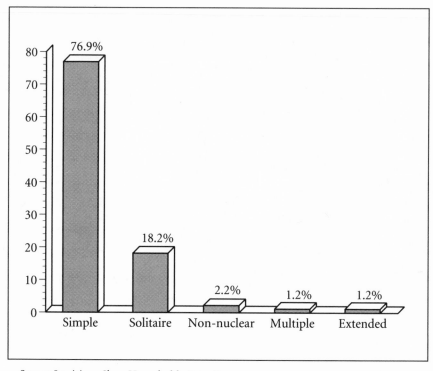

Source: Louisiana Slave Households Data Base.

market for their surplus chattels. The interstate trade that began after the closing of the foreign slave trade greatly accelerated after 1815, with New Orleans and Natchez both serving as major markets. Slave population in Louisiana increased by 99 percent from 1810 to 1820, a higher rate of increase than it would again exhibit. Prices for slaves rose slowly until near the end of the decade, then slumped slightly.[7]

The Panic of 1819 and the depression that followed did not affect the Mississippi Valley as gravely as it did many other parts of the nation, but it did slow the rate of expansion in the 1820s. Settlers still coursed into the region but not as eagerly as before. Shrewd planters of the lower South sometimes profited from the tendency of hard-hit upper South planters to sell slaves at lower prices immediately after the panic.[8]

Not unexpectedly for a comparatively early period of settlement, slave household composition between 1810 and 1819 was quite simple and lack-

FIGURE 2.2.

Louisiana Slaves in Simple Family Categories, 1810–1819, by Percentage

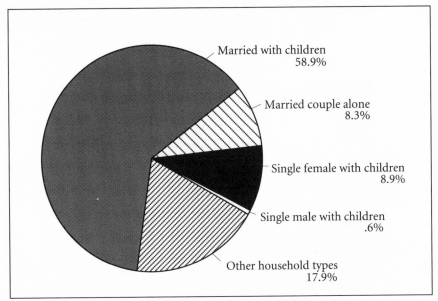

Married with children
58.9%

Married couple alone
8.3%

Single female with children
8.9%

Single male with children
.6%

Other household types
17.9%

Source: Louisiana Slave Households Data Base.

ing in generational depth (see figure 2.1). What is unexpected is that the composite community was remarkably stable, with nearly 60 percent of its members forming parts of standard nuclear family households—a proportion 10 percent higher than for the entire fifty-four-year period or for any other decade. Fewer slaves lived in female-headed single-parent households than in the general model, 9 percent compared to 14.5 percent of the population (see figure 2.2). A few slaves lived in complex household forms. The percentage who were solitaires was fairly high (as high as in the overall model), and a small percentage resided in households containing no relations, which can indicate a lack of maturity and integration in a slave society. Nevertheless, the communities of 1810 to 1819 exhibited a stability and maturity in their collective construction that seems out of step with the conditions shaping the decade—rapid demographic and economic expansion, three years of war, and a burst of intensive inflation followed by a major financial panic in the closing year.

Explanations for the seeming contradiction appear to be twofold. First, the most dramatic population increases occurred after 1815; the increase in the first half of the decade was considerably slower. Second, extant records indicating household affiliation of slaves from the early period are primarily associated with estate settlements, and slave communities established by the new migrants may not be adequately represented in this sample. To determine if this were true, the original sources for the 1810–19 sample were carefully examined. A few of the sampled communities were those of small planters who had migrated during the period, bringing with them, or purchasing later, one or two families and several prime field hands to aid them in clearing and planting. These owners were not large-scale planters by any means. The sample also included several larger slave communities associated with owners who had been in Louisiana for many years or who had recently migrated with their slave communities intact from nearby Mississippi. Therefore, it is in keeping with the cyclical development theory that these older communities would exhibit a mature construction usually associated with a later time period—including a high percentage of slaves in two-parent households, a relatively low percentage in single-parent households, and a token number in extended and multiple family households. Such cohesion reflects a late stage of development and does not necessarily correspond to a specific time period. These comparatively mature communities exert a disproportionate influence over the model for the 1810–19 decade partially because the longer-established communities contained more slaves than those associated with newcomer owners.

A community that exhibited a mature construction was that associated with cotton planter John O'Connor, who had been in the Felicianas since the late eighteenth century.[9] When he died in 1814, his estate of thirty-nine slaves included ten solitaires, two of whom were elderly individuals with kin on the plantation. The remainder of his slave force formed standard nuclear families. O'Connor's slave force contained no single parents at the time of his death. In addition to old American planters such as O'Connor, the 1810–19 sample also contained slave communities belonging to French-speaking planters identified as descendants of Europeans who had been in Louisiana for many decades. Therefore, upon close scrutiny, it is not surprising to observe stability and depth in the slave communities of this decade because many of those sampled were connected to planter families of some duration in the region.

The estates and slave community constructions of the newer migrants are more accurately reflected in the following decade. Likewise, the most serious effects of the Panic of 1819 on slave family construction are reflected in the 1820s.

LOUISIANA SLAVE HOUSEHOLD COMPOSITION, 1820–1829

The United States began the new decade in the throes of a major depression. Louisiana's population increased by 41 percent during the 1820s, but the rate of growth was less than it had been during the previous decade and smaller than it would be in the 1830s, the expansion slowed by the effects of the panic and depression.[10] Optimistic Louisiana planters continued to increase their slave forces but at a less frenzied pace than before. The slave population showed a greater increase than did that of the whole population—increasing by 59 percent between 1820 and 1830—but this, too, was much smaller than the rate of increase of the 1810–19 period.[11]

The panic seems to have had little effect on cotton prices. Cotton remained the premier money crop. Between 1819 and 1824, cotton prices fluctuated between a profitable 12 and 17 cents per pound but slowly decreased annually after 1825.[12] Despite the lower prices for the staple in the latter part of the decade, Louisiana, along with Alabama, Georgia, and Mississippi, was consumed by cotton fever. In 1827, Natchitoches, Louisiana, planters informed a northern passenger on a Mississippi River steamboat that "they could not get enough boats to bring the cotton down the Red." The northern man, having been subjected to constant "cotton talk" for months in the South, complained that he "still dreamed of cotton" even when safely en route to St. Louis and the North.[13]

Most Louisiana slaves worked in upland cotton production in the 1820s, but the decline in cotton prices during the second half of the decade, combined with the passage of a favorable sugar tariff in 1828, prompted some cotton planters to turn to sugar cultivation in areas where it was feasible. Because of these conversions and the sugar plantations established by migrating planters, the number of sugar estates increased from 308 in 1827 to 691 in 1830, a remarkable expansion for a three-year period.[14]

The constrictions of the economy in the early 1820s and declining cotton prices in the decade's latter years did affect Louisiana slave households.

FIGURE 2.3.

Louisiana Slaves in Major Family Household Types, 1820–1829, by Percentage

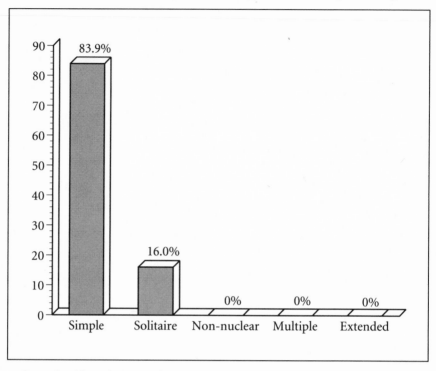

Source: Louisiana Slave Households Data Base.

Importation and purchase of slaves slowed somewhat, but the depression was not so severe or long-lasting nor were the prices for cotton so low that planters were forced to cut back greatly on their slave forces. Planters continued to migrate, buy, and build, but more cautiously. Therefore, slave families, households, and communities were not subjected to drastic changes imposed by their owners for economic advantage. A moderately constrictive period such as the 1820s did not encourage increased stability in slave family and household organization, but it did foster equipoise. Fewer slaves were bought and sold in such static periods, compared to volatile, high-profit periods, when slaves, like other commodities, were bought, sold, and traded with frenzied vigor, a circumstance highly disruptive of family and community life.

In the 1820s, most of the changes in household composition were minor (see figure 2.3). The percentages of slaves who were solitaires decreased

FIGURE 2.4.

Louisiana Slaves in Simple Family Categories, 1820–1829, by Percentage

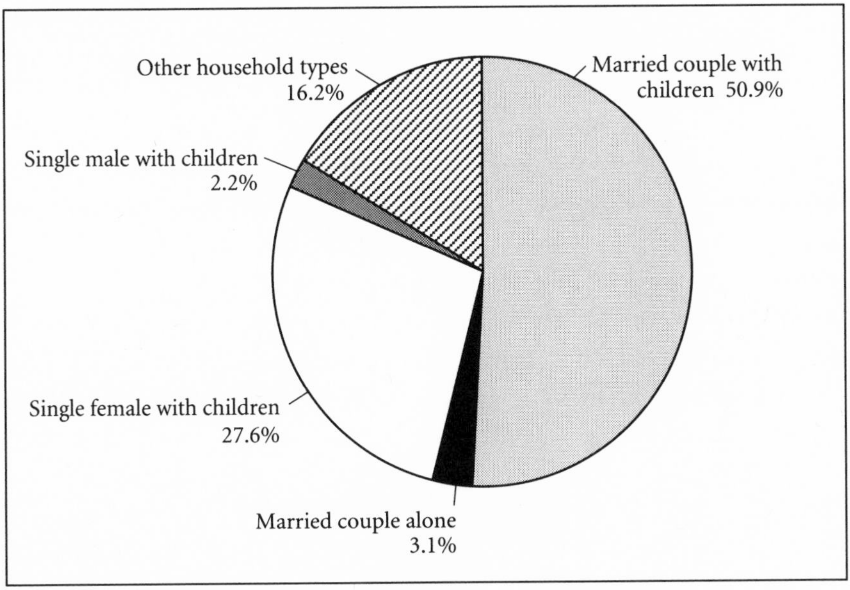

Other household types
16.2%

Married couple with
children 50.9%

Single male with children
2.2%

Single female with children
27.6%

Married couple alone
3.1%

Source: Louisiana Slave Households Data Base.

slightly, in keeping with the slower rate of slave importations. The mean size of the sampled slave communities dropped as well, reflecting both the slowed rate of expansion and the smaller estates of owners who had migrated during the previous decade. No complex forms were present, indicating that the old established communities of the previous period were less significant.

Simple families absorbed 84 percent of the sampled slaves, a higher percentage than was present in the overall model or in the previous decade. This does not indicate greater stability, however, but was partly owing to the lack of complex forms and to fewer solitaires, though the main reason was a leap in the number of slaves living in female-headed single-parent households (see figure 2.4). More than a quarter of the sampled slaves were members of matrifocal households, compared to less than one-tenth in the previous decade. The unusually high percentage of slaves in female-headed single-parent households is the major difference from the household com-position of 1810–19.

Explanations for this phenomenon are not clear. This increase in the proportion of matrifocal families might have been largely a temporary generational manifestation, with most units headed by young mothers who would soon marry, forming standard nuclear families. Or the women who headed such households might have been severed from previous mates by the slave trade or migration and were reluctant to remarry. The large number of female-headed households could also be attributable to greater disorganization within the sampled slave societies, reflecting the disruptions from the previous decade's expansiveness as well as the more unsettled conditions of the 1820s. The evidence is not conclusive. The population of the 1820s sample includes twelve more women than men, but this small gender imbalance does not indicate an overall shortage of males. There is no evidence that many owners were compelled to sell off male slaves because of financial exigencies, though fewer may have been purchased to correct existing gender imbalances.

Even a close scrutiny of the inventories within the 1820s sample with pronounced percentages of female-headed households does not supply a definitive answer. Most were cotton plantations in the Florida parishes (those that were part of West Florida before 1810) having between twenty-one and thirty-three slaves. These holdings had shortages of young, unattached males, indicating that many of the female-headed households were probably not bereft of husbands and fathers through choice.[15] The Florida parishes had been settled longer than most slaveowning regions of the state and had dense slave populations and plantation holdings so that some mothers heading households may have had husbands on nearby plantations.

The unusually high number of female-headed single-parent households in the 1820s remains a puzzle, but the phenomenon did not continue into the next decade and does not appear to have been of long-range significance.

LOUISIANA SLAVE HOUSEHOLD COMPOSITION, 1830–1839

Compared to the relatively static 1820s, the decade of the 1830s was extremely dynamic. Once more Louisiana's general population surged, with a 63 percent rate of increase.[16] The rate of increase among the slave population was slightly less than it had been during the 1820s primarily because of a set of restrictive laws passed after 1831 and in effect until 1834 prohibited the importation of slaves by professional traders. The acts, similar to those passed by other importing states, were written in the wake of the Nat Turner slave insurrection in Virginia and were designed to prevent the entry of potential slave insurgents into the lower South, as panicky upper South owners dumped suspected troublemakers on the interstate market. The prohibition of the trade was generally effective, although Louisiana planters could still obtain slaves by making personal buying trips to the Southeast or across the Mississippi River in Natchez. The process of buying slaves through such means was time-consuming, cumbersome, and costly, and planters overcame their initial fears and pressured the legislature to repeal the last of the restrictive laws by 1834. Soil exhaustion in the eastern seaboard slave states created a surplus of slaves and eager sellers, and the cotton boom of 1835–37 resulted in an even greater demand for slave labor in the Southwest than before. From 1835 on, slaves were imported into Louisiana in unprecedented numbers to meet the growing demands of both cotton and sugar producers. Even before the slave trade was reinvigorated, the ratio of slaves to the entire population was higher than it had ever been before in Louisiana, 50.8, because of the huge influx in the 1810–19 period and the more moderate increases of the 1820s.[17]

The new migration to Louisiana included substantial numbers of non-slaveholders, many of whom would purchase slaves in the state. These farmers who aspired to be planters joined experienced planters escaping the worn-out soils of the upper South.

By the 1830s Louisiana's allure for ambitious agrarians was twofold. Its lowlands beckoned potential sugar planters, and its upriver country promised riches in cotton. In the late 1820s and early 1830s, conditions favored sugar production more than cotton, and by 1839, Louisiana was producing most of the nation's sugar.[18] Drawing labor from the revitalized internal slave trade, sugar estates greatly expanded in the mid-1830s but stabilized somewhat in the latter years when the tariff was reduced and cotton prices rose.[19] The number of sugar estates declined by the end of the decade, primarily through consolidation when many of the more prosperous estates converted to steam-powered gins that increased productivity and reduced manpower requirements.[20] Despite these fluctuations, sugar remained profitable throughout the decade. Cotton holdings increased as

FIGURE 2.5.

Louisiana Slaves in Major Household Types, 1830–1839, by Percentage

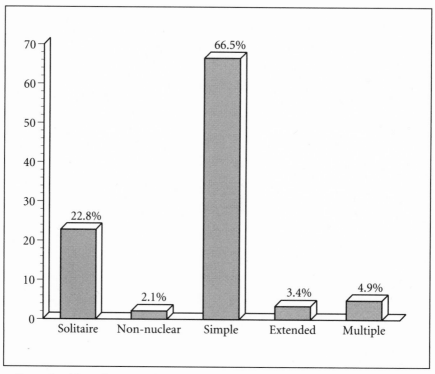

Source: Louisiana Slave Households Data Base.

well in the early and middle years of the decade, encouraged by the high prices from 1832 to 1838. The Panic of 1837 precipitated a serious decline in 1839–40, when cotton sold at only 8.6 cents per pound, but the worst effects of the panic on Louisiana's economy would not be felt until the 1840s.[21]

In general, the economy of the 1830s was affluent and inflationary, especially in the middle years. Prodigious profits could be gained in sugar and cotton, and both commodities were bought, sold, and traded in an extremely bullish market. In this intensely capitalistic, market-oriented period, slaves existed in a state of constant uncertainty. The flush era of the 1830s seriously undermined slave family, household, and community cohesion.

With the expansion of both cotton and sugar production in the 1830s and intensification of the slave trade to meet the demands of Louisiana's dual economy, the proportion of solitaires in the sampled communities

FIGURE 2.6.

Louisiana Slaves in Simple Family Categories, 1830–1839, by Percentage

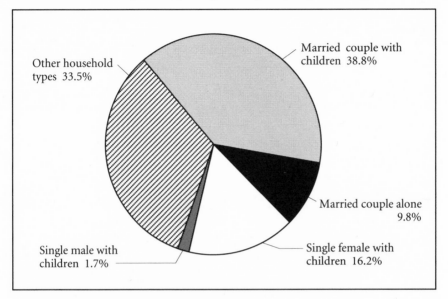

Source: Louisiana Slave Households Data Base.

climbed from 16 percent in the 1820s to 23 percent in the 1830s (see figure 2.5). Once more, males made up a significantly larger portion of the solitaires than did females. The percentage of slaves who were solitaires was larger in the 1830s than in any other antebellum decade and higher than that of the model for the entire period. This dramatic increase is almost certainly related to the acceleration of the interstate slave trade after 1834. Strong young slaves were in great demand, and both sugar and cotton planters were willing to pay premium prices to obtain them. Had there been no trade prohibitions, the percentage of slaves who were solitaires may well have reached one-third.

In consequence of the swelling of the ranks of solitaires, simple family households and their component groups declined proportionately (see figure 2.6). The proportion of slaves in female-headed households containing children dropped to a more normal 16 percent of the population. But standard nuclear families—fathers, mothers, and their offspring—now embraced only 39 percent of the population, a disturbing decrease from the 51 percent of the previous decade and an unfavorable contrast with the 49 percent of slaves forming such households in the overall sample. The sample and case studies suggest that a slave society in which 40 percent or less of its population was in the desirable norm indicates serious instability and disorganization. Many of the 1830s slave communities sampled were in a state of flux, disrupted by the changing economy and the unsettling effects of an intensified importation of laborers in the second half of the decade.

Slave communities of the 1830s were growing larger and more diverse. The 1830s sample shows small percentages in every major household category and a broader geographic spread than before. At least as many of the sampled communities of the 1830s were in sugar or cotton-sugar parishes as in cotton parishes.

The disturbing imbalances were found on both sugar and cotton plantations and so were not solely attributable to increases in sugar production. Many contemporaries and historians since have assumed that sugar production was more labor-intensive than cotton and that sugar planters were less concerned with gender and age balance, reproductive potential, and harmony and stability among their work forces. This question is explored extensively in the next chapter in which family household composition is examined by parish type.

Many Louisiana slave communities of the 1830s, regardless of the staple crop emphasis of their owners, were in a state of social disorganization, with a high incidence of solitaires and a low incidence of standard nuclear families, relative to the norm. This was unusual for Louisiana slave communities, particularly after two decades of healthy organizational patterns even in young slave communities. It appears that the high profits accrued by the aggressive planters of the 1830s were paid for by their slaves in increased anxiety and loss of internal cohesion.

It is important to differentiate between the effects of the prosperous but volatile conditions of the 1830s on slave community organization and those of the equally prosperous and expansive 1850s, when household organization was not disrupted. In the 1830s cotton and sugar planters flooded into the state, many bringing capital, slaves, and experience. These slaveowners were entrepreneurial, as would be those of the 1850s, but they were not simply expanding or increasing already well-established slave forces. Instead, they were attempting to construct a labor-efficient agricultural force as quickly as possible to take advantage of enticing but unstable markets in sugar and cotton. Always on the lookout for robust, youthful slaves and generally willing to trade or sell less productive slaves to get them, the highly speculative planter of the 1830s made frequent changes in his slave force, and sales and mortgages of slaves were extremely common. He attempted to stabilize his slave force, cease his frenetic buying, selling, trading, and mortgaging of slaves, and be concerned with the long-range improvement of his plantation and labor contingent only after his operation was well established and more solvent. He would then become more interested in social harmony, gender balances, and reproductive potential among his slaves. But for perhaps the majority of the new planters of the chaotic 1830s, these were not yet primary concerns. By contrast, most of the plantations in the 1850s sample were long established. The prosperity of that decade encouraged owners to expand their holdings but not to make numerous, threatening changes in existing forces.

LOUISIANA SLAVE HOUSEHOLD COMPOSITION, 1840–1849

The Panic of 1837 plunged the nation and even the booming lower South into a depression, and its effects were evident throughout most of the decade of the 1840s. Although the population of Louisiana continued to increase, the rate of increase was 16 percent less than that of the 1830s. The rate of increase among the slave population also dropped, by 9 percent.[22]

In the cotton districts, mortgages of land and slaves proliferated during the worst years.[23] Even planters who were not usually inclined to do so occasionally found it necessary to mortgage slaves to meet their obligations. One example was prominent cotton and sugar planter Thomas Butler, who wrote in 1842 of his intention to mortgage twelve slaves "to raise some money in these hard times."[24]

The export price of cotton in 1842 was only 6.2 cents per pound, and the highest price paid for middling cotton in New Orleans that year was 7.5 cents. In 1844, the price of cotton bottomed out at 5.9 cents, well below production costs; it rose briefly in 1846 only to plummet once again in 1848.[25] When prices plunged, cotton production decreased. In 1849 Louisiana made only 178,737 bales of ginned cotton, far behind Tennessee, South Carolina, Georgia, Alabama, and Mississippi.[26] Other cotton-growing

FIGURE 2.7.

Louisiana Slaves in Major Family Household Types, 1840–1849, by Percentage

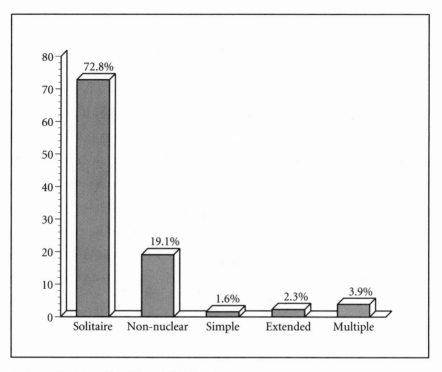

Source: Louisiana Slave Households Data Base.

states may have had no alternative but to produce more to compensate for the low prices. But Louisiana planters in large sections of the state did have an alternative, and hundreds turned to sugar production because sugar prices were not so adversely affected by the depression.[27] Stimulated by a higher tariff in 1842, the number of sugar estates increased to 1,536 by 1849, and the number of slaves in the sugar parishes more than doubled.[28]

The contraction of the economy in the 1840s had deleterious effects on the lives of many individual slaves, who were sold or mortgaged by planters in financial difficulty, but in general conditions in this constrictive decade—like that of the 1820s—prompted a return to a more normal family, household, and community organization. Slave household organization in the 1840s was still unstable, but it was moving toward greater equilibrium in comparison to the prosperous but disruptive decade of the 1830s.

FIGURE 2.8.

Louisiana Slaves in Simple Family Categories, 1840–1849, by Percentage

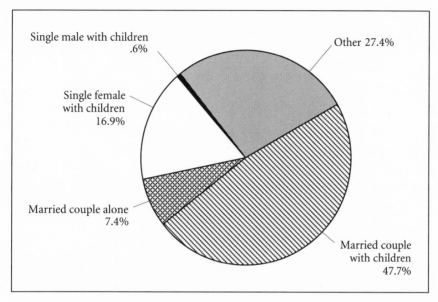

Single male with children
.6%

Other 27.4%

Single female
with children
16.9%

Married couple alone
7.4%

Married couple
with children
47.7%

Source: Louisiana Slave Households Data Base.

Planters in the most dire straits sold slaves they might have retained in better times, but most slaveowners simply stopped buying and tried to hold on to the slaves and other forms of capital that they had accumulated in the flush 1830s.

The slave household type most significantly affected by the depression was that of the solitaire. The percentage of slaves who were solitaires was reduced from 23 to 19 percent of the population (see figure 2.7). Some of the reduction was natural, as unattached slaves found spouses and formed families. But other slaves were sold by cotton planters to sugar producers or traders, and the hiring of cotton slaves to the sugar parishes was very common in the 1840s.[29] There is little evidence that large numbers of slaves were sold off to settle debts, but when such sales did take place, solitaires— especially young males—were the first to be put on the auction block. As more planters turned to sugar production, young male solitaires sold quickly and brought high prices, and many owners reasoned that selling solitaires caused little disruption to the slave community.

The configuration of slave domestic organization during the 1840s was improved over that of the previous decade (see figure 2.8). Not only were the numbers of solitaires reduced, but 73 percent of the slaves formed simple families, and 48 percent were members of two-parent households. A fairly large number of slaves, 17 percent, were in female-headed single-parent households, showing little change from the previous period.

In the 1840s cash-short planters relied more on natural increase and less on the slave trade. Since many cotton farmers and planters cut back on production during the depression, they bought fewer slaves, and existing communities had fewer adjustments to make. With a more stable population, slaves of many communities formed standard families and contributed to the development of kinship networks that would be well advanced by the next decade. Many of the communities that had formed during the first two decades of this study period included three generations in the latter 1840s.

Thus in the 1840s slave family and household organization underwent few major changes. In the absence of intense economic activity, slave communities were better able to assert their preferred forms. The lack of outside interference enabled them to build rather than just repair their besieged domestic structures.

LOUISIANA SLAVE HOUSEHOLD COMPOSITION, 1850–1859

The dual plantation economy of Louisiana recovered well from the doldrums of the 1840s, and prosperity continued through the decade of the 1850s. The size and number of slaveholdings increased, but the rate of increase in whole and slave populations slowed to about 36 percent, no more than 12 percent higher than the estimated percentages of natural increase.[30] The flood of migration of previous decades was reduced to a small stream. New residents and their slaves and slaves brought in by professional traders entered at a slower, more steady pace and were fewer in number. The calmer, more orderly influx of the 1850s was far less disruptive of the household and family compositions of Louisiana plantations than that of the 1830s, the other prosperous, expansive economic decade. The 1850s slowdown was not the result of a depressed economy. To the contrary, both cotton and sugar brought good prices in the period, although the costs of slaves rose exorbitantly.[31]

The soils of the old cotton districts of the lower South were seriously depleted by the 1850s. An overseer encountered by that insightful traveler Frederick Law Olmsted at Bayou Sara in West Feliciana Parish in 1856 boasted that "this was once a famous cotton region. When it was first settled up by 'Mericans, used to be reckoned the garding of the world, the almightiest rich sile God ever shuck down." But, he admitted, it was "gettin thinned down powerful fast now. nothin' to what it was."[32] An aura of decay and abandonment haunted the once "happy land" immortalized in the delicate drawings of John James Audubon. Uninhabited plantation houses; eroded, neglected fields; and empty, dilapidated slave quarters dotted the old road from Bayou Sara to Woodville and on to Natchez. The lodestone of opportunity had shifted, but exhaustion of land in the old cotton district did not result in great financial difficulty for most of its large planters. It did prompt a shift of slaves and other capital within the state, as many of the old planter families bought additional holdings in the still-fertile cotton lands of the northern and western parishes of the state or sugar estates in the coastal region.[33]

Cotton prices fluctuated from 1851 through 1855 but generally remained at profitable levels throughout the decade, and production rose markedly.[34] Louisiana's cotton production for the decade was surpassed only by that of Alabama and Mississippi, and planters in parishes such as Concordia broke national records for per acre yields.[35]

In cane sugar production, Louisiana had no equal or even close competitor among domestic producers. Sugar production reached an all-time high in the state during the 1853–58 seasons, but because prices were higher, it accrued substantial profits for producers even at the end of the decade, when production was lower. The tendency toward consolidation continued among sugar producers, and by the 1850s sugar production was as much an industrial undertaking as an agricultural enterprise.[36]

The record sugar yields and high cotton prices in the mid- and late 1850s produced a confidence approaching arrogance among Louisiana planters, leading to increased speculation in slaves. Among others, U. B. Phillips was convinced that speculation in slaves reached a veritable fever pitch, artificially increasing their value.[37] The slower rate of increase among slave populations during the decade demonstrates, however, that not all owners were caught up in the buying frenzy, and there was even an abortive attempt in the legislature to reintroduce African slavery to counter the inflated prices of slaves in the domestic market.[38]

The increase in prices of slaves during the 1850s was not prohibitively high, but it was dramatic. A twenty-eight-year-old field hand in the estate of Robert Perry in West Feliciana was appraised at $2,500 in 1858; in the 1857 Loisel estate sale, men in their twenties sold for nearly $2,000 each; and in Modest Guidry's 1859 probate sale, Zenon, twenty-eight, was sold for $2,500, seventeen-year-old Augell for $2,300, twenty-five-year-old Leander for $2,225, and twenty-two-year-old Hypolite for $2,430.[39] These slaves were experienced sugar laborers, but they were not specialized, skilled workers. The inflation of slave prices occurred rapidly. In 1851, a highly skilled sugar maker was purchased for only $900 from the estate of Alexis Blanchard, and prime field hands in their twenties sold for $800 each. The leap in slave prices began in the middle of the decade. At the Guidry sale in 1859, a mentally deficient ten-year-old was sold for $900, the same price that a valuable sugar maker had brought at the beginning of the decade.[40] The sharp rise in slave prices is further demonstrated by the records of a slave family consisting of parents and their five sons, appraised as a group for $2,150 in 1850. In 1855, the same man, woman, their newborn child, and the two youngest sons were sold together for $3,200. The three older sons, in their early teens, sold separately for a total sum of $4,735. The estate made $5,785 by holding the family for five years.[41] Nor were the high prices obtained only in local sales; the prices for slaves purchased from professional traders in New Orleans met or exceeded those of slaves bought at sheriff's sales, succession sales, or through private conveyances. Richard L. Pugh of Lafourche Parish paid premium prices in the New Orleans market from 1859 to 1861 for workers imported from Tennessee, South Carolina, Missouri, Florida, and Kentucky. Despite the high prices, as Joe Gray Taylor has observed, "planters were prosperous during this period and were convinced that more slaves would add to their prosperity."[42]

Speculation in slaves proved very profitable for those who bought early in the 1850s and sold late in the decade or in the prewar 1860s. After the mid-1850s buying was risky because prices were so extraordinarily high. The bloated prices encouraged ordinary planters to buy carefully, choosing only prime laborers who were really needed. The days of buying whole lots of slaves for speculation were over. Except for estate divisions, there was no incentive to sell slaves because they continued to increase in value through-out the decade. Despite the speculative activities of a small minority of planters, the prosperity of the 1850s did not greatly disrupt slave commu-nity development.

By the mid-1850s, Louisiana slave communities as a whole were probably as mature and stable as they had ever been or would be again. Units had increased in size so that although most holders still had twenty or fewer slaves, about half of Louisiana's slaves lived in units of fifty or more slaves, comparable to a small village. Slaves in these larger units usually found opportunities to marry within their own small society, and by the 1850s, such units frequently supported intricate kinship networks.

Household composition among the sampled Louisiana slaves of the 1850s reflected the prosperity and relative stability of the times and repre-sented a mature phase in the developmental cycle of many of the commu-nities. The majority of slaves, 75 percent, lived in simple families; solitaires accounted for 17 percent; complex forms contained nearly 8 percent (see figure 2.9). Almost none lived in non-nuclear forms. Within the simple family form (see figure 2.10), over 52 percent of the sampled slaves lived in standard nuclear families, and less than 13 percent lived in female-headed single-parent households. The most significant movement in slave family composition during the 1850s was toward internal cohesion, as exemplified by a decline in the proportion of the population without family connec-tions; a rise in the percentage of simple, standard nuclear, and complex forms; and a decline since the 1840s in the proportion in matrifocal households. More than half of the sampled slaves lived in families com-posed of a mother, father, and children. Another 8 percent were married, and some of these would eventually have children or had grown children. All others, except for the solitaires, formed parts of households made up of close kin. And even among the solitaires, many—perhaps most—had close relatives on the plantations upon which they resided.

This general profile shows a very balanced slave community organiza-tional structure relative to those observed in other time periods and in relation to the general model derived from the entire sample. If the general profile presented earlier (derived from the entire sample) represents the norm of 155 slave communities drawn during a fifty-four-year time span, the profile of the 1850s probably represents the best that the sampled slaves were able to achieve in their collective experiences.

FIGURE 2.9.

Louisiana Slaves in Major Family Household Types, 1850–1859, by Percentage

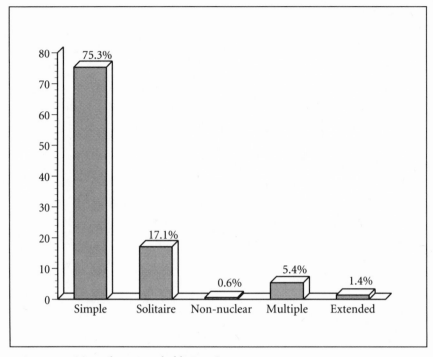

Source: Louisiana Slave Households Data Base.

LOUISIANA SLAVE HOUSEHOLD
COMPOSITION, 1860–1864

Even as war clouds were gathering in 1860, the Louisiana economy was in excellent shape. As the new decade began, prospects for profitable cotton and sugar production seemed boundless; rice production had increased; tobacco production had almost doubled; towns were growing throughout the state; and even the health of the people seemed to have improved, with lower mortality rates than in the previous decade.[43] Agricultural production was not seriously interrupted in 1861 after the war began. A banner sugar crop was produced that year, and J. C. Sitterson found that it was "harvested and manufactured into sugar without serious interference from war conditions."[44] Cotton, too, was grown and harvested with little diffi-

FIGURE 2.10.

Louisiana Slaves in Simple Family Categories, 1850–1859, by Percentage

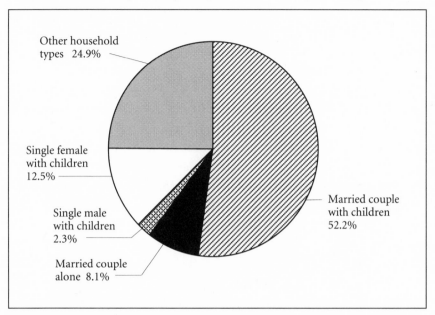

Source: Louisiana Slave Households Data Base.

culty in 1861. But Louisiana's plantation economy was wholly dependent upon external markets, and producing the staples that were in worldwide demand was only the first step. The commodities had to reach the intended markets before profits could be realized. Louisiana planters sold some cotton to New Orleans factors, but western and northern buyers withdrew from the cotton market. The same was true of sugar. Access to foreign markets was soon obstructed by the Union blockade. The huge sugar crop of 1861 found few buyers, and prices plummeted in 1861 to half those of the previous year.[45] Surplus cotton was stored, but, with most markets closed, there was little incentive to plant more in subsequent war years. Louisiana planter Kenneth Clark wrote a friend in 1861 that "all commercial interests are entirely destroyed. Cotton and sugar cannot be sold." Provisions were scarce and expensive, cash in short supply, and marketing almost impossible to achieve. And this was before New Orleans fell to federal forces in 1862 and many black belt parishes were occupied in late 1863.[46]

The effects of the Civil War on Louisiana's plantation economy and agricultural society were immense and have been chronicled in numerous secondary works as well as documented in planters' journals, diaries, and reminiscences, newspapers, and, of course, official records of both armies. Similarly, its effects on family and community life were devastating for all Louisianans, white and black. Many white as well as slave families were broken or dislocated by the war. A study of white family composition would probably show as much disruption and chaos during the middle war years as occurred in slave families. Unfortunately, records are very scarce for both groups. Parish records were often destroyed or were not kept as carefully as they had been during less trying times. Some estates were not probated for ten years. After 1861 there are few slave inventories appropriate for analysis. Additional sources are available, however, to assist in understanding the war's effect on the state's chattels. An excellent qualitative treatment of the Louisiana slave family during the Civil War is provided by C. Peter Ripley.[47] He documents the effects of Union conscription of slave husbands and fathers, the impressment and hiring of male slaves by the Confederacy, the dislocations associated with the removal of parts of slave communities to remote parishes or to Texas, and the contraband movement. Testimonies of former slaves provide poignant references to the effects of the war on their families, as do terse notations in planters' records.

Clearly, no matter how sweet was the taste of freedom, the fairly stable family and community life that Louisiana slaves had achieved by the 1850s was effectively destroyed by the dislocations of war. Much of the confusion and restlessness among Louisiana blacks in the 1863–65 period resulted from an attempt to adjust to quasi-freedom without the familial and community support they had before the war. Many families were never reunited, and some slaves searched for years for loved ones severed from them by the war or, previously, by sale.

The sample of slave communities for the 1860–64 period represents only a partial decade, and the sample is smaller than earlier ones. Because of the disruption in record-keeping during the war, extant records from the 1860s designating familial relations are rare. Many of the inventories available for analysis were from 1860. Therefore, the composition may not accurately represent the war years. Nevertheless, the sampled communities do reflect increased instability resulting from deteriorating conditions immediately before and during the Civil War. The proportion of solitaires declined from 17 percent in the 1850s to 15 percent in the 1860s (see figure 2.11). A

FIGURE 2.11.

Louisiana Slaves in Major Family Household Types, 1860–1864, by Percentage

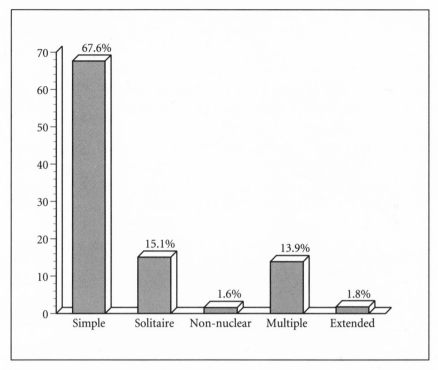

Source: Louisiana Slave Households Data Base.

corresponding decline occurred in the percentage of people who were members of simple families. Previously, 75 percent of sampled slaves resided in simple families, but in the 1860s, the percentage dropped to 68. Membership in standard two-parent nuclear families also declined significantly, to 45 percent, the lowest since the volatile 1830s (see figure 2.12).

Another departure in the 1860s sample from both the previous decade and the general model was a much higher percentage of members of multiple family households. Fourteen percent of the slaves lived in such units, and another 2 percent lived in extended family households. Most of these slaves belonged to units consisting of a parent or parents with an additional conjugal unit of a later generation, but practically all forms of multiple and extended family households were represented to some degree. In time of crisis, slave families absorbed needy relatives into established units. Single and married parents brought into their households widowed

FIGURE 2.12.

Louisiana Slaves in Simple Family Categories, 1860–1864, by Percentage

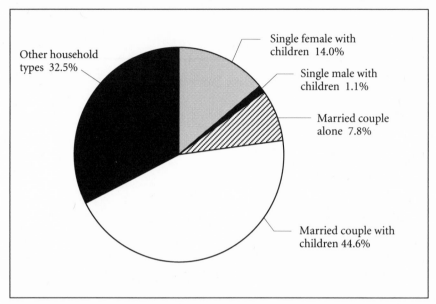

Other household types 32.5%

Single female with children 14.0%

Single male with children 1.1%

Married couple alone 7.8%

Married couple with children 44.6%

Source: Louisiana Slave Households Data Base.

or separated daughters, orphans, and grandchildren; couples took in siblings. This practice was, of course, common among family households of all races during that and other wars. Many of these complex forms resulted from the departures of young male slaves as a result of labor conscription, union seizure, removal to Texas, hire to the Confederate authorities, or death.[48] In September 1863, planter William Minor observed morosely that the slave "men [are] taken off & their families [are] in deep distress. . . . Bill Clarke was the only man who asked me to take care of his family—I will do all I can for them. . . . If the war continues twelve months longer all Negro men of any value will be taken. The women and children will be left for their masters to maintain which they can not do."[49] Minor's fears were realized on many plantations, and slave dependents often fell to the care of their own complex family households, sharing crowded quarters and increasingly meager rations. Some increase in these multigenerational forms was normal, however, because the 1860s represented a late developmental phase for most Louisiana slave communities.

It bears repeating that the sample was skewed because one-third of the sampled communities of the 1860s were inventoried in 1860. The household compositions of these communities closely resemble those of the latter 1850s; they were stable and family-oriented. Without these prewar inventories, the statistics regarding household composition in the 1860s sampled communities would have been far more distorted, imbalanced, chaotic, and more reflective of the turbulent times. The seventy-five slaves belonging to Alexandre de Clouet of St. Martin Parish in 1863 exhibited a household construction typical of the war years. Only one-third of his slaves were members of two-parent households, 21 percent were members of female-headed single-parent households, and a striking 23 percent belonged to multiple family households, in all of which parents had taken in grown children and grandchildren.[50]

A second and almost perfect example of the effects of the war on an old and stable slave community is drawn from records associated with the estate of David Weeks Magill. His slaves were part of a community built from his inheritance from his mother, Frances Weeks Magill Prewitt, who had inherited the ancestors of the community from the estate of her father, David Weeks. Frances and all of her children except for David perished in August 1856, when a hurricane destroyed Last Island, a popular resort area in Terrebonne Parish. At the time of her death, she was married to Buford A. Prewitt; her first husband, Augustin Magill, and another son had both died in 1851. The sole heir of her substantial property was young David Weeks Magill, the only survivor of her first marriage. He inherited a sugar plantation, L'Isle Labbe, valued at $35,000, various other tracts of land, and 113 family slaves.[51] Through reconstitution methods, it was determined that in 1856 these slaves lived in a community constituted very much like that of the model of the 1850s sample: stable and strongly dominated by families. Kinship systems were extremely well developed because most of the slaves were descendants of slaves belonging to the estate of David Weeks, who died in 1834, and a few were descendants of chattels from the estate of David Weeks's father.[52]

In the first two years, the war had relatively little effect on the daily life and family constructions of Magill's slaves, but all of that changed by 1863, when Union forces invaded the Teche country. The ill-fated last survivor of his family, young David Magill was by then an artillery captain in service of the Confederacy. A family slave said that he went as a substitute for his uncle William Weeks, but that claim has not been further substantiated. A petition of Magill's grandmother Mary Conrad Weeks Moore relates that her grandson died at the Battle of Vicksburg in 1863.[53] According to the recollection of one of William Weeks's slaves, his master went to the battlefield to search for his missing nephew. Magill's combat-mutilated body was found, but, according to the Weeks slave, the "only way he knowed it was him (David Magill), he have two gold eyeteeth with diamond in dem."[54] David Weeks Magill was only twenty-one at his death. He left no parents, wife, or children to mourn him, only a defiant grandmother, who would die in December 1863 while practically a prisoner in her Federal-occupied home, Shadows-on-the-Teche.[55]

Mrs. Moore was Magill's closest living relative, and in a deposition made a few weeks before her death, she explained to the court why an inventory could not be made of his "considerable estate consisting of a plantation and land situated in . . . St. Martin" and a contingent of slaves belonging to that plantation. She related bitterly that Magill's slaves had been removed "in April 1863 just before that part of Louisiana was invaded and overrun and pillaged by the troops of the United States . . . to another part of the State more out of the way of depredation by the Enemy."[56] Some of the slaves ran away, she said, but most were successfully transported to De Soto Parish. A few house servants remained behind at St. Martinsville. Later, William Weeks took some of the more valuable slaves to Polk County, Texas; others were conscripted for work in the Confederate ironworks in Texas, and several of the men were killed in an abortive insurrection near St. Martinsville in 1863. Some of the De Soto Parish slaves ran away and joined the Federal troops, and several died at the Battle of Mansfield in 1864. Unwittingly, for she had little sympathy for them, Mrs. Moore's long statement illuminates the severe disruptions that the war occasioned for this one slave community.

An accounting was finally made of the estate of David Weeks Magill's slaves in March 1865 by his overseer. At that time, sixteen slaves were in St. Martinsville and the remainder in De Soto Parish. The slaves in Texas and those who had run away were not inventoried. Of the 109 slaves in his estate in the few weeks before the war ended, 8 percent were solitaires (many of them elderly, for the young solitaires had long since left); 13 percent were part of extended or multiple family households; 50.4 percent lived in two-parent households; and 19.2 percent lived in female-headed single-parent households.[57]

A similar profile was found for the exiled slaves belonging to Evelina Moore Prescott and John Moore in De Soto Parish in 1864. There, ninety-one slaves were organized in the following proportions: 2 percent were solitaires, 38 percent lived in two-parent families, 9 percent were in female-headed households, and an astounding 41 percent lived in extended or multiple family households.[58] These examples show that the disruptions in slave family life and household composition were much more severe than indicated by the entire sample for the 1860s period, although the same general patterns prevailed.

DEVELOPMENT OF SLAVE
HOUSEHOLDS AND COMMUNITIES

Analyses of individual slave communities in a static time setting are of limited use in the study of general slave household organization. No matter how illuminating such studies are concerning the experience of a particular slave community in a particular place and time, there is no way to determine whether that community, time, and place in any sense represent a larger segment of slaves, in a larger setting, over a longer period of time. The study of many slave communities from a single state over several decades opens a wider window on slave household organization. As the foregoing analysis has shown, major variations from the general model emerged when the data were broken down into smaller time segments. Then a clear developmental pattern evolved that can be described as progressive; that is, slave communities, over time, proceeded from very simple to more complex household constructions. The analysis further suggested that communities grew in mean size and generally proceeded to what can be construed as a more stable construction. In addition, the statistical model, viewed by decades, revealed cyclical development, with the so-called stable features of slave community organization (relative gender balance, large numbers in simple families, relatively few solitaires, more two-parent than single-parent family households, and generational depth) occurring in a rising and falling upward curve, usually in response to external factors.

Historians of the family have long recognized that individual family households change over time according to the life cycles of their members.[59] In such studies, the measurements of household fluctuations are usually keyed to the ages of heads of households or their positions in their life course. Such a cyclical development was observed and noted in Louisiana slave communities.

Louisiana slaves were organized in several ways. They were organized by their owners into a recognizable unit for work and for habitation on a designated tract of land, and they were assigned living quarters. Slaves had little control over this organization, but within a relatively short time, the labor force congregated by the owner also formed a social organization, varying degrees of what is called a community. Within each of these communities, slaves organized further into smaller units: families and households (distinct from housefuls or mere co-residents). Eventually these families and households consolidated into kinship systems. The membership of all of these components changed constantly according to the life cycles of the individuals making up the families and households. Therefore, the household composition of a slave society may (and often does) simply reflect where the majority of slaves are in their own familial life courses. This study takes this natural, life-course-related cycle into serious consideration in its models and conclusion, but it only scratches the surface. The powerful forces of kinship and life course on slave family and household composition need much more study.[60]

In addition to the natural, collective life-course development alluded to above, a crisis-related cyclical pattern was revealed in both the quantitative analysis (broken down by time segment) and a series of case studies of communities traced generationally (three of which are presented in Part II). These studies demonstrate that many Louisiana slave communities went through often predictable cycles set in motion by crisis. The stages were basically the same whether the communities were formed as the result of in-migration from another state or were the labor force of a new or auxiliary plantation within Louisiana. The crisis that precipitated the cycle might be related to major disturbances other than migration, such as the sale of large numbers of community members, division of an estate, or a debilitating epidemic. How rapidly and how smoothly the communities passed through the building or rebuilding cycles depended on many factors—the health and condition of the slaves, the age and gender balance in the new society, the willingness of owners to correct imbalances, the financial circumstances of the owners, and the state of the economy as a whole, to name but a few.

Neither of these developmental cycles is necessarily time-specific. In Louisiana, they can be roughly related to time periods because many slave communities underwent very similar experiences at certain times as a result of external influences. But as demonstrated earlier in this chapter, an old slave community in the Felicianas inventoried before 1820 might display a mature and stable composition more generally associated with the 1850s construction for the majority of the sampled slave communities. Likewise, an 1840s community decimated by repeated estate divisions might conform to characteristics usually associated with the early stages of development, more frequently found in the 1820s and 1830s. Understanding the influence that these cycles had on the model of slave domestic organization can perhaps be clarified by reference to Appendix A, which is derived from both the quantitative and documentary study of Louisiana slave communities.

CHAPTER THREE

The Influence of
Parish Type and Size
of Holding

In earlier chapters I constructed a model for slave household composition in Louisiana from 1810 through 1864 and noted variations to that model by decennial intervals so as to develop a cyclical interpretation. Historical literature on slavery suggests that two other variables might result in significant differences in slave family, household, and community structure: the type of agriculture and the size of holdings associated with the plantations housing the sampled slave communities (the historical opinion is discussed in Chapter 8). Therefore, using the basic data from the larger statistical study, information was generated concerning household compositions associated with five parish types, categorized according to the prevailing type of staple-crop agriculture practiced there, and categories representing six sizes of slaveholdings. This chapter will present the results of these investigations, beginning with household analysis by parish type.

The method of classifying the sampled plantations into parish types was that devised by Joseph K. Menn in his seminal study of Louisiana's large slaveholders.[1] Based partly on their dominant staple crops according to the 1860 agricultural census, he divided Louisiana parishes into seven regions: sugar parishes, cotton-sugar parishes, Mississippi

River cotton parishes, north-central cotton parishes, Red River cotton parishes, southwestern undeveloped parishes, and southeastern piney woods parishes. Because there are insufficient records providing familial designations, the last two were not used in this study. In the latter portion of this chapter, the findings are based on six sizes of holdings: 1 to 19 slaves, 20 to 49 slaves, 50 to 99 slaves, 100 to 199 slaves, 200 to 299 slaves, and 300 to 399 slaves.

Scholars and the informed public have long surmised that the types of agricultural labor slaves engaged in gravely affected the quality of life—and perhaps the length of life—of Louisiana slaves. Influenced by contemporary observations, modern historians have often supposed that sugar operations were more destructive of slave family life than work on cotton plantations. On the former, family structure was less balanced because sugar production depended upon a labor force that was young, strong, predominantly male, and preferably single. According to this view, sugar production as practiced in mid-nineteenth-century Louisiana was so physically demanding that it was best performed by healthy young workers, and even among them, deaths and injuries exacted a terrible toll. Therefore, owners preferred their workers to be young male solitaires who could be replaced after a few years without undue disruption to the work force or the slave community.[2] If, indeed, sugar production was so strenuous and dangerous that it regularly killed or maimed young workers and discouraged the inclusion in the labor force of slaves who were not young, male, and unmarried, then the practice of this type of staple-crop agriculture obviously would be highly disruptive of family and community life. If these suppositions are true, slave communities in the sugar parishes should exhibit a much higher percentage of solitaires than in the model as a whole. Among the solitaires, a much greater gender imbalance should prevail, with males strongly predominating. And household composition in general should be less balanced than in the model or in the cotton parishes. Slave mortality rates should be higher in the sugar parishes as well, and a higher runaway rate could be expected, although this study did not test these last two variables.

These myths arose in the context of the bustling interstate slave trade of the 1830s and 1840s. Severance of ties with kin and friends was only part of the terror experienced by southeastern slaves sold to the lower South. Those sold for importation to Louisiana were convinced that they were going there to die. After sugar culture spread throughout the state, it was commonly believed in the North and Southeast that sugar production worked slaves to death within a few years (seven years, according to slave lore). A traveler in 1844 who encountered a slave coffle headed for Louisiana lamented that they were being sent "to perish in the sugar mills . . . where the duration of life for a sugar mill hand does not exceed seven years."[3] Whether he picked that number from slave folk belief is not known. Even southerners were concerned, and an 1830 New Orleans newspaper article on sugarcane culture estimated that the "loss by death in bringing in slaves from a northern climate, which our planters are under the necessity of doing, is not less than TWENTY-FIVE PER CENT."[4] The dangers of slavery in Louisiana's punishing sugar industry and unhealthy climate became a handy tool for abolitionists, and their tracts frequently commented on the perils associated with slavery in Louisiana and the lower South. The same horrific view was encouraged as a means of control by southeastern slaveholders as well, who often had only to threaten their slaves with sale to Louisiana's sugar fields to ensure their obedience. A dreadful fear of being "sold down the river" became so fixed in the minds of slaves that the phrase survives in general parlance today.[5] Lewis Clarke, who had been a slave in Kentucky, recalled that his master told the slaves that abolitionists "decoy slaves off into the free states to catch them and sell them to Louisiana or Mississippi."[6] Another former slave remembered the day that his two sisters were put on railroad cars bound for Louisiana: "The excitement was so great that the overseer and driver could not control the relatives and friends of those that were going away, as a large crowd of both old and young went down to the depot to see them off. Louisiana was considered by the slaves as a place of slaughter, so those who were going did not expect to see their friends again."[7] A modern historian contends that as the result of conversion to sugar production in many areas of the state, "Louisiana gained a reputation which made it the most terrifying of all the various hells of the deep South to which blacks from the older slave economies of the tidewater states could be sold."[8]

There is little doubt that the dramatic increase in sugar production in the 1830s and 1840s served as an impetus to the interstate trade. And it is also true that sugar was a more physically demanding crop than cotton, especially in its industrial aspects.[9] The round-the-clock labor required during the rolling of sugar was exhausting. Even the owners admitted the extreme rigors of the work. One stated in his will that a favored slave should not be obliged to work "during the sugarmaking time."[10] And accidents associated with sugarmaking probably were more frequent and serious than those associated with labor in cotton fields.

Yet there is some evidence that slaves who had been exposed to both types of labor preferred sugar production to work in cotton fields. A sugar planter in the Bayou Teche country stated that, in his experience, slaves "were much pleased with the change from cotton to sugar." He agreed that during rolling season the work was more demanding, "with the wood-cording and night watches, which they called 'towers' lasting three months." But he added that for most slaves "even this was better than the cold morning baths of cotton picking which often lasted from August to February, the most continuous labor of all the field crops." And he believed that slaves in the sugar country looked forward to the social opportunities associated with the sugar harvest.[11] Because he was a sugar planter, that observer may have been biased, but scattered records suggest that at least some slaves agreed with him.[12]

That the sugar districts were unhealthy cannot be denied. For all of its inhabitants, black and white, Louisiana was the deadliest state in the Union during most of the antebellum period, and the low-lying, semitropical sugar parishes were the most disease-prone in the state. Although there is little conclusive evidence that Louisiana slaves were driven to death by the labor and long hours connected with sugarmaking, coastal sugar slaves did die at an alarming rate from various fevers, as did white inhabitants of the sugar parishes. The fears of upper South slaves concerning the high risks associated with life in Louisiana were well-founded, and it is easy to see how the myth arose. Many sugar workers in the southern parishes did die prematurely, but the primary culprit was disease rather than overwork in sugar production.

Did sugar production or the insalubrious conditions in the sugar parishes undermine slave family formation and maintenance to a measurable degree, in comparison to cotton production? To answer this question, domestic organization among slaves in the sugar parishes was first compared to the model and then to sampled communities from cotton parishes and cotton-sugar parishes.

HOUSEHOLD COMPOSITION IN
SUGAR PARISHES

More than four thousand slaves in the sample resided in sugar parishes, providing a strong representation.[13] As shown in table 3.1, the proportion of solitaires in the population was 16 percent, lower than in the general model and in two of the cotton-producing areas. Although sugar plantations did not have a higher percentage of solitaires in their communities, there was a much higher male-favored gender imbalance; the solitaire group in the sugar parishes contained three and a half times more men than women. In fact, the sugar parishes had a greater gender imbalance across the board, with 2,252 males and 1,859 females (45 slaves were not identified by gender).

The comparatively low percentage of solitaires in the sugar parishes suggests that sugarmaking did not absolutely require young, single workers, although physical fitness was a requisite for some of the tasks. A close look at records that identify occupations on sugar plantations shows that many of the skilled workers were males in their thirties or even forties, and most of them were married.[14] Unskilled sugar fieldworkers tended to be young, and if they were single, they tended to be men.

The lower than expected percentages of solitaires and the male-dominated gender imbalance are the only important differences in household composition between the communities of the sugar parishes and the model. Contrary to the myth, in sugar parish communities a healthy 73 percent of the slaves lived in simple families, the same percentage as in the model. Within the simple family category, 49 percent of the sugar parish slaves were members of two-parent households (again, the same percentage as in the overall sample). And 13 percent of the slaves lived in female-headed single-parent households, very close to the 14.5 percent in the larger sample. Nor were percentages of slaves living in complex household forms within the sugar parish slave communities significantly different from the model. From these data, it appears that habitation in primarily sugar-producing parishes did not have major effects on household composition except that it fostered gender imbalance in the general population and especially in the singles category. But these conclusions rest only on comparison with the general model. Perhaps it would be more useful to

TABLE 3.1.

Percentage of Louisiana Slaves in Selected Family Household Types and Categories,
1810–1864, by Parish Types

Household type	General model	Sugar parishes	Sugar-cotton parishes	Mississippi cotton parishes	North-central cotton parishes	Red River parishes
Solitaires	18	16	19	23	14	7
Simple family	73	73	75	70	82	68
Married couple with child/children	49	49	49	45	60	45
Single female with child/children	14	13	16	14	17	16

Source: Louisiana Slave Households Data Base.

compare household composition of the sugar parish communities with
that of cotton-producing parishes.

HOUSEHOLD COMPOSITION IN
COTTON-SUGAR PARISHES

The portion of the sampled slaves who lived in parishes in which both
cotton and sugar were produced as staples on a large scale involved forty-
nine plantations upon which 3,135 slaves resided. In many respects the
household composition of communities in this parish type corresponded
closely to the model derived from the overall sample. An identical number,
49 percent, lived in standard nuclear families, and three-fourths of the
cotton-sugar parish slaves lived in simple families. The sex ratio was much
more balanced in the general population. But, interestingly, the proportion
of slaves in the solitaire category was higher by 3 percent than in the sugar
parish communities. The sugar parishes had fewer in the female-headed
single-parent household category than did the cotton-sugar parishes, by a
differential of 3 percent of the population. The higher percentages of both

solitaires and female-headed households in communities of the cotton-sugar parishes suggests that they were actually less stable in their household composition than were communities of the sugar parishes. Within the solitaire group, however, the percentage of males in the cotton-sugar communities was still about three times that of females, an imbalance similar to that exhibited in the sugar parishes, because of the inclusion of many sugar estates in the sample.

HOUSEHOLD COMPOSITION IN MISSISSIPPI RIVER COTTON PARISHES

Forty-five plantations containing 2,224 slaves were located in this parish type, which included the wealthy, sprawling Concordia cotton district. The solitaire category proved most telling. In this highly productive cotton region—renowned throughout the South for its spectacular yields—the percentage of solitaires was higher than in any other parish type—an astounding 23.4 percent. The bias toward male workers was not as pronounced as in the sugar parishes (14 percent of the population were male solitaires; 9 percent were females). This is not surprising because cotton-picking journals show that their dexterity made female workers equal in production to male workers. Intensive cotton production clearly required even more young, strong, preferably unattached male and female workers than did sugar production. No wonder that the demand for such slaves from the interstate trade was so intense in Louisiana.

Overall, the household composition of the Mississippi River cotton parishes was less stable than in the sugar parishes or the model, with 45 percent of the slaves in standard nuclear families and only 70 percent in the broad simple family category. Female-headed single-parent households, however, formed a near normal 14 percent of the population.

HOUSEHOLD COMPOSITION IN SUGAR PARISHES AND MISSISSIPPI RIVER COTTON PARISHES, 1830–1839

As a further test, household composition was compared for the two areas in the most expansive and disruptive period of all—the 1830s. In this tumultuous decade, the Mississippi River cotton parishes had an even more striking proportion of slaves in the solitaire group: more than one-third, exactly twice that found in the sugar parishes. Nevertheless, the sugar parishes continued to exhibit a greater imbalance toward males than cotton parishes. Twice as many men as women were solitaires. The differential was considerably less in the cotton parishes.

As was true in general during the disquieting 1830s, communities in both parish types compared unfavorably with the model for the large time span. Only 60 percent of the slaves in the Mississippi River cotton parishes formed simple families, and a dismal 37 percent were members of standard nuclear families. The situation was slightly better in the sugar parishes, but not by much. There, a respectable 71 percent of the slaves were part of simple families, but only 41 percent lived in two-parent households. These findings confirm the earlier analysis and suggest that planters in the Mississippi River cotton parishes during the cotton boom of the 1830s engaged in more activities (such as buying, selling, transferring, and hiring out of slaves) that were destructive to slave family and community life than were planters of the sugar parishes.

HOUSEHOLD COMPOSITION IN SUGAR PARISHES AND MISSISSIPPI RIVER COTTON PARISHES, 1850–1859

One other decade rivaled that of the 1830s in its prosperity and expansiveness, that of the 1850s. As a final comparison, household information was retrieved from the sample for the two parish types during that more stable but equally entrepreneurial period. In the sugar parishes a reasonable 17 percent of slaves were in the solitaire category; 13.6 percent of the population were male solitaires; 3.6 percent were females. The percentage in the solitaire category drawn from the cotton parishes was much improved— also 17 percent, with male singles making up 10.7 percent of the population and female singles accounting for 6.5 percent. The same close correlation to the overall model is found in other household categories. By the 1850s, slave communities in the sugar and cotton parishes varied little in their household compositions.

Although the most important trend is revealed in the comparison of the

two major staple-crop parish types, statistics were also generated in two
other parish types, both associated with cotton.

HOUSEHOLD COMPOSITION IN THE NORTH-CENTRAL COTTON PARISHES

Thirteen cases involving 577 slaves were located in this less important
cotton-producing region. Records showing familial relationships were
more difficult to locate in this area of the state. The communities in the
limited sample display an exceptional degree of stability and balance in
household and family organization. In these cotton parishes, where land
was less desirable and less productive, 60 percent of the sampled slaves lived
in families with both parents present, and only 14 percent were solitaires. A
very impressive 82 percent of slaves in this parish type were in simple
families.

HOUSEHOLD COMPOSITION IN THE RED RIVER COTTON PARISHES

The parishes belonging to the Red River cotton parish type were by the
1850s emerging as a high production area. Regrettably, only three plantations having clear household designations were found for this region. The
total population of the sample was 236 inhabitants. Because the sample is
small and the three communities may not have been typical, one must be
cautious in assigning significance to departures in household composition
from the model or other parish types. In fact, two of the communities
could not have been typical because they were transported into the area
from sugar and cotton-sugar parishes in the 1860s in an attempt to escape
Federal troops. (De Soto Parish was a favorite refuge for Teche planters in
1863 although its safety was short-lived because the Red River expedition of
1864 went through the area.)

On the sampled plantations of this parish type, only 7 percent of the
slaves were solitaires (a much lower proportion than in the model or in
other cotton-producing parish types). The other striking characteristic was

the very high proportion of slaves who lived in multiple family households (one-fifth). These are classic examples of household organization for the war years, when many of the young men who would have been solitaires were drawn off for labor on Confederate fortifications or in manufacturing operations, or were taken to Texas, or had escaped and joined the Union forces.

One Red River cotton parish community was not drawn from the 1860s and might project a more representative profile for the parish type. This was the Vienna slave community in Natchitoches Parish, one of several cotton plantations owned by A. LeComte in 1852.[15] His thirty-six slaves on this holding were distributed in the following proportions: 17 percent were solitaires (only slightly less than the overall model), 75 percent lived in simple families (compared to 73 percent in the entire sample), and 8 percent lived in multiple family households, the same as in the model. The only real difference from the profile generated by the entire sample of over ten thousand slaves was that 22 percent of Vienna's slaves lived in female-headed single-parent households compared to 14 percent in the large sample. Forty-seven percent of Vienna's slaves in 1852 were members of standard nuclear families, 2 percent less than the 49 percent of the model. Vienna's slave composition in 1852 is probably more typical of the parish type as a whole than that projected above because of the distortions that occurred in households during the war years.

The north-central and Red River cotton parishes did not exhibit the symptoms of disorganization that were detected in the household organization of the Mississippi River cotton parishes. Part of the reason for the discrepancy among the cotton-producing areas is that these two regions were not nearly as productive or as labor-intensive as the Mississippi River cotton parishes. The records located for the two less productive cotton parish types did not encompass nearly as many communities or individuals and are therefore much less reliable for generalizing about the influence of the dominant staple crop on household organization. The Mississippi River cotton parish sample contained nearly three times more slaves and plantation communities than did the other two cotton parish samples combined.

Whether sugar production was substantially more dangerous or unhealthy for slaves cannot be determined from household analysis alone. It is clear, however, that work in sugar production did not foster greater instability and disorganization in slave household composition than did labor in cotton-producing parishes.

As will be discussed further in later chapters, historians of slavery have found that slave life and labor often varied widely according to the size of holding upon which slaves labored. To test how size of holding affected household structure, the large sample of slaves from 155 communities, 1810–64, was analyzed by six size-of-holding groupings.

HOUSEHOLD COMPOSITION ON UNITS
WITH 1 TO 19 SLAVES

The aggregate census for 1850 confirms that 86 percent of Louisiana slaveholders reported owning fewer than twenty slaves (although probably no more than 70 percent of Louisiana's slaves lived in such units).[16] The sample does not reflect such a numerical dominance because slaveowners with twenty or fewer slaves left fewer court and plantation records than did more affluent owners of larger slaveholdings. Reliable records showing household affiliations for this group proved difficult to find. Nevertheless, twenty-two plantations or farms composed of fewer than twenty-one slaves were located that had clear family household designations.

Because most owners had slave communities in this size range and because historians have a particular interest in this category, more analysis has been done on this group than on some of the other categories.[17] The means in all household types and categories suggest that in the typical holding of twenty or fewer slaves the domestic composition was very simple, usually consisting only of solitaires and simple family households. Extended family households and multiple family households were rare, but units of co-resident siblings occurred occasionally. Based on the means of the total numbers of slaves in each household group, one finds that the average community in this sample consisted of fourteen people, eight of them males and six females. On such an average smallholding, three slaves typically had no apparent family affiliations, and two of the three solitaires were young males. The remaining eleven slaves were organized into two families: one was a standard nuclear family of seven members, and the other consisted of a mother and two or three children. Though this was the

TABLE 3.2.

*Percentage of Louisiana Slaves in Selected Family Household Types and Categories,
1810–1864, by Size of Holding*

Household type	Model	1–19 slaves	20–49 slaves	50–99 slaves	100–199 slaves	200–299 slaves	300–399 slaves
Solitaires	18.3	21	24	20	18	11	5
Simple family	73.1	77	71	70	74	80	77
Married couple with child/ children	48.7	48	45	44	51	56	63
Single female with child/ children	14.5	21	18	17	12	13	5
Multiple family	5.5	–	4	7	5	5	8

Source: Louisiana Slave Households Data Base.

profile suggested by the means, the compositions of smallholdings varied. Some consisted of several small standard nuclear families instead of one large family. And some occasionally included married couples without children, widowers with children, or brothers or sisters residing together. Basically, the small communities were composed of some combination of solitaires, standard nuclear families, and female-headed single-parent households, with more individuals in the standard nuclear families.

Of the entire sample of 296 individuals who resided on holdings with fewer than twenty slaves, 77 percent lived in simple families, 21 percent were solitaires, and 2 percent formed non-nuclear units (see table 3.2). Within the solitaires, males formed a much larger percentage of the total than did females, 16 percent to 5 percent. The percentage of solitaires on smallholdings was slightly higher than on the holdings with fifty to ninety-nine slaves and considerably higher than on most holdings containing over one hundred slaves. It was also higher than in the prototypical slave community for the entire period.

Only slightly fewer of the slaves on the smallholdings lived in standard nuclear family households than in the model (48 percent compared to 49 percent), but female-headed single-parent households accounted for more than one-fifth of the slaves in the sample. These two aspects of family construction on smallholdings raise questions: Why did smallholdings have such a high percentage of solitaires, especially males? And if male solitaires were so numerous on smallholdings, why were so many households headed by single females?

Smallholders were marginal producers of staple crops that usually required a gang-labor system if they were to make large profits. Owners and slaves often worked together; every individual's laboring capacity was of utmost importance. Because capital to buy and maintain laborers was limited, it was essential to smallholders that their few slaves had the physical capacity to perform a variety of tasks (some of which required strength, endurance, and skills generally associated with men, such as carpentry or blacksmithing), in addition to traditional fieldwork. Just as nonslaveholding farmers with limited funds to supplement their families' labor were more likely to hire young, single men rather than women, smallholders were inclined to buy or hire young male solitaires. Of course, some women (preferably members of settled families) were needed to help with domestic duties such as cooking, spinning, weaving, sewing, and child care, in addition to fieldwork. Women were also needed to reproduce the labor force so smallholders almost always included or encouraged at least one family unit (standard or female-headed) containing women with children or women of childbearing age.

Why were the male slaves of smallholdings often single? Smallholders tended to purchase young, unattached males. They could not usually afford to buy whole families. They occasionally bought couples, and they bought single females infrequently unless they had special skills. Nevertheless, small owners probably hoped their young male slaves would marry. The problem was finding appropriate mates within such small units. The marriage pool was generally very small; the only eligible girls were the daughters of the few nuclear families. Therefore, only a few of the male solitaires were fortunate enough to find mates within their community.[18] For this reason, small owners allowed off-plantation marriages much more frequently than did large holders.

One might also ask why smallholdings had a fairly high percentage of female-headed single-parent households if young male solitaires were frantically searching for wives. Once more, the answer is that the choices offered by smallholdings were so limited. The slave communities of the smallholding sample typically contained a few male solitaires (mostly young) and perhaps one female single parent. Frequently the male singles were men in their late teens or early twenties, whereas the woman heading her own household was often over thirty-five years of age. Perhaps one of the young men fathered some of the woman's children, but the two were unlikely to form a compatible, permanent couple. Many of the young men took as wives slaves of other smallholders, a pattern pervasive in slaveholdings of fewer than twenty slaves.

This was the normal construction for the sampled communities with fewer than twenty slaves and probably closely resembles that of most Louisiana smallholdings. Usually no more than half of the slaves on such holdings were full working hands. Slaves who were part of such communities were far more likely than slaves on larger plantations to have close, personal contact with their owners and overseers. If a small owner treated his slave property humanely, the resulting intimacy and informality could be advantageous for slave families and households, but if the owner was demanding or brutal, slaves would find it much more difficult to avoid his demands or escape his wrath by blending into the anonymity of a large slave population. And on very small units a sizable circle of friends and kin was not present for socializing or support in periods of crisis. Moreover, slaves on the smallholdings were especially vulnerable to separations through estate division because it was often impossible to split small slave constituencies equitably among numerous heirs. Life on a plantation with a slave force of fewer than twenty has been described in great detail by Solomon Northup, a slave in Louisiana for twelve years and one of the most reliable informants on the Louisiana slave experience.[19]

The sampled twenty-two slave communities with fewer than twenty members represented a wide range in the years in which they were inventoried, the type of agriculture in which they were engaged, and the parishes in which they were located. The slaves in the smallholdings sample belonged to French Creole planters and farmers as well as Americans. Among those sampled was the community of slaves belonging to the estate of Louis Breau in 1821. Four of the sixteen slaves on his Iberville Parish plantation were young solitaires, three of them men. The remainder of his slave force formed two standard nuclear families.[20] In 1841 "Sugarmaker Jim" and his wife and family formed part of a seventeen-person slave force in St. Mary Parish, which was also owned by French Creoles.[21] That community included, in addition to Jim and his family, another standard nuclear family household consisting of a woman and her children and four young male solitaires.

The same general pattern prevailed among the smallholdings of American planters. Among the nineteen slaves who formed part of Jane Lewis's estate in Concordia Parish in 1828 were three standard nuclear families, one elderly married couple, a unit consisting of a mother and children, and three male solitaires.[22] On a 160-acre farm in Pointe Coupee Parish, the appraisers of James Garvis's estate in 1846 inventoried "by room" three standard nuclear families and one female single parent with her offspring.[23] And as late as the 1860s, sampled small slave communities closely corresponded to the household composition suggested by the mean. In 1863, a community of thirteen slaves, consisting of two standard nuclear families and five solitaires, was widely dispersed among six buyers at the probate sale of John B. Evans in Avoyelles Parish.[24] Although many more examples could be cited, these should demonstrate that the typical household construction of communities in the sample with fewer than twenty slaves varied little from parish to parish, from one decade to another, from cotton farms to sugar holdings, and from Creole to American owners. It cannot be claimed that this model represents the household composition of the hundreds of smallholdings scattered throughout Louisiana in the nineteenth century, but the general trend appears to be consistent with the findings from qualitative sources concerning small slave communities (see Chapter 8).[25]

HOUSEHOLD COMPOSITION ON UNITS
WITH 20 TO 49 SLAVES

In the next size-of-holding category, 20 to 49 slaves, even more of the population was solitaires, 24 percent, and for the same reasons. Because more marriage choices were available, however, fewer slaves were in female-headed single-parent households. The proportion of slaves in standard nuclear families dropped from 48 to 44 percent, partially because 4 percent resided in complex forms usually built around standard nuclear families. The 20 to 49 category contained fifty-one communities and reflected the household organization of 1,618 slaves.

Slave communities containing fewer than fifty slaves encompassed more than half of the slave population throughout the antebellum period, although there was a steady trend toward larger holdings.[26] In general, slaves living in units containing under fifty slaves displayed a less stable household organization than did the larger units; their slave communities were more subject to changes resulting from their owners' financial reversals; and they probably worked harder. Moreover, they generally had fewer material comforts and certainly less opportunity for social interaction and community life.

HOUSEHOLD COMPOSITION ON UNITS
WITH 50 TO 99 SLAVES

Large slaveholdings, those containing fifty or more slaves, became increasingly prevalent in Louisiana during the 1850s, and in 1860, 48.4 percent of the total slave population of the state lived in units of fifty or more.[27] Many planters found that a holding of between fifty and one hundred slaves was the most effective working unit. When a population exceeded one hundred, planters often organized another "farm" with its own overseer, driver, quarters, and so forth. The holdings might be adjacent, but they became autonomous units, although kinship ties often existed between them and intermarriage was generally permitted.[28] This category included more of the sample than any other. Fifty-three slave communities were in this category; they contained 3,800 slaves.

The communities sampled in this size-of-holding category displayed a high percentage of solitaires in their total populations, 20 percent. The proportion of slaves in standard nuclear families remained an unimpressive 44 percent, about 4 percent less than in the overall model. Nine percent were members of complex forms, showing a greater diversity and some generational depth; this also helps explain the low percentage in standard nuclear families. The number of slaves living in single-parent households declined slightly, and those in female-headed single-parent households constituted 17 percent of the sampled population, a lower percentage than in the smaller communities. Like those in the preceding category, slaves in this middle-range grouping often had the worst of both worlds. Their units were too large for them to develop personal ties with their owners and too small to achieve a shield of anonymity. Moreover, the work expected of slaves on this size of holding was of a very high level because this was the typical labor force size associated with aggressively ambitious young planters. The household organization profile reflects these ambiguities.

HOUSEHOLD COMPOSITION ON UNITS
WITH 100 TO 199 SLAVES

In all categories containing over one hundred slaves, the larger the size of holding, the greater were the percentages contained in standard nuclear households. Conversely, the larger the communities, the smaller were the percentages in female-headed single-parent households and solitaires. Solitaires made up 18 percent of the community (the norm for the overall sample). Slaves in two-parent households formed a healthy 51 percent of the population, a dramatic improvement over the smaller holdings. The proportion of slaves who resided in female-headed households decreased to 12 percent. The 100 to 199 category also displayed increasing complexity, with 8 percent of its slaves in extended or multiple family households. In all aspects, this category had a much stronger, more stable, and well-balanced domestic organization than all smaller size-of-holding categories. This trend continued in the last two categories. The 100 to 199 category contained twenty-two slave communities with 2,819 inhabitants.

HOUSEHOLD COMPOSITION ON UNITS WITH
200 TO 299 AND 300 TO 399 SLAVES

These two categories contained far fewer communities in the sample but embraced many slaves. The 200 to 299 category contained five slave communities upon which 1,113 slaves resided. The 300 to 399 group contained 683 slaves belonging to two plantations. The trends observed before continued: the larger the holding, the more stable was its household construction. Its greater size made for a larger support network within the slave society, allowed more marriage choices, and, in most cases, provided a higher standard of living because of the wealth of the owners of such huge holdings.[29]

The proportion of solitaires decreased to 11 percent in the 200 to 299 group and constituted only 5 percent of the 300 to 399 category. This low figure suggests that young men and women on large holdings had more opportunities to form their own families, as is reflected in the high percentages in various simple family groups. In the 200 to 299 category, 56 percent of the slaves lived in standard nuclear families; only 13 percent were members of female-headed single-parent households. In the 300 to 399 category, an extraordinary 63 percent of the 683 slaves lived in two-parent households, and only 5 percent lived in families composed of mothers with their child(ren). In both of these very large slaveholding categories, multiple family households made up significant proportions of the population. For example, in the 300 to 399 group, 8 percent of the slaves lived in multiple family households. The higher percentages of slaves forming standard nuclear families in the large slave communities (where choices were more available) strongly indicates that this was the preferred family form for most slaves.

The foregoing analysis shows that although a norm can be established for the slave household composition of 10,329 Louisiana slaves, some variations existed from that norm according to the time period in which the slaves were inventoried, the parishes in which they resided, and the size of holding of which they were a part. Parish types do not appear to have had great bearing on slave household composition. The household organization of slaves who labored primarily in cotton production did not differ significantly from those who worked on sugar estates, contrary to popular, long-held assumptions. Indeed, the high-production cotton parishes had more solitaires and female-headed single-parent households and fewer numbers in the simple family and standard nuclear family household categories than did the sugar parish communities. This indicates a greater instability in communities associated with large-scale, intensive cotton production than in those involved in sugar production. In only one respect were the communities of the sugar parishes less stable—they exhibited a less healthy sex ratio.

The analysis of the sample by size-of-holding categories showed only one important trend: the larger the slaveholding unit, the greater were the opportunities for slaves to achieve a relatively balanced and stable society. It also showed that the broad category containing one to one hundred slaves, which encompassed most of Louisiana slaves, had a slightly less desirable structure than that projected by the model, with fewer people in standard nuclear families and more in solitaire and single-parent households. This implies that the model, which some may see as a more negative view of slave household composition than has been projected by revisionist historians, actually may err too much in the other direction; the model may be too optimistic, slightly skewed by a few very large holdings that exhibit a much more stable organization than was typical for Louisiana slaves.

Of the variables tested, the time period in which the communities existed had the greatest bearing on household composition. Slave communities in the sample responded to major economic trends, but they also displayed a long-range developmental cycle, from the simple to the complex and from relative disorganization to stability, although the cycles were often affected by external forces. Nevertheless, the slave communities, collectively, appear to have resumed their developmental cycles once they passed through a crisis precipitated by external factors. A period of economic expansion did not necessarily result in greater stability and cohesion among slave communities. In fact, the less change imposed from outside the community, the more progress a community was able to make toward establishing and strengthening bonds of family and kinship. During the 1850s general prosperity (combined with a slowed importation rate) coincided with the maturation of many of the slave communities formed during the 1820s and chaotic 1830s. This combination allowed the sampled slave communities to achieve and maintain their highest degree of diversity, stability, and internal cohesion of the entire period.

❧ ❧ ❧ ❧ ❧ ❧ ❧ ❧

PART II
The Developmental Cycle of Three Louisiana Slave Communities

❧ ❧ ❧ ❧ ❧ ❧ ❧ ❧

Part I presented an analytical model of Louisiana slave family and household composition, as well as major variations of that model, drawn from a sizable sample of slave communities for which familial relationships could be documented. It is also necessary to understand more specifically how slave communities developed and responded to economic and demographic factors as well as to owners' choices and circumstances. To perceive the cyclical development that was suggested in the quantitative analysis and to ascertain the symbiosis that existed between the destinies of masters and slaves, three communities will be analyzed in depth in the next three chapters, as the inquiry moves from a general to a particular view of Louisiana slaves' domestic organization.

Slave household composition cannot be fully understood apart from a study of the owners whose actions exerted a tremendous influence on their chattels' personal as well as economic lives. In Part II, questions will be posed and answered in respect to each of the slave communities: When did the owners come to Louisiana, and from where? What were the owners' backgrounds and motivations? Where did they obtain their initial slave forces and how? What happened to each of the owners in the Louisiana setting?

The major focus will be, of course, on the slaves attached to selected plantations. Answers will be sought to such crucial questions as these: What happened to the slaves of each set of owners? How were they affected by removal to Louisiana, by transfers, or by the splintering of their community through estate divisions? How were the slaves constituted into families, households, and communities, and how did that organization fluctuate? How were slaves' age and gender distributions, household composition, and family and kinship development affected by their own choices and preferences, as opposed to externally imposed factors?

THE SETTINGS

Two of the plantations whose slave communities are analyzed—Petite Anse and Tiger Island—were located at opposite ends of the elongated, verdant, fever-ridden parish of St. Mary. The third, Oakland, was located some one hundred miles away in the once-paradisiacal West Feliciana Parish. Oakland was established first, about 1809. Nathaniel Evans established Oakland as a cotton plantation in the northern part of what was then simply Feliciana, an area first inhabited by Tunica Indians. Europeans, most of them French, had settled some parts of the region by 1720, clustering along the west bank of the Mississippi at a spot known as Pointe Coupee.[1] Feliciana, the area on the river's east side, became part of British West Florida at the end of the Seven Years' War.[2] Only a stone's throw away, Pointe Coupee and the west bank, along with its French-speaking settlers, remained in Spanish territory. The Spanish regained control of the West Florida region, which included Feliciana, only twenty years later, in 1783, but the increased flow of immigration begun in the British period continued. Spain was generous in granting land to Americans, but nevertheless, local planters briefly rebelled against Spanish control in 1810. Taking advantage of Spain's deteriorating imperial status, the United States used the planters' rebellion as an excuse to annex Feliciana to the territory of Orleans by presidential proclamation. In 1812, Feliciana became part of the new state of Louisiana, and Oakland was located in the new parish of West Feliciana.[3]

From the 1790s on, upland cotton was the almost exclusive crop of the Felicianas.[4] The area's early and often ostentatious affluence was owing to King Cotton, although sugar was also grown in some parts of the Florida parishes by the later antebellum period. Many of the area's planters had made their capital in other fields—they were merchants, lawyers, and speculators before becoming agriculturalists.[5] A common ingredient may have been that described by the loquacious preacher and keen observer of planter life Timothy Flint. In 1823 he depicted Feliciana planters as "novi hommes"—self-made men. "Many of them," he explained, "are very opulent," producers of "vast quantities of cotton."[6] Nathaniel Evans, a merchant born in Ireland, was one of the self-made men described by Flint, and Oakland was established in such a milieu about 1809.

The slaves of Petite Anse and Tiger Island developed their communities in a somewhat remote setting. At the beginning of the nineteenth century, St. Mary was part of a sprawling, low-lying region of flat coastal plains, steaming swamps and marshes, moss-draped live oaks, and cypress-lined bayous. The larger region was called the Attakapas, dating back to the

French period. That part of the Attakapas in which St. Mary was located was known as the Teche country for the usually languid and navigable Bayou Teche upon which early planters depended for transportation. The region's primary villages, Franklin, St. Martinsville, and New Iberia, grew up on the banks of the Teche. Many early plantations fronted the Teche, the owners' houses adorning the higher west bank like a strand of pearls.[7]

In the late eighteenth and early nineteenth centuries, stock raising was a primary economic activity for slaveowners and nonslaveowners alike, and cotton, corn, and indigo were dominant crops. Cotton remained a major crop on the western prairies of the Attakapas, but it was slowly supplanted by sugar in the Teche area. Francis D. Richardson, owner of Bayside Plantation and an eloquent observer of life in St. Mary Parish, recalled seeing indigo vats along the Teche as late as the 1830s, but indigo production had waned long before that. Recent scholarship has revealed that the switch to sugarcane as the staple crop began earlier than previously believed. Glenn Conrad's research shows that "large-scale sugar operations began on the Teche in the years immediately before statehood, expanded significantly after the War of 1812, particularly with the slump in cotton prices, and really had 'caught the eye' of planters by 1830. In 1829 John D. Wilkins, a tobacco planter from Virginia, came to Louisiana, bought 8,000 acres . . . southeast of New Iberia and began a major sugar operation. His neighbors, the Patout family, began their sugar operation about the same time."[8] Conrad's study of settlement patterns in the Attakapas district has revealed that most land conceded to settlers in the region by colonial governments between 1764 and 1803 was to French Creoles (272 grants) and Acadians (154), but 95 grants were made to Americans. Twenty-one concessions were made to Spaniards and free blacks in the same period. During the American claims period (1811–25), various ethnic groups were required to reaffirm their claims for lands occupied during colonial times. Americans put forward 138 claims, again demonstrating that they were in the area early and stayed, although in far fewer numbers than the French Creoles and the Acadians.[9] The owners of both Petite Anse and Tiger Island first commenced their Louisiana sugar operations in the American claims period. The conversion to sugar and prosperity in the 1830s brought many more American planters to the region.

Conditions in the region during the first quarter of the nineteenth century were primitive. The Attakapas was still a frontier. It would be decades before many of the Americans had the time and capital to erect gleaming white mansions and handsome red brick sugarhouses as monuments to their success. Early American arrivals, such the Brashear, Marsh, Stone, Weeks, Towles, Conrad, Murphy, Moore, and Wilkinson families, had to cope with uncleared land, swollen bayous, and annual scourges of yellow fever and cholera. Settlements were scattered and sparsely populated; many neighbors were French-speakers. Shrewd speculators, the Creoles were quite willing to sell land to the Americans, but they often remained socially aloof.[10] It was in this setting that Petite Anse and Tiger Island plantations were established.

In 1818 Petite Anse was established in St. Mary by two enterprising New Yorkers, John Craig Marsh and William Stone. The luxuriantly vegetated "island" was surrounded on three sides by sea marsh and bayou waters.[11] Archaeological evidence suggests that Indians had long occupied the island, but Europeans as well as Americans had filed claims for portions by the late eighteenth century. The first Anglos to occupy their claims were the intrepid Elizabeth Hayes and her children, who lived there by 1790. Her descendants still retained a few arpents of her claim as late as 1869. Other parts changed hands frequently.[12] Marsh and Stone acquired most of the habitable area of the island, however, buying much of it from Jesse McCall and the estate of Alexander Bienvenu.[13] The plantation took its name from the bayou and from the landmass it partially encircled before meandering through the swamp to Vermilion Bay. Early settlers referred to all as "petite anse," little cove.

Though isolated in comparison to Oakland, Petite Anse Plantation was considerably less remote than Tiger Island. New Iberia was only ten miles away from Petite Anse, although in St. Martin Parish. That village could be reached from the island only by boat or along a narrow plank road flanked by a two-mile stretch of sea marsh on both sides.[14]

The final slave community in the case study was located on Tiger Island Plantation, at the eastern end of St. Mary Parish. The colorful name was given to the area by its first Anglo settlers, but long before their arrival, Chitimache Indians erected ceremonial and burial mounds in the area, on the opposite bank of the swelling of the Atchafalaya River later known as Berwick Bay. In 1797 the Spanish government granted the island to Thomas Berwick and his heirs. A son, Joseph Berwick, obtained the plantation site in 1811 but conveyed it to other parties. Between 1816 and the 1830s a physician, Dr. Walter Brashear of Kentucky, purchased most of the area known as Tiger Island and gave that name to the sugar plantation that he would eventually develop there.[15]

Walter Brashear had at least four sugar plantations in St. Mary: Belle Isle, Tiger Island, Golden Farm, and the Bayou Boeuf place. Among Brashear's holdings, Tiger Island was chosen as the case study because its records are the most complete. But the history of Tiger Island's slave community cannot be separated from that of Brashear's first Louisiana sugar plantation, the tragic Belle Isle overlooking the placid Atchafalaya Bay. It was here that Brashear moved his family in 1822.[16]

In these three settings, the slaves of Oakland, Petite Anse, and Tiger Island attempted to come to grips with their circumstances and obtain a modicum of stability and comfort in at least that area of their lives over which they could exert some control, their domestic organizations: the family, household, and community.

CHAPTER FOUR

Owners and Slaves

OAKLAND

Oakland Plantation was established in Feliciana in 1809, but much of its owners' early history transpired across an invisible line of demarcation along the thirty-first parallel separating West Florida from the territory of Mississippi. By the terms of Pinckney's Treaty of 1795, Spain agreed to honor the line as the boundary between its territory and that of the United States, allowing Americans access to the port of New Orleans for trade and deposit of goods. The area above the line of demarcation was surveyed in 1798, and the United States built Fort Adams, a military garrison on the Mississippi River, within the American sector. The village of Pinckneyville, technically in the Mississippi Territory, grew up as an agricultural trading center almost precisely on the line of demarcation. On the south side of the line, in Feliciana, the villages of St. Francisville and Bayou Sara served local planters in a similar capacity.[1]

Population growth was phenomenal in the lower Mississippi Valley by 1800, presenting exciting prospects for ambitious merchants such as Nathaniel Evans, a witty, articulate, and energetic Irishman for whom cotton planting never was much more than a diversion. Despite his ownership of Oakland Plantation between 1809 and 1819, his heart was always in the intricate, volatile world of buying and selling in the upriver portions of Mississippi and Louisiana.

Evans arrived at New York Harbor from Ireland in 1798. He quickly headed west and in 1800 made a propitious marriage to Sarah Bloomfield Ogden Spencer of Columbus, Ohio, whose family was extremely well connected in both Ohio and New Jersey. Within a year, Evans, his wife, and their infant son Francis moved to the territory of Mississippi, where he had been appointed as supply agent to the commissioner of United States troops in Tennessee and Mississippi, headquartered in Natchez.[2] While continuing in this capacity, he also established a general mercantile business at Fort Adams and a store in Pinckneyville.[3]

Evans's commercial activities were far-flung from the onset. He had a partner in Natchez and connections with import and export firms in New Orleans, New York, Cincinnati, London, and Liverpool.[4] The army at Fort Adams was his best customer.[5] Through his dealings with the military Evans renewed an earlier acquaintance with General James Wilkinson, now commander of the American troops at Fort Adams, and became a close friend of the paymaster, Lieutenant James Sterrett, later a New Orleans merchant.[6] Evans sold an impressive variety of goods to villagers, soldiers, and planters, but basically he was an upriver merchant who acted as a go-between for cotton planters of New Feliciana and western Mississippi and the staple merchant firms of New Orleans.[7]

The mercantile class of which Evans was a part enjoyed flush times in the lower Mississippi Valley until 1805. From 1806 to 1810, then again during the War of 1812, many of the merchants experienced serious financial difficulties. The New Orleans merchants were hardest hit. Evans and many of his Mississippi cohorts belonged to a merchant-creditor clique with strong Federalist connections, as did most of the New Orleans group. President Thomas Jefferson's military cutbacks had ominous effects on the area's economy even before the unsettling events surrounding the Aaron Burr affair and the implementation of the Embargo and Non-Intercourse acts. In a humorous but caustic letter to a friend in 1802, Evans, a Federalist, bemoaned the depressing economic effects of "these Republican times" on the prospect for a properly festive celebration of St. Patrick's Day.[8]

The revelations of the Burr conspiracy during 1806 and 1807 shook the

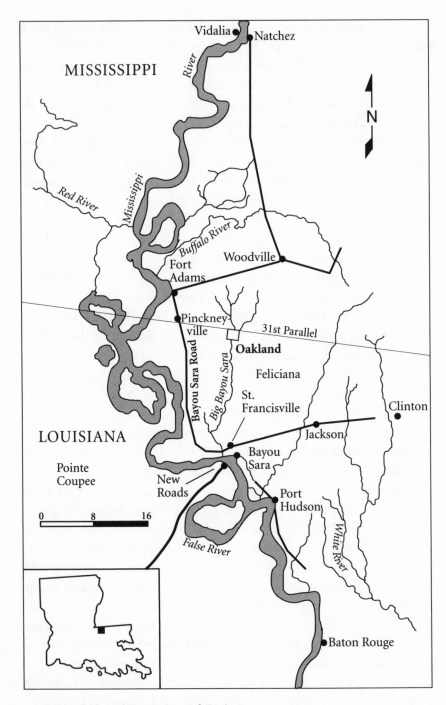

4.1 Oakland Slave Community and Environs

New Orleans banking structure and demoralized members of the merchant class, several of whom General Wilkinson accused of treasonable activities. Evans was personally acquainted with many of the major figures accused by Wilkinson, including Samuel Swartwout, Peter Ogden, and Daniel Clark. Some relatives of Evans's wife in New York were suspected of giving substantial financial support to the scheme.[9] Specific involvement by Evans cannot be documented, but he certainly knew about Burr's alleged plan to "revolutionize" Louisiana and sever the western states from the Union. It was widely discussed in his social circle. And one of Evans's closest friends, Samuel Swartwout, as well as his wife's nephew Peter Ogden, acted as couriers between Burr and Wilkinson.[10]

Between the confusion engendered by the Burr affair, the embargo on all foreign trade, and the weakness of the New Orleans banking structure, many merchant-creditors of the Natchez–New Orleans region were in a state of panic by 1807.[11] Evans weathered the crisis better than most merchants, but the disruption of "commerce regularity and confidence" (as fellow merchant O. H. Spencer called it) influenced his decision to diversify by investing in a cotton plantation.[12]

Another factor in his decision was the desire to provide a healthy, serene, and permanent home for his family. Until they moved to Feliciana in 1809, Sarah Evans and the four surviving children divided their time between small residences at Pinckneyville and at Fort Adams, the location of their main store.[13] Sarah had little taste for the commercial adventures and political intrigues that fascinated her husband and cousins. Ironically, one of the most blatant of the intriguers, Samuel Swartwout, was one of her chief allies in convincing Evans to establish a plantation. In a letter that deals primarily with the details of his arrest and imprisonment by General Wilkinson for his alleged role in the Burr affair, Swartwout advised Evans that his wife would "do better in the country, mistress of a farmer's family, you know you promised her that last year. . . . You & your amiable family will be amply compensated by so desirable a change," he assured his friend, because "you will make more by raising cotton than by your store."[14] Oakland was established in 1809, as much as for family considerations as for profit making, though the shrewd Evans no doubt expected returns in both areas.

Evans was away from Oakland as much as he was there, continuing his merchant activities without interruption. In his absences, the plantation was in the charge of Evans's overseer, Micajah Davis, and his wife, Sarah.[15] Evans's journals and correspondence demonstrate that he maintained a lively interest in the day-to-day operations at Oakland even when he was elsewhere. His interest in the plantation was greatest in the early years, and the 1811 account of his harvest is one of the earliest detailed records of cotton picking extant in the Louisiana records.[16] In it, he listed his slaves, kept count of their daily pickings, and made occasional comments on their character, assignments, and absences from the field. It is clear from the journal that the plantation was fully operational by 1811 with a slave force of forty, obtained locally and in the Natchez and New Orleans markets.

Oakland's early slave community probably considered Nathaniel Evans a good master in comparison to others they knew or had heard about. He was a good businessman and required consistent labor from his workers, but he was not insensitive to their needs. Few Oakland slaves were sold in his lifetime. He avoided separating families, as would his wife and son. He was concerned about the health of the slaves, providing adequate rations, smallpox inoculations for the children, decent clothing, and sturdy housing and furnishings.[17]

Almost nothing is known about the social activities of Oakland's slaves, but they had far more opportunities for social interaction with laborers from other plantations than did slaves on the other plantations in the case study. The St. Francisville–Bayou Sara area of West Feliciana was well populated with blacks, and local planters often exchanged, loaned, and hired out their slaves within the parish. Evans frequently participated in such arrangements. He sent slaves to town on errands on an almost daily basis, and a few skilled slaves were sent out "jobing" in the Mississippi Territory.[18] Therefore, many of Oakland's slaves had opportunities to get off the plantation, but to what degree they were allowed to do so for social purposes is not known. No records have been located to suggest that Oakland's slaves married off the plantation. The plantation generally possessed a good gender balance so perhaps there was no necessity for its slaves to seek mates elsewhere, or Evans might have prohibited such unions, as did many of his neighbors.[19]

Slaves ran away frequently in the Felicianas, but few escaped permanently. Most commonly, they hid out in the woods or swamps for a few days or weeks to evade work or avoid punishment. Although the number of Evans's runaways was small compared to those of some of his neighbors, he did have some. Jerry, for example, was off in the midst of the busy ginning season of 1811. Gundy, whom Evans had described on that year's roll as a "slowmotioned ox," was quick enough to elude his master for a month in June 1814, after which he voluntarily returned. Gundy was locked in the stocks for random periods throughout the month following his return, but he did not receive a lashing. In fact, no mention of whipping was found in the Oakland records. Bob ran away in 1819; his was apparently a more serious attempt. He may have planned to hide aboard a departing steamboat, for the overseer reported that, according to one of Bob's companions who was captured, "Bob was amin for the Red River."[20]

Life for the Evans family and the Oakland slaves was comparatively uneventful from 1811 to 1819. Despite disruptions in trade during the War of 1812, Evans's merchandising business prospered, and he continued to invest in land and other properties. The slave community increased to ninety-eight by 1819.[21] Although a few slaves were purchased, including some by Evans's brother in Bardstown, Kentucky, most of the increase came from births.[22]

An infant daughter had died in 1803 before the Evans family moved to Oakland, and a second daughter—an engaging five-year-old, Margaret Emma—died in 1811. The family was greatly affected by the little girl's death, and Evans's cotton journal shows that he took the slaves out of the fields, allowing no work to be done, on the day of her funeral.[23] The rest of the family remained healthy, and the two eldest children were sent away from Oakland to attend school.[24]

In 1819, just before a long-anticipated trip back to the land of his birth, Evans contracted malaria while on a trip to the coastal parishes. He died within a few days, at the age of forty-three.[25] His passing would ultimately cause successive waves of disruption in the previously quiet lives of Oakland's slaves.

At Evans's death, the running of the plantation was assumed by Sarah Evans. She conducted its business very ably with the assistance of overseers until her youngest son, John N. Evans, came of age and became her partner. She handled a considerable estate; it included 2,670 arpents of cotton land in Feliciana, 450 arpents on Buffalo Creek in Mississippi, town lots in both St. Francisville, Louisiana, and Fort Adams, Mississippi, as well as business inventories. In 1820 the federal census counted 108 slaves on the undivided estate.[26]

The estate was not settled for several years. During that time the slave community was essentially undisturbed, and the work force steadily expanded. In 1822 the probate court ordered a partition and final settlement.[27] The slaves were divided into four contingents between the widow and the three children. Two of the children, John and Cornelia, were still minors, and their slaves remained at Oakland for the time being, under the control of Sarah Evans, their mother and guardian. Francis Allison Evans was twenty-one and entitled to his share of the estate. He bought a plantation a few miles from Oakland.[28]

In defiance of her family, which had thwarted an earlier romance with a charming dancing master, young Cornelia married a dashing steamboat captain, John DeHart, who had been a business acquaintance of her father. By 1824, they had moved to the Indian Bend region of St. Mary Parish, taking with them Cornelia's share of the estate's slaves. The Oakland slaves, transported more than a hundred miles to DeHart's Orange Grove plantation, were severed from an extensive community of relatives and friends, which had been developing since the first decade of the century. On the Louisiana coast, they were required to make enormous adjustments—to new owners, to a radically different style of management, to dramatic changes in topography and climate, and to an unfamiliar type of agricultural production—sugar rather than upland cotton. How they fared will be related later in this chapter.[29]

Oakland's labor force was drastically curtailed when Francis Evans's slaves were removed to his plantation and Cornelia's to St. Mary Parish. In 1830 the combined holdings of Sarah Evans and John Evans, her son and now partner, amounted to only 82 slaves, 26 fewer than were present at Oakland a decade earlier, despite a dozen or more births.[30] The rebuilding of Oakland's labor force and the recovery of its slave community proceeded slowly until in 1841 Oakland had 111 slaves in residence.[31]

Sarah and John Evans operated Oakland as a partnership from the late 1820s until her death in 1851, although they carefully maintained separate accounts of their real and personal property. Separate records were kept in broad areas such as income and expenses but also in such specific areas as medical bills and issuances of food, tools, household goods, and clothing to the slaves. Although painstakingly differentiated in the records of Oakland, the partners' combined holdings functioned as a single social and economic unit, and the lines between the "property of S. B. Evans" and the "property of J. N. Evans" were indistinctly observed by the slaves themselves. The laborers freely interacted in both social and economic spheres, and many intermarried.[32]

Initially, Sarah Evans owned the largest share of the land attached to Oakland, but John soon expanded his holdings.[33] By her death, his holdings matched hers, and he had taken over many of the managerial functions. He married Mary Ann Chandler, a young woman wealthy in her own right, and began a household that would eventually include five children.[34]

The late 1820s and the 1830s were in most respects good times for the owners of Oakland, but not entirely so. Cornelia, the only surviving daughter of three born to Sarah and Nathaniel Evans, died on 31 December 1832, at the age of twenty-seven, leaving as her heirs in St. Mary Parish a husband and four young children.[35] When Cornelia died, the slaves of Orange Grove came under the exclusive control of her husband, Captain John DeHart, a hard, brooding man feared by the slaves. At her death, Cornelia owned thirty slaves at Orange Grove, all from the Oakland estate or their descendants. She owned one slave jointly with her husband, and he owned fewer than four at Orange Grove as his separate property. Acting as administrator of the estate and natural tutor of their children, Captain DeHart soon made changes among the former Oakland slaves that profoundly affected their future.

When she married DeHart, Cornelia Evans's slave property included two young couples, two unmarried women in their teens, and four families. The inventory and appraisement of Cornelia's estate in 1833 reveals the status of these slaves. The husbands of the two young couples were both absent—sold or dead. Their wives now had children, and one wife, Phyllis, had named her youngest son Armstead, after his missing father. Of the two unmarried women, one was still single and without offspring, but the other, still unmarried, had produced three children since she moved to Orange Grove.[36]

The first of the four standard nuclear families inherited by Cornelia was that of Little Harry and Liddy, who were married by 1817 and had a son, Manuel, by 1819. All were still alive in 1833, but the family had not increased. The second family was one of the oldest and most valued of the early Oakland slave community, headed by Peter and his wife, Rhoda, both regarded by their original owner as excellent workers. The couple lost one son in 1816, but two survived (Booker and Carlos). One additional son had been born at Orange Grove by 1833.

The last two families were severely affected by John DeHart's administration of Cornelia's estate, for he petitioned the court to sell both almost immediately after his wife's death. One of the families was that of Stepney, Milly, and their two children, Tom and Esther. The old master, Nathaniel Evans, had found no fault with them, but DeHart told the court that both adults were "of bad character" and that Milly was a thief. Less than two months after their young mistress's demise, the entire family was sold at public auction for $1,000.[37]

The final family that Cornelia had taken with her to Orange Grove was that of Jem Stack and Maria. They, too, had been part of the Oakland community since its founding. In 1833 the family of Jem and Maria included three children, Eliza, Caroline, and Billy. Again charging that the adults were "of bad character," DeHart sought the court's permission to sell the entire family. For undetermined reasons, Maria and the children were not sold, but Jem Stack was, separated from old Oakland friends, his wife of sixteen years, and his three children.[38] Witnessing his father taken off to auction in chains, never to be seen again, must have left a searing memory in the mind of the youngest, nine-year-old Billy, too young to understand the harsh realities of the system.

Eight years passed. Captain John DeHart sat at a table in his bedroom, reading while eating his solitary supper. It was an unusually hot, sultry evening for late October. The long shuttered windows opening on to the gallery were ajar to catch any cooling breeze that might stir. When a maid brought his meal about seven o'clock, DeHart sent her to retrieve a seine that had been left on the bank of the bayou. The errand took her out of the house for only a few minutes. No one heard the muffled shot, or would admit to it later, but when the girl returned to get her master's supper tray, she found him slumped over the table, his brains and hair splattered on the wall behind him.

The sheriff determined that Captain DeHart was killed by a powerful blast fired through an open window, the assailant hidden by heavy vines that curtained the gallery. The killer escaped in the dusk through the adjacent orange grove. An elderly slave working in the yard saw a figure emerge from the deeply shaded grove, mount a horse, and ride away at "full speed," but the figure was too far away to identify in the failing light, even as to race. At first it was rumored that a mysterious white man had shot DeHart. Another soon circulated that he was "shot at his own table" by his slaves, before the startled eyes of his children. In truth, DeHart was dining alone; his children were away at school.

A few days later, several Orange Grove slaves were arrested for the crime. The alleged shooter and ringleader was Bill, who, like his father before him, was regarded as a perpetual runaway. He was absent from the plantation at the time of DeHart's death but was arrested following his voluntary return to the plantation. Under questioning, he allegedly implicated four co-conspirators. Court records are no longer extant, and surviving newspaper accounts fail to explain how the young field slaves would have had access to a gun and a horse and why Bill came back to the plantation of his own accord. Within a month, all five slaves were convicted and executed. At least four of the five were descendants of Oakland slaves. Bill was Billy, the son of Maria and Jem Stack—the same boy whose father had been sold at De-Hart's order in 1833. Also among the slaves executed were Manuel, son of Little Harry and Liddy, and Carlos and Booker, sons of Peter and Rhoda. The executions wiped out most of the young male slaves in the Orange Grove community.[39] The agonized community was not dispersed, however. It stayed on at Orange Grove, which was run by overseers until the return from school of the DeHart's only son, John, Jr.

Cornelia's mother, Sarah Evans, mistress of Oakland, renounced her claim to the succession of Captain DeHart but served as guardian of his minor children. She took the girls back to Oakland to live and financed the medical school education of her grandson John DeHart, Jr.[40]

Despite the lethargic economy and family trauma resulting from De-Hart's murder, the decade of the 1840s was generally an expansive one for Oakland and a period of building for the Evans family as well as the plantation. The household included John's wife, two sons and two daughters, his mother, Sarah, and the three daughters of his deceased sister Cornelia.[41]

The Evans family was well respected, but it was not part of the extremely wealthy cotton aristocracy of the Felicianas. Its wealth in land and slaves did not approach that of the Turnbulls, Stirlings, Barrows, or even close friends such as the Butlers.[42] Though Oakland was not among the largest or even the most productive of the region's plantations, it provided a comfortable life for the family. And except for the death of John and Mary Ann Evans's one-year-old son in 1841, the 1840s were relatively tranquil as well as prosperous until the end of the decade. Then Mary Ann Evans unexpectedly died, followed within three years by the family matriarch, Sarah Evans.

Mary Ann Chandler Evans's death in 1849 deprived her family of a wife and mother, but it had no direct effect on the composition of the Oakland slave community.[43] Therefore, in 1850, Oakland's slave society was probably at its zenith as a well-balanced, socially integrated community.

Life at Oakland was well structured for blacks and whites alike. Whether the admirable organization and meticulous record-keeping at Oakland was attributable to Sarah Evans or her son is not known. Although in her seventies, Sarah still made the major decisions concerning her property, and in the 1850 census she is recorded as the head of a multiple family which included her widowed son John, his four children, and her three orphaned granddaughters.[44]

Also in 1850, the three daughters of Cornelia DeHart received three-fourths interest in the Orange Grove plantation and slaves in the form of a sale from their older brother, Dr. John DeHart, who had controlled the property during their minorities.[45] The estate division may have been in the form of a routine sale, or it may have been influenced by an acutely embarrassing incident that might have prompted a reevaluation of the troubled young physician's ability to manage the plantation for the other heirs.

After finishing his training, John DeHart, Jr., had returned to St. Mary Parish to practice medicine and to operate Orange Grove under the accusing eyes of a slave community that had suffered separations and abuse from his father and had been robbed, justly or unjustly, of five young men in a grisly execution. DeHart, too, must have held smoldering resentment against the silent company of slaves, whom he may well have held jointly responsible for the murder of his father. Perhaps it was the trauma of his father's violent death or perhaps an unconscious adoption of the abusive traits of his father that encouraged the development of sadistic tendencies in the young man. It is safe to surmise that the incident that occurred in June 1849 and came to light in an 1850 conviction was but the capstone of a series of mistreatments of his slaves. DeHart was accused by his neighbors and peers of "cruel mistreatment of a slave," a young mulatto named John. The slave was examined by experts who reported to the court that he had been whipped, burned, cut, and branded all over his torso, including his buttocks and testicles, by a small branding iron having the mark of a "d" encapsulated in a heart. The revelations shocked DeHart's family at Oakland but were not news to the thirty-five slaves at Orange Grove, who must have often heard the young man's tortured screams. Brought to the Fourteenth Judicial Court by charges made by fellow planters in St. Mary Parish, Dr. DeHart was found guilty and fined a token $200 by a lenient judge who had been one of the appraisers of his father's estate.[46] In compliance with a court order, the slave was sold.[47] DeHart left the parish after the incident.

Shortly after the judgment against her grandson in St. Mary, Sarah Evans wrote her will at Oakland. Her estate was to be divided among her children or their living descendants, but she also made several special bequests. She left her grandson John DeHart "*all the money* I have extended to him in giving him a medical profession," and she ordered that her granddaughters should have the services of the servant woman Celeste "as long . . . as they remain at their Uncle John's."[48]

That same year, 1850, the slave community numbered 138 individuals, jointly owned by Sarah Evans and John N. Evans. Once more the increase was primarily owing to births, which occurred regularly among the new families formed in the late 1830s. The sale of only two slaves, both young, male solitaires, can be specifically documented for the entire 1819–50 period, both taking place in the 1840s.[49] Besides the expected deaths of infants, a puzzling series of deaths occurred among older children and young adults in the 1840s, with at least four in 1845 alone.[50]

Records for the 1830–50 period are especially rich and include many informative lists of slaves. Some are enumerations for tax purposes, others are rolls, but most list recipients of various domestic or occupational items. These lists lack the precision of court records, and they are frustratingly inconsistent. Some do not provide ages of the slaves, and others do not enumerate the entire slave force. But used together with other sources, they fill in many blanks and are especially helpful in determining relationships among Oakland slaves. These dozen or more lists provide documentation upon which reconstitutions of families can be partially based, help bridge the period between the early Oakland community and that of the 1850s when precise records are again available, and provide some insight into the material culture of Oakland slaves.[51]

The slave community at Oakland in 1850 had almost fully recovered from the partitions of the 1820s. Kinship was developing, age and sex distributions were near normal (assisted by John Evans's steady purchases of young potential mates in the 1830s), and young families were forming and expanding at a rapid pace. The community was little affected by the division of the estate of their young mistress, Mary Ann Evans, who died in 1849, but the death of the old mistress, Sarah Evans, in February 1851, had a serious impact.[52]

Sarah Evans survived her husband, Nathaniel, by thirty-two years. She provided continuity in ownership for the older slaves. It was she who loved Oakland the most, who was always present, who had been young with the oldest slaves, who had nursed some of them in sickness and childbirth, and who had held the plantation and much of the slave community together in the critical decade after her husband's death before her son became a partner. It was she who planned the gardens, expanded the plantation, and built the great house. It was she who encouraged families, and it was she who, in her will, urged her son John to buy the older servants from the estate so they would not have to leave their home. For these reasons, many of Oakland's slaves grieved the death of the old woman. But all of the slaves, whether they were saddened or indifferent to the passing of yet another owner, were concerned about the repercussions of her demise, for she was a primary owner. At the partition of her estate in 1852, forty-five Oakland slaves were destined for removal. Thirty were drawn by DeHart heirs. Fifteen were inherited by Francis Evans and transferred to his nearby plantation; their adjustment would be eased because his slave community was closely linked to that of Oakland through kinship and frequent visitation. John Evans acted as the administrator of his mother's estate. In that capacity, he made several adjustments in the appraiser's distributions to keep husbands and wives and parents and children on the same plantation.[53]

Once more, the slaves inherited by the DeHarts faced a difficult adjustment. For slaves of the 1851–52 partition, the removal must have been even more difficult than for those of the 1822 and 1833 successions. Some of the slaves displaced in 1851 left a home they had known for forty years and were severed from several generations of friends and relatives. The Oakland community had surely learned of the difficulties experienced by the slaves taken to Orange Grove, and the slaves inherited by the DeHarts must have faced their journey to St. Mary Parish with great trepidation.

The death of Sarah Evans was the last occasion for an estate division of Oakland slaves. John Evans, with his children, was sole owner of Oakland and would remain so until his death nearly forty years later. Oakland's slave community consisted of 115 members (down from 138 in 1850) after all the heirs had received their shares. This included the slaves Evans purchased from other heirs to prevent separating families.[54]

In 1860 Evans was listed on the federal census as a fifty-year-old planter with property valued at $164,000. His household included his daughters Cornelia, twenty-two, and Corinne, sixteen, and his son Frank, fourteen, each credited with personal property valued at $5,000. Of the DeHart nieces, only Louisa, twenty-eight, remained at Oakland. Evans's household also included a new wife, his children's former governess, Marian Darcy, whom he married in 1860. Evans would have a second family with Marian, surviving members of which inherited Oakland.[55]

The Civil War had a monumental effect on the families and communities of the Felicianas, as it did throughout Louisiana and, indeed, most of the South. Some areas were more directly affected than others. Heavy fighting took place at Berwick Bay, and in 1864, the battles of Mansfield and Pleasant Hill were bitter, costly engagements for both sides. But as Charles P. Roland states, the only battle of "major proportions" in the Louisiana plantation districts was the siege of Port Hudson, near West Feliciana.[56]

Although relatively little fighting took place in Louisiana compared to other parts of the South, the state did not escape physical destruction. Indeed, slaveowning parishes were ravaged by confiscations, pilfering, vandalism, and neglect as armies of both sides destroyed anything that could be of use to the enemy. Planters forsook their homes in frenzied flights to the northern and western parishes and then to Texas. Confused and demoralized slaves abandoned their plantations or refused to work. And opportunistic and often brutal marauders intimidated the vulnerable, black or white, and stole what they could find.[57] Except in a few locations, the greatest losses of property in Louisiana did not come from cannons and combat but from what Roland calls the "winds of destruction—blown from friend and foe alike."[58] The Felicianas did not suffer from as much pillaging and destruction of plantation homes as did those parishes on the

Mississippi River between Baton Rouge and New Orleans, but the area was not entirely spared. In March 1863, Union troops invaded the Florida parishes, engaging some Rebel infantry, then retreated after extensive looting.[59] Their visit terrified the residents of the Felicianas, who braced for their inevitable return.

Even while life went on as usual on plantations such as Oakland, reminders of the conflict were everywhere. Residents of both East and West Feliciana parishes heard the frightening sounds of war and saw the cannon flashes from nearby Port Hudson, located between St. Francisville and Baton Rouge, even before the major siege began.[60]

On 23 May 1863, General Nathaniel Banks and thirteen thousand troops of the Union army crossed the Mississippi River at Bayou Sara, a short distance from Oakland. As the troops made their way across the Felicianas, slaveowners found their slave forces diminished nightly, the boldest chattels stealing away in the dark to follow the Union troops. More Federal troops followed, and soon the Confederate stronghold at strategic Port Hudson—key to control of the Mississippi River—was under deadly siege. The siege continued for forty-five days and included twenty-one days of intense combat and two unsuccessful major assaults. On 6 June, Ellen Power wrote in her diary, "They are still fighting at Port Hudson, how much our poor men must suffer." She was correct; the siege took a terrible toll in lives and injuries on both sides. The outcome was inevitable, even though the surrender of Port Hudson came only after the Confederate commander learned about the fall of Vicksburg on 4 July 1863. As Joe Gray Taylor observed, "Banks had surrounded Port Hudson and the results that military action could not achieve quickly starvation would achieve slowly." Supplies ran out, and the exhausted Rebel troops were reduced to eating rodents by the time of the surrender.[61] The defenders of Port Hudson were in such pitiful shape that some of the victors willingly shared their provisions with them.

Slaves in the Oakland vicinity began fleeing their plantations in small numbers when Federal troops first entered the area, but following the surrender of Port Hudson they left by the hundreds. Among those who had waited until Port Hudson fell were Evans's slaves at his Hazlewood Plantation. He noted in his journal that "the Hazlewood negroes all ran off to the Yankees on the ninth of June 1863" and later recorded the names of twelve who were "reported dead at Port Hudson." Among these were five children under the age of five, an old man, and six men and women in their twenties.[62] The death toll among contraband slaves was very high. Conditions were unhealthy for the soldiers and worse for the slaves, who swarmed into makeshift refugee camps at Port Hudson and Baton Rouge. Many slaves in the camps died from exposure and contagious diseases, and most of the casualties were the old and the young children.

The pattern exhibited by Evans's Hazlewood slaves (presumably also by his Oakland slaves since only forty-two were left on the plantation in early 1864) was found throughout West Feliciana and adjacent parishes. Not only the young and healthy but also the elderly, sick, crippled, and even blind slaves made their way to Port Hudson in search of freedom. Some women literally rose from childbed to join in the exodus, with their newborn infants bundled in their arms. Throughout invaded areas of the state slave families argued over the decision to go or to stay. Some wives left without husbands and grown children without their parents. In many cases, however, there was no argument. All left who were physically able to do so. One Louisiana mistress wrote that all of her slaves had fled to the Federal lines "save one invalid family . . . and a young man . . . who remained with his sick wife."[63] At the magnificent manor house on Rosedown Plantation, also in West Feliciana, Martha Turnbull painstakingly listed the slaves who "ran off at the siege of Port Hudson" and later noted on the back of the list those who had died "with the Yankees." Her list, compared with Rosedown's inventories, provides information on the ages and conditions of slaves who joined the contraband camps in West Feliciana Parish. Turnbull later estimated that "very near 450 negroes were liberated by the Yankees belonging to M.H.T [herself] & the Estate" of her deceased husband, Daniel Turnbull.[64]

In 1864, only forty-two slaves still lived at Oakland, a fraction of the former community. This number was even more diminished by 1865, when John Evans and his family began to adjust to a new plantation system using contracted laborers.[65] At emancipation—a new beginning for Oakland's slaves as free people but an end for them as an intact community—the slave society closely resembled that of the 1809–11 period. In 1811, the household composition of Oakland's forty slaves could scarcely qualify them as a community. In 1865, Oakland's freed laborers were about the same number or less, and, once more, were barely recognizable as a community.[66]

PETITE ANSE

About a decade after Nathaniel and Sarah Evans established Oakland with dreams of a long, comfortable, and genteel life as cotton planters, two northern families came to the southern part of Louisiana with similar hopes of wealth and eventual leisure. Their ticket to status and success was sugar, not cotton, and prospects for success were good. Some Creole and American planters were already demonstrating the profitability of sugar production in the Attakapas. John Marsh and William Stone acted quickly, buying the most promising land on Petite Anse, a bayou-created island where sugar was already being grown on a small scale. Upon their arrival in 1818, the overseer Jesse McCall already had a cane crop in the field, a welcome sight and good omen, they thought.

John C. Marsh was born at Rahway, New Jersey, in 1789 but lived in New York City at the time of his departure for Louisiana. His wife, Eliza, and baby daughter Sarah accompanied him by boat to the South, but their son George remained in school in New Jersey. Three more daughters and a son who died in infancy were born in Louisiana.[67] Marsh and his family arrived in 1818. The following year his partner William Stone also moved from New York City to Petite Anse, with his wife, Euphemia, and their son David.[68] Both families lived on the island for at least part of the time during the 1820s.

In 1820, the Stone-Marsh partnership owned thirty-one slaves, fourteen males and seventeen females, most of them purchased in the Northeast. Almost all were working-age hands; only two small children were listed in that year's census.[69]

The Marsh and Stone families' common business interests and long friendship continued until the mid-1820s, when a series of personal tragedies began to mar their undertaking. Eliza Marsh died on a trip back east in August 1826, and her youngest daughter, Helen, died on the island shortly thereafter.[70] By October, William Stone had also succumbed.[71] A stunned John Marsh attempted to run the plantation alone, with a slave force that the same fevers had diminished to twenty-eight, fewer than the partnership had six years earlier despite natural increases and some purchases.

Two years after his partner's death, John Marsh married Stone's widow, Euphemia. Perhaps because he thought it would be a healthier environment, in 1828 he bought land on both sides of the Teche and moved his family there before 1830.[72]

Marsh's second marriage was short-lived. Euphemia and a young daughter born to the marriage both died in the late winter or early spring of 1836.[73] Marsh was only forty-seven when his second wife died, but he appears to have lost interest in life as a sugar planter and abandoned his plantation for months at a time—perhaps associating it with the loss of so many loved ones. He spent much of his time in the Northeast after 1836 but continued to maintain his home in New Iberia.

In the early 1830s, the slave population of Petite Anse ranged from fifty to sixty; it is difficult to determine with precision because Marsh frequently rotated his Petite Anse and New Iberia slaves. In early 1839, Marsh officially conveyed an undivided one-third of Petite Anse and its seventy-one slaves to his only son, George, who had been active in operating the plantation since 1836.[74] George Marsh resided in the family home at New Iberia for part of the year, but he worked on Petite Anse for long periods and by 1840 claimed it as an official residence. That year his Petite Anse household consisted of himself and six other men who appear to have been employees. Among the Petite Anse slaves, George owned thirty-eight in his own right, nineteen of each gender.[75]

The 1840 census of St. Martin Parish credited John Marsh with eighty-eight slaves, but they included his two-thirds of the Petite Anse slave force as well as town servants.[76] An 1839 Petite Anse inventory indicated that the partnership of John C. Marsh and George Marsh owned seventy-one slaves.[77] Several more were certainly born between the 1839 appraisal and the 1840 census enumeration, but the discrepancy in numbers suggests that John Marsh kept a fairly large contingent of laborers in New Iberia in addition to those he owned in partnership with his son.

John Marsh traveled frequently during the 1840s and was rarely in Louisiana for more than a few weeks at a time. After being in Baltimore for much of 1840, he moved to New York City by 1845.[78] Despite his frequent absences, the 1850 census for St. Martin Parish still described him as the head of a household that included his son-in-law William Robertson, his daughter Eliza, and their three small children.[79] Marsh had conveyed most of his Louisiana property to his children by 1849, deeding Petite Anse to George Marsh, Sarah Marsh Avery and her husband, Daniel David Avery, and Margaret Marsh Henshaw and her husband, Ashbal B. Henshaw.[80]

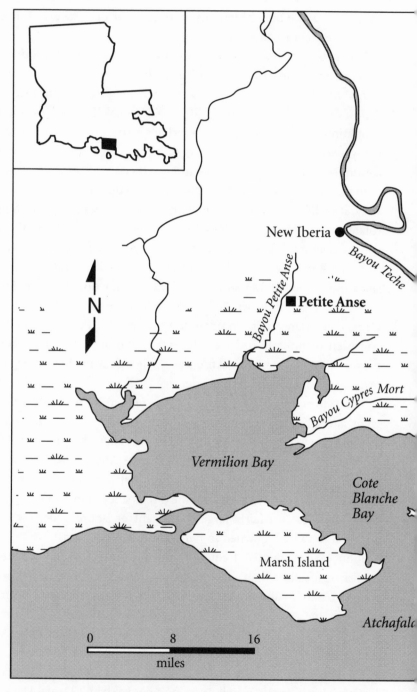

4.2 Petite Anse and Tiger Island Slave Communities and Environs

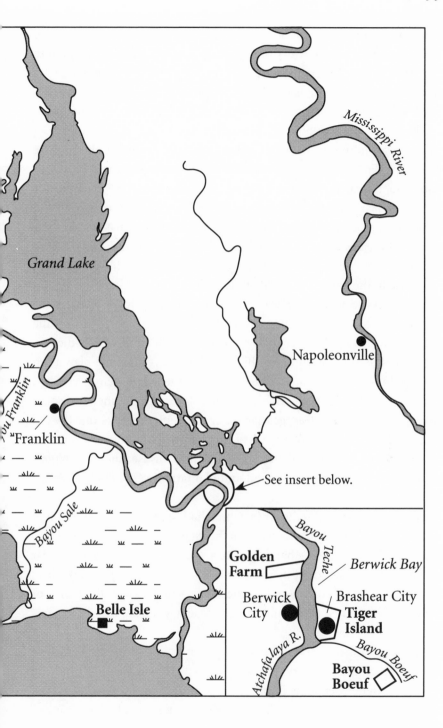

Mississippi River

Grand Lake

Napoleonville

Bayou Franklin

Franklin

See insert below.

Bayou Sale

Belle Isle

Golden
Farm

Bayou Teche

Berwick Bay

Berwick
City

Brashear City
Tiger
Island

Atchafalaya R.

Bayou Boeuf

Bayou
Boeuf

Daniel and Sarah Avery and their five small children continued to reside in East Baton Rouge, where Avery practiced law, but the Henshaws moved to Petite Anse in 1849, where they are enumerated as part of George Marsh's household in the 1850 census returns. That year, George Marsh was reported as the owner of eighty-five slaves on Petite Anse, but they were actually held in partnership with two of his sisters and their spouses.[81]

In the 1850s John Craig Marsh lived in Rahway, New Jersey, although he died at the East Baton Rouge home of his eldest daughter in 1858.[82] Meanwhile, the Henshaws had tired of island life. Before he departed for the East in 1851, John Marsh conveyed the New Iberia property to the Henshaws, George Marsh, and the Averys, but the other owners sold their shares to the Henshaws. The Henshaws moved from Petite Anse to New Iberia that same year. In 1854, they conveyed their one-third interest in Petite Anse to the Averys, giving them two-thirds ownership of the plantation and slaves, with George Marsh retaining the remainder. Even as the majority owner of Petite Anse, Avery left the daily operations of the plantation up to his brother-in-law George Marsh until Marsh died in December 1859.[83] An inventory of his estate in 1860 valued the plantation and its eighty-nine slaves at $54,516.92. In 1860 the federal census credited the partnership of Marsh and Avery with 104 slaves, but this included some of Avery's slaves.[84] After George Marsh's death, Petite Anse became the full property of Daniel D. and Sarah Avery and their heirs. Within a generation the century-old name of Petite Anse fell into disuse and was largely forgotten, and by the 1870s the land and plantation were known as Avery Island, as they are today.[85]

Oddly, the destiny of Petite Anse, which had been a sugar plantation at least since 1816, came to be associated in the 1860s with the antithesis of that product—salt. Even more than sugar, that rare commodity was in great demand by the armies of both South and North in the Civil War. Because of its salt deposits, Petite Anse became a powerful pawn in the hands of generals of the United States and the Confederacy during the Teche campaign.

Petite Anse's inhabitants had been aware of its saline springs at least since the early nineteenth century, probably earlier.[86] But it was not until the early 1860s, under demands imposed by war, that the owners discovered the island's full potential for salt production. The Averys had a salt evaporating plant on Petite Anse in 1861 and sold salt to the Confederacy. The operation, based on evaporation of salt-bearing brine from the springs, was tediously slow and did not produce salt in volume. In 1862, while dredging out one of the springs, Avery's slaves accidentally struck a huge bed of solid rock salt some sixteen feet below the surface. The importance of the discovery was quickly recognized, and the family put the salt mine in the hands of the Confederacy. An elaborate saltworks employing hundreds of slaves was erected, and Petite Anse soon became a major supplier of salt and salt-cured beef to the southern states.[87]

Transportation of the products from the Petite Anse saltworks was complicated by the appearance of Federal troops in the Berwick Bay area in 1862. And by spring 1863, it was obvious that a full-scale Federal invasion of the bayou country was imminent. Before their retreat, Confederate armies in St. Martin and St. Mary parishes attempted to destroy anything that could be of direct assistance to the invading troops, from cotton, ammunition, and serviceable vessels to salt. Northern troops arrived in New Iberia on 16 April 1863. In a controversial action, they proceeded to Petite Anse to destroy what remained of the saltworks, perhaps fearing that it might again fall into Confederate hands.[88] Between the destruction by the retreating Rebels and the invading Federals, almost nothing of service to either remained on Petite Anse after 1863.

Many members of the Avery family fled to Texas in 1863 in advance of the invasion, taking most of the Petite Anse slaves with them. Others remained on the island or nearby, and with the occupation of the Teche country by Federal troops they were among hundreds who abandoned the area's plantations. After the war, a fraction of the former slaves wandered back to the only home many had ever known, and a freedman account book for 1866–67 documents the return of a dozen or more of the Petite Anse workers.[89] Some of these were descendants of the original contingent that belonged to Stone and Marsh.

With the exception of the war years, when the placid, verdant island was transformed into a virtual fortification and mining enterprise, life on Petite Anse was unmarked by dramatic events since its founding in 1818. House servants and skilled workers occasionally rotated between New Iberia and the island, but most Petite Anse slaves remained on the plantation until they died. The bayou-encased island was their constant habitat except for occasional approved trips to New Iberia or sporadic, unsuccessful runaway attempts. The rare runaway attempts seemed to be primarily motivated by a dislike for the isolation rather than a reaction to mistreatment. Few slaves were sold, and there is nothing in the record to suggest excessive discipline or abuse. Males and females were regularly purchased, usually as individuals, occasionally in small families, and never in a large lot. They were quickly assimilated into the existing community, and many single adult purchases married within a year.

A fairly large number of slaves dropped off the lists from 1826 to 1860. It is probable that most of these died. Although the slave population of Petite Anse doubled between 1826 and 1836, many of the additions were new purchases. The growth of the slave population from sixty in 1836 to eighty-nine in 1860 was unimpressive considering the large number of documented purchases. Surviving records do not provide systematic information on deaths, but a very high mortality rate appears to have been the primary factor in the slow growth rate on Petite Anse because inventories show that births occurred with normal regularity.[90]

The quiet monotony of life and labor on the island was punctuated primarily by births, courtships, marriages, deaths, and the occasional excitement provided by end-of-the-year celebrations. Throughout most of its documentable existence, the Petite Anse slave community was well-balanced and stable. This is all the more remarkable when one considers how very atypical were the slave community's beginnings.

A few bonds of kinship, friendship, and prior sense of community were usually transferred with slaves who migrated with their owners. In the new location, the core force retained and shared vivid recollections of the old place and former associations. This bond of prior association in some ways sustained these slaves, providing a basis for the building of a new sense of community, but it also made it difficult for some migrating slaves to relinquish old emotional commitments and build new ones. As will be seen, this was the case on Tiger Island, where a new community was only slowly and painfully constructed. But a very different situation existed on Petite Anse. No core force from a single plantation migrated with the owners. The Petite Anse slave force was hurriedly assembled—but not in the South from slaves already familiar with plantation agriculture and acclimated to southern environmental and cultural conditions. Rather, the owners of Petite Anse constructed their initial work force from New Jersey slaves and New York indentured servants procured only a short time before the implementation of a strict anti-slave-trading law in New Jersey.

Most northern blacks who were still enslaved in 1800 lived either in New York or New Jersey. New York passed a Gradual Abolition Act in 1799, and New Jersey lawmakers followed with a similar act in 1804.[91] In each case, children born to slave mothers after 4 July of the year the law was passed were considered freeborn but were legally required to serve their masters for periods ranging from twenty-one to twenty-eight years before manumission was effective. New York passed additional legislation in 1817 freeing as well those born before 1799.[92]

The provisions of New Jersey's 1804 Gradual Abolition Act were weak and easily circumvented. The law did not require the abolition of slavery among slaves born before 1804, and it assured the servitude of slaves born after 1804 for twenty-one years for females to twenty-five years for males. New Jersey slaveholders nevertheless resented the legislation. They found the prospect of a large free black population ominous and threatening. They considered gradual abolition laws unconstitutional and the first step toward a general abolition. They also saw the legislation as financially ruinous, denying them the legitimate labor of their slave property's increase, while requiring the children's upkeep during their dependent years. For these reasons, and because it was increasingly difficult to find profitable employment for slaves in the state, many New Jersey owners were anxious to sell their chattels, especially the young ones bound for eventual emancipation.[93] In-state buyers were few. Therefore, sales of New Jersey slaves for exportation to the South not only continued after 1804 but increased— especially after the abolition of the African slave trade in 1808 and the expansion of cotton production into the lower South precipitated by Eli Whitney's improved cotton gin. These factors not only encouraged the sale of surplus slaves from the upper to the lower South, they also encouraged the sale of northeastern slaves, against the spirit of gradual emancipation enactments.

To curtail spiraling slave exports, the New Jersey legislature passed a more stringent law in 1812. It increased penalties for violations but allowed slaves to be transported out of the state with their own consent, given privately and freely to two officers of the court.[94]

Both the 1804 and 1812 laws were repeatedly and blatantly violated. The appetite for additional slave laborers was particularly voracious in Louisiana, which was expanding its production of both sugar and cotton. In the changing economy of New Jersey, advertisements for the sale of prime-age slaves ran in newspapers for months without success, despite assurances from the sellers that the chattels would be "sold cheap" and on "liberal terms."[95] In the same period, New Jersey papers noted labor shortages in the lower Mississippi Valley.[96]

In response to these circumstances, violation of the New Jersey laws became a systematic business. It involved New York ship captains such as William Lee of the brig *Mary Ann*, who, sailing without a manifest, attempted to slip a blatantly illegal cargo of New Jersey slaves into the New Orleans harbor. It involved New Jersey speculators, slaveowners, and magistrates. And it extensively involved planters from Louisiana or those planning to settle there.[97] All these people found ways to circumvent the consent provisions of the 1812 law. Slaves were bribed with promises of quicker emancipation in the South or threatened with bodily harm if they appeared reluctant to consent to removal.[98] In many cases, slaves who were sold for out-of-state transport never saw the magistrates who signed their consent forms. Judges such as Jacob Van Wickle (sometimes spelled Van Winkle) colluded with slave dealers and purchasers, occasionally to the shock and outrage of sellers, who found that they unwittingly had become parties to schemes to sell slaves south. Some New Jersey individuals were involved in more than misrepresentation, kidnapping slaves and indentured servants for sale to the lower South. A man whose black indentured servant was illegally taken for exportation described Van Wickle's house near South Amboy as "almost like a garrison," serving as a holding pen until the hapless slaves and servants were placed on brigs bound for New Orleans, which often sailed without manifests. Among those individuals in New Jersey who were involved in slave exportation schemes were, in addition to Van Wickle, Peter Ferron Henry of West Windsor and Lewis Compton of Perth Amboy.[99] Compton, who acted as an agent for Marsh and Stone in acquiring and transporting their New Jersey slaves, was the subject of an indignant article in the *New Jersey Journal* of 16 June 1818. Compton had bought four slaves in Bergen County, ostensibly for his own use. Suspecting that he might try to export the slaves, the sellers rode to Compton's house in Perth Amboy the day following the sale and confirmed that the slaves had been taken directly to the "grand repository at south Amboy" to be loaded on southbound ships along with many others. After filing a complaint against Compton, the men were allowed to reclaim their slaves.[100]

Publicity regarding such circumventions of the abolition statutes directly influenced the unanimous passage, in the fall of 1818, of an act that absolutely prohibited the exportation of slaves or black servants from New Jersey.[101] The act specified heavy fines and prison terms for violations.

The bill was under discussion throughout the late winter and spring of 1818. By summer, it was clear that it had the support needed to pass. During that time, those involved in the export of slaves plied their trade with an even greater urgency. In the months before the stringent new law became operative, the *New Jersey Journal* reported that at least four shiploads of northern slaves legally left Perth Amboy for New Orleans. Other ships attempted to smuggle their human cargoes, some of them obtained illegally, into the lower South. Still other slaves were taken overland.[102]

William Stone and John Marsh acquired many members of their early Louisiana work force in a frantic buying spree and a dramatic race against time before implementation of the new law. Just before the law's passage, Stone and his agents, Lewis Compton and William Rayburg, bought a dozen or more slaves, most of them purchased between 28 September and 25 October 1818. Twelve slaves were from Bergen, Hunterdon, Middlesex, and Essex counties; all were between the ages of fourteen and twenty-five; and most were purchased from different owners.[103] Earlier in the summer, Stone and Marsh had contracted for at least eleven indentured servants, all of them blacks or mulattoes. Most were from New York; they allegedly agreed to serve in Louisiana for terms ranging from three to five years.[104] Consent forms were required for the removal of indentured servants as well as slaves.[105]

The reasons why Marsh and Stone decided to compile a labor force made up of northeastern slaves and servants cannot be precisely determined, though they may have included these men's inexperience as planters, misinformation concerning the prices and availability of laborers in the South, and a desire for workers with known and specialized skills.[106] They may have been persuaded that the lower cost of slaves in New Jersey was significant enough to offset the risks and expenses of transporting them to Louisiana, although they later learned that such was not the case.[107]

Marsh and Stone were certainly not alone in buying slaves from the Northeast. Many Louisiana planters made buying trips north between 1812 and 1818. Foremost among these was Charles R. Morgan, a New Jersey native who had become a planter in Pointe Coupee, Louisiana, in 1800, one of the first Americans in the settlement. He was also the brother-in-law of Jacob Charles Van Wickle, judge of the Court of Common Pleas in Middlesex County, New Jersey. Morgan and Judge Van Wickle's son Nicholas Van Wickle became notorious in New Jersey during the summer of 1818 for their flagrant circumvention of the 1812 law's consent requirements. Through questionable means, the pair removed at least sixty slaves from the state just before the implementation of the strict 1818 law.[108] Judge Van Wickle himself bought most of the slaves, in his son Nicholas's or Morgan's names, and housed them until they were shipped out. He also signed the consent documents.[109] The Van Wickles and Morgan were not just obtaining laborers for their own use. They were deeply involved in speculation, and Judge Van Wickle was clearly a party, as a July 1818 notice in a New Orleans newspaper makes clear: "Jersey negroes appear to be peculiarly adapted to this market—especially those that bear the mark of Judge Van Winkle [Wickle], as it is understood that they offer the best opportunity for speculation. We have the right to calculate on large importations in the future."[110]

Judge Van Wickle also signed some of the consent agreements for slaves bought by Stone, Marsh, and their agents, and Compton was involved in both the purchase and transport of the slaves bound for Petite Anse. In addition to bills of sale and consent documents, a remarkable letter has survived in which William Stone, still in the East, graphically describes to his partner in Louisiana some of the perils associated with removing their slaves from New Jersey and the Northeast.

> Compton started out from Amboy on the 25 Oct with 4 negroes by land and George that ranaway from me was one of them[.] Williamson & Dehart started with him with 4 negroes[.] Rayburg & somebody else also started from Sumervil with a wagon load[.] they got as far as reding in the state of Pensylvania[.] there they was stoped and taked to Lebonen for trial where the negroes was all taken away from them and set at liberty.[111]

Stone's letter went on to inform Marsh that Compton duly rounded up the slaves and had them jailed for "safekeeping." Once more the slaves were liberated and sent to Philadelphia. Compton and DeHart rushed to Philadelphia to recover the chattels and were themselves arrested and jailed for falsely imprisoning the slaves. The authorities returned the slaves to New

Jersey. Despite the problems, Stone confidently predicted that the slaves could be successfully reclaimed in New Jersey and safely transported to Louisiana. He informed Marsh that

> all the talk in Jersey is about Lewis Compton[.] they [Compton and De Hart] intend to sease on them [the slaves] again and take them out if posible[.] the Legeslator of N. Jersey pased a law on the 25th Oct—a compleat prohibition of the trades but the negroes was out of the state before the law was know[.] therefore the opinion is, they can take them yet, as they was taken away from them [Compton and DeHart] by force.

Stone also informed Marsh that their actions had caused some difficulties with his neighbors in New York City.

> there was two of the straight coat gentry this afternoon at your house to enquire about phebe[.] they understood she was to be taken away to the state of Louisiana to be put under the lash[.] I order them out of the house and told them that if they ever came in again pimping for negroes to spoul them I would send them out faster than they came in.[112]

He closed with an assurance that he and his charges would leave for Louisiana within a fortnight.

As he predicted, Stone convinced the New Jersey courts to return the slaves to him. At least six of the confiscated New Jersey slaves eventually arrived at Petite Anse, as did most of those transported by other agents. Marsh had previously brought most of the indentured servants and house slaves with him by ship. The New Jersey slaves, combined with the New York servants, constituted the bulk of the small contingent of workers on Petite Anse from 1818 to 1822. This small, bewildered assemblage of northern slaves intermarried with new purchases and, with steady additions through the years, developed into an unusually strong, mature, and stable community by the 1850s.

TIGER ISLAND

Unlike Oakland, where the major crisis affecting slave household development was estate division, the primary crises for Tiger Island slaves were the migration process and the owner's aggressive business practices. At Petite Anse, too, first-generation slaves were severely marked by the migration process, but after that initial trauma, the owners allowed and even encouraged a natural community development. Tiger Island slaves had multiple and continuing adjustments to make—to the challenges of migration, sales, rotations, and transfers and to the manifold hardships associated with setting up new plantations. Since the original Tiger Island slaves were virtually all transfers from other Brashear holdings, their story must include the years before a sugar estate was hacked out of the densely vegetated near-wilderness known as Tiger Island. Ultimately, the story must go back to Kentucky, the memories of which persisted in the collective consciousness of Brashear's slaves for several generations, as will be related in more detail in Chapter 6.

Walter Brashear, who established Tiger Island and three other plantations in St. Mary Parish, had little prior experience as a planter before migrating to Louisiana, and he had none as a sugar planter. He was primarily a practicing physician. But in spite of his relative inexperience, he—like so many others—was confident of his future success. Brashear was attracted to the adventure of starting a plantation in a near-wilderness, but he was also determined to make a fortune.

Brashear was born in Maryland, lived part of his childhood in Virginia, and moved with his parents to Bullitt County, Kentucky, in 1784, joining other Brashears who had already established salt-trading posts and farms in the frontier region.[113] Walter's father, Ignatius Brashear, was a Kentucky trader and an Indian fighter of considerable local reputation. He farmed and owned a few slaves, as did several of his sons, including Walter.[114] Theirs was a hardworking pioneer family with little financial security or social pretensions. Walter, the most studious of the offspring, attended Transylvania University in nearby Lexington, became an accomplished Latin scholar, and subsequently read medicine under the noted physician Frederick Ridgely. After two years of additional medical studies at the University of Pennsylvania, he spent an exciting period as ship surgeon aboard a merchant vessel engaged in the China trade.[115]

After several adventures, including one in which he was allegedly threatened with death if he failed to cure the wife of a Chinese potentate, Walter Brashear settled down to a more sober existence. He established a brisk medical practice in Nelson County, Kentucky, married Margaret Barr, the attractive daughter of a distinguished Kentucky family, in 1803, and quickly acquired town property in Bardstown, where he practiced, and a four-hundred-acre farm on Cox Creek.[116] In 1806 Brashear made medical history with a successful amputation at the hip joint of the leg of a young Bardstown slave. His feat earned him several impressive offers, including the prestigious Chair of Surgery at the Paris Academy of Science. He refused the offer and continued to practice medicine at Bardstown. His skill earned him the respect of the community, but the financial rewards were inadequate for the life-style he desired. He diversified further, investing in a distillery, a cotton gin, and several additional real estate ventures, none of which proved profitable. In 1808 he initiated a promising career in politics, serving a term in the Kentucky legislature.[117]

The next year Brashear visited the Attakapas district of Louisiana. Struck by the beauty and the potential of the region, he arranged to buy the future site of Belle Isle, primarily as an investment.[118] By 1815, he was committed to the pursuit of a new career as a sugar planter in Louisiana, abandoning the practice of medicine.

Brashear's decision to leave the medical profession was not an impulsive one. In 1802, shortly after finishing his medical training, he wrote his future brother-in-law that he intended to combine medicine with other, more lucrative business endeavors. He mused that a merchant was free to retire, but a physician was not. He admitted to a burning ambition, but not for himself alone; he wanted the means to be of service to his future family and "to my poorer relations and older brothers."[119] Brashear decided to pursue his goal in the beckoning sugar fields of Louisiana only after his efforts to combine medicine with more profitable business operations proved disappointing. In spite of a thriving medical practice, he was in serious debt by 1814, with mortgages on his land, town buildings, slaves, and even his medical equipment.[120] A vague dream became a serious undertaking. He proceeded to sell out his Kentucky holdings but, even then, the removal would have been difficult without the financial support of Margaret's brothers, Robert R. Barr and Thomas T. Barr, who enthusiastically endorsed his plan and served as informal co-partners in the endeavor, an arrangement that ceased only with their deaths in the 1830s.[121]

The removal of Brashear's slaves from Kentucky was piecemeal. Most accompanied the family in 1822, but a few left earlier, during Brashear's annual trips to the Attakapas. Some of the slaves sent to Louisiana had been attached to Brashear's or his wife's families for many years. He owned twenty-two slaves in 1810, according to the federal census, and that number was substantially increased by 1819–22, although not all were taken to Louisiana.[122]

In 1819, Brashear took several skilled workers with him to Louisiana, including Eli, a brickmaker and distiller. Despite his serious drinking problems, Eli possessed skills that were difficult to find in Louisiana, and his personal weaknesses would be tolerated by Brashear for thirty years or more.[123] Some of the other slaves that Brashear took to Louisiana in 1819 were not so fortunate. Within days of their arrival, Brashear sold three of the Kentucky slaves to local planters. One of these was a forty-year-old man, but two were boys, one of them only eleven.[124] Always short of cash in his expansive phase, Brashear rarely let sentimentality get in the way of profit making. Although he was not yet an official resident, Brashear had eighteen slaves in St. Mary Parish in 1820, according to the federal census.[125]

As he prepared for his final move, Brashear selected the youngest, strongest, and most skilled of his Kentucky slaves and negotiated trades or purchases of others from family members and neighbors. In March 1822, Brashear transported sixteen slaves and a manager to St. Mary by steamboat so that they could "pitch a crop" before the white family and other slaves arrived.[126] Two months later, Brashear, his family, and a few servants left for their new home aboard the steamboat *Fayette*. At the same time, the remaining migration slaves were en route by flatboat, under the supervision of sixteen-year-old Robert Brashear.

According to plan, the Brashears began their new life at Belle Isle in 1822. At that point they were a young, vigorous family with seven healthy children ranging in age from the adventuresome Robert, sixteen, to the quiet, frail, one-year-old Thomas. The two oldest daughters, Rebecca and Caroline, temporarily remained in boarding schools in Lexington.[127]

Their new home was undeniably a showplace.[128] The plantation commanded a magnificent view, not only of Atchafalaya Bay but of the gulf beyond. Family members and slaves alike enjoyed fishing, bathing in the warm waters of the gulf-fed bay, and watching the bustling steamboat traffic. But for the slaves from Bardstown and Lexington, accustomed to the rolling green hills, limestone and granite cliffs, clear, swift-running streams, and crisp, cold winters of Kentucky, the semitropical terrain and climate of the Gulf Coast must have seemed strange and forbidding. It also proved to be deadly.

Despite the plantation's elevation and the sound and spacious home that Brashear built for his family in St. Mary Parish, the area's unhealthiness was soon apparent. The middle daughter, Mary Eliza, who often expressed dissatisfaction with her new home's "want of society," died within a year after the family's arrival. The older daughters, Caroline and Rebecca, joined the family on Belle Isle after finishing school, but Caroline died at Belle Isle in 1831. Then, in 1832, a third child, Walter, Jr., who was described by his mother as a "stirring and industrious child," died suddenly at St. Joseph's Academy in Bardstown. Margaret Barr Brashear, who would have preferred the life of a noted physician's wife in Paris, Philadelphia, or even Lexington, steeled herself to accept her many losses with the expected stoicism. Informing her daughter Fanny about the death of a family slave but also musing on the recent death of her young son, Margaret wrote, "How frail, how uncertain is life and how good we should be to . . . meet our end with fortitude and resignation."[129] Less than two years later, she too was dead, followed by her daughter Rebecca within a few months. It is not fully documented, but Margaret may have died in childbirth or shortly thereafter. An infant son, Darwin, is reputedly buried near her at Belle Isle.[130] In just over a decade, Walter Brashear had lost his wife, three daughters, and at least one son, perhaps two. All but one of these deaths had occurred at Belle Isle.

Through the years, illness also plagued the slave community at Belle Isle and at Brashear's other holdings, including Tiger Island. Belle Isle was especially vulnerable to fevers and cholera, brought in from New Orleans and carried by sailors on the steamboats entering the parish through Atchafalaya Bay. Several of the Kentucky migrants died within a few years of their arrival, but the highest death toll occurred in the 1830s, when the new slaves were believed to be acclimated. For the slaves, fevers were more common but less deadly than cholera. In January 1833, two hundred slaves died of cholera in St. Mary and St. Martin parishes, although family letters claimed that, because of his medical skills, Brashear lost far fewer than did his French Creole neighbors.[131]

Despite his family losses, Brashear was beginning to make a great deal of money by the late 1820s, both in his sugar operations and in the raising of fine-blooded cattle on Belle Isle. Encouraged by the possibility of accumulating great wealth, Brashear engaged in almost reckless expansions in the late 1820s and 1830s, heavily mortgaging his property to buy more. The frequent changes that Brashear made in his work force from 1822 to 1842 not only included buying and selling slaves but also transferring laborers from one to another of his expanding landholdings. The slave community that had been fragmented by the migration and frequent sales was once more disrupted when Brashear mortgaged Belle Isle and sixty slaves in 1831 to finance the acquisition of Tiger Island, an undeveloped plantation on the east bank of Berwick Bay.[132] By the early 1840s, he had bought two additional sugar plantations—Golden Farm, on the more densely populated and accessible west bank of Berwick Bay, and the Bayou Boeuf Plantation about eight miles south of Tiger Island.[133]

Belle Isle had become increasingly oppressive for Brashear after the deaths of his wife and most of his children, and he gladly moved his residence to Golden Farm in the fall of 1838. Thereafter, Belle Isle was largely devoted to cattle raising and logging, with only a skeletal slave force in residence.[134] Brashear's personal servants and oldest Kentucky slaves accompanied him to Golden Farm, but the most robust and prime work-ing-age slaves were sent to Tiger Island. Tiger Island showed the potential to become the family's sugar bonanza. In the early and mid-1830s prac-tically every slave strong enough to cut cane was temporarily sent to the new holding.[135]

In the expansive 1820s and 1830s, inventories, bills of sale, mortgage documents, and family records show that the Brashear slave communities underwent constant change. The original community was not only affected by the migration, unhealthy living conditions, and sales of individuals, it was also disturbed, in the short run, by Brashear's buying habits. He occasionally bought whole lots of slaves, rather than a few individuals or families that are more easily assimilated into an existing community. For example, in 1830 he bought twenty-three slaves at one time and in a single lot.[136] All but three were solitaires, and eighteen were male solitaires between the ages of fourteen and twenty-eight. The recent imports, ac-quired in New Orleans, increased Brashear's slave community by 40 per-cent. In the long run, the community would benefit from these new additions, but in 1830 their arrival must have been disruptive. Most of the newcomers were unknown to each other. If they were typical of new imports, they were either deeply depressed or filled with frustrated rage.[137]

Their introduction as a large group was likely to cause confusion, resentment, and jealousy in a small, closely knit, but unstable community bound by common memories.

Brashear made the large purchase of slaves in anticipation of setting up another sugar plantation. He invariably sent his strongest slaves to Tiger Island, and for most of the younger slaves it became a permanent home. The new holding was raw and isolated even in the 1840s. Life was monotonous and lonely, and the work was far more demanding than at either Belle Isle or Golden Farm. Just as the migration slaves longed for Kentucky, Tiger Island workers of the first decade were anxious to return to Belle Isle or to rejoin Brashear at his new home, Golden Farm.[138] As a result of Brashear's acquisitions, his slaves were divided into at least three major contingents in the late 1830s and 1840s, splintering the Belle Isle community and destroying any internal cohesion it had achieved in twenty years.

The isolation, the unbalanced age and sex distribution, the harsh work expectations, the fluctuating makeup of the labor force, the inexperience of Brashear's sons in plantation management, and the frequent absenteeism of Brashear and other family members resulted in many runaway attempts and other discipline problems at Tiger Island in the mid-1830s. Walter Brashear instructed his son Robert to "give Hale a particular charge about the management of the Negroes or he will have them running off before you get back. I think you should have an understanding privately that when you are not at home not more than five lashes should be given without consulting you."[139] A major crisis was averted in 1838 only after a strong-willed and charismatic slave, Jim Roy, was removed from the island and sold. Brashear wrote his daughter that "Jim Roy had the island under his dominion when I went down and after I had obtained the mastering I left it and the very same day he assumed the dictatorship. Rose [the overseer] brot him up yesterday and he goes not back again."[140]

In 1840 Walter Brashear's household at Golden Farm consisted only of himself, his lone surviving daughter, Frances, and one of his two sons, Thomas. The other son, Robert, was probably at Tiger Island and was not enumerated. Again, inexplicably, Brashear is credited with only sixteen slaves at Golden Farm, eight of them adults. These were his house servants. Perhaps at the time of the enumeration, the main body of his Golden Farm workers were temporarily at Tiger Island or Belle Isle and escaped the attention of the enumerators.[141]

Restless to undertake new endeavors, Walter Brashear began to divest himself of some of his property and responsibilities in the early 1840s. Satisfied that his sons had properly served their apprenticeship in plantation management at Tiger Island, Brashear in 1842 conveyed to each of his children, Robert, Thomas, and Frances, an undivided one-third interest in the harsh but fertile Tiger Island plantation and its 106 slaves.[142]

Brashear was a wealthy man by the early 1840s. Most likely because he was deeply involved in politics, he simply wanted to divest himself of the time-consuming duties connected with large-scale sugar production. But he was also influenced by economic conditions. Several poor sugar crops combined with the instability of banking as the result of the Panic of 1837 encouraged him to diversify and apply more of his time and money to other enterprises. He became more financially conservative in the 1840s, but the capital he had amassed in the flush 1830s had enabled him to make the timely purchases of his three additional holdings.[143]

In 1844 Frances Brashear married New Orleans merchant Henry Effingham Lawrence, providing her father with a business and political confederate as well as a son-in-law.[144] The entrepreneurial New York–born Lawrence was frequently absent from St. Mary, his wife, and his growing family in the late 1840s. Frances and the children preferred Belle Isle to her father's new plantation and spent much of their time there; Lawrence joined them when his business and political activities permitted.[145]

In 1850 Walter Brashear's household at Golden Farm, as described in the federal census, was made up of himself, a seventy-five-year-old planter with real estate valued at $25,000 and forty-nine slaves, his son Thomas, twenty-nine, also a planter, and several white skilled workers, one from Ohio and two from Ireland. At Tiger Island, Robert Brashear, forty-four, was enumerated only with his wife Nancy Royster Brashear, thirty-one, and their ten-month-old son Walter. Value of the Tiger Island real estate was estimated at $100,000, of which Robert owned one-third, and the island contained 111 slaves.[146]

In 1852 Walter Brashear made further disposition of his plantation holdings, conveying to Frances Brashear Lawrence the Bayou Boeuf Plantation and twelve slaves. She, in turn, relinquished her undivided one-third interest in Tiger Island to her brothers, who became full partners in the most profitable of all the Brashear holdings.[147]

The period between 1838 and 1856 was generally a forward-looking, happy, and prosperous one for the Brashear family. Walter Brashear served several terms as a representative in the state legislature. He and his eldest son, Robert, prominent Whigs, were frequently consulted by the national party on local and state political issues well into the troubled era of sectionalism in the 1850s.[148] The Brashear business interests continued to grow. In the early 1850s Robert erected a sawmill on the east side of Berwick Bay, and Thomas operated a ferry from the west to the east bank.[149] Both sons, daughter Frances Lawrence, and father Walter Brashear continued to produce impressive quantities of sugar on their various plantations, and Walter expanded his herds on Belle Isle. By 1853, all were deeply engaged in a town-building scheme at the bay edge of Tiger Island.

In the early 1850s, Brashear and his capitalistic son-in-law Henry Lawrence laid the groundwork for developing a remote plantation area into a dynamic railroad terminus and port of entry, offering rail and steamboat transportation from New Orleans to Texas, via Berwick Bay.[150] The years from 1853 until emancipation were filled with both uncertainty and excitement for Tiger Island's slaves. In the 1850s the Brashears were instrumental in the construction of a town, Brashear City, on the site of a Tiger Island cane field. And in accordance with Walter Brashear's vision, Brashear City did become a major railroad terminal and port of entry, providing travelers with rail and steamboat connections from New Orleans to Texas by the summer of 1857.[151] The arrival of the railroad, the stream of visitors, and the incessant docking and departing of steamboats were marvels to all Berwick Bay residents, including slaves, but the events initially had little direct effect on the plantation. The majority of Tiger Island slaves still worked in the cane fields, but the new activities did help break down some of the early isolation and created improved social opportunities. The brothers were less aggressively entrepreneurial than their father, and after they assumed ownership, Tiger Island's slave community finally began to stabilize, in part because the owners engaged in almost no sales and transfers.

Then death interceded. Robert Brashear died in late 1856, leaving as his primary heirs his wife, Nancy, son Walter, and co-partner and brother, Thomas. The inventory and appraisement associated with Robert Brashear's death show that Tiger Island had 139 slaves in 1857. In 1859, before his elder brother's estate was settled, Thomas Brashear also died.[152] Tiger Island had 150 slaves that year. Walter Brashear served as the administrator of his sons' estates, but before a settlement could be reached, he too died, on 23 October 1860, at the age of eighty-five.[153]

Robert's widow bought Tiger Island from the other heirs. In 1860, she was credited with 103 slaves and was described in the population schedules as a thirty-nine-year-old planter with property valued at $150,000. Her household consisted only of her son Walter, age ten, and two of her Royster relatives. At nearby Bayou Boeuf Plantation, Henry E. Lawrence and Frances Brashear Lawrence owned property (real estate and personalty) with an estimated value of $130,000. Their household included their five children.[154]

The inventory of Walter Brashear's estate, filed in November 1860, amounted to $133,952[155] and included fifty-five slaves, Belle Isle, Golden Farm, several steamboats, interest in the shipyards at Berwick, and town property. The appraisers grossly underestimated the value of much of his property, perhaps for the benefit of the heirs. Belle Isle was bequeathed to young Walter, the only son of Brashear's deceased son Robert. Golden Farm was willed to his only surviving daughter, Frances Lawrence.[156]

Most Louisiana residents were gravely affected by the Civil War, but those of the Berwick Bay area suffered more than most. In some respects still little more than a "raw railroad town," Brashear City nonetheless had grown steadily in the late 1850s. It was much trafficked by travelers, but it had only a few hundred permanent residents in 1860, when it was officially incorporated. The precocious village perched on the edge of Tiger Island Plantation had become "a main artery of traffic into the interior of Louisiana and west to Texas."[157]

The Tiger Island slaves were divided between Nancy Royster Brashear and Frances Brashear Lawrence and their children. The division separated no simple families, but, on paper at least, it totally dispersed kinship groups and friends. Had the plantations remained intact, the division would not have been devastating because Tiger Island and Bayou Boeuf plantations were only a few miles apart. The war changed that prospect. In 1863 Tiger Island's slaves, and those of the entire region, were subjected to many additional changes as the war literally reached their doorsteps.

Brashear City's strategic importance converted the raw new town that was Walter Brashear's pride into a muddy, wagon-rutted campground for thousands of military men and machines. Its few streets and buildings were wholly inadequate for the hordes that gathered there. One of the occupation soldiers called Brashear City a "poor specimen of a squalid southern village," and a contraband slave more graphically described its deterioration by calling it a town that was "borned and hadn't growed."[158] The town changed hands several times in 1863. It was ransacked by the war-weary troops of both armies, and marauders and wandering displaced, sick, and hungry slaves added to the general havoc.[159] That summer of 1863 the town was described as a sea of tents, harboring thirty thousand Federal soldiers waiting to invade Texas. A Federal officer wrote that "so many troops have been here that there is nothing left to win . . . chickens and forage is equally unattainable."[160]

The turmoil engendered by the Federal invasion of the Berwick Bay–Brashear City area might have been a fair exchange for Tiger Island's slaves if it had meant an early liberation. But for most, that liberation did not come swiftly, and for some, not at all. Hundreds of the slaves from the area were moved by panicky owners. Henry Lawrence moved a contingent of the Bayou Boeuf slaves to Bayou Mallet, where they soon scattered.[161] Many of these were Tiger Island slaves whom his wife had recently inherited. Robert Brashear's widow, Nancy Royster Brashear, took her part of the Tiger Island slaves to Texas, where she would remain for a decade. Both she and Lawrence sold a few young men to Texas cattle drovers.[162]

Amid the confusion, some Tiger Island slaves managed to escape the plantation and join other fugitives. Their numbers were so great that the contraband contingent formed a major appendage to the occupation forces. Physically able males were generally recruited by the Federal forces. John Ogee was a Brashear City slave who ran away from his plantation. He explained their motives: "The Yankees comed 'bout a mile from us and they took every ear of corn, kilt every head of stock . . . and feed their teams and themselves. . . . When we think of all that good food the Yankees done got, we jus' up and jine up with them. We figger we git lots to eat and the res' we jus' didn't figger." John ran away with his father and two other men from his plantation; they all were volunteered for service in the Union army. John survived the fighting in Mississippi, Georgia, and South Carolina, but his father was killed. He had no regrets about leaving his plantation and slavery but, concerning his enlistment, he said: "I wishes I hadn't after I got there. When you see 1,000 guns point at you . . . you wishes you'd stayed in the woods."[163]

Only a small fraction of the area's slaves who ran away to the Federal camps became soldiers. Most—tired, malnourished, confused, but exhilarated—hovered in makeshift camps near those of the soldiers. They formed a contraband camp in Brashear City that was the largest anywhere in Louisiana.[164] For many, the camp became a grave instead of a refuge. Confederate troops retook Brashear City for a short time in 1863. According to a *New York Tribune* correspondent who was there, members of the Confederate Texas cavalry attacked the contraband camp and "slaughtered" its occupants. He claimed that "when in camp a few weeks previous, I found as many as 6,000 old men, women, and children. Of these, 2,000 or 3,000 were removed before the attack." He contended that the remainder were brutally killed by the Confederates.[165]

It is not known how many members of the Brashear slave communities were able to reunite after the war. Probably a very small percentage of those sold or removed to Texas had the physical and financial resources to return to Brashear City. Some did not survive the war. A few remained with the Brashear family and leased land on the plantation for a token payment of a rooster a year.[166]

Both the white family and the slaves associated with Walter Brashear's Louisiana experiment were widely scattered by the war.[167] The port town he had envisioned was in ruins, and in 1876 its name was changed from that of its founder to that of a northern industrialist who made a fortune in railroads and shipping—Charles Morgan. His capital and verve reinvigorated the economy of the coastal area, and Brashear City became Morgan City, as it is known today.[168]

The pattern of destruction, reconstruction, and dispersal exhibited among Walter Brashear's slaves is tragically familiar in the history of Louisiana slave communities. Their former community fragmented by migration, Brashear's slaves painfully reconstructed a semblance of a community on Belle Isle by the late 1820s despite constant assaults on it by Brashear's frequent changes in the labor force. In the 1830s and 1840s, with the expansion of his holdings, that cohesion was almost entirely lost, and the slaves on each of his three plantations had to renew their efforts to forge a coherent domestic structure. A slave community comparable to that which existed at Oakland and Petite Anse in their most mature phases was never achieved on Tiger Island. But the slaves of Tiger Island did make enormous progress by the 1850s, when the deaths of primary owners, followed by the disruptive effects of the war and emancipation, finally and permanently dispersed the Brashear slave communities.

The next two chapters will analyze how the domestic structure of Oakland, Petite Anse, and Tiger Island slaves was affected by the events and owners' decisions related in this chapter, with particular attention to the impact of estate divisions, migration and transfers, and economic contractions and expansions. The following chapters will provide further evidence of a domestic structural preference arising from within the slave culture. Determining the origins of this preferred structure is beyond the scope of this study but deserves a book in and of itself. I suspect that the structural prototype that was described in the first two chapters evolved over several centuries. The wellspring of its functions, if not its forms, appear to be in the African past. It was shaped, through the years, by the special conditions and needs of an enslaved people. And it was molded further by Western mores, slave Christianity, and a traditional southern emphasis on family and kinship pervasive both in the broad folk culture and in planter society. In any case, in this book I am content to describe and analyze slave domestic organization, leaving the tracing of its origins to others.

CHAPTER FIVE

Gender and Age
Distribution and
Household
Composition

This chapter explores the internal domestic structure of Oakland, Petite Anse, and Tiger Island slave societies. It seeks further to validate household development patterns observed in the larger sample and to determine possible variations and hidden patterns that might emerge in a more detailed, in-depth analysis of three communities drawn from the larger sample. It also assesses the influence of gender and age distribution on slave household composition in the three communities.

An analysis of a slave community's inhabitants as they were distributed by gender, age, and household groups at several points in time can be a valuable index to social changes and continuities in that society. It can shed light on the community's potential for work and reproduction and the degree of stability and social harmony that can be expected. The most stable and socially integrated slave communities were nearly balanced in their ratios of men to women, had generational depth (that is, enough members of older generations to afford continuity, supply a sense of kinship, and fulfill certain socialization functions), sufficient men and women between the ages of seventeen and forty to provide the bulk of the labor and to reproduce themselves, and enough children to assure that such was the case in the future. The community would contain a wide variety of household types, including complex forms, solitaires, and single-parent households, but most slaves would be members of standard nuclear families. How successful were the slave communities of Oakland, Petite Anse, and Tiger Island in achieving this profile?

GENDER AND AGE DISTRIBUTION OF OAKLAND SLAVES, 1811–1819

As demonstrated in figure 5.1, early Oakland's gender distribution was balanced or nearly so. The main imbalance—and it was not a serious problem—was a preponderance of females in the seventeen-to-thirty-four age group. In 1811, females outnumbered males two to one in the critical seventeen-to-twenty-eight age category, although the differential is less if the span is broadened to seventeen to thirty-four. The trend continued in 1817, with females outnumbering males in both primary reproductive age groups, but the differentials were slightly smaller. The gender imbalance among young adults was practically corrected by 1819, when the ratio of males to females was only one to three percentage points apart. The genders were well distributed throughout the 1819 population, although women still formed a slightly higher percentage than did males. This situation is somewhat unusual among the Louisiana slave communities examined in this book. The preponderance of females in the young adult age categories, however, did not result in an abnormally large number of female solitaires who were unable to find mates, nor did it result in an unusually high percentage of female-headed households.[1] In the economic sphere, the smaller number of men than women in the young adult categories might have had more impact. At Oakland, female labor was used as extensively as that of males in many areas, particularly in cotton picking and chopping. Women were also used in planting and clearing, but only men appear to have been used for plowing, ginning, pressing, and hauling and in most plantation crafts such as smithing and brickmaking.[2] The shortage of men in the seventeen-to-thirty-four age group probably proved a slight economic disadvantage to Oakland's owners in the plantation's first two decades of operation.

FIGURE 5.1.

Gender Distribution of Oakland Plantation Slaves, 1811–1857

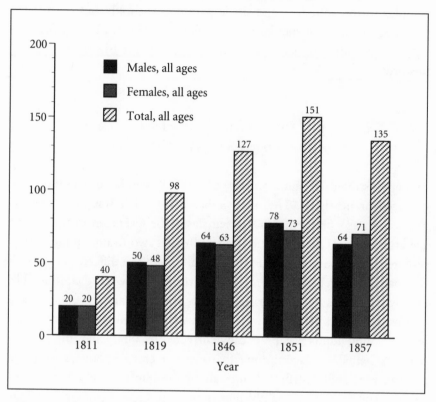

Source: Oakland Data Base.

In its first inventory in 1811, taken several years after the plantation was established, Oakland's slave community was heavily skewed toward the young, a tendency that persisted in the 1819 inventory. The mean age for all slaves in 1811 was eighteen, in 1814, nineteen, and in both 1817 and 1819, twenty. Children sixteen and under made up 43 percent of the total slave population in 1811, and in 1814 that percentage was even higher. In 1819, ten years after the plantation was established, the zero-to-sixteen age category still contained 40 percent of the slaves, and nearly one-third of them were under the age of eleven.

A disproportionately large number of children is common in young, rapidly expanding slave societies. That pattern was found on Petite Anse, Tiger Island, and numerous other plantations and is typical of a young, vigorous slave society in its second phase.[3] The large numbers of very young slaves in 1819 did not diminish the reproductive potential of the society, for well more than half of the population was in the seventeen-to-forty category in 1819.

The most unbalanced age feature of early Oakland was the exceedingly small number of slaves in the group over age forty, fluctuating between 8 and 9 percent of the community's members from 1811 to 1819. This paucity of older slaves is also very typical of communities in their first and second phases. Oakland's early community shows more depth and maturity than most in their first two decades. Although no females over the age of fifty-eight were present in 1819, a sixty-two-year-old male lived at Oakland, and 5 percent of the slaves were in the forty-seven-to-fifty-two age range.[4]

Since a slight gender imbalance was present in the prime-age years, the number of slaves of those ages is of considerable interest and possible significance. Although the seventeen-to-twenty-eight age category encompasses only eleven years and that of seventeen to thirty-four just seventeen years, these periods are critical in household development. Marriages were generally first entered into and first births normally occurred among people in the first category. The second category includes the first, but it generally represents the outside limits for first births. Most of the slave women in the Louisiana sample had given birth to their last recorded child by their mid-thirties. This category also had peak labor capacity, although most slaves certainly aged seventeen to forty were capable of productive labor. At Oakland, women tended to outnumber men in all of these categories, but the situation became more balanced by 1819.[5] And throughout the 1811–19 period, the overall percentages of slaves in the seventeen-to-forty age grouping was quite respectable, ranging from 46 to 54 percent (see table 5.1).

GENDER AND AGE DISTRIBUTION OF
OAKLAND SLAVES, 1846–1851

The division of Nathaniel Evans's estate in 1822 resulted in the exodus of many slaves to plantations of his heirs. How did the estate division affect the age and sex distribution of the community that remained? The question is important, for if a decent balance was maintained despite the

TABLE 5.1.

Oakland Plantation Slaves in Major Age Categories, 1811–1857

Year	Ages 0–16		Ages 17–40		Ages 41–65+	
	n	%	n	%	n	%
1811	17	42.5	20	50.0	3	7.5
1814	28	44.1	29	45.6	6	9.1
1817	33	38.5	45	53.5	7	8.0
1819	39	39.6	51	51.7	8	8.0
1846	55	43.3	51	40.1	21	16.5
1850	66	47.5	49	35.1	23	16.2
1851	74	49.0	52	34.4	25	16.5
1852	58	50.8	40	35.0	16	14.0
1857	72	53.6	44	32.5	19	14.0

Source: Oakland Data Base.

division, the community could be expected to recover from the losses much more quickly. Unfortunately, inventories that can be precisely analyzed for age and sex distribution are not available for the late 1820s and the 1830s. Sources for these years are sufficient to trace the Oakland community during decades of rebuilding after the partition, but they are not appropriate for statistical analysis, even via reconstitutions. Those data are not again available until the 1840s. But in the interval, most families can be followed, and overall growth patterns can be determined.

At the time of Evans's death, the slave community consisted of 98 individuals. In 1820, the federal census credits his estate with 110 slaves, with a perfect gender balance. But by 1830, only 82 slaves were enumerated for Sarah Evans at Oakland. Inexplicably, the slaves of Sarah and J. N. Evans were not enumerated in the 1840 census, but information compiled for taxation purposes confirms that Oakland's slave community in 1834 contained only 84 people. Tax documents further show that the combined holdings of the Evans partnership was 99 individuals in 1835 and that 111 slaves lived at Oakland by 1841.[6] The precise age and sex distributions of Oakland's slave community at these various junctures cannot be determined, but a recovery process is evident in the inventories, which show formation of new families, rapid reproduction in families established earlier, and purchases of individuals of both sexes. Age and sex distribution among Oakland's slaves can again be analyzed with precision in 1846.

The inventories of Oakland's slaves in 1846, 1850, and 1851 are analyzed as a group because they all represent the combined holdings of Sarah and J. N. Evans. The community continued to recover from the 1822 losses, with steady increases and healthy gender distributions. The slave population increased from 127 in 1846 to 151 at the end of 1851.[7] The overall gender distribution remained remarkably balanced, and the percentages of males and females in the seventeen-to-thirty-four age category was almost equal. The gender problem had been solved by time and propitious purchases, but Oakland's slave community still had an obstacle to overcome in the 1846–51 period before it had a stable structure. That problem related to its distribution by age rather than gender, and it arose at least partially from the estate division.

Oakland's age distribution continued to be skewed toward the young during the 1840s and early 1850s, as shown in table 5.1. The mean age fluctuated between twenty-one and twenty-two from 1846 through 1857. In 1846 children under seventeen continued to be heavily represented, making up 43 percent of the total slave population, the same proportion found in 1811. By 1851 children aged zero to sixteen composed nearly half of Oakland's inhabitants, indicating a healthy birth rate but also contributing to social imbalance.

In the same period the over-forty age group was also increasing; by 1851 it formed 17 percent of a maturing slave society. One-tenth of Oakland's slaves in 1851 were over the age of fifty-three, another signal of increasing generational depth and greater social integration (see table 5.2).[8]

The most serious age distribution problem was now with the middle group. After 1846, Oakland had a shortage of young adults, and the trend worsened in the 1850s. The problem began with the 1822 division and was deepened by the 1851–52 division following Sarah Evans's death. As can be followed in table 5.1, the proportion of slaves in the seventeen-to-forty group dropped from 40 percent of the population in 1846 to 34 percent in 1851. The increases in the groups sixteen and under and over forty contributed to the slave community's overall social balance, yet the group that fulfilled most of the society's labor and reproductive functions was reduced to about a third. This could place heavy labor demands on older slaves and older children and might limit marriage choices as well.

TABLE 5.2.

Mean Ages of Oakland Plantation Slaves, 1811–1857

Year	Males	Females	Total slaves
1811	18.7	18.2	18.4
1814	21.6	17.3	19.4
1817	21.5	18.4	19.9
1819	20.8	19.2	20.0
1846	22.7	21.9	22.3
1850	20.8	20.6	20.7
1851	21.4	22.7	22.1
1857	20.0	22.2	21.1

Source: Oakland Data Base.

GENDER AND AGE DISTRIBUTION OF OAKLAND SLAVES, 1852–1857

The death of Sarah Evans and the partition of her estate reduced Oakland's slave force from 151 to 114, but the smaller community displayed a perfect gender ratio with males and females each numbering 57.[9] In 1857 the slave community consisted of 135 individuals, with a slightly higher percentage of females than males.[10] Gender imbalance was not, therefore, a major problem at Oakland in its last phase, and gender distribution was little affected by the partition.

The age distribution problem, however, became even more serious after the estate division. Children (nursing infants through sixteen-year-olds) formed more than half of the plantation's population in 1852, even after the removal of many by the partition. By 1854 they made up 54 percent of the community—too high a proportion for a well-integrated, productive slave society under normal circumstances. But considering the small number of slaves in the seventeen-to-thirty-four age category from 1846 to 1857, it was fortunate that a new generation was rapidly approaching years of peak labor and reproductive potential.

Although the sixteen and under age group continued its remarkable increases, the category of older slaves slowly contracted. The proportion of slaves over age forty had increased to 17 percent by 1851 but declined to 14 percent by 1852–57 (after the partition), lower than at either Petite Anse or Tiger Island in a comparable stage. This contraction occurred even though John N. Evans had made a conscious effort to retain the oldest family slaves at Oakland after the division. What happened was that the 1811 slaves had begun to die out by the mid- and late 1850s. In the 1852 division Evans had relinquished too many of the established families with heads of households in their forties (families with many youngsters in their early and mid-teens). Therefore, Oakland had too few slaves in the over-forty and the middle categories. The young families Evans had helped create through his purchases of young males in the mid-1830s were rapidly producing children, but the estate division had seriously diminished the two other categories—the one so necessary for social stability and continuity of traditions and the other equally necessary for economic proficiency and reproduction. The slaves in their twenties were doing well at reproducing themselves, however, despite their too small numbers.

In 1852 Oakland's community still had a dearth of young adults, and, in that category alone, the old bugaboo of gender imbalance reasserted itself—although in reverse. In 1852, slaves in the seventeen-to-twenty-eight age range constituted about one-fifth of the population; if the range is extended to seventeen to thirty-four, they composed one-fourth. And slaves in the seventeen-to-forty range still made up only 35 percent of the population, about the same as in 1850 and 1851. In 1852, men outnumbered women nearly two to one in the seventeen-to-twenty-eight age category (in which first marriages and first births were most likely to occur), although the differential was less marked in the seventeen-to-thirty-four and seventeen-to-forty groupings.

The contraction of the young adult group that had been taking place at least since the 1840s (and probably started in the late 1820s and 1830s as a result of the first division) had not been corrected by the time of the last available inventory in 1857. In that year, the percentage of slaves in the seventeen-to-twenty-eight age category was lower than at any point since the establishment of Oakland—15 percent—and the category displayed a severe gender imbalance, with the percentage in the population of males from this age group exactly twice that of females. Although the large numbers of slaves in the sixteen and under age category (which was well balanced by gender) would eventually remedy this unnatural situation, the highly critical seventeen-to-twenty-eight age group had dwindled to an alarming degree by 1857. If the age range is extended to seventeen to thirty-four, the gender ratio is much improved, but slaves in the category still encompassed only 23 percent of the overall population. The percentage of slaves in the large young adult category, seventeen to forty, was at its lowest point in the history of the community.

The problem with the age structure at Oakland from 1846 to 1857 (and no doubt earlier, too, although the data are not available) was attributable in part to a natural cycle—the dying off of early generations and rapid expansion in the zero-to-ten age group; some improvement would have occurred naturally by 1860. Another contributing factor may have been a rash of childhood deaths in the 1830s, diminishing the number of slaves who would have been young adults in the late 1840s and 1850s. The primary reason was estate division and the decisions made by administrators and heirs in the two divisions. At least twelve of the youngest offspring of the slaves who left Oakland after the 1822 partition would have been in the seventeen-to-thirty-four age group. At least ten of the older children who left Oakland in 1822 had children of their own by 1857 who were in their late teens and twenties. Among the slaves who were parceled out to heirs other than Oakland's owner in 1851–52 were thirteen who would have been in the seventeen-to-thirty-four age group during most of the 1852–57 period. The conclusion is obvious. Assuming that they had all lived, at least thirty-four more slaves would have been in that age category at Oakland if the estate divisions had not taken place.

Oakland's age and sex distribution at three points in its development suggests that it made good progress but was handicapped to a degree by the estate division.

HOUSEHOLD COMPOSITION AMONG OAKLAND SLAVES, 1811–1857

Throughout most of the 1811–19 period, Oakland's household structure was very simple with only two household types present—predictably, solitaires and simple families. But even within this relatively brief time span, significant changes occurred within the various categories of the simple family and in the solitaire household type. In 1811, solitaires constituted 47.5 percent of Oakland's forty slaves, nearly as high as members of simple families, 52.5 percent (see table 5.3).[11] It certainly was not unusual for an early community to have a high proportion of solitaires. What was unusual at Oakland was the female dominance in the solitaire category and a female-favored gender imbalance in the young adult group as a whole. This suggests that although a high percentage of solitaires is a common characteristic of slave societies in early stages of development, males do not necessarily dominate the group. When a solitaire group is numerically dominated by males, additional variables are usually also present—a particular type of agricultural production and geographic conditions or cultural biases among owners.

The Oakland slave population began a steady move toward a more balanced household structure quite early. By 1814 the proportion of solitaires had dropped by 11 percent, and the gender differential had almost evened out.[12] The proportion of solitaires at Oakland declined another 11 percent by 1817. Because many of the female solitaires had married or formed single-parent households, they represented only 7 percent of Oakland's slaves by 1817, whereas the proportion of male solitaires had increased to 19 percent.[13] Not only had the female dominance in the solitaire type disappeared by 1817, but the type was skewed toward males. At the time of Evans's death in 1819, the proportion of solitaires was reduced to a more reasonable 22 percent of a population of ninety-eight. Male solitaires continued to constitute a larger proportion of the general population than women, 13.2 percent to 9 percent.[14] The general trend was a steady decline in the solitaire group as the population increased and a steady increase in the numbers and percentages of the population who were male solitaires.

All slaves who were not solitaires were organized in simple family households throughout most of the 1811–19 period. In 1811, one-tenth of the slaves were married but childless. An additional 35 percent were members of standard nuclear families, averaging 3.5 members. There was only one female-headed single-parent household in 1811 because most of Oakland's young women had not yet married or entered into child-producing relationships. Seven of the ten female solitaires in 1811 were between the ages of ten and seventeen, most of them new regional purchases.

In 1814, 63 percent of Oakland's slaves still lived in simple households. The proportion in standard nuclear families rose slightly to 37 percent of

TABLE 5.3.

Oakland Plantation Slave Household Composition, 1811, 1814, 1817, 1819

	Oakland slaves, 1811				Oakland slaves, 1814			
Household type	Total slaves	Number of units	Mean size of units	Percent of total slaves in type	Total slaves	Number of units	Mean size of units	Percent of total slaves in type
Solitaire	19	19	1	47.5	23	23	1	36.5
Non-nuclear	–	–	–	–	–	–	–	–
Simple family	21	7	3	52.5	40	14	2.8	63.4
Married couple alone	4	2	2	10.0	4	2	2	6.3
Married couple with children	14	4	3.5	35.0	23	7	3.2	36.5
Single female with children	3	1	3	7.5	13	5	2.6	20.6
Single male with children	–	–	–	–	–	–	–	–
Extended	–	–	–	–	–	–	–	–
Multiple	–	–	–	–	–	–	–	–

Source: Oakland Data Base.

the population, and that of female-headed households sharply increased (absorbing some of the decrease in female solitaires), now constituting more than one-fifth of the population.

By 1817, the proportion of slaves living in simple family households had grown to 71 percent of the population. Several marriages had taken place since 1814, creating a notable rise in the category of married couples without children. The proportion of slaves living in standard nuclear families stayed about the same, but the size of the double-headed family increased to 3.8 members, or parents and two children.

	Oakland slaves, 1817				Oakland slaves, 1819		
Total slaves	Number of units	Mean size of units	Percent of total slaves in type	Total slaves	Number of units	Mean size of units	Percent of total slaves in type
22	22	1	25.8	22	22	1	22.4
–	–	–	–	–	–	–	–
60	20	3.0	70.5	72	22	3.2	73.4
10	5	2	11.7	8	4	2	8.1
31	8	3.8	36.4	54	14	3.8	55.1
19	7	2.7	22.4	10	4	2.5	10.2
–	–	–	–	–	–	–	–
3	1	3.0	3.5	–	–	–	–
–	–	–	–	4	1	4	4.0

Some complexity was evolving by 1817, and for the first time a type of household appeared other than solitaires or simple families. A younger sister of the wife lived with a young couple, forming a laterally extended family. Other than this, Oakland's slave community remained uncomplicated, and it still involved no more than two generations.

By 1819 the household structure began to resemble that achieved at a much later date by migration communities. Oakland's 1819 community exhibited many mature characteristics that did not appear at Petite Anse and Tiger Island until the 1840s and 1850s. By 1819 solitaires had declined to make up slightly more than one-fifth of the population, well distributed between males and females. This was still higher than the 18 percent in both the model and the 1810–19 sample, but not markedly so. Simple families were in strong ascendancy, absorbing nearly three-fourths of the residents (the same proportion exhibited in the model and close to the 77 percent in such families among the 1810–19 sampled communities). Over half of Oakland's slaves lived in families with both parents present, with a mean membership of four, higher than the percentage in standard nuclear families in the overall model (49 percent), and only 4 percent less than that of the 1810–19 sample. Another 8 percent of Oakland's population were married couples. The number of female-headed single-parent households had decreased; members of these units now made up only one-tenth of the population (about the same as in the 1810–19 communities but lower than the model). Finally, the 1819 community had a multiple family household whose members accounted for 4 percent of the community. The percentage is so small as to be numerically insignificant, but it signifies an early appearance of generational depth.

All of these characteristics—decrease in solitaires, rise in families involving married heads of households, decline in single-parent households, the development of complex forms, and the achievement of three-generational depth—indicate that at an amazingly early date Oakland was approaching the prototype of a stable, mature slave community with a healthy social structure. The strong trend toward stabilization was, however, diminished by the death of Nathaniel Evans in 1819 and the subsequent division of his slaves among several heirs.

An extraordinary record in the Evans papers—a cabin list—provides additional information on the personal lives of Oakland's slaves.[15] The Oakland quarters bill is one of only two cabin lists that I found in the Louisiana records that are clearly identified as such.

HOUSEHOLDS AND HOUSEFULS:
THE CABIN LIST OF OAKLAND

Historians of the family have long been aware of a nagging discrepancy between what they call households and housefuls, and nowhere is that discrepancy more apparent than in slave communities.[16] Cabin lists reveal that actual living arrangements of slaves often differed markedly from their household and kin identification. Persons who identified themselves and were recognized by their peers and owners as a family household did not always reside together if the facilities did not permit it (for example, a very large multiple family unit might occupy more than one cabin). The more common occurrence was for persons who were not part of the same family household, or even kin group, to occupy the same dwelling, making up a "houseful" but not constituting a "household."

Oakland's list of cabin residents of the field quarters does not include its entire slave population; house servants are excluded, and a few known field hands are not mentioned. But the names of occupants of fifteen cabins are provided, and these listings can be profitably compared to the household and family identifications of those individuals (see Appendix B).

Only Cabin 8 was inhabited exclusively by solitaires. Four men lived together, none of them known to have been related. All other solitaires were spread out among established families. Only two married couples were allowed the privilege of having cabins all to themselves. Andy and Phyllis lived in Cabin 11, and John and Sarah occupied Cabin 13.

Even though the quarters list included several standard nuclear families, only one of these families had a cabin for its exclusive use. Cabin 4 was the home of Isaac, Anarky, and their two children. Two recently married couples shared Cabin 9—Big Harry and Susan and Jem Stack and Maria. Standard nuclear families usually had additional occupants in their cabins—most often, single-parent families or solitaires. Randolph, Harriet, and their daughter shared Cabin 3 with Grace and her two children. A similar situation existed in crowded Cabin 5, occupied by Jack, his wife, Milly, and their son, as well as single parent Jenny and her four children.

Cabin 7 harbored two women and their children—Hannah and her four children and Tall Jenny and her two. Hannah had a husband, Jacob, who was on the 1817 roll, but he is not on the cabin list. Perhaps he was hired out for part of that year. When he was at Oakland, he probably resided in the cabin with his wife and children and Jenny's family.

In the remaining cabins, families lived with various solitaires who were unrelated to them. In Cabin 10, Jerry, Nancy, and their children resided in the same dwelling with Gundy, a thirty-three-year-old solitaire. The residents of Cabin 15 included solitaire Jem Gillum as well as Alex Carpenter, his wife, and their child. Several families shared cabins with female solitaires. In Cabin 14 Alex and Nancy had Tenah with them. Will, Winney, and their children shared Cabin 6 with Dorcas and her baby, which was born a few months after the listing. In Cabin 12, Peter, Rhoda, and their children had Betsy living with them. These young women were not adopted daughters who were considered part of the family household. Rather, the arrangement was usually a temporary one of convenience or necessity, similar to boarding in free society.

Although only the Oakland list is analyzed here, other confirmed or suspected Louisiana cabin lists were compared, and they manifested the same general patterns except that communities in a later stage were likely to have more multiple family households, which generally occupied cabins by themselves or sometimes overflowed into contiguous cabins. On very large holdings, male solitaires tended to reside together rather than being parceled out among established families. In *Time on the Cross* Fogel and Engerman suggest that family formation was encouraged by owners' offering single-family-occupancy cabins to young, two-parent families. The inference is that most families did not have to share cabins with nonfamily members. This did not prove to be the norm among the Louisiana plantations I examined. Very rarely did a standard nuclear family have the privilege of a cabin for its exclusive use—and even then only if that family was larger than the average or was very favored. Genovese's interpretation of the 1850 and 1860 census reports led him to conclude that "five to six slaves—one family unit—occupied a cabin." In the Louisiana cabin lists, however, those five to six people were often a family plus a solitaire or two small households. According to my evidence, John Blassingame was more correct in asserting that "most of the cabins contained at least two families."[17]

The 1817 cabin list demonstrates that although slaves maintained a strong sense of identity with their own families and households, their residency arrangements were often determined by other variables. These factors ranged from the preference or dictates of the owner and the availability of housing, to choices made by the slaves themselves—perhaps in response to special needs of some community members for the sharing of domestic duties, for security, or in the case of sick, old, young, or pregnant solitaires, for care and nurturing. At Oakland, the living arrangements of slaves represented a compromise between the preferences of the owners and the slaves. Owners wanted to use available cabins economically, but they were also cognizant of the problems that could arise if incompatible groups and individuals were assigned to the same small physical space. Slaves of each household probably would have preferred to have exclusive occupancy of a cabin. This was not often permitted, but the slaves appear to have had some choice in their cabin mates, if not in the decision that cabins must be shared.

Slave family households often coexisted with other individuals or groups in a single residence, but they did not surrender their family or household identification by such co-residence. Cabin occupancy in Louisiana and probably throughout the South took on a variety of forms depending in part on the stage of the community's development. Oakland's 1817 list is representative of an early community that had achieved little generational depth but had defined social organization and young but established families. The discrepancy between the household organization and living arrangements of Oakland slaves shows their adaptability to circumstances not of their own making. It also demonstrates their strong sense of family, kinship, and household identification—none of which was weakened by their changing living arrangements, as long as such arrangements were built on combinations of existing households and included persons who were somewhat compatible in age. The list in Appendix B demonstrates the differences between the household organization and the cabin residency of Oakland's 1817 community.

HOUSEHOLD COMPOSITION AMONG
OAKLAND SLAVES, 1846–1851

As was the case with the age and sex distribution analysis, household analysis of Oakland's community is not possible for the decades of the late 1820s, 1830s, and early 1840s, although households can be traced through those decades with relative ease. By the mid-1840s, statistical analysis is feasible once more (see table 5.4).

The population of Oakland's slave community in 1846 was 127; it reached 151 by 1851.[18] In 1846 solitaires made up one-fifth of the slaves. Male solitaires still predominated, constituting 15 percent of the slaves, while females accounted for only 5 percent. By 1851 the proportion of solitaires had declined to 15 percent of Oakland slaves, but male singles still con-

TABLE 5.4.

Oakland Plantation Slave Household Composition, 1846, 1851, 1852, 1857

	Oakland slaves, 1846				Oakland slaves, 1851			
Household type	Total slaves	Number of units	Mean size of units	Percent of total slaves in type	Total slaves	Number of units	Mean size of units	Percent of total slaves in type
Solitaire	25	25	1	19.6	22	22	1	14.5
Non-nuclear	3	1	3	2.3	3	1	3	1.9
Simple family	95	–	–	74.8	122	29	4.2	80.7
Married couple alone	6	3	2	4.7	8	4	2	5.2
Married couple with children	70	17	4.1	55.1	92	17	5.4	60.9
Single female with children	14	6	23	11.0	17	6	2.8	11.2
Single male with children	5	2	2.5	3.9	5	2	2.5	3.3
Extended	–	–	–	–	4	1	4	2.6
Multiple	4	–	–	3.1	–	–	–	–

Source: Oakland Data Base.

stituted a higher proportion of the population than did females, 9 percent to 6 percent. The composition of the ranks of solitaires in 1846 is of interest. Most of the males were young men who had not yet married, but only one of the six female solitaires was of an age suitable for marriage and child-bearing; she was twenty-two. The other women were all in their fifties. This pattern continued in 1851 and thereafter. Most of these older single women were house servants who had long been in the service of the Evans family.

One unit of co-resident siblings present both in 1846 and 1851 consisted of the three orphaned Jackson sisters—Sarah, Jenny, and Henrietta. Al-

	Oakland slaves, 1852				Oakland slaves, 1857		
Total slaves	Number of units	Mean size of units	Percent of total slaves in type	Total slaves	Number of units	Mean size of units	Percent of total slaves in type
17	17	1	14.9	5	5	1	3.7
6	2	3	5.2	2	1	2	1.4
91	25	3.6	79.8	100	23	4.3	74.0
2	1	2	1.7	4	2	2	2.9
82	22	3.7	71.9	73	15	4.8	54.0
7	2	3.5	6.1	15	5	3	11.1
–	–	–	–	8	1	8	5.9
–	–	–	–	7	2	3.5	5.1
–	–	–	–	21	3	7	15.5

though they surely lived with adults when very young, they are consistently identified as a household until the mid-1850s, when one married and the other two became unmarried mothers.[19]

As would be expected, the vast majority of Oakland's slaves lived in simple family households—75 percent in 1846 and an impressive 81 percent in 1851. Great variety was present within the simple family group in both periods. Married couples and their children composed a strong 55 percent of the population in 1846, and married couples without children made up another 5 percent. Single-parent households also encompassed a fairly substantial 15 percent. These figures are somewhat misleading, however, because several of the single heads of such households were widowed parents who had been part of standard nuclear families until their spouses' deaths. Four percent of Oakland's 1846 community were male-headed single-parent households—all of them headed by widowers.

In 1851 the proportion of standard nuclear families had risen to 61 percent, and another 5 percent were married couples without children. Such a high proportion of families with both spouses present is a strong indication that Oakland was an unusually stable slave society at this point. The percentage of single-parent households in 1851 was unchanged from that in 1846.

Some complex forms existed in the 1846 and 1851 slave communities of Oakland, but they did not appear with as much frequency as one would expect in a society of such generational depth. In 1846 a man headed a household composed of his widowed and "diseased" daughter-in-law (whom he took care of) and his grandchildren. By 1851, the daughter-in-law had died, and he headed an extended household unit with his orphaned grandchildren. These units made up 4 percent of the population in 1846 and 3 percent in 1851.[20]

By 1851, Oakland's slave community had almost recovered from the effects of the division of Nathaniel Evans's estate in 1822. The household structure was very balanced, with a high percentage of the slaves living in households composed of standard nuclear families. Marriages and new families were starting, and kinship was as extensive as it could have been considering that some members of the progenitive generation had been removed during the first estate division.

HOUSEHOLD COMPOSITION AMONG OAKLAND SLAVES, 1852–1857

In 1852, the population of Oakland's slave community was reduced to 114 (from 151 the previous year) because of the settlement of Sarah Evans's estate.[21] This was a considerable drop considering the births that had taken place and the slaves that Evans had purchased from heirs in addition to his own share of his mother's estate. The overall gender balance was perfect, with 57 slaves of each gender.

Household composition was simplified by the estate division. Complex forms were no longer present in 1852, and no male-headed single-parent units remained. Solitaires made up about the same percentage of the population, but some important differences were present within the type. In 1851, male solitaires, mostly young, amounted to 9 percent of the population, and females, mostly old, made up 6 percent. In 1852, the 7 percent of the population who were female solitaires and the 8 percent who were male solitaires represented a loss of four young, healthy male singles and the retention of seven solitaires over the age of fifty-four. Three of them were seventy and over, and the remaining three were in their sixties.[22] Evans, like his mother, was reluctant to sever old family slaves from the home plantation.

In 1852, two co-resident sibling groups were present, constituting 5 percent of the population. The additional unit included the children who in 1851 had lived with their devoted grandfather. He had been drawn by the DeHart heirs and was removed from the plantation. Fortunately, Evans managed to buy him back, and by 1853 he was reunited with his grand-children at Oakland.

The number of slaves living in simple families remained high but dropped very slightly by 1852. Again, several changes took place within the general type. John Evans, like his father, made a strong effort to keep together his standard nuclear slave families. Although he had fewer total slaves in 1852, standard nuclear families composed an even higher percent-age of his slaves than they had in 1851 (72 percent compared to 61 percent). The proportion of single-parent households decreased sharply from 1851 to 1852, to less than half the percentage of the community they had made up before the division.

Comparison of the household compositions of Oakland in 1851 and 1852 shows that, in the estate division proceedings, John Evans was determined to hold on to the old family servants and to established family units, especially those who had intermarried with his slaves. In the one case of a husband and wife still separated after the division, John Evans bought the husband within a year and reunited the couple. John Evans was clearly influenced by sentimentality in the makeup of his inheritance from his mother and in his shaping of the Oakland slave force in the two years after the division. His choices probably reduced Oakland's working capability but preserved about as much social harmony and continuity at Oakland as was possible under the circumstances. As a consequence, Oakland's household structure quickly recovered and resumed the expansive pattern temporarily arrested in 1851–52.

At its last reliable inventory, in 1857, Oakland presented an extremely stable, almost ideal slave household organization despite the effects of two devastating estate divisions. Not only was it stable and well balanced, it was also diverse, with its population of 134 distributed among all five major household types.[23] Only 4 percent were solitaires (compared to 17 percent in the 1850s sample and 18 percent in the model). An additional 1 percent (2 persons) lived in a non-nuclear unit (again, precisely the same percentage as in the model and the 1850s sample).

Oakland's slaves in 1857 were strongly concentrated in families despite the somewhat disproportionate age distribution. Almost all adults in the society were or had been members of stable families. Three-quarters of the slaves were in simple families, slightly more than the 74 percent of the 1850s sample and the 73 percent of the model. And within the simple family type, 54 percent were members of standard nuclear families, 5 percent more than resided in such households in the model and 3 percent more than in the 1850s model. Married couples without children made up another 3 percent. The only slight exception to the general improvement was the higher proportion living in single-parent households in 1857—17 percent of the population compared to 15 percent in 1846. This statistic is deceiving. Only one of these households was headed by a male, a recent widower, but he had seven children in his family; they alone swelled this category to 6 percent of the population. Female-headed households embraced only 11 percent of the population, in contrast to 13 percent of such units among the 1850s sampled communities and 14 percent in the model. Two of the new female-headed households were made up of two of the three orphaned Jackson sisters who had been co-resident siblings. Sarah Jackson, now eighteen, had a two-year-old son by an unnamed father. Her fourteen-year-old sister Henrietta had a newborn son, also by an unidentified father. The other women were in their thirties and forties and had been listed on previous inventories as single-parent heads of households.[24]

The 1857 inventory of Oakland's slaves also shows a pronounced complexity in the reappearance of extended forms and in the variety displayed within these forms. Only 5 percent of the slave population lived in extended family households, but they included units of both upward and downward extension. A young couple, Woodson and Hena, included in their household Hena's aged grandfather, Old Isaac, obviously an example of familial concern. This was one of the few cases of upward extension encountered. And Old Alex was back at Oakland again, heading a household composed of his young, orphaned grandchildren from whom he had been temporarily separated by the partition.

As was also found at Tiger Island and Petite Anse during their most mature phases, Oakland had a high incidence of multiple family households in its last documentable inventory in 1857. Three multiple family units were present, with a mean size of seven people. The twenty-one slaves in these units constituted 16 percent of Oakland's slave community. Together, extended and multiple family households encompassed a significantly high 21 percent of Oakland's bondspeople. Oakland had a higher percentage in multiple family households than found in the 1850s sample, but the proportion was not far from the 14 percent in such units in the 1850–65 sample. Oakland was an old slave community, first established in 1809. It is logical that it would reach a mature point and would have highly developed kinship lines by the late 1850s. Considering that married couples with children were also involved in the multiple family households, the incidence of families involving married couples was remarkably high.

Although insufficient documentation is available for household analysis, additions to the 1857 rolls show the births and deaths of the 1858–60 period. These suggest that the household composition of Oakland remained basically the same through 1860, with slight increases in the numbers of standard nuclear families and multiple family households.

An 1864 roll of Oakland slaves demonstrates the profound effects of the Civil War on its household composition. The list shows only a remnant of the 1857 community remaining on the plantation.[25] Many of the 1857 families were entirely absent. A few individuals from the familiar slave households of previous inventories were listed, but in not a single case was a household intact. All were fractured—divided by departure, death, or disagreement. Of the forty-two slaves left, thirty were females and twelve were males. One-fourth of the remaining slaves were house servants, who characteristically stayed with their owners longer than did fieldworkers. Whether they tended to do so out of self-interest or emotional attachment to their owners is debatable. The mistress of another Louisiana plantation, from which all the field slaves had fled, commented concerning her house servants who stayed: "The . . . household host[,] adverse to leaving pleasant homes for an uncertainty, did not then leave, but like Irish retainers [they] were consumers not producers."[26] Many of the Oakland slaves who remained in 1864 were economic liabilities rather than assets. No more than one-third were able-bodied adults; the others were old, infirm, or children. Little household or family organization remained among those who stayed.

GENDER AND AGE DISTRIBUTION OF PETITE ANSE SLAVES, 1826

Petite Anse's slave community was formed by 1822, but records appropriate for statistical analysis are not available until 1826, when the appraisal of William Stone's estate provided an accurate and detailed inventory of Petite Anse slaves.[27] Although not divided into family/household groupings, the inventory serves as a very satisfactory basis for analysis of age and sex distribution at an early stage of the Petite Anse slave community's development. Once more, gender distribution will be considered first. The twenty-nine slaves of Petite Anse in 1826 formed a community that was clearly labor-intensive and consisted almost entirely of young, single, adult workers. But it was well balanced in gender, particularly within the age groups most conducive to successful reproduction and optimal work performance. The favorable gender distribution is reflected in the sex ratio. The ratio for males per female was 1.4 among slaves of all ages, and in the adult categories, 1.2 males were present for each female. In the seventeen-to-twenty-eight age group, males outnumbered females (in their proportions in the general slave population) by 7 percent, but the differential dropped to a more acceptable 3 percent in the seventeen-to-forty category. Such differentials were greater in 1826 than they would be later, but they are still smaller than those exhibited in many other coastal slave communities. For example, the differential in the percentages of men and women in the seventeen-to-forty category on Tiger Island in its first-phase inventory (1842) was more than 38 percent, and Oakland also had a gender imbalance in its earliest inventory (1811), with a 13 percent differential in the seventeen-to-twenty-eight age category and a 5 percent differential in the seventeen-to-thirty-four group, although in Oakland's case females predominated.[28]

Major skewing in the 1826 gender distribution at Petite Anse occurred only in the ten and under and over-forty age groups, with males strongly predominating in both. In the small community present in that year, the ten and under group consisted entirely of two infants, both males, and the only slaves over forty on the plantation were also males. It was coincidental that the only surviving children were boys, but the predominance of males in the minuscule over-forty population might have been contrived. An absence of women over forty—and especially over fifty—was a common feature of migration communities still in their first decade of operation. The small number of women over forty in such communities was usually the result of owners' choices. Migrating planters rarely brought older slave women to remote, newly established plantations in Louisiana unless the women were trained house servants, had other specialized skills, or were part of valuable family groupings that the owners chose not to break up. In the case of Petite Anse—a community first populated almost entirely with slaves bought for the migration—it is logical that the owners would buy few or no female slaves past prime work and childbearing ages.[29] Most of the males chosen for migration were also young, but it was not uncommon for migration contingents to include men in their mid- and late thirties and even forties if they were skilled or experienced workers such as blacksmiths, bricklayers, or carpenters.[30]

The population of Petite Anse in 1826 was unequally distributed within the major age groups. Such maldistribution was, however, typical for any early-stage community. Like Oakland at its first inventory analysis, more Petite Anse slaves of 1826 were in the seventeen-to-forty age category than in either of the other two groups (see table 5.5). Only 7 percent of Petite Anse slaves were under the age of eleven and 14 percent were sixteen and under. Seven percent of its slaves were over forty, leaving a heavily skewed 79 percent of the community in the seventeen-to-forty age bracket. Small percentages of very young and old slaves are typical of all first-generation holdings, but Petite Anse's profile is also that of a migration community in its first phase, accounting for the much larger percentage in the seventeen-to-forty category. A similar profile was found at Brashear's first plantation, Belle Isle, but was not found at Tiger Island—a start-up operation begun two decades after the initial migration.

Despite its few children, the slave community of Petite Anse in 1826 was young both in its organization as a slave society and in its members' mean age, as seen in table 5.6. The mean age for all slaves was twenty-five. The mean dropped by 1836 and did not climb back to twenty-five until 1860.

TABLE 5.5.

Petite Anse Plantation Slaves in Major Age Categories, 1826–1860

Year	Ages 0–16		Ages 17–40		Ages 41–65+	
	n	%	n	%	n	%
1826	4	13.6	23	78.8	2	6.8
1836[a]	29	48.7	26	43.4	4	6.5
1839	33	46.2	32	44.8	6	8.4
1845[b]	27	33.6	34	42.2	19	23.6
1860[b]	32	36.9	34	39.1	20	22.8

Source: Petite Anse Data Base.
[a]One infant of unidentified gender is not included in the computation.
[b]Three infants of unidentified gender are excluded.

The reason is apparent. In 1826 there were almost no children present because permanent pairings had not yet begun or were just commencing.[31] As more infants and children entered the community, the mean age dropped until the natural cycle produced larger numbers of older adults to offset the growing number of children.

Like other new holdings, the 1826 community had far too few young slaves and lacked generational depth. The important middle group did have a fairly good gender balance, however, and the owners bought many potential mates in the 1820s and early 1830s, providing a basis for new family formations and births to correct the first-mentioned deficiency.

GENDER AND AGE DISTRIBUTION OF
PETITE ANSE SLAVES, 1836–1839

Petite Anse workers made admirable strides toward correcting these problems in the middle period. The population doubled to sixty by 1836, and in 1836 it had increased to seventy-one.[32] Inventories for both middle years show a near perfect general gender distribution, a marked improvement over that of 1826 and much better than that of other St. Mary Parish sugar estates, including Tiger Island, at a roughly comparable stage of development.[33] In 1836 the sex ratio for Petite Anse was 1.1; in 1839, females slightly outnumbered males with a 0.9 ratio. Among the adult slaves (over age

TABLE 5.6.

Mean Ages of Petite Anse Plantation Slaves, 1826–1860

Year	Males	Females	Total slaves
1826	24.2	25.8	25.0
1836	16.7	18.5	17.6
1839	20.6	18.8	19.7
1854	17.7	21.4	19.5
1860	28.5	21.9	25.2

Source: Petite Anse Data Base.

sixteen), the sex ratio was 1.0 in 1836 and 1.1 in 1839. Moreover, the differential in the percentages of males and females in the earlier society had evened out to 1 percent by 1839 (see figure 5.2).

In its age distribution trends, Petite Anse followed a predictable course in keeping with the developmental cycle. First-decade migration communities characteristically exhibit a first phase in which age distribution is strongly skewed toward young adults, with few children and even fewer slaves over forty, and Petite Anse corresponded to this pattern. By the 1836–39 inventories, Petite Anse had entered a second phase, with 46 to 49 percent of the slave population consisting of children sixteen or under. Between 35 and 37 percent of the slaves of the 1836–39 period fell in the important seventeen-to-thirty-four age category, with the lower percentage in 1839. During the same period, 43 to 45 percent of the slaves belonged to the seventeen-to-forty grouping. Petite Anse was a youthful, dynamic, expanding slave society, with 74 percent of its people younger than twenty-nine in 1836 and 86 percent below the age of thirty-five. A slight correction was made by 1839, when more than 80 percent of the slaves were under thirty-five, but only 67 percent were younger than twenty-nine, adding to the middle group, which needed expanding.

The over-forty age group remained small. In 1836, only 7 percent of the slaves at Petite Anse were over forty, and only 2 percent were older than forty-six. No slaves were over the age of fifty-two. The over-forty category increased its proportion of the community to 8 percent in 1839, but once more, the individuals older than forty-six amounted to only 3 percent of the community and no slaves were older than fifty-two.[34]

FIGURE 5.2.

Gender Distribution of Petite Anse Plantation Slaves, 1826–1860

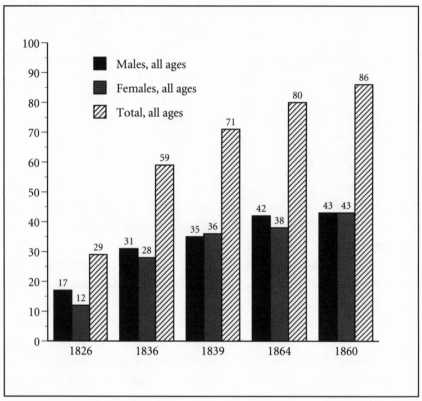

Source: Petite Anse Data Base.

The young dominated Petite Anse's demographic profile from 1836 through 1839, but the community was prototypical of a second-phase, first-generation migration community. And a slight progression toward a more balanced age distribution was noticeable, even in three years.

GENDER AND AGE DISTRIBUTION OF
PETITE ANSE SLAVES, 1854–1860

The gender ratio was good in Petite Anse's second phase, and by its most mature documentable stage, that of the 1857–60 period, the gender distribution was near ideal (see figure 5.2). Gender differentials were acceptable in all young adult age categories, even though males formed a slightly higher percentage of the population. The 1860 Petite Anse slave community was perfectly balanced in its overall gender distribution. A minor skewing continued in the sex ratio of slaves in the primary working and reproductive age categories, with as much as a 5 percent differential in the percentage of males over that of females.[35]

In its age distribution, Petite Anse exhibited a very balanced profile by 1854–60. In 1854 the numbers and percentages of children in the society were in good proportion to the rest of the population. About one-fourth of the slaves were under the age of eleven, and slightly more than one-third were sixteen or under (compared to nearly half in 1836). By 1860, 37 percent were under seventeen.

The proportions of middle-aged and elderly slaves in the community increased. The over-forty group, which embraced only 7 percent of Petite Anse's slaves in 1836, contained more than one-fifth of the slaves in the late 1850s. In 1860, 16 percent of the slaves were over forty-six, and 9 percent were over fifty-two. Although owners might not be pleased with the increased number of slaves whom they had to maintain in years of declining productivity, the increases were indicative of a more mature and stable society, with kinship developed to the third and fourth generations.

In the same period the proportion of slaves in the middle range remained steady. The seventeen-to-forty grouping accounted for 42 percent of the slaves in 1854 and 39 percent in 1860, only a few percentage points from that of 1836.[36]

By 1860 Petite Anse had achieved an excellent gender ratio, a good distribution of ages, and a generational depth that is all the more remarkable for a coastal sugar plantation plagued by diseases that took a heavy toll of the very young and old. In its age and sex distributions at least, Petite Anse had attained a society that was as structurally balanced as one could expect considering nineteenth-century life expectancies and its constitution as an unfree population. Petite Anse of the 1854–60 period provides an excellent example of a mature society in its household composition as well.

HOUSEHOLD COMPOSITION AMONG
PETITE ANSE SLAVES, 1826

The earliest inventory of Petite Anse slaves, that of 1826, was not divided into households by the enumerators, and insufficient evidence is available from other sources to reconstitute the community into family household groupings. It is nevertheless apparent that the community of twenty-nine slaves contained only two families with children—one a standard nuclear unit, the other a female-headed single-parent household. No other family organization is obvious, and many of the young workers were solitaires.[37]

HOUSEHOLD COMPOSITION AMONG
PETITE ANSE SLAVES, 1836–1839

The first Petite Anse inventory allowing a clear determination of slave family household types was done in 1836 (see table 5.7). The domestic structure was still uncomplicated even though the community had been building for nearly two decades and was in the second phase of the developmental cycle. Predictably, the sixty slaves fell into the two major types—simple family and solitaire. The simple family household category accounted for nearly three-fourths of the slaves, precisely the percentage in the Louisiana household model and higher than that of the 1830s sample. The healthy portion of its society in families suggests that Petite Anse was more stable in its domestic structure than most of its counterparts in the expansive but unsettled decade of the inventory. Solitaires constituted the remainder of the habitants.[38]

Within the simple family household type, the standard nuclear unit dominated. In 1836, 43 percent of the plantation's slaves lived in families consisting of a husband, wife, and children. This was a high percentage for the tumultuous 1830s, higher than that exhibited in the sampled communities of the decade, although lower than that found in the 1810–64 model. The 1836 standard nuclear family of Petite Anse contained a mean of 4.3 members, or parents and two children. The only other simple family households present in 1836 were those made up of single mothers and their offspring. Eighteen slaves lived in such units (with a mean of 3.6 members), composing 30 percent of the total population, a much higher percentage than in the 1810–64 model or even the 1830s sample.

In 1836 more than one-fourth of the slave community was made up of solitaires, and the percentage of male solitaires was double that of females. The proportion of solitaires was higher than in the model (18 percent) although close to the 23 percent of the sampled population for the 1830s. Still, such a high percentage of solitaires was a sign of instability, particularly because of the marked gender imbalance in that category. Coupled with the higher than average percentages of single-parent female-headed households and the absence of complex forms, the swollen ranks of the solitaires demonstrate that the community was not as stable as its 73 percent in simple families might suggest. Fortunately, the community was changing very rapidly, and a marked improvement was made within three years.

In 1839, among a population that had grown to seventy-one, a remarkable 86 percent were part of simple families, although no complex forms had yet appeared. The remaining 14 percent were solitaires, a significant reduction since 1836. Some of those who had been single in 1836 had married so there were five married couples without children. Well more than half of the slave population formed families consisting of both parents and their children, and only three households contained female single parents and their children. The mean size of the two-parent family was 4.5, a slight increase over that of 1836. Families composed of a mother and children declined fractionally in mean size, from 3.6 to 3.3 members.[39]

The household organization of Petite Anse slaves in the 1836–39 period was still simple and in an early stage of development, but the changes within the only two household types present show that the society was proceeding toward a more complex and balanced construction. Population was increasing; the percentages of solitaires and single-parent households were decreasing, and the percentages in standard nuclear families were expanding over time—all of which can be expected of a maturing slave society. By 1839 marriages were taking place at an accelerated pace, as were the formations of first families, which would provide foundations for future kinship networks.

Despite its youthfulness and relative immaturity, the Petite Anse slave community of the 1836–39 period was already far more stable and balanced than Tiger Island's was in 1842, even though the migration of the owners and initial laborers of both plantations took place within a few years of each other. Even so, Petite Anse in 1839 was still composed basically of atomized units of young unrelated families and of solitaires with no known linkage between most of them.

TABLE 5.7.

Petite Anse Plantation Slave Household Composition, 1836, 1839, 1854, 1860

	Petite Anse slaves, 1836				Petite Anse slaves, 1839			
Household type	Total slaves	Number of units	Mean size of units	Percent of total slaves in type	Total slaves	Number of units	Mean size of units	Percent of total slaves in type
Solitaire	16	16	1	26.6	10	10	1	14
Non-nuclear	–	–	–	–	–	–	–	–
Simple family	44	11	4	73.3	61	17	3.5	85.9
Married couple alone	–	–	–	–	10	5	2	14.0
Married couple with children	26	6	4.3	43.3	41	9	4.5	57.7
Single female with children	18	5	3.6	30.0	10	3	2.3	14.0
Single male with children	–	–	–	–	–	–	–	–
Extended	–	–	–	–	–	–	–	–
Multiple	–	–	–	–	–	–	–	–

Source: Petite Anse Data Base.

HOUSEHOLD COMPOSITION AMONG PETITE ANSE SLAVES, 1854–1860

By 1854, the Petite Anse slave community was considerably more complex and exhibited intricate kinship networks.[40] Among a population of eighty-three, including three infants for whom gender identification was not provided, the slaves were divided into solitaires, all categories of simple family households, and multiple family households. Solitaires in 1854 accounted for 16 percent of the population, the slight rise owing to pur-

	Petite Anse slaves, 1854				Petite Anse slaves, 1860		
Total slaves	Number of units	Mean size of units	Percent of total slaves in type	Total slaves	Number of units	Mean size of units	Percent of total slaves in type
13	13	1	15.6	13	13	1	14.6
–	–	–	–	–	–	–	–
35	8	4.3	42.1	28	9	3.1	31.4
2	1	2	2.4	2	1	2	2.2
29	6	4.8	34.9	21	6	3.5	23.5
2	1	2	2.4	5	2	2.5	5.6
2	1	2	2.4	–	–	–	–
–	–	–	–	–	–	–	–
35	5	7	42.1	48	3	1.6	53.9

chases and divorces. A gender imbalance was still present among the singles; 14 percent of the society consisted of unattached males. Another possibly disquieting change was a dramatic reduction in the percentage of slaves in simple families, fewer nearly by half than had lived in such units in 1839. Only one childless married couple was present, and just 35 percent of the population lived in standard nuclear families (now with a mean size of 4.8, or parents and two to three children).[41] But the percentage of slaves in single-parent households had been reduced to near numerical insignificance. Only 5 percent of Petite Anse slaves lived in the two households headed by single parents, one headed by a woman, the other by a man, each containing only one child. These contradictions do not, however, mean that the society was regressing. The strange configuration was actually a sign of increased stability because of the development on Petite Anse by 1854 of powerful kinship networks clustered in large, sprawling, multiple family units. In 1854, 42 percent of the population lived in multiple family units, precisely as many as lived in simple family households and more than were part of standard nuclear units. These multiple family households were examples of the only other household type present on the island because there were no extended families or households of co-resident siblings.

The last available inventory of the Petite Anse slave population was done in 1860; it listed eighty-nine slaves. Of these, 14.6 percent were solitaires, consisting of ten men—four of them over the age of fifty-seven—and three women. The percentage of the population who were solitaires is slightly lower than in the 1810–64 model but is the same as in the 1860s sample. The remaining slaves were organized either in simple family households (31 percent of the population), or they constituted multiple family households, which accounted for 54 percent of the slave inhabitants.

Among the simple family households in 1860 were one childless married couple and two female-headed single-parent households, with a mean of 2.5 members. The percentage of 1860 Petite Anse slaves in female-headed households was lower (by more than half) than the proportions exhibited in either the model or the 1860s sample, but this is primarily because some Petite Anse single mothers with a child or children were absorbed in multiple family units. About a quarter of the population consisted of two-parent households, with a mean size of 3.5 people. Ordinarily such a low percentage of slaves in standard nuclear families would indicate extreme instability, but it should be kept in mind that the three multiple family units contained nine married couples, most of them with children.[42]

As was true in 1854, the multiple family households, all examples of downward extension, assumed an unusual dominance in the island's domestic structure. The standard nuclear family accounted for six units as opposed to only three units in the multiple family category, but forty-eight people were embraced in the three multiple family units, whereas less than half that number formed part of standard nuclear units.

By 1860, three pervasive kinship groups numerically dominated the internal social structure of the Petite Anse slave community; they will be described in the next chapter. The percentage of Petite Anse slaves in multiple family households in 1860 was much higher than in the model or in the sampled communities of the 1860s. Proportionally, however, more Louisiana slaves were part of multiple family households during the 1860s than in any other decade studied (14 percent), so Petite Anse corresponded to a broad trend toward expansion of this form in the later phases.

In some respects, Petite Anse's household development could provide a model for the ideal migration community. From a state of social disorganization in 1826, it evolved by 1836 into a young society with a domestic structure that was simple and only slightly imbalanced. Although naturally lacking generational depth and diversity, it exhibited a healthy organizational structure for an early first- or second-phase slave community. By the 1854–60 period, Petite Anse was well balanced in age and gender distribution and distribution of household types, partly because of the natural developmental cycle and partly because the owners had periodically brought young families and single females (as well as young males) into the community. The major aberrant feature was an unusually large number of slaves living in multiple family units. Most of these, however, were extremely stable units built around a standard nuclear family core.

Petite Anse slaves, in a relatively isolated setting and undisturbed by estate divisions, massive sales, and transfers, forged a remarkably balanced and stable community for an unfree people who are limited in many of their choices. Petite Anse also showed a natural progression in its household development as its population increased from twenty-nine in 1826 to eighty-nine in 1860. From a state of social disorganization in 1826, it moved to a very simple construction in 1836–39, to one that in 1854–60 included a wide variety of household types, including complex forms.

The shattering of prior bonds by the migration and by the additional adjustments required of the northern slaves who constituted the majority of the initial workers at Petite Anse resulted in a long period of imbalance in their domestic organization. In the late 1830s the community began a steady recovery, assisted by infusions provided by Marsh's purchases. By 1860 the community displayed all the attributes of a mature, third-phase society, unusual only in the extensiveness of its kinship groupings.

GENDER AND AGE DISTRIBUTION OF
TIGER ISLAND SLAVES, 1842

Of the three communities in the case study, that of Tiger Island had the most severe challenges to overcome in attaining a balanced domestic structure. The major obstacle was a crippling gender imbalance that, without intervention by the owner, would be almost impossible to overcome naturally without the passing of many generations. Tiger Island was first manned in the late 1820s or early 1830s; a partial listing of slaves exists for 1833, but the first inventory appropriate for age and sex analysis is that of the 1842 community.[43] This inventory in some respects reflects the second phase in the developmental cycle, but the age and sex distribution is typical of a new holding manned primarily with transfers from older holdings of the same owner.

In 1842, 106 slaves lived at Tiger Island; their distribution by gender and age groups was far from optimal (see figure 5.3). The most serious problem related to gender distribution, for males made up a disproportionately large part of the community—63 percent, compared to 37 percent females. The gender imbalance was most marked in the categories over the age of ten—in other words, slaves old enough to provide some labor. Males over age ten accounted for 43 percent of the population, whereas females in the same age classification accounted for less than one-fifth of the slaves. The gender skewing was found in all adult groups. Men of prime working age, seventeen to forty, made up about one-third of Tiger Island's slaves, and women in this same age bracket encompassed only 12 percent of the plantation's workers.[44] The portion of the population who were males between the ages of seventeen and thirty-four was 24 percent compared to 10 percent for women. These differentials in the numbers and percentages of young adult slaves show that opportunities for marriage and nuclear family formation were demographically limited.

The very serious gender imbalance at Tiger Island was no accident. Tiger Island in 1842 was a labor-intensive new holding with a deliberately heavy preponderance of young, single males. Such an imbalanced, male-favored sex ratio was most unlikely to have occurred naturally. Such ratios were found on plantations where immediate work capacity was primary, and social harmony and reproduction were secondary considerations. Skewed gender ratios were almost always the result of deliberate choices made by

FIGURE 5.3.

Gender Distribution of Tiger Island Plantation Slaves, 1842–1860

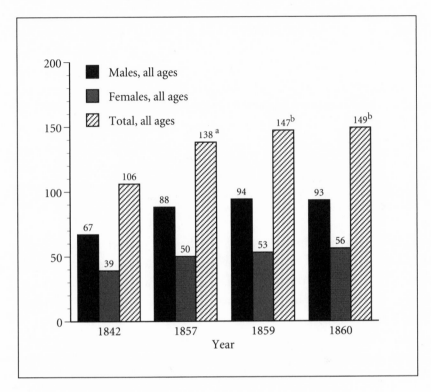

Source: Tiger Island Data Base.
[a]One infant of unidentified gender excluded from computations.
[b]Three infants of unidentified gender excluded from computations.

owners. Richard Dunn, in his study of the slaves of Mount Airy Plantation in Virginia from 1799 to 1828, found an average male-female ratio of 55.7 to 44.3 percent, considerably less distorted than the 62.6 to 36.4 percent ratio at Tiger Island in 1842. Even so, Dunn considered the sex ratio at Mount Airy significantly imbalanced. He attributed the imbalance to the actions of the owner, John Tayloe III, who frequently transferred in male slaves while selling off females, retaining only "enough females . . . to perform domestic tasks and to assure a healthy rate of natural increase."[45] Brashear did not sell off females, but he did not transfer as many women as men to Tiger Island, and he often rotated women who were there back to Golden Farm, replacing them with young men as they became available.

TABLE 5.8.

Tiger Island Plantation Slaves in Major Age Categories, 1842–1860

Year	Ages 0–16		Ages 17–40		Ages 41–65+	
	n	%	n	%	n	%
1842	51	48.1	47	44.3	8	7.5
1850	65	58.5	37	33.3	9	8.1
1857[a]	61	44.2	56	40.5	21	15.2
1859[b]	64	43.5	60	40.8	23	15.6
1860[b]	60	40.2	62	41.6	27	18.1

Source: Tiger Island Data Base.
[a]One infant of unidentified gender is not included in the computation.
[b]Three infants of unidentified gender are excluded.

A persistent gender imbalance was not the only problem faced by Tiger Island slaves in their attempts to attain a stable, sustaining domestic organization. In 1842, they also had to contend with a marked age imbalance, with well over half of the slaves under the age of twenty-two and 94 percent under forty.

Like Petite Anse and Oakland, early Tiger Island was a young society. The mean ages of slaves at Tiger Island was even lower than that of the other two plantations in their early phases. The mean age for all slaves was only nineteen in 1842—that of males, twenty-two, and of females, sixteen.[46] Children under the age of ten contributed strongly to the low mean age because they constituted 38 percent of the population. And as demonstrated in table 5.8, children sixteen and younger composed 48 percent of Tiger Island's slaves in 1842.

A small percentage of the 1842 slaves were over forty, very comparable to the proportion at Petite Anse and Oakland in the 1840s. Not a single slave, male or female, was older than fifty-eight.[47] Many of the Tiger Island slaves had parents and other older relatives at Golden Farm or Belle Isle, but there is no evidence that they had opportunities to visit.

Despite the small number of older slaves, the population of Tiger Island did not cluster in the middle age bracket between seventeen and forty; the 44 percent of the population in this age category is a reasonable proportion in a society with high work expectations. About 19 percent of the community was composed of slaves in the seventeen-to-twenty-eight range, and if the range is extended to seventeen to thirty-four, 35 percent of the population is encompassed. Therefore, no serious problem existed in the proportion of the population available for work and family formation; the difficulty lay in the gender imbalance within those significant groupings. In its general youthfulness and lack of older slaves, Tiger Island's 1842 community resembles that of Oakland and Petite Anse in their first inventories, but Tiger Island had been in operation since the early 1830s and should have shown more improvement by 1842. The next inventory, that of 1850, is therefore a telling one. Because a slave community was not an open society in which inhabitants were free to leave or to bring in others to correct imbalances, the responsibility for improving the gender imbalance at Tiger Island was borne largely by its owners—the Brashear family.

GENDER AND AGE DISTRIBUTIONS OF
TIGER ISLAND SLAVES, 1850

The 1850 age and sex distribution figures may not be as reliable as those taken from the court documents, but an interim inventory was needed. The 1850 statistical profile was derived from the enumeration of Tiger Island slaves attributed to Robert Brashear in the slave schedules of the 1850 federal census. Such enumerations provide only the numbers, ages, and genders of the slaves. Their reliability is suspect because the statistics appear to deviate strongly from the pattern established by the four inventories (1842, 1857, 1859, 1860) that provide much more detailed information on the slaves and have been cross-checked with each other as well as with other sources. Although the 1850 enumeration may be less than satisfactory, it is included because it provides interim data between the first available Tiger Island inventory in 1842 and the inventories of 1857, 1859, and 1860 compiled as part of the estate probate process.[48]

The community in 1850 encompassed 111 persons. Of these, 55 percent were male, and 45 percent were female. In the seventeen-to-forty age category, in which imbalance created serious problems for the community, about one-fifth of the slaves were male and 14 percent were female—imbalanced to be sure, but much less seriously than before, if the figures are correct. I do not believe the gender distribution figures are correct, however. It is hard to believe that the male-to-female ratio decreased from a 27 percent differential in 1842 to a less than 10 percent differential in 1850, then again increased to a 27 percent differential seven years later.[49] More likely, for the federal census a busy overseer or lackadaisical census enumerator correctly tallied the total number of slaves but only estimated age and gender designations. In any case, a gender imbalance of some degree persisted at Tiger Island in 1850 as it had in 1842.

Earlier trends in the age distribution of Tiger Island slaves continued. The society in 1850 was still demographically dominated by the young. Forty-four percent of the slaves were under ten, even more than in 1842; 77 percent of the population was under the age of thirty-four, and 92 percent were younger than forty-one. The mean age of slaves in the 1850 enumeration was lower than it had been in 1842—now it was fifteen for females, twenty for males, with an average of eighteen for all slaves, as can be seen in table 5.9.[50] In its overall configuration, the age distribution was less balanced than before. Fifty-nine percent of the slaves were enumerated as sixteen or younger, whereas only one-third fell into the seventeen-to-forty age bracket, and the percentage in the over-forty category stayed about the same. Like the gender figures, the age statistics appear to be broad estimates of questionable reliability.

GENDER AND AGE DISTRIBUTION OF TIGER ISLAND SLAVES, 1857–1860

Tiger Island's slave population had reached 139 by 1857 and rose to 152 in 1860, the last available listing.[51] That increase did not, however, improve the distorted gender distribution. The ratio of males to females in 1857 was precisely the same as in 1842; 63 percent of the slaves were males, and only slightly over 36 percent were females, a very unhealthy discrepancy. The percentages were about the same in 1859, but a very slight improvement was noticeable in 1860. Males then constituted 61 percent of the population, compared to approximately 38 percent females. Simply through natural means (reproduction of both genders and the dying off of the generation having the disproportionate number of males), the proportion of females was finally beginning to increase, but that increase would not be large enough to be significant in 1860.

Because a male-favored gender imbalance was a prevailing feature of

TABLE 5.9.

Mean Ages of Tiger Island Plantation Slaves, 1842–1860

Year	Males	Females	Total slaves
1842	22.2	16.0	19.0
1850	20.0	14.9	17.5
1857	24.6	19.5	22.8
1859	23.4	20.3	22.3
1860	24.4	20.5	22.5

Source: Tiger Island Data Base.

Tiger Island's community throughout its documentable history, the problem should be stated in a larger perspective. How did the skewing occur? Why was it not corrected? Did other owners in the area have similar imbalances? Many planters—such as John Tayloe at Mount Airy, as revealed by Dunn's study—preferred a labor force dominated by males.[52] Walter Brashear initially stocked the plantation with a strong preponderance of males, as reflected in the 1842 ratios, resulting in a distortion that was not offset by natural increase by 1860. His motive was the same as Tayloe's, a conviction that male labor was more productive, thus more profitable.[53] He and many others reasoned that sugar production required the strength and stamina of males rather than the dexterity that often put female cotton pickers on an equal production level with male workers. Brashear, and to a degree his offspring, was interested in retaining sufficient young females to provide a reasonable reproduction rate, but he was primarily interested in the short-term economic benefits that he perceived would accrue from a heavily male-dominated labor contingent. His preference was manifested not only on Tiger Island but on his home plantation, Golden Farm, on which in 1850 males composed 73 percent of the labor force and nearly half of the slaves were men over age seventeen.[54]

Russell Menard, working with colonial records of slaves from four Maryland counties, also found a "striking preponderance of males." He, too, attributed the imbalance to owners' preference as well as the effects of African immigration. Menard cogently suggests that such skewed ratios "placed definite limits on the opportunities for family life among slaves; the dispersed ownership pattern prevented slaves from taking full advantage of such possibilities for contact with persons of the opposite sex as the sexual imbalance permitted. Together they placed formidable barriers in the way of affectionate relationships between men and women, denying many blacks a fundamental human opportunity."[55] Although Menard writes of a different time, place, and condition, his remarks are applicable to Tiger Island at its first inventory in 1842. The coastal area which Brashear preferred was sparsely settled, secluded, and primitive, and most St. Mary Parish planters established their home plantations in the more accessible and developed part of the parish, along the Teche, reserving the coastal and island areas for experimental outposts.[56] Island plantations such as Tiger Island were generally managed by overseers for absentee owners or by sons of the planter as practical preparation for the establishment of their own holdings.[57] The inhospitable conditions and physical isolation of the island sugar plantations in St. Mary persisted well into the 1840s. Most of them were, like Tiger Island, manned with predominantly male work forces, many of whom were solitaires. The insularity of the island plantations (most, like Tiger Island, could only be reached by boat) severely restricted social intercourse and limited marriage choices to the plantation. Tiger Island was surrounded by a series of waterways and swamps. It was effectively cut off from the well-traversed plantation country of the parish until the 1850s. Except for a few holdings along Bayou Boeuf, Tiger Island slaves of the 1840s and early 1850s did not have the opportunity to travel to other plantations in search of appropriate mates. The Brashears made no effort to buy young women who might provide suitable mates for the surplus male solitaires, and the slaves themselves were prevented from doing so by geographic conditions and—probably—plantation rules. There is not a single mention of an off-plantation marriage, although one slave was accused of having a white Cajun woman as a lover. Thus the Tiger Island sex ratio imbalance presented a serious social problem for its slave inhabitants, as will be discussed later in the section on household analysis.

As was shown in the statistical analysis by parish type, such an imbalance was not the norm in Louisiana, even on sugar estates, but it was very common. When a marked male-dominated imbalance did appear, it was almost always correlated with a high incidence of solitaires, most of them young.[58] There is virtually no evidence that heavy male-to-female ratios were the result of higher mortality rates among women. Owner preference appears to be the overwhelming reason for the imbalances, which were found more frequently but not consistently among planters who engaged in sugar production. Nor does the preference appear to be related to culture; French as well as American planters often preferred heavily male-dominated slave forces. For example, out of a slave force of forty-two on an Iberville Parish sugar plantation owned by Antoine Duprey in 1855, 38 percent of the slaves were male solitaires, and all but two were prime-age males. The entire community contained only seven adult women, and all but one of them was married; the exception was a single mother.[59] Also in Iberville, the 1852 estate inventory of Ulgere Baugnon exhibited an even more striking imbalance. Seventy percent of his slaves were male; 55 percent were solitaires, and 48 percent were male solitaires. Only one single woman was on his plantation who was of an age appropriate for childbearing. In Louis Landry's 1831 estate inventory in Ascension Parish, the appraisers listed 36 males and 17 females. More than 55 percent of his slaves were singles, and 47 percent were single males. Colonel Charles Morgan's Pointe Coupee estate inventory for 1848 shows 197 males to 89 females; 37 percent of his slave community was composed of solitaires. The pattern was even more pervasive on other island and coastal plantations of St. Mary Parish. A sugar plantation owned by Olympus Young on Bayou Boeuf, bordering Tiger Island, had a similarly high ratio of males and solitaires. In 1860 males constituted 53 percent of his work force and singles 32 percent, almost all of them men. The 1857 estates of Nicholas and Celeste Prevost Loisel contained 40 males to 22 females. Forty-nine percent of their slave community were solitaires; 41 percent were both male and solitaires.[60] Although numerous others could be cited, these should suffice to show that Brashear's decision to maintain a gross gender imbalance among his slave workers was not unusual, even though it was not typical.

In spite of the continuing gender imbalance, Tiger Island made some progress by the 1857–60 period toward attaining a more stable construction, and the age distribution of the community did improve. The mean age of Tiger Island slaves rose to twenty-three in 1857, dropped back to twenty-two in 1859, and settled at twenty-three in 1860, still low but considerably higher than it had been in 1842. By 1860 40 percent of slaves in the community were under the age of seventeen, roughly comparable to the proportion on Petite Anse in the same period and 13 percent lower than at Oakland. The figures, though slightly high, showed an expanding community and were in good proportion to the other age categories. The middle grouping, consisting of slaves in the seventeen-to-forty prime-age category, embraced about 42 percent of the work force, also comparing favorably to that of Petite Anse and Oakland at their final inventories. Tiger Island made particularly good progress in achieving generational depth by the 1857–60 period. In 1842 less than 8 percent of Tiger Island's slaves were in the over-forty age bracket, even though the Kentucky migration had been twenty years earlier and the plantation had been in operation a decade. But by 1860 the over-forty category contained 18 percent of the slaves, and 6 percent were over fifty-eight—a dramatic increase with important repercussions for the slave society. It demonstrated that kinship was likely well developed and that older slaves were available to provide advice, support, continuity, and a sense of history for the slaves at Tiger Island.

The age and sex distributions of a society are important in determining how that society is structured into households and families. In the simplest of situations, a slave child in the 1842 Tiger Island community was most unlikely to know its grandparents, or even aunts, uncles, and cousins. By 1860 he or she had a very good chance of having some of these relatives around. A young man of twenty in the 1842 Tiger Island community would have a very difficult time finding a wife and would probably remain single for at least ten years. The chances of finding a mate for a young man in 1860 were only slightly improved. In 1842 it appeared that Tiger Island's slave community would have little chance of achieving a stable structure with a preponderance of standard nuclear families, with generational depth, and with a healthy balance of men and women, adults, elders, and children. Such a condition was not entirely obtained by 1860, but admirable progress had been made. In spite of the demographic odds against them, the slaves formed families—some of them unorthodox, as will be shown in the next chapter—that, by the end of the recorded period, had achieved surprisingly well-developed kinship networks. Tiger Island was unable to correct its severe gender imbalance, but it made significant progress in other areas of its population distribution and in 1860 was moving toward a more balanced configuration, even in regard to gender, with virtually no assistance from the outside.

HOUSEHOLD COMPOSITION AMONG
TIGER ISLAND SLAVES, 1842

In 1842, at its first full inventory, the demographic facts weighed heavily against the formation of a stable community at Tiger Island. It had a crippling gender imbalance and a heavily skewed age distribution, and it was organized only into solitaires and simple family households, with solitaires composing well more than a third of the population. The island plantation had only recently assumed a permanent work force, however; its membership had fluctuated widely since the early 1830s. It is therefore not surprising that far more of its population was solitaires than in the model (18 percent) or among the sampled plantations of the 1840–49 period (19 percent). Nevertheless, the slaves of the remote outpost moved resolutely toward such a community in the eighteen years before their social organization was dispersed by the war and estate division in the early 1860s (see table 5.10).[61]

When Brashear transferred Tiger Island to his children in 1842, its slave household structure was starkly imbalanced. The most seriously skewed element was the large proportion of singles among the general population. Thirty-eight percent of the plantation's slaves were solitaires, almost all of them men, as the result of Brashear's transfers of most of his young, single male workers from Belle Isle to Tiger Island between 1833 and 1842 and his confining most of his purchases to males.[62] Not all of Tiger Island's problems can be attributed to the migration process, however. The gender and household imbalances may have begun then, but the slaves of 1842 were twenty years away from the migration, and many of them had been purchased since that time. Their society's instability was primarily owing to the starting up of a new plantation rather than to migration. The imbalance was also a result of Brashear's unwillingness to correct imbalances present at Belle Isle since the 1822 migration and his constant meddling with the composition of the slave force after that time, allowing little opportunity for any of his slave communities to attain a stable structure.

Sixty-two percent of Tiger Island's 1842 slaves resided in simple family units, less by 11 percent than in the model or the 1840s sample. The composition of the simple family units also reflects the instability of the 1842 community. Less than 30 percent of the slaves were part of standard

TABLE 5.10.

Tiger Island Plantation Slave Household Composition, 1842, 1857, 1859, 1860

| | Tiger Island slaves, 1842 | | | | Tiger Island slaves, 1857 | | | |
Household type	Total slaves	Number of units	Mean size of units	Percent of total slaves in type	Total slaves	Number of units	Mean size of units	Percent of total slaves in type
Solitaire	40	40	1	37.7	35	35	1	25.1
Non-nuclear	–	–	–	–	2	1	2	1.4
Simple family	66	14	4.7	62.0	102	24	4.2	73.0
Married couple alone	–	–	–	–	10	5	2	7.1
Married couple with children	31	6	5.1	29.2	60	13	4.6	43.1
Single female with children	35	8	4.3	33.0	28	6	4.6	20.1
Single male with children	–	–	–	–	–	–	–	–
Extended	–	–	–	–	–	–	–	–
Multiple	–	–	–	–	–	–	–	–

Source: Tiger Island Data Base.

nuclear families, which had a mean size of 5.1 members. This mean size is higher than one would expect of a new community but appropriate for a ten- to twelve-year-old society created from transfers and purchases. The portion of Tiger Island slaves in two-parent households compares unfavorably with both the overall model and the 1840s sample; in the model 49 percent of the sampled slaves were in standard nuclear households, and in the 1840s sample 48 percent were in such households.

In 1842, more slaves were part of female-headed single-parent households than were members of standard nuclear families. About one-third

	Tiger Island slaves, 1859				Tiger Island slaves, 1860		
Total slaves	Number of units	Mean size of units	Percent of total slaves in type	Total slaves	Number of units	Mean size of units	Percent of total slaves in type
25	25	1	16.6	24	24	1	15.7
2	1	2	1.3	–	–	–	–
94	21	4.4	62.6	98	21	4.6	64.4
6	3	2	4.0	4	2	2	2.6
61	13	4.6	40.6	70	14	5	46.0
25	4	6.2	16.6	20	3	6.6	13.1
2	1	2	1.3	4	2	2	2.6
4	1	4	2.6	7	2	3.5	4.6
25	3	8.3	16.6	23	3	7.6	15.1

lived in such families, having a mean size of 4.3 members (compared to 14 percent in the model and 18 percent in the 1840s sample). One might question why so many women headed their own households when a large group of male solitaires was available. Since there was a serious gender imbalance at Tiger Island, and women were few, it would seem that those women would have had a wide choice of mates. No evidence has been uncovered to indicate that they had husbands belonging to other owners. That eight women remained single mothers under such circumstances suggests uncertainty and insecurity, a distinct unwillingness among the first-generation females to take on new, permanent alliances, possibly after having been severed from earlier spouses or sweethearts. In any case, subsequent records indicate that the vast majority of these women never married. No slaves were part of male-headed single-parent households in 1842.

The lack of extended and multiple family households at Tiger Island is a final indication that the community was still in an early stage of social organization and shows the deep disruptions caused by the migration and worsened by subsequent sales, purchases, and transfers. No members of a generation earlier than that of the heads of household were present, and no grandchildren were contained in 1842 households. Other slave lists show that Brashear kept the older migration slaves at his residence at Golden Farm; the average age there in 1850 was thirty, compared to eighteen at Tiger Island in 1842.[63]

HOUSEHOLD COMPOSITION AMONG
TIGER ISLAND SLAVES, 1857

A fifteen-year interval occurs before the date of the next reliable list showing family structure among the slaves of Tiger Island. By 1857 the slave community had grown only modestly, from 106 to 139, but its household structure had become far more diverse. Without the importation of additional young women into the community, it would take several more generations for the initial sex ratio imbalance to be corrected by natural increase, but a healthier ratio did exist than before, particularly in the solitaire category. The proportion of solitaires had decreased to about one-fourth of the population, a drop of 13 percent since 1842.[64] The solitaires were still overwhelmingly male—thirty-two men and only three women.

No multiple family or extended family households were found on Tiger Island in 1857, but the society was much more diverse than it had been in the early 1840s. Although nearly three-fourths of the slaves lived in simple families of various types, there was one household of co-resident siblings— sisters who formed a household. Within the simple family type there was much more variety. All four subtypes were present. Marriages were taking place regularly. The most noteworthy change in the household structure

from 1842 to 1857 was the increase of persons living in households associated with married couples. If the five married couples without children
were added to the standard nuclear families, half of the population would
be accounted for. Forty-three percent of the slaves lived in standard nuclear
families, a nearly 10 percent increase since 1842. The percentages of Tiger
Island slaves in female-headed single-parent households decreased similarly. Another 3 percent of the population formed part of male-headed
single-parent households, both headed by widowers. Although the percentage of persons living in standard nuclear family households is still low
in comparison to the model, it is a significant improvement, and, coupled
with decreases in the numbers and percentages of solitaires and female-
headed households, it indicates greater stability than before.

HOUSEHOLD COMPOSITION AMONG
TIGER ISLAND SLAVES, 1850–1860

In most respects the Tiger Island community had changed little by 1859,
but the percentage of solitaires had dropped to less than half of what it had
been in 1842.[65] Of these solitaires, twenty-three were men and only two
were women, showing that a scarcity of marriageable females was still a
problem. All of the men who had the opportunity to make a match had
done so. The prospect of finding a wife was grim for the single males who
remained.

Only three of the 1857 married couples were still childless, and 41 percent
of the plantation's slaves now lived in standard nuclear families. Eighteen
percent of the population consisted of single-parent households, but the
percentage in female-headed units had decreased by 3 percent. A new
development in the 1859 structure was the emergence of complex family
household types. A laterally extended family household consisted of a
young couple with the wife's sister. Three households were of the multiple
family type, all examples of downward disposition of the secondary unit.

In 1860, Tiger Island's slaves exhibited a much improved domestic
structure.[66] Only 16 percent of the slaves in the community were solitaires,
lower than the 18 percent in the model and higher by only 1 percent than in
the sampled population for the 1850s. A severe gender imbalance remained

in the solitaire grouping. One of the two female solitaires had married, seventeen-year-old Fanny, leaving as the only female solitaire sixty-one-year-old Becky, a widow. A few teenaged girls remained in their parents' households, but most of these young single women were closely related to the unmarried men and therefore not available as wives.

In 1860 a far more representative proportion of the community lived in simple family households and, within that type, in standard nuclear families. Sixty-four percent lived in simple family households, and 46 percent formed part of standard nuclear families, containing a mean of 5.0 members. This is more than the 45 percent in such households in the 1860s sample and not appreciably below the percentage in standard nuclear families in the overall sample. Sixteen percent of the population were part of single-parent households, but only 13 percent resided in units headed by females—about the same percentage as in the model and the 1860s sample.[67]

Tiger Island's slave community in 1860 had five complex family households containing one-fifth of the population. This is considerably higher than the 18 percent in such forms in the overall sample but not far from the 16 percent in such forms among the 1860s sampled communities. Two extended families were present, both with lateral extensions involving siblings of one of the married partners. The multiple family households (15 percent of the slaves) were still all composed of a later-generation conjugal unit living in a parental household, along with other children of the heads. If one includes with the other two-parent units the extended and multiple family households that were headed by a married couple, nearly 70 percent of the 1860 slaves lived in double-headed households, a substantial change from the 29 percent in such households in 1842.

One must recognize that the same slave community could and often did exhibit marked differences in its household structure from one period to another, sometimes in a relatively brief period—in Tiger Island's case, only eighteen years. If the Tiger Island analysis had commenced in 1833, it would have been judged a clearly matrifocal structure. If it were analyzed only in 1842, the findings would suggest that it was inherently disorganized and hopelessly imbalanced, dominated by male solitaires and female-headed single-parent households. An analysis of Tiger Island over time demonstrates that these were but early stages in an evolution to a society that by

1860 closely resembled the model suggested by recent historians of the slave family—one dominated by simple families and characterized by two-parent households. Although Tiger Island remained somewhat imbalanced in its age and sex distribution, it made excellent progress toward a more balanced, stable, and family-oriented society in the relatively short period from 1842 to 1860.

CHAPTER SIX

Marriage, Birth, and Kinship Patterns

The degree to which a society's inhabitants enter into marriages, maintain lasting relationships, promulgate families, and develop extensive kinship systems can reveal much about its cohesion or lack of it. The slaves of Oakland, Petite Anse, and Tiger Island attempted to build these pillars of a strong society, often against discouraging obstacles.

INCIDENCE OF MARRIAGE

As was seen in the household analyses given in previous chapters, willingness to enter into marriage and the ability to find mates are less prevalent in highly disorganized, early-stage communities than in later ones. As a slave society becomes more stabilized, its people increasingly seek expression of their family-oriented values by marrying and starting families, although single status and single parenthood continue to be viable alternatives for both sexes. Table 6.1 shows that in all three slave communities the number of married couples increased over time in keeping with a general progression toward greater stability. The number of married

TABLE 6.1.

Slave Husbands' and Wives' Mean Ages and Age Differences, Oakland, Petite Anse, and Tiger Island Plantations

	Oakland		Petite Anse		Tiger Island	
	1814	1857	1836	1860	1842	1860
Number of married couples	10	21	6	16	6	21
Percent of total slaves who were married	32	31	20	39	11	28
Mean ages of wives	27.2	33.3	24.3	35.0	24.6	29.2
Mean ages of husbands	30.8	39.3	30.8	38.1	32.1	39.5
Mean age difference, all cases	7.8	6.4	6.5	5.6	7.5	11.3
Number of cases, husbands older	7	17	6	15	6	19
Number of cases, wives older	2	2	0	1	0	2
Mean age difference, husbands older	8.1	7.4	6.5	5.8	7.5	11.6
Mean age difference, wives older	10.5	5.0	0	3.0	8.0	8.0

Source: Oakland, Petite Anse, and Tiger Island Data Bases.

couples at Oakland more than doubled between the 1814 and 1857 inventories, as it did at Petite Anse between 1836 and 1860. And at Tiger Island from 1842 to 1860 the number of married couples tripled.

Since all three slave communities also increased in population over time, the increase in numbers of married individuals is not particularly noteworthy. But a similar trend in the percentages of those married in the total slave population was detected on two of the plantations. And on all three, expected cyclical, life-course-related fluctuations were present.

Only Oakland had no increase in the percentage of married slaves from its first inventory to its last. In 1814, 32 percent of the slaves were married, and in 1819 just before the first estate division, that proportion had risen to over 40 percent. After the setback caused by the estate division of 1822, the proportion of married individuals declined slowly to 28 percent in 1851–52, then rose to 31 percent by 1857, the last inventory. Clearly, the two estate divisions checked a more marked improvement.[1]

At Petite Anse, married people composed one-fifth of the 1836 population and nearly 40 percent in 1860.[2] The percentage had decreased in 1854 because of two divorces and the deaths of several married slaves, but by 1860 remarriages and new marriages had corrected the drop. The percentage of married persons in the 1860 community was quite healthy, especially considering the large number of children in the population and the greater number of older people than on previous inventories.

Tiger Island's married couples increased their numbers by threefold between 1842 and 1860, and the percentage of married people in the community had more than doubled since 1842, when only 11 percent of the population were married. But at its last inventory in 1860, still only 28 percent of Tiger Island's slaves were married.[3] One reason for the small numbers was that the community was much younger than the others. Tiger Island did not have a documented slave force until 1833 or a permanent body of workers until 1842. In contrast, though Oakland's first suitable inventory was in 1814, its slave force had been functioning since 1809. The 1836 inventory of Petite Anse reflects the community at a midpoint in its development; it was begun in 1818. Tiger Island's community was understandably less stable than the others. Considering its youth and Walter Brashear's unconcern with gender balance, the Tiger Island society made remarkable progress by doubling the percentage of its slaves who were in stable married relationships in eighteen years.

MEAN AGES OF SPOUSES

The increase in the mean ages of spouses is also to be expected in a still youthful but slowly aging society. In such societies, even though new couples are constantly being established, age increases among the surviving older couples cause the mean age of spouses to rise. As shown on table 6.1, the mean age of wives at Oakland increased by six years and that of husbands by eight years from 1814 to 1857. At Petite Anse in 1860 the mean age of wives was higher than it had been in 1836 by eleven years, and that of husbands was higher by seven years. In the Tiger Island slave community between 1842 and 1860, the mean age of wives increased by four years and that of husbands by eight years.

MEAN AGE DIFFERENCES
BETWEEN SPOUSES

The age differences between spouses might be another factor in determining the stability of a slave society. More stable societies generally conform to a pattern also found in free and white societies of the period, when husbands and wives generally differed in age by six to eight years or less, and husbands were older than wives in the majority of cases.[4] This pattern prevails in the case study communities. In the two more stable societies—Oakland and Petite Anse—the age difference between spouses was never larger than the norm and decreased over time. The mean age difference between spouses at Oakland decreased from eight years in 1814 to six years in 1857; at Petite Anse, the mean age difference decreased from seven to six years. At Oakland, the number of marriages in which husbands were older increased dramatically, while the number in which wives were older stayed the same. At Petite Anse, the number of older husbands in 1836 was six, and no wives were older than their husbands; by 1860, husbands were older than wives in fifteen of the marriages, and a wife was older than her mate in only one marriage. This same trend was present at Tiger Island, with cases of older husbands increasing from six to nineteen and those of older wives from zero to two. This steady trend of marriages in which the husbands were older by about six years prevailed at Oakland and Petite Anse over a long period of time. It suggests that when potential spouses were available, as they were on both plantations, women chose to marry men older than they but by no more than seven years or so. But it was not unusual or socially unacceptable for women to marry men younger than they by about the same age spread, five to eight years.

Although Tiger Island conformed to the above pattern in that the number of marriages in which husbands were older increased over time, it did not conform to the trend concerning decreasing age differentials between spouses. At Tiger Island, age difference between spouses increased from a high-normal 7.5 years mean age differential in 1842 to a much higher than normal 11 years in 1860 (and in 1859 the age differential was 12 years).[5] A closer look at Tiger Island's marriages in 1859–60 provides explanations for the aberration to the pattern found on the other plantations. Severe gender imbalance in the ages appropriate for marriage compelled some Tiger Island slaves to form couples with considerable age differences. On Tiger Island in 1860, husbands and wives were the same age in only one case. The husband was older than the wife in 90 percent of the marriages, and in most cases the husband was significantly older, by an average of 12 years. In one case a husband was 45 years older than his wife, and in two cases, 30 and 32 years separated the spouses. In all but one of the other husband-older cases, age differences of at least five years prevailed.

In 1860 two Tiger Island slave women were married to younger men, but the average age distance was eight years. In one case the wife was older by four years, but in the second case, Maria was forty-one to her husband's twenty-nine. This was a second marriage for Maria, who had two sons by a husband who was sold.

One spouse was ten or more years older than the other in nine Tiger Island couples out of twenty-one (or 43 percent of the cases). This age differential was much higher than usually found in other contemporary Louisiana slave societies, including those of Petite Anse and Oakland.

One contributing factor to the large age differential among Tiger Island married couples might have been the high mortality rate on the disease-plagued island. Family letters and notations on slave inventories from 1825 to 1860 suggest that slave mortality was alarmingly high on the island.[6] Therefore, one could suspect that the 1860 marriages involving partners with an age difference of thirty and forty years were second marriages for the men after years of being widowers. Petite Anse appears to have had an even higher mortality rate than Tiger Island, and yet the age discrepancy there was not as high. The possibility that the large age discrepancy was related to second marriages was investigated, and it appears very unlikely that the males who married much younger women did so after long periods as widowers. Instead, the men were generally single before marrying their much younger wives. In 1842 Sam Ferrygood was listed as an unmarried man in his middle years, but in 1860 he had been married for at least seven years to America, who was thirty-two years younger than he. The same is true of Henry Todd. Single and in his mid-thirties in 1842, Todd was married to Esther, thirty years his junior, by 1857, and by 1860 they had two small children. Likewise Moses, forty-five years older than his wife, Polly, had been married to her since at least 1857. He, too, had been single in 1842.[7] There is no evidence that these men had earlier marriages even of short duration.

A more convincing explanation for the significant age differences within Tiger Island married couples is that the extremely limited marriage pool, caused by gender imbalances and the isolation of the island, prevented a wide choice of spouses in more appropriate age ranges. Few women were available as wives until the mid- and late 1850s, when some of the female children of the 1840s finally reached ages appropriate for courtship and marriage. In the intense competition for these few eligible young women, the older single men proved more successful than the younger men. They were more successful partly because they were respected and established members of the community but also because most of the young men were related to the eligible girls—and Louisiana slaves observed a strong taboo against consanguinity. There had been no large influx of transferred or purchased males since the late 1830s. Since Walter Brashear conveyed the property to his sons in 1852, the sons had not interfered with the demographic makeup of the labor force.[8] Few slaves had entered and few had left the island except through births and deaths. Although the sons had ceased the lopsided buying that had caused the shortage of young women, they had not corrected the problem by bringing in new laborers of both genders, especially females of reproductive age.

Another factor influencing the May-to-December marriages might have been the youthfulness of the Tiger Island slaves in 1860. The average age in 1860 was still only twenty-three, despite the presence of many older slaves. In 1857, when many of the marriage choices were being made, 39 percent of the slaves were under age seventeen. The few females available for marriage were young and quickly spoken for, and the older, more mature and established, and unrelated men were the more likely choices for marriage. All of these factors contributed to the formation of matches that might not have been considered appropriate if not for the limited marriage pool.

LONGEVITY OF MARRIAGES

An additional telling factor in determining the stability of slave family households is the extent to which marriages endured before being dissolved by death or separations, either forced or voluntary. Slave marriages on all three plantations in the case study were of long duration if both partners lived. Separations by owners, by the choice of the married partners, or through estate division, gifts, or transfers were relatively rare once the plantations were in operation.

The most destructive force in slave marriages on the three plantations was an exceedingly high mortality rate. Of the ten married couples at Oakland in 1814, all were still married in 1819, but by 1846 only two of the couples were still present and married. These were Milly and Jack and Nancy and Jerry. Nancy and Jerry's long marriage was dissolved by his death by 1852, and she was sent to St. Mary Parish as the result of the estate division following her mistress's death. Milly and Jack were still married and at Oakland at its last full inventory in 1857, both of them in their sixties. They had been married at least forty-three years. At that time they were still an active couple, heading their own household, which included one of their sons, a daughter, and several grandchildren. Neither Jack nor Milly appears on a listing of slaves still at Oakland in 1864, but it appears they were alive elsewhere, for in another notation, listing both names, his death is given as occurring in 1867. Their marriage apparently endured from at least 1814 until 1867 and perhaps for the entire life of Oakland Plantation to that point. One of the other eight married couples of 1814 was drawn by Cornelia DeHart and taken to Orange Grove in St. Mary Parish in 1822. This couple, Peter and Rhoda, left the ranks of Oakland couples, but their marriage lasted until the early 1850s, over thirty-five years, and was dissolved only by death. All of the other marriages ended with the death of one of the partners by the late 1840s, and few remarried.[9]

By 1817 five additional married couples appeared on the Oakland rolls.[10] All of these new marriages were intact in 1819–22, but not a single one endured at Oakland until 1846. Four of the couples were separated by death, but one couple—Harry and Liddy—was sent to Orange Grove after the 1822 estate division, and they were still married there at my last accounting of that community in the early 1850s.

Ration lists and partial inventories between 1822 and 1846 show that many additional marriages commenced in the late 1820s and 1830s.[11] In 1846 eighteen married couples were present who were not married in 1819. Of these, seventeen couples were still at Oakland in 1851 when Sarah Evans's estate was inventoried (both spouses in one couple had died). The partitioning of Sarah's estate in 1852 resulted in the exodus of two of the seventeen couples of 1851: Charity and Henry, inherited by the DeHarts, were sent to Orange Grove, and Gunny and Vicy were transferred to the plantation of Francis Evans. One marriage, that of Robin and Patsy, was dissolved by death, but after her young husband's demise in early 1852, Patsy was sent to Orange Grove. One couple was separated by the estate division—Jem Gillum and Mary (he had belonged to Sarah Evans and she to John Evans). Jem was sent to Orange Grove, and Mary remained at Oakland. Therefore, thirteen of the seventeen 1851 couples remained intact at Oakland after the division. In 1857, at Oakland's last inventory, thirteen of the eighteen couples of 1846 were still there and still married. Though numerically the same as in 1852, the couples were constituted slightly differently. One marriage was terminated by the death of a spouse; Squire had lost his wife, Ellen. But another couple was reunited. John Evans had begun negotiating to reunite Jem Gillum and his wife, Mary, shortly after their separation, and they were together again at Oakland within a year and a half.[12] Judging from the age of their eldest known child, three of these couples had been married for twenty-one to twenty-seven years; seven had been married from thirteen to nineteen years.

Seven of the 1846 couples appear on a partial listing for 1860, and it is elsewhere documented that one additional couple remained together. But by 1860, death or the war had apparently divided or removed from Oakland all couples whose marriages dated back to the 1840s except for one. Herbert and Fanny were still at Oakland, having been husband and wife for over thirty years. One of the spouses from four other couples remained, but the other eleven couples entirely disappeared, although they may have vacated the plantation with their marriages intact.[13]

At Petite Anse, only two simple family units were recognizable in the 1826 inventory. One was female-headed, and the other was a recently purchased standard nuclear family consisting of Perry, Hanny, and their infant son. This was the first documented slave marriage at Petite Anse, but it was brief because both young parents soon died.

Six married couples were present on the plantation in 1836, and all of these were still intact at the next inventory in 1839. Four of the marriages continued in 1854, and three pairs were still united at the last inventory in 1860.[14] In every case in which a marriage commenced by 1836 was dissolved, it was because of the death of a partner, and only one of the widowed parties remarried.[15] Among the six 1836 couples, four had been married for at least eighteen years before they were separated by death, and three of the couples had been together for periods ranging from twenty-six to thirty-five years.[16]

The next wave of marriages, beginning between 1836 and 1839, consisted of eight additional couples. These couples did not fare as well as those who were married before 1836. None were still married to the same partner in 1854. Two couples were divorced, and in the four remaining couples one of the partners had died. Of those marriages dissolved by the death of a partner, only one individual remarried. Two couples' marriages ended in divorce. One pair did not remarry. In the case of the other couple, the husband (Ned) did not remarry, but the wife (Gracy) quickly remarried. Gracy's marriage to her new husband, Archy, lasted for at least seventeen years.

No marriages can be documented at Tiger Island in 1833, the date of its first inventory, but that could be because the labor force there was still being rotated from Belle Isle and Golden Farm. By 1842 the plantation had a more permanent contingent, but out of 106 slaves only six couples were married, probably both because of a shortage of appropriate matches and a reluctance on the part of single mothers to marry. It is also indicative of the general instability of the still amorphous society. Judging from the age of their eldest children in 1842, most of the couples apparently were not newly married.

Three of the married couples of 1842 were still married in 1860. One of the six marriages was broken by the sale of the husband, but the wife eventually remarried and sustained another long relationship. In the second of the dissolved marriages, the husband died, but his wife and children were still present at Tiger Island in 1860. In the third, the wife died, but the husband and at least one of their sons were still part of the community in 1860.[17]

Because Tiger Island did not have a stable population until the early 1840s, longevity of marriages is difficult to determine. Most of the twenty-one married couples present in 1860 were young. In addition to those already mentioned, it is possible to determine the longevity of a few other Tiger Island marriages by examining the ages of the oldest known children in residence. The marriage of Aaron and Rhoda, for example, had endured for at least twelve years, and Jerry and Maria—the still young progenitors of a vigorous Tiger Island clan—had been married for at least twenty-seven years.

As was true of Oakland and Petite Anse as well, most of Tiger Island's dissolved marriages were the result of deaths rather than divorce or separations. Only one separation or divorce at Tiger Island is known to have been instigated by a slave spouse; it involved a young wife who left her husband to marry his brother.[18] As mentioned before, one couple was separated when the owner sold the husband.

In 1860 the Tiger Island slave community was still relatively young and expanding through marriages and births so the permanence of its unions over time cannot be determined. Only a few slaves stayed on the plantation as freed people. Many were taken to Texas, and nothing is known of their marriages. Among the few who stayed on the plantation were Sam Ferrygood and his child bride, America, who were still married in the mid-1870s.[19]

AGES OF SLAVE WOMEN AT MARRIAGE AND FIRST BIRTH

One of the most debated areas in slave demography concerns the ages at which slave women began sexual activity, married, and first gave birth. Despite the abundant records, birth lists are not available for Oakland, Petite Anse, and Tiger Island. Therefore birth and marriage data had to be extracted from the inventories (both complete and reconstituted). Two samples were taken. One was of married and unmarried women who bore their first child between 1803 and 1824, excluding all mothers who commenced childbearing later because they were unlikely to have completed their childbearing period before the years of the last available inventories. The primary purposes of this sample were to determine roughly the childbearing range for women of the case study communities, the mean number of children they bore during their supposed fertile years, the mean interval between births, and the mean age at which they last gave birth.

The other sample consisted of women under age thirty, drawn over the entire recorded period for each community but not repeating the same woman. This sample was confined to women under thirty because they

TABLE 6.2.

Mean Ages at First Birth of Slave Mothers under Thirty at Oakland, Petite Anse, and Tiger Island Plantations

	Oakland 1811–1857	Petite Anse 1836–1860	Tiger Island 1842–1860
Number of cases, married mothers	24	15	14
Number of cases, unmarried mothers	15	7	6
Mean age at first known births to married mothers	20.2	19.1	17.5
Mean age at first known marriage of married mothers	19	18.7	16.9
Mean age at first known births to unmarried mothers	20.6	18.1	16.5
Total number of mothers, married and unmarried	39	22	20
Mean age at first known birth to married and unmarried women	20.2	19.1	17.5

Source: Oakland, Petite Anse, and Tiger Island Data Bases.

were more likely still to have their firstborn children in their households. At Oakland, married and unmarried mothers under thirty had their first recorded birth at 20.2, at Petite Anse, 19.1, and at Tiger Island, 17.5. The ages are substantially the same for married and unmarried mothers at Oakland, but at Petite Anse and Tiger Island unmarried mothers gave birth about a year earlier than did married mothers (see table 6.2).

The slightly higher mean age for Oakland women at their first known birth is probably owing to the longer sampled period and the larger number of cases. The differences between the means generated for the two more stable communities—Oakland and Petite Anse—are not large enough to be significant. The mean ages at first birth for Oakland and Petite Anse mothers are lower than found on many plantations of the Southeast but not to a striking degree. The means at these two plantations remained steady from inventory to inventory, indicating that these communities were relatively stable and that availability of females of appropriate age made an overly intense competition among the males for mates unnecessary. That women were not generally well into their twenties before first giving birth suggests that sufficient men were also available for marriage and reproduction.

The situation at Tiger Island was different. Just as broad age differences between spouses were not surprising because of Tiger Island's isolation and the age and gender differentials of its slaves, it is also to be expected that the young females in great demand generally married and bore their first children at an early age. The average Tiger Island wife married at slightly under seventeen years of age (almost two years earlier than did the wives of Oakland and Petite Anse), and two of the women apparently conceived near the onset of puberty, at the ages of twelve and thirteen. Tiger Island's unmarried women gave birth at an even earlier mean age, 16.5 (compared to 20.6 at Oakland and 18.1 at Petite Anse). Young women were scarce at Tiger Island, and considerable sexual pressure must have been brought to bear on even its very young women as they sexually matured, encouraging both early marriages and early pregnancies.

Mean age at first birth was computed for the sample of women, both married and single, who gave birth between 1803 and 1824. The findings differ little from those for the under-thirty sample; at Oakland, the twenty-one women from the 1803–24 sample gave birth at a slightly later mean age (20.7, compared to 20.2); the nine Petite Anse women from the 1803–24 sample had their first known child one year later, at 21, compared to 19.1. The thirteen Tiger Island women still had the earliest mean age at first birth, 18.4, although it was slightly higher than that of the under-thirty sample for the plantation (17.5).

Statistics on last births and birth intervals are approximations. Because of the inconsistency or absence of reliable birth and death records, adjustments for mortality were not made. A substantial gap exists in the Oakland records so figures for last births and mean number of children are omitted, and birth intervals for that community are based on the first several children, before the estate division interrupted the records. Despite these problems, it is possible to determine a general idea of childbearing patterns on the three plantations.

At Oakland, the interval between births was thirty months. At Petite Anse, using the childbearing records for all nine women as the basis for the calculations, the mean interval between births was four years, but this average is strongly distorted by a single case, that of Sawney's wife, Maria, whose first and second children were born twenty-four months apart. Sixteen years elapsed between her second and third recorded births, a period during which she may have had aborted pregnancies, stillbirths, or infants who died without having their births recorded. If Maria is removed from the sample, the mean interval between known births of the eight remaining women was thirty-four months, about what could be expected in a rural, agricultural society with little knowledge of birth control methods. Removing nine months for the pregnancy, about twenty-four months elapsed between the previous birth and conception of another child, a common period of lactation among slave women.

At Tiger Island, in a sample of thirteen women, the mean interval of slightly under thirty-four months between births is also considerably skewed by several cases in which the mothers had long intervals of no recorded births, followed by several births in rapid succession. Single mother Matilda, for example, had a four-year interval between the birth of her first known child and her twins, followed by an eleven-year interval before the birth of a fourth child in 1839. She then bore several more children, with only brief intervals between births. Rhoda, the wife of Aaron Smith, had a six-year interval between the births of her third and fourth children. Mary Brien had an eight-year interval between her third and fourth children, and other examples could be cited as well. These occasional long intervals distort the average, which would otherwise be about twenty-four months between births, but they occur often enough to require accounting. Certainly study of a larger and more concrete sample of Louisiana slave mothers must be done before solid interpretations can be offered. I compared the Tiger Island and Petite Anse slave women's birth interval patterns with those of William T. Palfrey's slave community (also at St. Mary, during roughly the same time period), for which excellent birth records exist.[20] The comparison suggests that occasional intervals of four or five years between births were probably not periods of infertility but periods in which regularly spaced pregnancies had ended in miscarriages, stillbirths, or early infant deaths. Very long periods without recorded births, however, followed by the resumption of regularly spaced pregnancies, suggest periods of abstinence, possibly because of separation from a long-term partner. Demographic historians are currently exploring the effects of diet and illness on the fertility of men and women; a long illness could account for some of the wide intervals between births.

At Petite Anse, the women produced a mean of five known children over their childbearing years, compared to a mean of seven borne by Tiger Island females. Tiger Island women probably bore more children because they commenced childbearing several years earlier than did the Petite Anse women, thereby extending their childbearing years. Tiger Island women, in great demand by the large number of single males seeking mates, both married and produced first children at earlier ages. On both plantations, the women gave birth to their last child at the mean age of thirty-four. If women who died before that age are excluded from the sample, the mean age at last recorded birth was thirty-six for Tiger Island and thirty-seven for Petite Anse, very close to the findings of other historians.

All three plantations showed a lack of consistency in the ages of women at their last recorded birth. Some women had long periods of fertility, while on the same plantation other women ceased childbearing at a relatively young age. For example, at Petite Anse three women had children while in their forties. Arena, the wife of Augustus, bore children over a span of twenty-one years. Maria Houston's first child was born when she was twenty and her last when she was forty-six. Sawney's wife, Maria, bore children over a twenty-year period. By contrast, Milly's nine children were all born by the time she was thirty-six. Although they lived on the plantation as husband and wife for at least fifteen more years, Milly and her husband had no more recorded births after her thirty-sixth year. The inconsistency in ages at last births was also found at Oakland and Petite Anse.

FAMILY AND KINSHIP

A progressive trend toward family and kinship development is apparent in the household analysis of Oakland, Petite Anse, and Tiger Island slaves, from the foundation of their permanent slave force to their last full inventory before emancipation. Once more, the vulnerability of slave domestic organization is revealed. In both migration communities the trauma of separation from prior family and kin networks was overcome with difficulty. After two decades during which slaves built new family and kindred ties at Brashear's home plantations, the start-up of Tiger Island with transferred and newly purchased slaves set back family and kinship development there and exacted a cost in social stability. At Oakland, estate divisions dispersed family and kinship groups twice. Kinship developed fairly naturally only at Petite Anse, and it was there that family and kinship networks were most pervasive in 1860.

Each slave community's persistence in forming family units (an inclination that grew stronger as the years passed) demonstrates its high regard for family and kinship. The great value that slaves placed on family and kin was recognized, if not always respected, by their owners. This is particularly apparent at Oakland and Petite Anse, where the owners made concerted efforts to keep family groups intact and, through purchases, to maintain a viable marriage pool. Even at Tiger Island, the owners' forwarding of messages between the Kentucky migrants and their relations in Bardstown and Lexington shows that they recognized the intensity and durability of the ties between separated slave kin.

Oakland Many of the early workers at Oakland married and quickly began families, but that bright beginning was dimmed by Nathaniel Evans's death and estate partition in 1822. Some kinsmen were separated, and other entire families were removed from the plantation and area (such as Peter, Rhoda, and their children, who left no kin behind at Oakland).[21] As they sought to rebuild their fractured work force, Sarah and John N. Evans bought many young, unattached slaves in the 1830s and 1840s, and this contingent produced most of the families that were present in 1857.[22] By 1850, Oakland's slave community was as strong and stable as it would ever be. Family formation and kinship development would have been extremely intricate by 1860 if it had not been disrupted by the estate division following the death of Sarah Evans in 1851.[23] This division again separated Oakland slaves from a bevy of relatives. The division hit the oldest kin groups hardest; most of the new families had been bought by John Evans, and they were directly affected only if they had intermarried with Sarah Evans's slaves.[24]

As in 1822, the ordeal was greatest for the slaves inherited by the DeHarts, who were transferred to the ill-fated Orange Grove Plantation in St. Mary Parish, where they would have little or no opportunity to interact with their friends and families in West Feliciana.[25] The transfer to the Attakapas must have been particularly difficult for the family of Henry and Charity, who were members of one of the earliest and largest kinship groups of

Oakland. Charity had been a child among Nathaniel Evans's early workers, the daughter of Nancy and Jerry, whom Evans had owned since 1809. Charity's father, Jerry, was twenty in 1814 and already married to seventeen-year-old Nancy. They had at that time an infant daughter, Phoebe, who died early. Two more daughters were born by 1817—Charity and Ellen. Both lived to marry and have their own families at Oakland. Jerry died in the 1830s, but Nancy lived to raise two orphan girls, Susannah and Kitty.[26]

Jerry's widow, Nancy, her four daughters, and their families were greatly affected by the 1852 estate division. One daughter, Charity, her husband, and their children were drawn by the DeHarts. Nancy and two of her other daughters, Kitty (adopted) and Ellen (along with Ellen's children) were drawn by John Evans and remained at Oakland. The remaining daughter, Susannah (adopted), and her husband and children were drawn by Francis Evans. John Evans soon traded the mother, Nancy, and the youngest adopted daughter, Kitty, to the DeHart heirs in exchange for several slaves who were married to his workers.[27] It is not known whether he was also accommodating the wishes of Nancy, Charity, and Kitty, who might have wanted to stay together even if they all had to leave Oakland. In any case, Nancy moved away from Oakland at the age of fifty-four, leaving in West Feliciana two daughters, several grandchildren, and a lifetime's accumulation of friends and memories. At Orange Grove, however, she would be with her daughter Charity, her son-in-law Henry, her adopted daughter Kitty, and nine grandchildren.

With the departure of Charity, Henry, and their children, Oakland lost a vital branch of two old and respected kinship lines. Charity's husband, Henry, was the offspring of original Oakland slaves, Jacob and Hannah, who had, in addition to Henry, at least one daughter and four other sons.[28] Surviving members of Henry's family remained in West Feliciana, the property of the two Evans brothers. Henry and Charity's marriage had been very productive. By 1851, they had nine healthy children ranging in age from six months to eighteen years, the youngest named Jacob, for Henry's long-deceased father. Family and kin obviously meant a great deal to the couple, for they named two more of their children for grandparents: Little Nancy and Little Jerry, for Charity's parents.

Even at Orange Grove, Charity and Henry's family was not impervious to further separations. The appraised value of their large family unit was $3,675 in 1851, far more than the value of the other single family units inherited by the DeHarts. To effect an equal distribution, Henry and Charity's immediate family was further divided among the four DeHarts. Henry and Charity formed a lot with their four children under the age of ten, as required by Louisiana law. They and fourteen-year-old Charles Henry were allotted to Louisa DeHart. Sarah DeHart drew two other sons—Albert and Jerry—as well as their grandmother Nancy and aunt Kitty. The remaining children (Willis and Joice) were drawn by Dr. John DeHart. The legal separation on paper did not necessarily involve physical separation; they were all initially sent to Orange Grove. But Sarah DeHart married a Mississippi planter shortly thereafter, and it is not known whether she took her slaves with her.[29] The transfer of Henry and Charity, their children, Charity's mother, and her younger sister separated parents from grown children and grandchildren and divided siblings, as well as a host of aunts, uncles, and cousins from both Charity's and Henry's lines.

It is true that Henry and Charity's family was not thrust in the midst of utter strangers because Orange Grove was originally peopled with Oakland slaves. Henry and Charity might have dimly remembered some Orange Grove slaves with whom they had played as children at Oakland. And Nancy would have been well acquainted with Peter, Rhoda, Harry, and Liddy with whom she and Jerry had picked cotton as high-spirited teenagers. But only Harry and Liddy were still at Orange Grove in 1852 to greet their old friends from Oakland. They had six daughters and six grandchildren on the plantation, although their firstborn, Manuel, was among those executed in 1841 for the murder of Captain DeHart. Nancy's close friends Peter and Rhoda were dead or sold, for an 1854 listing shows not a single member of their family left on the plantation. Two of the sons, Carlos and Booker, were among those executed; what happened to the others is not known. Maria—the mother of Billy, the alleged ringleader in the murder of DeHart—never remarried after the sale of her husband, but she eventually had two more daughters by an unknown father. By 1854 she headed her own household, which included two grandchildren, at Orange Grove. She, too, would have been there to help ease the adjustment of Nancy, Charity, and Henry, although her own experience in St. Mary could hardly have encouraged them.[30]

Nancy's other daughter, Ellen, and her sizable family remained at Oakland, but Susannah, her husband, and two children were sent to Francis Evans's plantation.[31] For Susannah, separated from her sisters and mother and the children from their maternal grandmother, her closest kin at her new home, except for her husband and children, was her brother-in-law's mother, Hannah. Of Hannah's once large family, only Henry—now at Orange Grove—and her youngest daughter, Retty, remained. Retty, twenty-six, was also at Francis Evans's place, as was Hannah's four-year-old grand-daughter and namesake, Little Retty.[32]

Another example of family and kin separated by Sarah Evans's estate division was Gunny and Vicy, who, with their nineteen-year-old son Washington, were inherited by Francis Evans and removed from Oakland. Both were part of Oakland's earliest labor force. Vicy had her daughter Mima at the age of seventeen, but she remained unmarried for about ten years. By 1834, she and Gunny had married and were parents of two-year-old Washington. By the 1840s, Vicy's daughter Mima had married a new purchase, John Briton, and had started her own family with a daughter named Vicy after her grandmother. They would eventually have many more children. Mima, her husband, and children would remain at Oakland after the estate division, whereas her mother and stepfather became the property of Francis Evans and were transferred to his estate, which was, fortunately, close enough to Oakland to allow for occasional visits.[33]

These are only a few of the Oakland family and kinship groups that were disrupted by estate divisions. Scarcely a family was not affected. Kinship was so advanced among the older Oakland residents by 1851 that it would have been difficult to make a division that did not sever parents from adult children and grandchildren or separate adult siblings and their families from each other. Although separation of kinsmen beyond the standard nuclear family was perhaps less traumatic than separation of spouses or parents and minor children, it was nevertheless extremely painful. Owners often commented upon the sadness of parents whose nearly grown children were sold or transferred.

The Oakland community continued to be family-based, but another generation would pass before kinship would be as extensive as before. Most of the families present at the last inventory in 1857 were headed by individuals who had been purchased by John Evans in the 1830s and 1850s as part of the rebuilding process after his father's demise. The new purchases intermarried extensively; only a few married offspring of the original laborers. By 1857 they were in their late thirties or forties and had large and growing families that would soon reach marriageable ages. Among these couples were John Briton and Mima, Peter Barlow and Ailsy, Jim and Jane West, and Peter Murphy and Susan. Thanks to Evans's timely purchases, kinship would soon flourish anew at Oakland. But for the slaves at Oakland belonging to the original kin groups whose relations were dispersed between three holdings, this was little consolation.

Petite Anse Some of the laborers brought to Petite Anse from New Jersey and New York by William Stone and John Marsh founded major kinship groups with lines extending until 1860, but these generally resulted from unions with nonmigration slaves. The strongest kinship groups present in the last recorded inventory were produced by slaves brought into the labor force during the 1820s and 1830s. Therefore, even when estate divisions did not result in the exodus of many slaves, the kinship networks of the earliest generation appear to have been less vigorous than those produced by later unions.

Peter was one of the few New Jersey slaves to found a lasting kinship line on Petite Anse. He was bought as a boy of eleven or twelve in 1818 and appeared as a twenty-year-old solitaire on the 1826 inventory. In 1827 he married eighteen-year-old Milly, who had been purchased the year before from a New Orleans slave dealer. By 1836 they had five children: John, Mary Ann, Jerry, Margaret, and Peter, Jr.[34]

In 1854 Peter and Milly had been married for about twenty-seven years. Their household consisted of Mary Ann, Jerry, Margaret, and Peter, Jr., as well as three additional children born since the previous inventory: Henrietta, Dave, and Jane. In addition to their own children, Peter and Milly's household also contained a two-year-old grandchild, Catherine, the daughter of Mary Ann, who was unmarried.[35]

Peter and Milly still appear as a married couple on the 1860 inventory. Most of their children, including some with spouses, are listed directly after them, although they were appraised separately. Whether these grown children and their families lived with their parents cannot be determined because no cabin lists have survived. But it is certain that they were considered part of a kinship group headed by Peter and Milly and formed part of their multiple family household. Old Pete (as he was now called) and Milly headed a large clan, which included single daughters Margaret, Jane, and Mary Ann along with Mary Ann's two children; Henrietta and her husband, Allen, and their two sons; and Dave and Peter, Jr. Another son, Jerry (along with his wife and children), appears elsewhere on the inventory, as part of the multiple family household of his wife's parents, Gus and Arena.[36]

Peter is a prime example of a migration slave who intermarried with a new purchase, had a long marriage, and promulgated a major kinship group on the island. By 1860 three generations of his line were present on Petite Anse, many of whom formed a portion of his large, sprawling household.

In many ways, however, Peter is exceptional. The most enduring family and kin groups at Petite Anse emanated from slaves bought in Louisiana. For example, Sylvia was the progenitor of one family still present on the island in 1860. She had been bought from a New Orleans trader on 20 April 1826, when she was twenty-two and pregnant.[37] In 1836 she was the still unmarried head of a household that contained her two sons, John Congo and George (also called Roy), and two daughters, Effy and Mary Ann. By 1839, she had married Edmund, ten years younger than she, who had been bought between 1836 and 1838.[38] Edmund and Sylvia had no known children together. She had died by 1854, as had her daughter Mary Ann. Her sons, John Congo and Roy, were still at Petite Anse, as solitaires. Effy was either in New Iberia or was mistakenly left off the 1854 inventory, for she reappears on the 1860 list as the young wife of a former widower. Roy also appears on the 1860 inventory as the husband of the sixteen-year-old daughter of John and Maria Houston. John Congo is not listed on the 1860 inventory, but he had not died, for he alone among Sylvia's descendants was listed among the freedmen having a credit account with Petite Anse owners in 1867.[39]

Sawney was another purchase from the 1820s who founded a major kinship group on Petite Anse. He was bought by Stone and Marsh at the estate sale of Jesse McCall in St. Martin Parish, 23 December 1824.[40] Portions of Petite Anse Plantation were purchased by Stone and Marsh from McCall, and Sawney may have been born on the island. If so, he was the only known member of the early slave force with previous ties to the plantation. Sawney married Maria about 1833 or 1834, possibly earlier. In 1836 they had a daughter, Betsy Ann, and another daughter, Sarah, was born by 1839. In 1854 Sawney and Maria's household consisted of themselves, Betsy Ann and Sarah, now in their upper teens, and two-year-old Lucy. An additional daughter, Fanny, was born in 1860. By that year Betsy had married Gus and Arena's son Bob and had produced a grandchild for Sawney and Maria. The eldest daughter, Sarah, was married to John and Maria Houston's son Tom, and they had a four-year-old daughter, Rosana.

Along with Cane and Gus, Sawney was one of the acknowledged leaders of the Petite Anse slave community. He and many of his progeny continued to work on Petite Anse after emancipation.[41]

The most extensive kinship group on the island in 1860 was formed by one of the few families that had been purchased as a group in the 1820s, Augustus or Gus, his wife, Arena, and their nine-month-old daughter Fanny, bought together in Adams County, Mississippi, on 19 May 1827.[42] In 1836, Gus, the plantation's blacksmith, lived with Arena and their sons Foster, Bob, and Little Gus. The eldest daughter had died by 1839, but another daughter, Celia, had been born. By 1854 Gus and Arena, both in their forties, had six children, including three grown sons and three daughters. In addition to Celia, the daughters were Rachel and Lavenia, both born since the previous inventory. The family proliferated, and in 1860 it consisted of Gus, Arena, their youngest daughters, Rachel and Lavenia, and their son Gus, now twenty-two. Listed consecutively and forming part of a solid kinship grouping were Foster, Bob, and Celia, along with their spouses and children. With their parents' households, these young families formed part of a large multiple family household unit.[43]

One of the most unusual families emanating from the 1820s purchases was that of Harriet. Described in her bill of sale as an eighteen-year-old mulatto, Harriet was bought by William Stone from a Charles County, Maryland, planter on 17 November 1823.[44] She served as a maid or cook for the Marsh family for the remainder of her life.

Harriet and "her children," Ben, Lizzie, and John Henry, are all mentioned in a family record of house servants at Petite Anse.[45] Ben was Harriet's very light-skinned son by an unnamed local white man. He was born after 1826 but before 1836, for he appears on the latter inventory with his mother, Harriet, although his age is not stated.[46] Northern-born Marsh disapproved of both concubinage and the casual sexual freedom that many Louisiana white men took with attractive slave women; therefore, I do not believe that Ben was an illegitimate offspring of the Marsh family. Marsh may not have known who Ben's father was, but he did have unusual compassion for the "neither black nor white" children of his slave community, and he took a special interest in the boy. Ben was kept in New Iberia most of his youth and was trained as a house servant. Eventually, Marsh freed him. For that reason, Ben usually does not appear on subsequent inventories with his mother, although they kept in close contact.[47]

In 1839 Harriet was enumerated in a household consisting of herself, her slave husband, William, and a one-year-old daughter Elizabeth, whom they called Lizzie.[48] Lizzie was the only one of Harriet's children who had a slave father. William died in the early 1840s, and Harriet eventually bore another son by a white man whom Marsh identified only as "Hoyt." That child, John Henry, may have been reared in Harriet's home during his early years, but he, like his half-brother Ben, was not enumerated with the other slaves because he was marked for eventual manumission.[49] The 1854 inventory of Petite Anse slaves mentions only Harriet and her daughter Lizzie, omitting both boys. Trained as her mother's helper, Lizzie would eventually replace Harriet as the cook at Petite Anse. Harriet was no longer listed on the 1860 Petite Anse inventory, but Lizzie was, along with her husband, Butler, and their two-year-old daughter Cora.[50]

Harriet's two mulatto sons were of constant concern to Marsh and his family. In 1856, John Marsh signed a document manumitting John Henry, stating that "Hoyt," John Henry's "reputed father," had paid for his son's freedom by the "building of a sailboat for me called Little Red." Hoyt apparently had some occasional business dealings with Marsh, perhaps on short-term contracts as a carpenter or overseer. In a letter of 1845 George Marsh had written his father about plantation matters and incidentally mentioned that "Hoyt is in N Orleans." In the 1856 manumission document, Marsh stated that the "boy John Henry is now in the charge of my son George Marsh." But two days before, Marsh had written George to tell him that Casimere Pinta "informed me this morning that he had got a good place for John Henry to get his schooling . . . in the city [New Orleans]." Marsh was obviously willing to undertake the cost of tuition and boarding for the boy, but John Henry—if he ever did attend school in New Orleans—returned to Petite Anse. His name was among those in the freedmen account records for the plantation in 1866–67.[51]

Harriet's oldest son, Ben, married Georgianna, the young daughter of Maria Houston, by 1850. In 1853 Georgianna lived with her two small children in the household of her mother and stepfather, but Ben was in Rahway Township, New Jersey, with his old master, John Marsh, who was attempting to find occupational training and a degree of acceptance for the young man. In a letter of 16 May 1853, Margaret Marsh Henshaw wrote her father in New Jersey, asking him to "tell Ben that his Mother [Harriet] is now with me [in New Iberia] on a visit of pleasure, she is well and sends her love to him. Lizzy [Ben's half-sister] is confined to her bed with measles. His baby [with Georgianna] is well and the very image of him—I sincerely hope that Ben is ere this put to a trade, he will never be worth one cent until he is made to work and earn a living." A month later Marsh wrote back that he had been unsuccessful in placing Ben in New Jersey. "Ben is now in sight mowing. . . . I shall probably send him back . . . as he cannot be placed here at a trade with comfort to himself as he is neither white nor black and would become the butt of other apprentices."[52]

Ben returned to Petite Anse and was emancipated by the same 1856 document that freed John Henry. In that document Marsh provided that Ben, his "servant boy," would become free on 1 April 1859. Marsh informed his heirs in that same record that Ben had agreed to pay fifteen dollars per month in the three-year interval before his emancipation became effective. It appears that in the interim Ben was allowed to hire out his own time or was paid wages by the family.[53] During the three-year period, Ben was to be supervised by William Robertson, the husband of Marsh's daughter Eliza.

Ben's emancipation was effective in 1859 so he is not listed as a slave on the 1860 inventory. But his wife, Georgianna, appears, along with their five children, including an infant son who was named Ben for his father.[54] Both Ben and Georgianna remained family servants for many years.[55] Despite John Marsh's efforts in their behalf, Ben and John Henry were not able to make lives for themselves off the plantation. Since a stigma against mulattoes should not have prevented their assimilation into at least some respectable trades in New Orleans, one might suspect that family ties were equally important in drawing Ben and John Henry back to Petite Anse.

Harriet's daughter Lizzie was strong-willed and independent, causing frequent clashes with the overseer, but she was a family favorite. During her mother's temporary absence in 1854, Lizzie was left in charge of the house servants at Petite Anse, although she was only seventeen.[56] Daniel Avery, the attorney husband of Sarah Marsh, wrote of problems with Lizzie at Petite Anse in a letter to his wife in Baton Rouge: " 'Jim' [the overseer] yesterday told me for the first time that during my absence he had much trouble with 'Lizzy' who was either at the Millers or had my houseful of his Negroes, & that was the way the fowls were stolen & my Bridle missing &

unless some steady woman was placed to stay with him & Lizzie sent away he would not stay after I left, as he could not control her."[57] Despite the overseer's low opinion of Lizzie, she matured into a very responsible woman. She married William Butler, and both are mentioned in the Avery papers as esteemed family servants of long duration.[58]

During the 1830s, Marsh expanded his Petite Anse slave force and replaced deceased members, buying as many females as males. There were only two children under age eleven among his 1826 contingent, and he was sensitive to the value of a labor force that could reproduce itself. One woman Marsh bought about 1833 is noteworthy in two respects. She became the progenitor of a large family of Petite Anse slaves, and she left an informative account of her journey from Norfolk, Virginia, to New Orleans as a newly purchased slave. The woman was Maria, generally referred to as Big Maria before her marriage to John Houston to distinguish her from several other Marias on Petite Anse. Big Maria was part of a group of slaves purchased by Marsh from the cargo of the *Ajax,* a coastal slave-trading vessel.[59] She often related the story of her voyage to Louisiana, and it was transcribed by an Avery family member when Maria was in her seventies. She and her fellow slaves sailed from Norfolk to New Orleans aboard the *Ajax* on a journey that she said took two months. Before her sale, Maria and her brother Thornton were owned by Henry Phillips of Fredericksburg, Virginia. Her brother remained on Phillips's farm, but Maria was sold to a trader, separated from her only kin, and crowded aboard a ship bound for the lower South. On the long, painful voyage from Norfolk to New Orleans, "when the wind failed," Captain Bangs would "call out the fiddler," making the women dance "to start the breeze," according to Maria. When revenue officers came aboard the ship to check credentials, a frightened young Maria believed them to be pirates. And as the ship finally neared the crowded port of New Orleans, she saw a massive "poplar grove," mistaking the masts of sailing vessels docked at the port for the familiar slender, silvered trunks of poplar trees of her home. Maria's story may have been embellished by time, but it indicates that her transportation to Louisiana as slave cargo was both a terrifying and adventuresome experience for a naive eighteen-year-old girl who had probably never been off her master's farm.[60]

The 1836 Petite Anse inventory listed Maria as a single parent, heading a household that included her children Francis, Perry, and Evelina or Vina.[61]

Vina was Maria's daughter by a William Hudson, a white man. At Vina's birth in 1835, John Marsh had agreed to emancipate the child when she reached the age of twenty-one, according to the terms of a bargain struck with Hudson, her "reputed father," who paid him $100.[62] Until she reached that age, Marsh put Vina in charge of his grandson John Marsh Henshaw. Vina remained with the Henshaws in New Iberia and does not appear on subsequent Petite Anse inventories with her mother, Maria. As Marsh had promised William Hudson, Vina was emancipated in 1856.

Maria was still single in 1839. Her household included Francis, Tom (the same person as Perry), and an infant daughter Georgianna. By 1844 she had married John Houston, who had been purchased at a public auction in New Orleans in 1837 and was single before his marriage to Maria. Houston, a highly skilled brick mason, was among the most valuable of Petite Anse's slaves.

By 1854 Maria's family and household were drastically altered. Both Maria and her husband were in their forties. They headed a fourteen-member multiple family grouping. Francis and Tom, now young adults, remained part of their stepfather's and mother's household, as did Georgianna and her two small children fathered by Ben, Marsh's mulatto servant. Maria had borne another daughter, Maria, Jr., shortly after the 1839 inventory. John Houston was the likely father, although they were not yet married. In 1854, Maria, Jr., now fourteen, had a newborn infant by an unknown father. Both resided in the household of John and Maria. The exact year of John and Maria's marriage is not known, but Maria's last five children, all enumerated on the 1854 inventory, were John's.[63]

In 1860, the multiple family household headed by John and Maria Houston had increased to eighteen members and included four nuclear families. John and Maria and their five younger children formed one family. Maria's son Tom, his wife, and their daughter formed a second. John and Maria's oldest daughter, Helen, and her husband, Roy, formed the third. The last of the multiple family components was formed by Maria's daughter Georgianna, the wife of Ben, now manumitted, and their five children. Maria, Jr., was now regarded as a twenty-one-old solitaire because she had apparently lost the baby (named Vena after Maria, Jr.'s, sister) born to her in 1854. She no longer resided with John and Maria.[64]

Some members of John and Maria Houston's family remained associated with the plantation for half a century. In the 1866–67 accounts listing freedmen appear the names of John and Maria Houston, their son William Houston, and their daughters Rebecca and Matilda, the latter having married one of the sons of Peter and Milly Stephens.[65] Georgianna and her husband, Ben Keller, remained Avery family servants. Maria, Jr., also remained a house servant after emancipation and eventually married Aaron from a nearby plantation. Of the family, at least Maria Houston was still alive and with the Avery family in 1883.[66]

Petite Anse's owners purchased other slaves in the 1830s, but one that had particular impact on the subsequent development of the slave community was a group bought by Marsh at an estate sale in Pointe Coupee Parish in 1838.[67] Among them was John Pierre, his wife, Aime, and their daughter Clemence. John Pierre had died by 1854, but Aime (now Americanized to Amy), headed a household that included Clemence and her two children Emile, two, and an infant, Rosana.[68] In 1860, Amy lived as a solitaire. Clemence was married to Gus and Arena's son Foster, and in their household lived Emile, her child before marriage, and three additional children, one of whom was named Foster for his father.[69] Among the same group of slaves bought at the Pointe Coupee estate sale was Fanny, forty-nine, and her fifteen-year-old daughter Mary Ann. Both were house servants, and Margaret Marsh Henshaw took Mary Ann as her particular charge. A lively girl who soon attracted many suitors, Mary Ann often proved to be a challenge for her mistress. Margaret Henshaw's siblings made amused comments on her apparent difficulties in dealing with Mary Ann and her admirers. In a June 1845 letter George Marsh told his sister Margaret that "Mary Ann has become quite a bug—has already had three proposals and receives a *killing* . . . glance from every passing *Buck*." Also in 1845, Sarah Avery asked her brother George on Petite Anse, "How does Mary Ann flourish. I hope you will keep a strict watch over her on Margarets account for she has had too much trouble with her to lose her now entirely." She further commented that Mary Ann was "naturally bad enough. I never saw anyone but Margaret that could begin to find her in her sly capers."[70]

By 1854 Mary Ann was living in the household of her mother, Fanny, with a five-year-old son George. Sadly, by 1860 the once sprightly Mary Ann was permanently bedridden, unmarried, and still the mother of only one son.[71]

The major kinship groups of the Petite Anse slave community in the 1854–60 period were formed from the slaves present before 1840—mainly those just discussed in detail. But throughout the decades of the 1840s and 1850s Marsh and his sons-in-law continued to buy young slaves, some of whom married into the old kinship groups by 1860. Because of a staggering death rate, the owners were not able to sustain a healthy rate of increase, and the work force reproduced itself only in the first generation. Largely through the constant infusion of young purchases of both genders, however, the owners provided nonrelated potential mates for the children of the early slave residents as well as vigorous young workers for the sugar operation.

Tiger Island Many of Tiger Island's slaves were severed from prior kinship connections twice—by the migration from Kentucky to Louisiana and by the start-up of an additional plantation in the late 1830s and early 1840s. Despite these and other disruptive actions taken by the Brashears, the Tiger Island slave community continually sought to attain a society defined by family and kinship. In their quest, the slaves overcame many obstacles, beginning with those connected with the migration process. The Walter Brashear family repeated a common pattern among slaveholders relocating in the lower South. Planters and farmers migrating to the fertile and inexpensive lands of the Southwest usually brought with them only the younger and more choice slaves, later fleshing out their work forces through purchases and trades, replacing the migration slaves who failed to acclimate and died early or those that could not adapt to the new work expectations. The old slave community was almost always dissolved by the migration. The generation of slaves who were severed from their birthplaces and most of their kin (certainly parents, grandparents, aunts, uncles, and cousins, and often siblings, spouses, and older children as well) suffered protracted periods of grief and homesickness. Although they understood it was unlikely, migration slaves nevertheless cherished hopes of going back to Kentucky, Virginia, Maryland, Georgia, or the Carolinas to see the old home place once more and to be reunited with lost kinsmen and childhood friends.[72] Migrating white families endured similar periods of displacement and adjustment, but the planter class was often able to maintain ties with its former home and distant relatives through correspondence and occasional visits.

For migration slaves, the pain of separation subsided very slowly, as families and then communities began to form. By the second or third generation at the new plantation, kin networks were usually sufficiently developed to provide a web of security and stability around individual members of the community. Individuals born in an advanced-stage slave society surrounded by kin often had little understanding of the utter desolation experienced by migration slaves or individuals sold away from their communities. Walter Brashear's slaves went through this painful, migration-spawned pattern of destruction and reconstruction, first described by Herbert Gutman in his seminal work on the black family.[73]

Brashear's early slave force in Louisiana had great difficulty adjusting to the loss of their prior community. Their discontent was often reflected in a reluctance to form lasting relationships and in messages or inquiries sent back home through the correspondence of their owners. Only the more privileged migration slaves had this opportunity, but the messages movingly demonstrate their longing for loved ones in Kentucky. Walter Brashear's wife included the following message from Belle Isle slaves in a letter to her daughter in Lexington, Kentucky: "In your next letter tell Rachel how her relations come." She added, "Poor little Hannah says ask Miss Caroline if she sees Daddy to give my love to him." Another letter mentioned that a migration slave begged for word of his brothers. Brashear family members frequently traveled back and forth between Lexington, Kentucky, and their holdings in Louisiana, and they usually cooperated in forwarding the slaves' messages to their Kentucky kin and relating responses. In 1827, for example, Walter Brashear, visiting in Kentucky, instructed his wife in Louisiana to "tell Lowny his family is all well and his friends very glad to hear he is in good health."[74]

A more detailed look at some of Brashears' migration slaves reveals some of their difficulties in adjustment and their high regard for family and kin remaining in Kentucky. Most of the young male solitaires whom Brashear brought to Louisiana from Kentucky did not marry and disappeared from the record after 1831. Among these were several slaves from Margaret Barr Brashear's inheritance, including Andrew and Peter, as well as some Walter Brashear owned in his own right, such as Lowny.[75] The deaths of a few are documented in the records of the 1830s, but it is unlikely that so many died after having survived acclimatization, and some must have been sold.

Another Kentucky slave who never married was Brooks. Only thirteen or fourteen years old at the time of the removal, he was one of those slaves who seemed genuinely devoted to his master and his master's family.[76]

Brooks was particularly fond of Walter Brashear, Jr., who died at school in Kentucky. Both of the young men loved Belle Isle and its sleek, free-ranging cattle. In 1830 Brooks sent a message to Walter, Jr., via a letter from Rebecca Brashear. It expresses the affection he held for his young master, but—more significant—it demonstrates a persistent awareness of kinship even among slaves who had been separated from their families as children.

> Brooks wishes me to write you that he has been very ill for the last twelve months but is now getting well. He wishes you to see his brother and say to him that he almost thinks of him as a stranger as it has been almost eight years and he has never written to him to let him know where and how his brothers or sisters are. . . . He should have acted differently had their situations been reversed.
>
> He says when you [were] here you requested him to look after your cattle which he has done faithfully and now he can have the pleasure to let you know they increase very fast and all look well. He requests me to say to you that he *adores* you and intends one day or other to be your devoted slave.

Brooks died in a cholera outbreak in 1849, along with several other young men.[77]

Another of the young male solitaires from Kentucky was Eli, the brick-maker whom Brashear sent ahead to construct Belle Isle's house and outbuildings. He, too, never married or fathered any known children, although he lived into the 1850s.[78]

An additional slave artisan who did not marry in Louisiana was Sight. He was part of the Barr inheritance and was employed both at Belle Isle (while Brashear still operated it in partnership with the Barr brothers) and at the home of David and Emily Barr Todd in Franklin (Emily was Margaret Brashear's sister). He could not adjust to his new surroundings. Todd wrote relatives in Kentucky that "Old Sight is here & expressing a wish to go back to Kentucky—indulgence to him will not answer a good purpose—he has drank hard this winter & spring."[79] Sight drops off all Brashear and Todd records shortly thereafter, so perhaps he was sent back to Kentucky.

Isaac and Fanny Henderson were a married couple in their thirties when they removed to Louisiana with the Brashears. Fanny died by 1831, but Isaac Henderson remained part of Walter Brashear's slave community until he, too, died, about a decade after his wife. The couple remained childless in Louisiana.[80]

A young mother, Rachel, was also among the Kentucky migrants, along with her two small children. She and her children first appear as Walter Brashear's slaves on a Kentucky mortgage document of September 1814. Rachel is listed below Bill, thirty-two, who might have been her husband, and they were all identified as part of Margaret Barr Brashear's inheritance from her father.[81] Bill remained in Kentucky. One of Rachel's children died during the migration or shortly thereafter, but a daughter, Ellen, lived with her mother at Belle Isle.

Rachel's parents, Ben and Sabina, were slaves of the affluent Barr family. In an 1822 letter to her daughter in Lexington, Margaret Barr Brashear asked her to "give Rachel's love to Ben and Sabina [and] tell them she is well."[82]

Between her arrival in Louisiana in 1822 and her death in 1830 after a long illness, Rachel gave birth to several additional children—Elisha, Carillo, and a girl, Sabina, named for her Kentucky grandmother. A Brashear daughter announced the birth in a letter to her sister in Lexington with the comment that baby Sabina was "as white as Ellen," the infant's older half-sister.[83] The baby grew into a beautiful woman and was bought by a white man for his concubine in 1849, along with her own small child. In 1850 Frances Brashear Lawrence wrote that "Sabina has gone to Gibbons Point and taken up her avende. I wonder if she lives in the same house with him, or if he has put her up in a house there?"[84]

The father of Rachel's Louisiana-born children (Elisha, Carillo, and Sabina) is not known, but it might have been Carillo, who appears as a twenty-five-year-old solitaire on an 1825 list.[85] He is not in the 1831 records, and Rachel had died in 1830. Her orphaned younger children were reared by her close friend, possible relative, and fellow Kentucky migrant, Milly.

Rachel's oldest known child, Ellen, moved to Louisiana at the age of eight or nine. Like her mother, she had been part of Margaret Brashear's inheritance.[86] Also like her mother and her younger sister Sabina, Ellen appeared to be white. She spent most of her life as a slave at Belle Isle. But in the start-up phase of Tiger Island, she was among the young slaves transferred. She was present on the island in 1833, in a household with two young boys, Ben (named for his grandfather in Kentucky), five, and Patrick, two.[87] Patrick might have been the son of Hannah Jones, who accompanied young Frances Brashear to school in the 1830s, leaving her children on the plantation in the care of friends or relatives.

Ben was Ellen's son with another migration slave, Franklin, to whom she was married for several years. Franklin had a wife or sweetheart named Milly in Kentucky (not to be confused with the Milly who raised Rachel's orphans in Louisiana). Some affection lingered, for he attempted to contact Milly in 1832, provoking Margaret Brashear to write her daughter in Lexington, "I do not know who wrote Franklin's letter to Milly—as he has taken our Ellin to wife. I think it was not worth his while to have written to her at all, but he is a great rake at any rate."[88]

The marriage between Ellen and Franklin did not last, but whether because of divorce or Franklin's death is not known. In any case, Ellen appears on an 1848 Golden Farm inventory as the single mother of sons Elias, nine, and Patrick, one. Her older son Ben was on his own, and the earlier Patrick had probably been emancipated, as will be related in the story of his presumed mother, Hannah. Ellen apparently named her baby son Patrick after the boy she had kept for several years. By 1848, Ellen had three daughters—Josephine, seven, Caroline, four, and Susan, three—in addition to Elias and Patrick. These children were fathered by a Brashear slave, Billy Brown, but he and Ellen did not share a household as a married couple.[89]

Ellen had become very sick by late 1849. Despite efforts by Frances Brashear Lawrence to heal Ellen's chronically diseased leg by taking her to a hot springs in Arkansas, she died in 1850.[90] Ellen's daughters Caroline and Josephine were among the valued servants whom Walter Brashear bequeathed by name to family members in his will. They were still alive at the outbreak of the Civil War, as was Elias, who appeared on a Golden Farm inventory in 1861.[91]

As was the case with many of the Kentucky women, Milly—another migrant—did not marry in Louisiana. She did, however, found a major kinship line on Tiger Island. She was listed as aged thirty on the Tiger Island list of 1833, already the mother of five children between the ages of twelve and two: Maria, Jenny (named for her mother in Kentucky), Ann, Sandis, and Horace. She was also rearing Rachel's children, Sabina, Elisha, and Carillo. Nine years later, Milly's biological children also included Esther, nine, and Leven, five.[92]

Milly died between 1843 and 1847, but her surviving children remained at

Tiger Island and proliferated. By late 1842 the eldest, Maria, was married to the strong-willed Jim Roy and had two children by him (Coleman and Delphy). Jenny, the second of Milly's daughters, was married to Ed Davis in 1842 and had a small daughter, Laura. Ann disappeared from the lists and probably died, and Milly's adopted children had been transferred to Bayou Boeuf Plantation.

By 1857, Milly's children had formed solid alliances and were fostering a new generation of Tiger Island slaves. Esther had married Henry Todd and had a small daughter. Sandis had married and had six children, ranging in age from one to fifteen. Maria had remarried, to Henry Brient. Jenny, like her younger sister Esther, had married an older man who was her mother's contemporary, Ed Davis. In addition to Laura, they had four children. And Laura, whom Jenny had borne at the age of fourteen, was married to Alfred and had her own infant (Joe), born when she was fifteen. Joe's birth marked the fourth generation of Milly's line to be born on Tiger Island. By 1860, the deceased Milly's blood descendants on the island numbered at least twenty-eight, including four great-grandchildren. Including her adopted children, grandchildren, and great-grandchildren, her descendants numbered thirty-five.[93]

As far as can be determined, Hannah also remained a single parent in Louisiana. She was the personal maid of Walter Brashear's daughter Frances for many years. When she was little more than a child, Hannah had accompanied her mother (also named Hannah) and five siblings to Brashear's Belle Isle plantation, leaving her father behind in Kentucky. It was young Hannah who in 1822 had sent the poignant message to "ask Miss Caroline if she sees Daddy to give my love to him."[94]

While barely in her teens, young Hannah gave birth to a daughter, Clarissa, and, four years later, to a son, Sinclair. Both children probably had the same father, but he was not named. No more children appear with Hannah on plantation or court documents for eleven years. Nevertheless, she did have another child, Patrick, born about 1830, who is never listed with her in the inventories. His existence is documented in the will of Robert R. Barr, the brother of Margaret Barr Brashear. Barr was an early partner in Brashear's sugar undertakings and a frequent visitor to the plantation.[95] Barr was almost certainly Hannah's lover and the father of Patrick. Barr wrote his will in 1832, while at Belle Isle. Part of it reads, "It is my will that Walter Brashear or his family shall inherit no part of my estate as legal heirs until Hannah Jones and her son Patrick are emancipated & sent to Kentucky and $2,000 paid to trustees for their support and the education of Patrick Jones."[96] Barr died within four years, but Hannah was not emancipated as he had willed. It is possible, though I have been unable to confirm it, that Patrick was emancipated and sent back to Kentucky to the Barr plantation. It appears that Patrick was placed in the care of Ellen between 1832 and Barr's estate settlement in 1836 or 1837 and was thereafter manumitted.

Robert Barr's wishes for Hannah were never carried out by Walter Brashear. Brashear's daughter Frances did apparently sympathize with her deceased uncle's attempt to force Brashear to manumit Hannah and her son. Hannah lived in Lexington for much of the mid- and late 1830s, serving as Frances's personal maid while she was at school. Perhaps after 1836 Patrick was there also. Frances pressed her father to free Hannah and allow her to remain in Kentucky. In response to one of Frances's inquiries, Brashear tersely replied in 1838 that "Hannah Jones cannot be freed in Kentucky as there exists a law of the state which prevents her returning to it. The object can be attained here under certain forms prescribed by the laws of Louisiana." He did not offer to pursue the matter, but he did add that "Hannah's children are quite well and growing finely."[97]

Hannah was back in Louisiana by 1841. Perhaps recognizing that she would probably die a slave, she either resumed a former union or began a new one and gave birth to five additional children in rapid succession: Edward, William, Alice, Mary, and Sophia. By 1848 she was also a grandmother. Her eldest child, Clarissa, now twenty-two and a single head of household, had two children of her own—Cornelius, two, and an unnamed infant.[98]

Hannah and many of her younger children died before 1860, but among the slaves who remained with the Brashears after most had fled to the Federal forces were the older children, Sinclair and Clarissa. Clarissa, still single, was listed with her own large family, including Cornelius, Isaac, Daphne, Becky, Thomas, and Lewis.[99] The older children and their offspring had become permanent members of the Tiger Island slave force.

Yet another migration slave who remained single in Louisiana was Queny, although she headed another family that lasted for at least thirty years. Queny had two children who accompanied her in the 1822 Kentucky migration—Henry Todd and Matilda, both of them teenagers. On an 1825 list of Belle Isle slaves, they were on their own and Queny was described as thirty-three and single, although a son Augustus would have been born by then. She was on Tiger Island in 1833, listed with her son Augustus and daughters Flora and Courtney.[100]

Queny was not a permanent resident of Tiger Island. Like others of the original Kentucky slaves, she spent most of her life at the Belle Isle and Golden Farm home plantations with the old master, Walter Brashear. She lived at least through 1861 and was listed, at the age of seventy, as part of Walter Brashear's estate, along with her daughter Flora, her son Augustus, and a bevy of grandchildren.[101] Queny's daughter Courtney lived only to early adulthood, but her daughter Rachel was a Brashear family favorite, bequeathed by Brashear to one of his granddaughters. One of Flora's daughters, Fanny, was likewise left to a Brashear grandchild. Augustus never married. Flora married a Golden Farm slave, Oliver, by 1845, and in 1860 they had at least seven children. Oliver and Flora were among the slaves for whom Henry and Frances Lawrence provided land at the end of the war.[102]

Unlike Hannah and Queny, who stayed on Tiger Island only temporarily, Queny's daughter Matilda remained on the island from 1833 until the slave community was dissolved in 1860–61, the unmarried head of a large and vigorous clan. Matilda bore children from at least 1824 through 1857. Her first five children, as listed in 1842, were Corilla, Anne, Rhody, Annette, and Allen. By 1850 she had, in addition, Quincy, Mina, Webster, and Stuart—the youngest only two years old. She was also rearing a twelve-year-old orphan, Primus, the son of the deceased Maria. Corilla, Anne, and Annette had died or were transferred by 1850. Rhoda married Aaron Smith, a Tiger Island man who was her mother's contemporary. He had been purchased with seventeen other men and four women in a single lot in 1830.[103] Rhoda and Aaron had a lasting marriage despite a fourteen-to-eighteen-year age difference, and by 1860 they had five children, ranging in age from three to sixteen. The same inventory shows Matilda at the age of fifty the formidable head of a household of six children, ranging in age from seven to seventeen.[104]

Henry Todd, the eldest son of Queny and the only male adult to appear on the 1833 mortgage list for Tiger Island, resided on the plantation for the remainder of his life as a slave. He, too, had been brought to Louisiana from Kentucky in the early 1820s, as an adolescent. He was still unattached in 1842, but as he neared the age of fifty, he married Esther, the seventeen-year-old daughter of Milly, who had been one of his co-workers on the island in 1833. By 1860 they had two small daughters.[105]

The six adults constituting the first known generation of Tiger Island slaves have already been discussed; they were Hannah, Queny, her adult children Henry Todd and Matilda, Milly, and Ellen. They were the first Tiger Island slaves with ties to the Kentucky slave community although other Kentucky slaves on Belle Isle or Golden Farm were occasionally transferred to Tiger Island. Five of the six were women, and all had small children. All but one of the children had been born in Louisiana, presumably at Belle Isle, suggesting that new alliances were formed in Louisiana, although none of the women had married the fathers of their Louisiana offspring.

Cut off from their prior familial antecedents, the fourteen families of the 1842 Tiger Island inventory had provided the basis for a supportive kinship system by 1860. By 1842, many of the migration slaves were no longer at Tiger Island, but their progeny continued to increase, and several new kinship groups were formed.

The most vigorous lines, however, resulted from alliances begun by newcomers. One of these families was formed by Jerry and Maria Key. Maria's origins cannot be determined from existing records, but Jerry was part of a lot of young men between the ages of fourteen and twenty-six who were purchased in 1830.[106] Jerry, twenty at the time of his purchase, married Maria, daughter of Belle Isle slaves originally from Kentucky. Jerry and Maria had a young family on Tiger Island in 1842, and by 1860 they had eight known children and eleven known grandchildren, or nineteen direct descendants.[107] All of the surviving children produced by the long marriage between Jerry and Maria Key themselves married and formed standard nuclear families at young ages.

A second family of 1842 consisted of Jim Roy and Maria. Roy's origins are unknown; he was probably purchased in the early 1820s. He was sold by the mid-1840s. Maria was a daughter of Milly, a Kentucky slave and one of Tiger Island's first settlers. Jim and Maria had two known children and a grandchild by 1860, although by that time she had remarried.

A third family from 1842, that of single parent Mary Brien, had produced four known children and one known grandchild by 1860. A fourth family was that of Daniel Atter and Eliza, who had six known children and two known grandchildren in the 1860 community, although Daniel Atter died about the time of his last child's birth. A fifth family, that of Henry and Eliza Cox, included seven known children and two grandchildren by 1860. The sixth couple, Bob Willis and Betsy, had produced six known children but no grandchildren by 1860. In the seventh family, single mother Scilla had given birth to ten known children and by 1860 had ten grandchildren as well. The eighth family was also headed by a single mother, Matilda, who had ten known children and five grandchildren by 1860. The ninth family was headed by Ed and Jenny Davis, who included among their progeny by 1860 three natural children, two adopted children, and four grandchildren. Although she and two of her daughters did not survive until 1860, Lucinda contributed four known children to the Tiger Island kinship; likewise, Maria did not survive, but her son Primus continued her line. The twelfth family was begun by Becky, another old Kentucky slave, who had at least three children and five grandchildren on the island in 1860. As observed earlier, Milly had borne seven known children and raised three adopted children. Along with various natural and adopted children and great-grandchildren, she had thirty-five descendants who lived at least part of the 1842–60 period on Tiger Island. The fourteenth 1842 family consisted of Violetta and her children. She died early, and two of her five children were adopted by Ed and Jenny Davis, the female child eventually having two children of her own.

In all, the fourteen 1842 families had by 1860 produced at least 145 blood descendants, most of whom still survived on Tiger Island. Every known match was made without indulging in consanguinity, but the families headed by Scilla and Jerry Key intermarried heavily. Finding nonkin to marry would have become an extremely acute problem by the time the grandchildren and great-grandchildren of the 1842 community had reached sexual maturity. They would be to a large extent a generation of cousins. Fortunately, emancipation intervened, freeing the young slaves to seek mates off the plantation.

The records of Oakland, Petite Anse, and Tiger Island have allowed the backward tracing of the families that contributed to the kinship networks of the last recorded community. The naming of children after parents and especially grandparents—both those present and in Kentucky—demonstrates affection and a respect for familial continuity and kin identification. Household composition reveals that slaves in the three communities often ministered to the needs of family members, orphaned kin, and nonrelated, dependent children who might be considered fictive kin in the framework of existing households. The role of kinship beyond that contained in individual households and families was probably equally supportive to that of individual families in providing slaves with continuity, stability, and even limited economic assistance, but it is much more difficult to document and measure. Social historian Robert Wheaton has warned that "the emphasis which household censuses put on co-residence tempts one to ignore the kinship system as it extends beyond the household." He points out that because households leave a "clearer historical and, particularly, legal record," the connections between the household structures and the larger kinship systems of which they are part are often obscured. He warns that "we can understand household structure only within the larger context of the kinship system."[108]

1. *Solitaires were households unto themselves. In the early stages of community development most solitaires were young singles, but in later stages they were often middle-aged or elderly widows or widowers or never-married individuals whose children had left the household.* (Century Magazine [April 1886]; courtesy The Historic New Orleans Collection, 1974.25.23.26, Museum/Research Center, New Orleans, La.)

2. *This photograph illustrates one category of the simple-family household type—that of married couples alone. Its membership varied widely according to the life course of slaves, embracing briefly young, newly married but childless couples and, more consistently, childless mature couples and those whose children had departed the household.* (Appleton's Journal of Literature, Science, and Art, *2 July 1870; courtesy* The Historic New Orleans Collection, 1974.25.23.37, Museum/Research Center, New Orleans, La.)

3. About 14.5 percent of the slaves in the Louisiana sample were part of female-headed single-parent households. Although this percentage by no means constitutes a matriarchal structure, in slave society single parenthood was viewed as a viable option for slave women to a greater degree than was true of contemporary white society. (Harper's Weekly Magazine, 21 February 1863)

4. This domestic scene illustrates the most common form of the simple family, the standard nuclear unit consisting of both parents and their children. (Courtesy The Historic New Orleans Collection, 1974.25.23.39, Museum/Research Center, New Orleans, La.)

5. *Bemused young parents and a shocked grandmother watch their offspring's hijinks. If this grandmother lived in a household headed by one of the parents, this group would serve as an example of an extended family with upward extension.* (Appleton's Journal of Literature, Science, and Art, *2 July 1870, courtesy The Historic New Orleans Collection, 1974.25.23.18, Museum/Research Center, New Orleans, La.*)

6. *If the man with the fiddle is a brother of the head of household and shares his residence, this group could serve as an example of an extended family with lateral extension. (Sketch by A. W. Thompson in* Harper's Weekly Magazine, *8 February 1868)*

7. *A common form of the non-nuclear family household in Louisiana was that of co-resident siblings living as a domestic unit in old age or prior to marriage. (Courtesy The Historic New Orleans Collection, 1974.25.23.63, Museum/Research Center, New Orleans, La.)*

8. *This 1856 sketch of a Mississippi river plantation shows Louisiana agriculture during one of its most prosperous decades. (Sketch by Henry Lewis, in* Das Illustrirte Mississippithal *[Düsseldorf, 1857])*

9. *The Whitney cotton gin prompted a major expansion into Louisiana after the War of 1812. (Drawing by William L. Sheppard, ca. 1868, courtesy The Historic New Orleans Collection, 1974.25.13.27, Museum/Research Center, New Orleans, La.)*

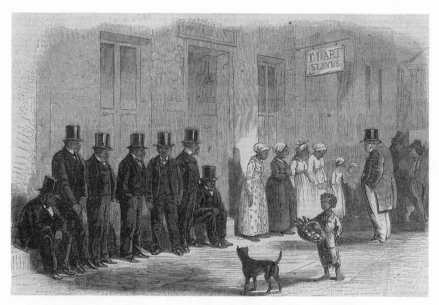

10. Potential buyers look over house servants for sale at a New Orleans slave pen. Most such chattels were victims of the interstate trade. (Harper's Weekly Magazine, *24 January 1863*)

11. This engraving of an 1842 sale in the rotunda of the St. Louis Hotel in New Orleans was probably of an estate. (Engraving by M. Starling in J. S. Buckingham, Slave States of America, *vol. 1 [London, 1841])*

12. *Gender discrimination was common in Louisiana agriculture. With some notable exceptions, cane cutters and sugar boilers were generally male, as were cotton ginners and heads of plow gangs and picking teams.* (Harper's New Monthly Magazine, June–November 1853)

13. Sugar manufacture involved long hours and exposure to dangerous, unguarded machinery and open boiling vats. (Harper's New Monthly Magazine, June–November 1853)

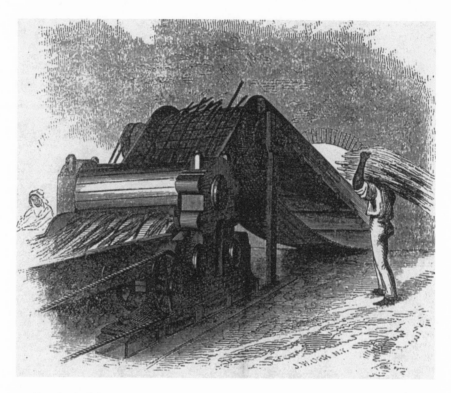

14. Despite its labor-intensive aspects, many slaves looked forward to the communal social aspects of the sugar-making season and the relative autonomy they were allowed during the long night watches. (Harper's New Monthly Magazine, *June–November 1853*)

15. *Life and labor on a smallholding such as this cotton farm were not necessarily easier for slaves than on large plantations. A smaller community and marriage pool were available, and slaves on smallholdings were especially vulnerable in estate divisions. (Courtesy The Historic New Orleans Collection, Museum/Research Center, 1974.25.13.13, New Orleans, La.)*

16. *Cotton production engaged the labor of almost all able-bodied slaves at Oakland during Nathaniel Evans's period of ownership.* (Harper's New Monthly Magazine, December–May 1853/54)

17. Despite the risks and unhealthy conditions, Louisiana slaves by the thousands sought refuge in contraband camps attached to federal encampments. This drawing of contraband children dancing a break-down at a camp near Baton Rouge, Louisiana, shows the residents of the camp as well as wives and children visiting their husbands and fathers now in Union service. (Frank Leslie's Illustrated Newspaper, *31 January 1863*)

18. *Some of Oakland's slaves fled to the federal lines near Port Hudson. Here such contraband slaves are shown working on fortifications in the Port Hudson area in 1863. Baton Rouge can be seen in the distant background.* (Frank Leslie's Illustrated Newspaper, *9 May 1863*)

19. Jacob Stroyers, whose two sisters were sold to the lower South, remembered how relatives and friends gathered at the depot to say good-bye, singing hymns of consolation. Hannah Blair, a slave wife whose husband was sold to Louisiana in 1860, dictated a letter to him in 1861 that reads in part, "Our boy grows finely. I do wish you could see him but as that cannot be I will learn him to always remember you, he has not forgot you. Even now if we ask him where you are he will say that you are on the cars." (After the Sale: Slaves Going South from Richmond, *a painting by Eyre Crowe* [1853], *courtesy the Chicago Historical Society, Chicago, Ill.*)

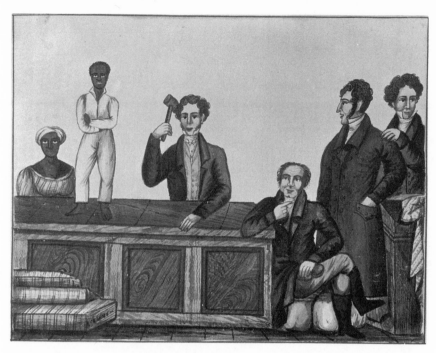

20. *Despite Louisiana's legal prohibition against separating slaves under ten from their mothers, such sales were commonplace among out-of-state imports auctioned in New Orleans. No Louisiana law prohibited the separation by sale of older children from their parents. (Courtesy The Historic New Orleans Collection, 1941.3, Museum/Research Center, New Orleans, La.)*

21. *Charles Taylor and Angelica Broujoy were among the numerous Louisiana off-spring of miscegenation involving slave mothers and their owners or overseers. (Detail of an engraving in* Harper's Weekly Magazine, 30 January 1864*)*

22. *When the Union troops liberated the bayou country, one puzzled officer inquired as to why a very elderly man was among the crowd that greeted them. "Uncle, freedom will do you no good; for you are just on the edge of the grave." The old slave replied that he rejoiced for his children who would live free.* (Harper's Weekly Magazine, *9 May 1862*)

23. *Louisiana slaves considered a funeral a highly significant communal observance. Note the broad gender and age representations at this Louisiana slave funeral and burial. (*A Plantation Burial, *a painting by John Antrobus [ca. 1860], courtesy The Historic New Orleans Collection, 1960.46, Museum/Research Center, New Orleans, La.)*

24. Slaves en route to visit their off-plantation spouses and children were often stopped by patrols and required to produce passes. (Frank Leslie's Illustrated Newspaper, 11 July 1863)

25. Strong nurturing tendencies were documented in Louisiana slave households and communities in all phases of development but were especially strong in mature communities with advanced kinship networks and generational depth. (Courtesy the Negro Almanac Collection, The Amistad Research Center, Tulane University, New Orleans, La.)

PART III
Patterns

CHAPTER SEVEN

Images and Influences

In Part III, the quantitative models and case studies presented in earlier chapters will be placed in the larger historical and cultural context of Louisiana slavery and slavery scholarship in general. Drawing upon both contemporary sources and modern scholarship, I will address broad cultural and historical factors that influenced the slave families, households, and communities of Louisiana. Some of these factors threatened slave domestic organizations; others served as fountains of strength and support. First I will discuss perhaps the most formidable foe of domestic unity and peace—familial separations.

SEPARATIONS

In his memoirs Louisiana planter Francis D. Richardson relates a story concerning the African slave progenitors of some of his Bayside Plantation workers. The incident he describes addresses topics that will be further developed in this chapter—the devastating impact of enslavement on the enslaved and the intense, enduring regard held by slaves for their families, kin, and communities.

205

After the terror of capture, the long, frightening voyage, the humiliating sale at Charleston, and the exhausting trip to the plantation in Statesboro, Georgia, the thirty Africans felt little except numbness. Impassively, they trudged after their new owner through the door of his house. A black man who remembered a little of their language told them that they were to be shown to their new owner's family because newly arrived Africans were a curiosity to them. One and then another of the Africans began to pick out faces at the end of the crowded, dimly lit hall. The faces were unmistakably African. The slaves shrieked with joy; they laughed, cried, and danced. Their capture and enslavement had been but a long and terrible dream. They were back in Africa, and—looking straight at them—were their lost families and kinsmen, rejoicing as well. After the slaves were brought under control, the interpreter explained to the alarmed owner that the African chattels had mistaken their own images reflected in a large mirror at the end of the hall for their families in Africa. For those Africans at Statesboro, the nightmare of enslavement and separation from home and family was not an apparition as they had hoped; it was a tragic reality. The hope of being returned to their home and reunited with their families and friends died hard with the Africans. Disappointment and despair discouraged many of them from forming permanent relationships or bearing numerous children. Richardson remembered that the female Africans bought by his grandfather at Charleston had borne few children, and he believed that such was "the case with Africans imported generally."[1]

A few of the Africans and many of their direct descendants experienced a similar sense of estrangement two generations later when they were wrenched from their families and friends to be transported to Louisiana's sugar fields as part of Richardson's inheritance from his grandfather in Statesboro.

Through the years Africa became less tangible and more mythical to African-American slaves. The idea of an ancestral homeland increasingly became part of a rich body of legends told by the elders. Through their tales and acts, the African elders also transmitted an intense devotion to family and kin and an overpowering dread of separation. The wound of separation never seemed to heal for African-born Judy, slave of the Douglas family in Louisiana. Even after half a century she continued to grieve for her "old mudder in Africa" and begged Emily Douglas to write a letter to her.[2] Similar feelings were expressed by slaves separated from loved ones by the interstate trade such as a man in Louisiana's bayou country, who told a visitor of his longing to see his "old mudder" in Virginia, from whom he had been sold away at the age of thirteen.[3]

By 1808, the African slave trade was legally closed, but slave trafficking intensified within the southern United States, with tragic implications for slave families, households, and kin.

SEPARATIONS CAUSED BY THE INTERSTATE TRADE

During the peak of the internal slave trade, from 1815 through 1840, thousands of future Louisiana chattels were separated from family members in the upper South by the brutal combination of interstate sale and forced migration. Though slowed after the depression of the late 1830s and early 1840s, the interstate slave traffic was again brisk by 1850. According to Clement Eaton, most of the slaves in the interstate trade were young, "prime field hands." Eaton and U. B. Phillips contended, in Eaton's words, that though "a considerable number of the slaves taken to the lower South were transported by emigrating masters . . . the majority were probably delivered by professional traders." Eaton also acknowledged that the "worst feature of the internal slave trade was the break up of Negro families." Kenneth Stampp agreed that a "large proportion of the slaves who were transferred to the Southwest—perhaps a majority of them—reached their new homes through the facility of the interstate slave trade."[4]

This consensus was challenged in the 1970s by Robert Fogel and Stanley Engerman, who argued that the internal slave trade was small compared to the numbers of slaves who migrated with intact families when their owners relocated. They also asserted that historians have grossly exaggerated the numbers of families separated by the internal trade. Using many of the same records, Richard Sutch and Herbert Gutman reached the opposite conclusion. Joe Gray Taylor, in *Negro Slavery in Louisiana*, had an informative section on the trade as it affected Louisiana, but he did not enter the debate. Eugene Genovese believes that the extent to which families were separated by the trade will probably never be known. But Michael Tadman has recently produced convincing evidence that the domestic slave trade did often separate slave families.[5] Indeed, much more work must be done before a definitive conclusion can be reached about the volume of the internal slave trade and its effects on slave families, especially because many of the New Orleans records omit mention of familial status.

The interstate trade could separate slaves from family members at several junctures. In the exporting states, economically pressed owners sold slaves to traders to settle debts; in most of the cases involving family separations, southeastern owners sold husbands apart from wives and children, unmarried children in their late teens away from parents and younger siblings, and mothers and their youngest children away from their children over age ten, but no laws prevented southeastern sellers from dividing families in any combination. Young adults sold south invariably left older kin behind—parents, grandparents, aunts, and uncles. Traders involved in the interstate traffic often assured sellers that families would be kept intact but ignored these comforting pledges once en route. If a child, especially an infant, proved to be a burden to the trader, it was sold cheaply at the first opportunity.[6]

Even if slaves reached the New Orleans slave pens with their family units intact, they were not safe from separation. New Orleans traders often divided married couples if they could obtain higher prices by selling them separately, and older children were routinely sold apart from their parents. No documentation proved familial relationships; the slaves were unknown in Louisiana, and their protests were unlikely to be heeded in any case. Therefore, women were easily sold apart from their children under age ten in the New Orleans slave marts, despite the state prohibition. Solomon Northup recounts the case of a woman whose ten-year-old son was sold apart from her at a New Orleans auction. She expected to be able to keep her five-year-old daughter with her, in accordance with Louisiana law, but at the mother's sale, the trader refused to relinquish the little girl because she was light-skinned and would bring a high price as a "fancy girl" in a few years.[7] Slaves were often sold in small family units even in the New Orleans market, but without tracing the history of each family back to its plantation of origin, there is no way of knowing whether the entire family was represented in the sale. The ages of many women—in their late twenties and early thirties with only infants or very small children present—suggest that they were separated from older children and perhaps husbands at the point of original sale or were sold separately in New Orleans.

The experience of being sold to the lower South was "dreadful bad," according to one Louisiana slave, who vividly recalled the day he last saw his family.[8] Another explained how his parents and their four youngest children (including him) were sold to a trader, leaving six older children behind. "That way I was sold but never alone," but "our family was divide[d] and that brought grief to my parents."[9] When Virginia slave Jim Blair was brought to Louisiana by traders, he left a wife and five children behind.[10] Perhaps the most vivid description of the effects on families and communities when slaves were sold to traders for transport to Louisiana is that of Jacob Stroyer. He, along with relatives and friends, "young and old," gathered at the depot where the sold slaves were being boarded. The crowds were so agitated that it was difficult for the overseer and driver to control them. Some of the older slaves quietly sang "little hymns . . . for the consolation of those that were going away." A few of the slaves inside the cars were leaving cruel masters and were fiddling and dancing, but most were crying, Stroyer's two sisters among them. As the train pulled away, he recalled that "we heard the weeping and wailing from the slaves, as far as human voice could be heard."[11]

The vast majority of the slaves transported from the Southeast to Louisiana through sale lost touch with their old homes and families. Unless the sold slave found some way to send a message, the old community had no way of knowing his or her whereabouts. Isolation, poverty, and lack of education limited extensive searches even after the war, although some Louisiana slaves made extraordinary efforts.

A few Louisiana slaves successfully contacted their loved ones through letters written for them by obliging owners, some of which have survived in planters' papers. These letters and the responses to them are testimony to the dislocations to family life wrought by the interstate slave trade, as well as to the powerful love that bound even separated slave families.

One example is an 1861 letter written by a slave wife in Jonesboro, Tennessee, to her husband in Louisiana. He had been taken to New Orleans by traders and was subsequently purchased by Richard Pugh of Lafourche Parish in 1860. The letter reads, in part:

We received the letter that your Master so kindly wrote to us and you can not ever think how glad we was to hear from you and Jake. I had almost given up the thought of ever hearing from you again. We did not [know] what part of world you was so you may know I was glad to hear that you and Jake was together. . . . We are all . . . doing tolerable well. Our boy grows finely. I do wish you could see him but as that cannot be I will learn him to always remember you, he has not forgot you. Even now if we ask him where you are he will say you are on the cars [railroad cars]. his grandfather send his love to you.[12]

The letter continues with news of relatives and friends and affairs of the plantation. It is signed "Your loving wife Hannah Blair."

Two other letters involve a family of female slaves spanning three generation, all of whom were separated by the trade. The first woman was Jane Dennis, owned by T. D. Jones in Maryland until he sold her to traders about 1850. She was sold apart from at least some of her children, including Eliza. Eliza Jones grew up, had at least two daughters—Tillie and Jennie—and was a devoted nurse to her invalid mistress until she died. After his wife's death, Eliza's owner decided that "the only alternative presented to me was to quit housekeeping or part with you [Eliza]," suggesting that he sold her for financial reasons.[13] Until his ominous announcement that she would be sold, Jones admitted that Eliza was loyal and hardworking. Her anger and despondency at the prospect of being parted from her home and children provided Jones with the justification he sought to soothe his conscience—she was ungrateful and faithless. Jones sold Eliza and Tillie to traders. The other daughter, Jennie, remained with him in Maryland.

Assisted by Thomas Butler, her new owner in Louisiana, Eliza contacted Jones concerning the possibility of regaining her daughter Jennie. She received an ambiguous reply relating that he had received the request and that her daughter's "countenance lightened up with smile" when he read her the news about her mother and sister. But, Jones claimed, the child was content to stay with her master, and he was "reluctant to part with her." In in a classic example of blaming the victim, he admonished Eliza for behavior which he inferred led to the separation: "Your tender & affectionate services to your afflicted former Mistress created in me an attachment for you that nothing but your ingratitude & faithlessness could have broken. . . . Up to the period of this sad event you were as fine a servant as I ever knew."[14] Jones had not reached a decision concerning Jennie's future at the time he replied, and Butler's records do not indicate whether he was able to purchase Jennie.

Perhaps the unfulfilled desire to be reunited with her daughter impelled

Eliza Jones to try to contact her own mother, Jane Dennis. Again with the cooperation of her owner, Eliza heard that her mother might be on a St. James Parish plantation. She wrote a letter of inquiry and received a reply in 1861. In the letter she dictated, Jane Dennis wrote that she was "truly glad" to hear from her daughter. Her age and poor health prevented her from coming to see Eliza, but she implored Eliza to come to her plantation for a visit, for "I should like very much to see you once more before I die."[15] Considering the support that Butler had given Eliza in her quest, there is a good chance that the old woman's request was fulfilled.

SEPARATIONS CAUSED BY MIGRATION

Although they were not part of the internal slave trade, slaves who accompanied migrating owners joined the westward flow of laborers. Few slave communities were transported intact. Separations were in some cases unavoidable but were common. Migrating slaves generally had no choice but to leave family members behind, especially if they were involved in an off-plantation marriage. Some slaves were given a choice, and it was often a painful one. Annie Carmouche, a planter's wife in Louisiana, recalled that when her parents left Virginia in 1845 the slaves faced a dilemma: "Some of Father's slaves had married slaves belonging to other people. Father asked each one before leaving Virginia which they preferred, to be sold to the owners of their wives or husbands, or that he should buy them [the spouses of other owners] if they wished to leave Va. None . . . wanted to be sold, others he bought, some did not want to leave Va. thus preferring separation."[16] Elderly childless or unmarried slaves were usually reluctant to leave their home state if given the choice.[17]

As was demonstrated in the case studies, migrating planters took only selected members of their slave forces, selling the others with the plantation or to family members. Migration slaves were subjected to less trauma than were those sold to traders, but they nevertheless traveled to a distant and unfamiliar destination with only part of their community or kin network to support them. As their heavily loaded wagons pulled out of sight of the old home place in the East, migrating slaves realized that they had little chance of ever again seeing the people and homes they left behind.

SEPARATIONS CAUSED BY TRANSFERS

By the 1840s and 1850s Mississippi River cotton planters were expanding into the coastal parishes, establishing sugar plantations in parishes such as Terrebonne and St. Mary. Transfers of slaves between distant multiple holdings became increasingly common. Young males were frequently sent to the sugar parishes from the cotton districts. Their absences from the home plantation sometimes lasted only for a season, but occasionally the arrangement continued for years or became a permanent separation from families and friends.[18] Owners knew that hiring out and transfers of slaves were injurious to their family and community life. Only a few, however, based decisions on that knowledge. One who did was J. T. Jeter, who had plantations near New Orleans as well as in Pointe Coupee Parish. When he decided to move his residence to the Pointe Coupee Plantation, he deliberated over whether to transfer the New Orleans house servants. He knew that "they did not want to come" and to compel them "would make them dissatisfied and influence the others to be."[19] Several were married to slaves of other New Orleans owners, and their pain of separation would be acute. Finally, Jeter decided to take only the unmarried servants.

Separation of parents from their children of any age caused distress within the slave community.[20] Nevertheless, parents did not always protest the transfer of their children but might resign themselves to the separation if they thought it would better the child's condition in slavery. Such was the case on the Moore plantation in St. Martin Parish. Polly, the nine-year-old daughter of Prissy, a Moore family servant, was described by her mistress as a "light mulatto, not much fit for the field [but] . . . will in time I think do for the house." The child was sent to New Orleans from St. Martin Parish to "wait on and learn from Mrs. Randolph." Mrs. Moore expected Prissy to object to a long and perhaps permanent separation from Polly, but instead Prissy "said she would rather [Polly] should go then to stay in the cabin or go in the field."[21]

SEPARATIONS CAUSED BY
LOCAL AND REGIONAL SALES

Louisiana was a buying rather than a selling state. After a work force had stabilized, most owners did not usually sell workers unless they were unproductive, considered troublemakers or confirmed runaways, or in the case of a serious financial reversal. Private sales and local sheriff's sales or estate auctions did take place with regularity, but these sales did not involve as many family separations as did the interstate trade. I have perused thousands of bills of sales in parish courthouses relating to local buyers and sellers. Most involve the conveyance of small families or young solitary males and females between the ages of fifteen and twenty-five and records of children referred to as orphans.

The hard times of the early 1820s and the 1840s did compel many planters to mortgage their slaves and occasionally to sell a few to cover debts. Lewis Stirling instructed his son at Arbroath Plantation to turn ten slaves over to Mr. Lyons, who had just purchased them. Stirling added, "These negroes will probably be somewhat distressed at being sold and you must say what you can to reconcile them. Tell them (which is the fact) that I owed Mr. Lyons and had no other way of paying him."[22] Private sales, foreclosures, and sheriff's sales did not often divide nuclear family members, but they always separated the slaves from their community.[23]

Although they were exceptional, some Louisiana planters in every parish had no compunctions about breaking up families in local sales. Most commonly, they separated spouses and older children from their parent or parents, transactions that were entirely legal. And occasionally, children under ten were falsely represented as orphans and were sold apart from their mothers.[24] Another practice was to sell a woman, giving title to her alone, but allowing her to take with her an infant or small child. If she were bought in a large lot of slaves, the fact that she had the child at the time of the sale might go unnoticed for years. Meanwhile, the new owner would maintain the child and assume it was his property but had no legal claim to it. Eventually the original owner would appear to claim the working-age child or demand payment. Christopher Adams and Isaac Erwin of Iberville Parish were notorious for such activities, as well as misrepresenting slaves in sales, and both had the sale of a plantation and its stock of slaves annulled for such fraudulent practices.[25]

SEPARATIONS CAUSED BY ESTATE DIVISION

As was seen in the Oakland case study, estate division was a major cause for family disruptions among Louisiana slaves. One example, certainly not an isolated case, was that of slaves belonging to the estate of Alexander Stirling, a native of northern England and an early settler of Feliciana. Separations among his slave families were all the more regrettable because he sincerely wished for the families and community to remain intact as long as possible. In his 1806 will, Stirling carefully directed that his slaves should remain together until his youngest son was twenty-one. At that time, the slaves could be partitioned among his heirs but "without separating the Negro families without their consent."[26] Further, he provided for the immediate manumission of Katy [Caty], and when Stirling's son John reached his majority, Hercules and Terrence were also to be freed. Stirling died in 1809, and his estate went into probate in West Feliciana Parish. Katy was manumitted, and most of the other slaves were sent to a sugar plantation in St. Mary Parish, where their labor would accrue more profit for the estate. Stirling's youngest son came of age in 1818, allowing the delayed division to take place. Alexander Stirling, Jr., immediately took eight slaves as his share, including two teenaged children who were separated from their parents and siblings. Rather than drawing lots, the other heirs wanted the slaves sold at an estate sale so they could bid only on the most desirable workers. In one sale held in West Feliciana, nineteen slaves were sold, separating several children over age ten from their parents. In a second sale, held in St. Mary Parish, the remaining slaves of Stirling's estate were sold to a wide variety of Stirling relatives and local planters. Three of seven immediate families were separated. Between Alexander Stirling's death and the last estate sale, more than a dozen families were separated by partition or sale. These included the family of Hercules, whom Stirling had ordered manumitted when Stirling's youngest son reached his majority. When his owner died in 1809, Hercules had a wife, Madeline, and three children, Caesar, Mary, and Clary. Three more children were born to them before 1818, Betty, Harry, and Adam. Clary and Mary had died by 1818, but Caesar, now eighteen, was listed below his parents and young siblings. At the St. Mary probate sale in February 1819, Hercules, now free, was exempted, but his wife and three youngest children were sold to one planter and his oldest son to another. Without his family, Hercules's freedom must have seemed a hollow victory.[27]

The most usual division made in families by estate partition or probate sale was that of husbands or fathers from wives and children or of parents or a mother from children over age ten. An example of the latter was Milly, who headed a household on the Read plantation consisting of herself, three sons ranging in age from twelve to twenty, and a daughter-in-law. In her mistress's estate sale, Milly and her sons were sold to different owners, although the daughter-in-law remained with her husband.[28] Occasionally, in the estate's interest, a mother was illegally separated from a child under age ten. In such cases, the mother-child relationship was not mentioned on the partition records, although it was described on earlier inventories and appraisements. Such was the case of Charity, slave of Job Bass. After his wife's death, Bass retained Charity, but her eight-year-old son Winchester was awarded to another of his wife's heirs.[29]

The separation of wives and husbands or young women and their small children horrified critics of the slave system and often caused guilt and remorse among the owners, but the breaking up of old, established kinship groups was equally painful for members of the slave communities. The unusual slave community of sugar planter Philemon Nicholas Prevost in 1850 consisted primarily of three large matrifocal kinship groups. They were those of Chalinette, sixty, Adelaide, fifty, and Emerenthe, forty-five, and their respective children and grandchildren. Chalinette and her descendants were divided among three heirs after their owner's death; Adelaide and her extended family were distributed among two heirs; and Emerenthe was severed from all nine of her descendants, her family partitioned among five heirs.[30]

Owners knew that separating families through estate division was inhumane. Some tried to avoid it by meticulously delineating slave family relationships in letters to future heirs, enjoining them to respect the blood ties of slaves in any partitions. Rachel O'Connor wrote to her sister-in-law in great detail concerning the kinship lines of her slaves: "I send to you . . . a list of negroes names and the family they come of, which I pray you and your sons to take care of, for my sake after I am in my grave."[31] Others gave instructions in their wills. Catherine Turnbull of Solitude Plantation requested in her will that "my slaves be divided in that manner (equal parts, 6) as near as can be, without dividing families, which in no case is to be done if it can be avoided."[32] John Palfrey of St. Martin Parish wrote a will bequeathing a considerable estate to his sons but "requiring however that in case it should be necessary to effect a partition by means of a sale or by division into lots that my slaves be sold or disposed of by families so as not to separate parents from their children or children from their parents without their consent." He then gives an interesting definition of what constituted to him an inviolable slave family and what did not. "When the young people have families of their own," he explained, "I consider them as alienated from the Parent stock & forming a New Branch."[33]

Affluent heirs sometimes purchased portions of families that fell to other heirs or effected trades. Wealthy John Moore of St. Martinsville and his daughter Evelina S. Prescott of St. Landry Parish exchanged inherited slaves, and he paid the difference in their value "to prevent the separation of families."[34] It will be recalled that John Nathaniel Evans bought the wives and children of his slaves from heirs of his mother's estate. In many cases, however, heirs were not able or willing to make purchases or trades to keep families together. On 24 January 1861, young Kate Stone, daughter of a woman planter, wrote: "Other Pa only came on business and went back to Vicksburg carrying with him Ashburn's Negroes, who are to be divided out among the heirs. Separating the old family negroes who have lived and worked together for so many years is a great grief to them and a distress to us. I wish Mamma had been able to buy them all in and keep them here." On 27 January she wrote that her mother had drawn two slaves from the estate of her brother, and she also recorded the names of nine who were apportioned to other relatives. A favorite slave, Sydney, was drawn with her youngest children by Kate's aunt. Kate noted, "It is hard for Sydney and her older children to be separated. We are so sorry but cannot help her."[35]

OTHER MEANS OF SEPARATING SLAVE FAMILIES AND HOUSEHOLDS

Family members could be separated by a variety of other means, either permanently or for long enough periods to have serious effects on the family. These included gifts of slaves to the owner's children, grand-children, or other relatives or a long-term loan of a slave to a relative (especially common with house servants). In some cases, slave children were removed from their parental households although kept on the same plantation. As Dinah Watson explained, "My old missy done take me from my mammy when I's a small baby and raised me." In another case, his owner, who was also his father, took J. W. Terrill away from his slave mother when he was six weeks old, giving him first to the owner's mother, then to his sister. The boy was not allowed to interact in any way with his slave mother and her two children by a slave.[36] Children sometimes became household pets and were eventually trained to be house servants. But in Terrill's case, removing him from his mother's care was part of a series of sadistic abuses.

Ironically, the liberation of one member could break up a family. Often owners manumitted one member of a slave family, leaving the rest enslaved. The natural children of an owner and a slave woman were sometimes manumitted and sent north by their father, while the slave mother remained on the plantation. Or one member of a married couple was manumitted, causing the family to face a terrible decision. Would the manumitted spouse stay on the plantation with his or her family, free in name only? This was the choice Ben made on Petite Anse. In some cases, however, the manumitted individual left his family. Hiram Bradley, a slave of the Jeter family in Louisiana, was manumitted in 1859 and given a job as carriage driver with his previous owner's brother in Philadelphia. According to Annie Jeter, the owner's daughter, when Hiram left his wife in Louisiana, he promised to "save up and buy her." In 1861, she came to his former master seeking word of him, saying that "she had been faithful to him believing he would keep his promise."[37] He had by that time remarried in Philadelphia.

Slaves in Louisiana were separated from their families, households, kin, and community in a wide variety of ways, ranging from sales and migration to gifts, transfers, and even manumission. Families were vulnerable to breakup by other, more universal means as well—marital separation or divorce and, most commonly, the death of family members. Early death was the single greatest culprit in separating children from parents and husbands from wives, both among slaves and their owners.

The numerical incidence of slave family separations is still debated among historians, but perhaps the sheer numbers have been given too much importance. A single sale or partition involving the permanent separation of family members or even the rumor of one sent shock tremors throughout an entire slave community. Slaves reasoned that if their master allowed even one family to be separated, all were endangered.

LACK OF AUTONOMY

The deliberate separation of its members was the most ominous threat to the majority of slave families, but other, more subtle factors were also capable of destroying much of the unity and mutual dependency that slaves forged in their domestic organizations. Perhaps the most powerful threat of all was the absence of autonomy decreed by the slave system. One of the most perceptive works about slaves' lack of autonomy is John Boles's *Black Southerners*, even though the topic is treated briefly. Boles recognized that lack of autonomy was a critical factor in undermining individual, family, and community development among slaves, but he also pointed out an irony. As conditions for slaves generally improved in the nineteenth century over those of the eighteenth century, "now there was too much to be lost. Although the human desire for autonomy and freedom still burned in the breasts of peaceful slaves, sensible strategy cautioned against community-threatening actions."[38]

Restrictions on autonomous actions of Louisiana chattels were pervasive. Although not warranting great risk taking, each restriction whittled away at the integrity of the slaves' internal society. Every time an owner or overseer verbally or physically abused a member of the slave family or community who was powerless to react, the structure was undermined. Every time the community was forbidden to congregate for religious purposes, for a wedding, for a funeral, for recreation, or to settle an internal dispute, its authority was undermined. Every time an owner overruled a parent's order to a child, or interfered in a marriage, or arranged a match, the family was under attack. And every time a slave woman was violated by a white authority figure, the family and the community were also violated. Space does not permit further exploration of most of these abuses, but I will discuss the threat to the family provided by both forced and voluntary miscegenous relationships.

MISCEGENATION

No extended studies have been done on miscegenation involving Louisiana plantation slaves, although the mulatto concubines of New Orleans have been frequently alluded to in historical and literary sources. Such a study is beyond the scope of this work, but judging from Louisiana plantation records, recollections of former slaves, and especially court records, miscegenation involving white men and slave women was common. Miscegenous relationships between white women and slave men no doubt occurred in the Louisiana plantation country, but because of the powerful stigma attached to them, they were far less common and more carefully concealed.[39] The few cases I have encountered involved slave men and white women who were not of the planter class.

Most quantitative estimates for the incidence of miscegenation are based on the percentages of mulattoes in the slave population, generally drawn from the 1850 and 1860 census slave schedules, although quantitative evidence has also been extracted from ex-slave narratives. Historians from W. E. B. Du Bois to modern cliometricians have wrestled with these and other sources and have reached different conclusions. Fogel and Engerman's estimates in 1974 are the lowest. They suggested that in 1850 the proportion of mulattoes in the general slave population was from 4.5 to 7.7 percent and in 1860, 10 percent.[40] Gutman and Sutch find these estimates too low, but, accepting the 4.5 percent figure for the sake of illustration, they projected that slave women between the ages of fifteen and thirty had a 58 percent chance of being the object of a white man's sexual advances at some time. If they were attractive, the odds were considerably higher. Their findings correspond to comments made by a Louisiana planter that were recorded by Frederick Olmsted: "There is not a likely-looking black girl in this state that is not the concubine of a white man." Alton Moody estimated that about 24 percent of Orleans Parish slaves were mulattoes and that in parishes with smaller slaveholdings, such as Lafourche, it was about 26 percent. In the northern river parishes, however, only from 9 to 13 percent of the slaves were mulattoes. Du Bois's calculation that mulattoes made up from 13 to 15 percent of the general slave population was considered reasonable by Genovese, writing decades later.[41]

Recently, historians have picked up on Moody's finding that miscegenation was far more common in urban than in rural areas and on smallholdings with a lower black-to-white ratio than on large holdings with a high black-to-white ratio. Steckel's analysis of the 1860 slave schedules confirmed that one of ten slave children was a mulatto and that the percentages of mulatto children were highest on smallholdings in urban settings and lowest on large but isolated rural plantations with relatively few whites and a large slave population. Stephen C. Crawford's analysis of ex-slave narratives similarly concluded that a higher percentage of mulattoes existed on small plantations than on large ones. He also found that at least one in six female-headed single-parent households contained mulatto children and that house servants were much more likely to bear children by a white man than were field slaves.[42]

Impressionistic sources as well suggest that miscegenation was common in Louisiana. Among owners in their youth and unmarried planters the practice was so widespread as to be almost expected. Chris Franklin recalled that "dey lots of places where de young massas has heirs by nigger gals," and Gabriel Gilbert stated that "old massa have sev'ral boys. Dey went after some of de slave gals. Dey have chillen by dem. Dem gals have dere cabins and dere chillen, what am half white."[43] It was a brutal rite of passage for planter-class youth to sneak down to the quarters and compel slave girls to have sex, an event fraught with sexual excitement and, possibly, danger, for irate slave husbands, lovers, or fathers occasionally did take reprisals. Irritating one's own papa or uncle was part of the vicious ritual as well. In 1838, planter Bennet Barrow noted that he had discovered his nephew in the quarter and mused on a proper punishment. Local white youths often audaciously prowled the quarters of plantations other than their own, looking for slave women, or bribed or coerced slaves into serving as procurers. In 1837, the same planter had commented in his journal that "white men sending for some of my women by one of my boys 'one-eyed Sam'—a load of buck shot will be the dose if I can . . . find them." He further noted that he held a "general whipping frolick."[44] One-eyed Sam was no doubt one of the objects.

A habit accepted if not openly condoned in planter society as part of the excesses of youth was expected to be set aside when the young men married. Former concubines were often allowed to marry slave husbands. Victor Duhon, the light-skinned, blue-eyed offspring of a planter father and a slave mother, recalled that after his father's marriage, his mother married a slave from a neighboring plantation and had several children with him.[45]

Treatment of former concubines differed from owner to owner, plantation to plantation. Some were sold after the master's marriage, but not always. On the Broussard plantation, according to former slave Gabriel Gilbert, "after a while dem boys marry. But dey allus treat dey chillen by de

slave womens good." A case in point is George Kenner of Ashland Plantation. His long relationship with a slave woman while he was a bachelor
produced seven children. When he married, he sent his former concubine
to St. Louis, Missouri, along with the four youngest children, and provided
for them there. Kenner died unexpectedly without having legally manumitted his black family. His former mistress and children in St. Louis
spent many years negotiating with the Kenner family, both in and out of
the courts, attempting to reclaim the older children remaining in Louisiana.[46]

Whether the sexual relationship between a white man and a slave
woman was casual or long-lasting, characterized by affection or loathing,
each relationship was deeply threatening and disturbing to the slave community, acting as a constant reminder that the community could not
protect its daughters, wives, and mothers. The slave community and its
individual members responded with a low, simmering rage that occasionally blazed into verbal or physical confrontations. At Rosedown, a protective older slave woman, Sylpha, after repeatedly arguing with the overseer
over his "familiarity" with slave girls, took her complaint to the owner.[47]
Eben, distraught over discovering his future wife having sex with the
overseer, angrily informed both the owner and the overseer's wife.[48] Even
though such conduct was considered grounds for dismissal, overseers
frequently used their power over their slave charges to force sexual favors.[49]

For a slave woman or her defenders to resist an overseer carried great
risks. To refuse or challenge an owner was almost unthinkably hazardous.
Therefore, slave communities usually lived with the shameful knowledge
that they could not protect their members from sexual as well as economic
exploitation by whites. A former slave in Louisiana recalled a slave husband's helplessness when a white man appeared at his cabin to have sex
with his wife, ordering him out. The husband had "to go outside and wait
'til he do what he want to do." The former slave recalling the incident sadly
observed that the husband had no real choice; he "couldn't do nothin 'bout
it."[50] Pushed beyond endurance, slave men and women did sometimes
spontaneously fight back against the outrages to their persons and their
families, usually with tragic consequences for them. A slave man in Concordia Parish who objected to his owner "taking" his wife was tied up by
his thumbs and whipped to death by an overzealous overseer.[51] Some men
might have deliberately sought wives off the plantation to avoid the possi-

ble trauma of watching their mates submit to beatings or knowing of their rape.[52] The burden of mutely and passively witnessing such atrocities damaged slave morale collectively as well as individually. The devastating effects of a miscegenous relationship on a small community of slaves is recounted by Solomon Northup in his autobiography. He and his fellow slaves were supportive but helpless as they observed the slow destruction of a spirited young woman caught between her master's lust and her mistress's jealousy.[53] Likewise, parents lived with the constant fear that their daughters would catch the eye of a white man.

Miscegenation affected all the slave principals involved. Slave males, frustrated and angry, were the most likely to inform or to take physical action against white rapists. The most pervasive bitterness, however, was felt by the slave women, forced into submission and often irrationally blamed by their white mistresses or even their own slave husbands or lovers.[54] That bitterness can be seen in the case of Melissa, forced to become her master's concubine while still a very young girl. She subsequently bore him two children, Eli and Anna, whom she gave away after emancipation "because they reminded her of him."[55]

The children produced by miscegenous relationships were also victims. Owner-fathers' guilt or indifference or the jealousy of their wives or children sometimes prompted them to abuse or even sell their slave children and concubines. J. W. Terrill was a slave born to a white father and a slave mother in De Soto Parish. Shortly after his birth, Terrill's father took him away from his mother but required her to have sex with him after she took a slave husband. The boy's life was made a living hell with constant beatings. In addition, his father forced J. W. to "wear a bell . . . strapped 'round my shoulders . . . bout three feet from my head in a steel frame. That was my punishment for bein' born into the world a son of a white man and my mammy a negro slave." The child wore the bell night and day until he was seventeen; his father's sister removed it when his father died.[56] Another case was that of the slave child Anna and her mother, who were starved and beaten—and Anna nearly blinded—by their owner and Anna's father, Tom Bias.[57]

In these cases, the mulatto children born of miscegenous relationships were rejected by one or both of their parents. In all cases, the offspring occupied a very shaky and confusing position. As former slave Agatha

Babino put it, "Some of de masters had chillen by dey slaves. Some of 'em sold dere chillen and some sot 'em free."[58]

Guilt, concern that children of their blood were destined to a lifetime of servitude, and sometimes genuine affection moved many Louisiana masters who fathered slave children to seek their emancipation.[59] The dilemma was especially taxing for white fathers who had children enslaved by others—and compounded if the white father was not wealthy. Some of these men made long-term arrangements, paying the owner of their child a token sum at its birth but allowing the owner the labor of the child until it was grown.[60] William Boyce, on his deathbed, wrote a will instructing that his property be used to buy and emancipate his two natural children, Mag and Louisa, slaves of Colonel Winfrey Lockett. Boyce's estate, valued at only $840, was insufficient, and there is no evidence that the children were ever purchased by Boyce's family or emancipated.[61]

It is because of their desire to emancipate and provide for their slave children that we know how common miscegenous relationships were among the planter gentry in Louisiana. Almost every major planter family had at least one member whose alliance with a slave woman became a subject of court records. Two prominent examples are those of William Weeks, whose family had plantations in West Feliciana, St. Mary, and St. Martin parishes, and John Turnbull, one of the West Feliciana Turnbulls of Rosedown and Solitude fame.

William Weeks, an Englishman by birth, in his will of 2 October 1817 emancipated his "three mulatto slaves . . . Edward Wilson Curtis, Mary Ann Curtis, and William Curtis, children of Anne Marie Curtis." He provided money for their support and education in Cincinnati, Ohio. The children's mother was also emancipated, in a separate document, but she remained in West Feliciana until her death in 1828, probably without ever seeing her children again after their departure for the North with Weeks's agent, Joseph Hodgson. It appears that until his death in 1834, David Weeks, William Weeks's son, did all he could to honor his father's wishes in regard to the children. But after David Weeks's death, his heirs put up a strenuous legal battle to set aside the will.[62]

Likewise, John Turnbull's miscegenous relationship is revealed in the legal protests of angry relatives. In his 1855 will, Turnbull acknowledged that he had five children by the slave woman Rachel, aged twenty-three. He instructed that they be emancipated and receive one-third of his estate, which was more than $80,000. Turnbull died the next year, and relatives battled all the way to the state supreme court to block both the emancipation and the legacy. They were unsuccessful in setting aside the manumissions, but they did succeed in depriving Rachel and her children of most of their intended inheritance.[63]

Sale or the threat of sale, physical abuse, and restrictions or intrusions into almost all areas of human activity, even the most intimate, posed powerful threats to the psychological health of slaves as individuals and as domestic groups. To combat such humiliating, demeaning, and spirit-crushing assaults, slaves found resources in their own culture. Humor, storytelling, and music were exceedingly important, but only family and kinship (especially marriage and parenting) and religion will be discussed.

MARRIAGE

Earlier chapters have described the changes and continuities in Louisiana slaves' domestic organizations. It was shown that slave families and households took many forms in Louisiana, depending on circumstances and developmental cycles, but most were built around a conjugal unit—either that of a parent and child or a husband and wife. Slaves accepted families headed by unmarried parents more readily than did their white contemporaries, but they, too, preferred a family unit consisting of both parents and their children. And they put great stock in marriage.

Slave marriage presented in microcosm much of the ambiguity of the slave's status in southern society. On one hand, owners allowed, sanctioned, and sometimes encouraged slaves to marry (they were similarly ambiguous about slaves as parents). On the other hand, no southern state, including Louisiana, recognized the legality of slave marriages or the legitimacy of offspring. In some parts of the state, owners allowed ministers or priests to perform slave marriage ceremonies (and baptisms), and by the 1850s most owners had probably given in to their slaves' preference for a "Scripture wedding" rather than a simple broom-jumping ritual.[64] Even so, the only legitimacy slave marriages had was derived from their recognition by the owner and the slave community.

Owners initiated some slave marriages in Louisiana, but they usually yielded if the slaves involved objected strongly. The prevailing pattern was for the initiative to rest with the slaves, but the owner's approval was required before the marriage could take place. Slaves often conducted courtships without their owners' knowledge or approval, but consent was necessary for the formal setting up of households or the recognition of the couple as a marital unit.[65] Some former slaves indicated that parental consent was sometimes required as well. In most cases, owners quickly granted permission.[66] William Minor, however, absentee owner of plantations in Ascension and Terrebonne parishes, required the "posting of banns," so to speak. Among his list of regulations was that "marriages must not take place until after a month's notice of the intention to be given by parties."[67]

Owners did not always grant permission to marry. Freedman Willie Williams recalled that "some not 'lowed to git married."[68] An example is the case of the ill-fated courtship of Sam and "Mrs. Irwins Charlotte," drawn from a planter family's correspondence: "About two weeks ago Sam came out here to ask my leave to marry Mrs. Irwins Charlotte. I told him no that he need not think taking a step of that kind would prevent my sending him . . . I went in and told Charlotte that Sam had to go to you this winter. I endeavored to shame her, but she thought herself young enough for him. Her mistress told her that she would sell her if she took Sam. I have not seen him since."[69]

Even though their marriages had no legal basis, most Louisiana slaves entered into their unions with solemnity and joy. When weddings were allowed, they became community observances and social occasions rivaled only by Christmas and end-of-harvest celebrations. As one mistress observed, "anything like a wedding sets them crazy."[70] Louisiana slaves were not always permitted to exercise their predilections for ceremonies commemorating important individual and community events such as marriages. When a wedding ceremony and celebration were not permitted, the lack was sorely felt by the slave community, which made careful distinction between a marriage and a wedding. A Vermilion Parish former slave stated that on his plantation no "weddin' 'lowed. Dey ju' gits married."[71] One could enter into a marriage without a wedding ceremony, just as one could be buried without a funeral, but neither was considered proper by Louisiana slaves. Owners knew that their slaves desperately sought legal and religious sanction for their marriages and would occasionally indulge their slaves, engaging or allowing priests or ministers to perform a ceremony. Such ceremonies involved at the least a reading of some Scripture and an appearance of recording the marriage. The great majority of slave weddings took place on plantations, but some were performed in white churches, presided over by white ministers.[72] A few owners attempted to give their slaves the assurance that their marriages were being legally contracted, calling in justices of the peace or local judges to perform the ceremonies. The slaves were rarely fooled.[73]

Slaves were especially eager to have their marriages recorded "in the book," meaning a plantation ledger, journal, or day book kept by the owner or overseer. Unfortunately, few Louisiana owners systematically recorded marriages, and even births and deaths were noted irregularly. Because of this laxity, valuable information concerning slave marriages is either lost or difficult to retrieve. When slave weddings were noted, they were generally mentioned in passing in a planter's or overseer's journal as part of a normal daily entry. In some of the Catholic parishes of south Louisiana priests recorded slave marriages, but they did not do so consistently.[74] Even though planters, priests, and ministers were usually neglectful in recording slave marriages, the emphasis placed by slaves on having their names put "in the book" as a married couple illustrates their concern about obtaining legitimacy for their matches, a concern that continued into freedom.

Almost as important to Louisiana slaves as the reading of Scripture and the recording of their ceremonies in a book was participation by the slave community, both as witnesses at the ceremony and as celebrants at a dinner and dance afterward. The desire for communal wedding celebrations went deeper than simply an understandable excuse for a holiday, special foods, and recreation. Rooted in the social organization of Africa, the communal celebration was a vital facet of the slaves' search for marital validation, for in such celebrations, the married couple received the ritual sanction and support of the society.[75]

Longevity of Marriages Because conditions in Louisiana were so unhealthy, the prognosis for a long married life was not good for either white or black couples. Slave mortality was even higher than that for whites, but nevertheless, the duration of slave marriages in Louisiana appears to have been about the same as for those in the white population. Of the slave marriages that were dissolved, a small minority were terminated by the slaves themselves and a slightly larger percentage by the actions of the owner or his heirs, but by far the majority ended with the death of a spouse.[76]

Off-Plantation Marriages Off-plantation marriages present a problem for household analysis of slave populations. It is very difficult to determine their frequency or assess what they meant in terms of functional families. If visits from a husband or father were brief and infrequent, the female-headed single-parent household was just that, even if the woman head of household had a husband on another plantation. This is especially true if the husband or father was unavailable to assist the family with day-to-day problems as well as crises. Many of the classic functions associated with marriage and parenthood were compromised by enslavement; separate residency and frequent absenteeism added other serious limitations. In my analysis, I have generally not interpreted divided families as operating household units unless I had some evidence that they functioned as families on a regular basis.

It is difficult to determine how common off-plantation marriages were in Louisiana or elsewhere. Blassingame held that they were common, and Crawford's and Paul Escott's analyses of the ex-slave narratives concur.[77] I have found little evidence that they were common in Louisiana except on smallholdings, where marriage choices were so limited as to convince owners that the merits outweighed the risks. Owners of male slaves on holdings of any size accrued little advantage from such marriages, for the slave husbands tended to be restless and dissatisfied at home and any offspring brought no financial benefit. Therefore, many slaveholders—at least those whose papers have survived—had either formal or informal proscriptions against such matches. Admittedly, these were usually large holders.[78]

Even the slaves involved in such alliances often found off-plantation marriages difficult to maintain. Solomon Northup related that "Uncle Abram's wife lived seven miles from Epps'. . . . He had permission to visit her once a fortnight, but . . . truth to say, he had latterly well nigh forgotten her." Especially after patrols became stricter and more pervasive following Nat Turner's 1831 insurrection, off-plantation marital or courting visits were risky, even dangerous. Planter's wife Priscilla Bond recorded in her diary that "the Negro man who has been staying in the yard a good deal, and who I suspect was Minty's beau, was taken out of the kitchen last night . . . and shot so dreadfully in the face that they say he must die. I suppose the men [a neighborhood patrol] were drunk. We had never seen anything amiss with 'Dave' and allowed him to stay here at nights." In a similar incident, a slave of Alfred Dusperier was shot and killed by a slave patrol near New Iberia when his startled, unbroken horse galloped after the patrollers shouted at the slave to stop. The man was on the way to visit his wife on the Dubuclet place, with his master's "full assent and standing permission."[79]

Marital Separations Historians continue to differ concerning the incidence of marital and familial separations resulting from the slave trade. Blassingame was convinced that many marriages were broken through sale. I agree that the interstate trade to the lower South severed many young adults from their spouses and other family members. Yet current historical opinion tends to concur with evidence I found in Louisiana suggesting that stationary owners dissolved few slave marriages.[80] In the relatively small number of cases in which owners did separate spouses, they rarely did so simply for financial advantage. More often, a husband was sold away from his wife or family as a punishment for independent or disobedient behavior—and to impress the rest of the community with the control the master had over their lives.

Marital Discord and Devotion Likewise, my findings confirm that slave marriages were not often terminated through separation or divorce, either at the instigation of the owner or the slave couples. Nevertheless, one should not assume that slave marriages were unusually blissful. As much marital discord existed among slaves as among their free contemporaries— possibly more, given the stress of their lives. References to marital squabbles are frequent in both white and black sources. The owner of Airlie Plantation recorded on 13 July 1862 that he "punished Stephen for mistreating his wife." Similarly, Bennet Barrow of Highland Plantation recorded in 1838 that "Hemps gave his wife Hetty a light cut or two & then locked her up to prevent her going to the Frollick." And on another occasion Barrow reported that his slave Jack had whipped his wife, Lize, then escaped to the woods.[81] The frequency of reports of domestic violence in planters' records involving slave men against their wives suggests that a pattern usually attributed to the black male's frustrations experienced under the debilitating systems of tenancy and segregation might have been present during slavery as well. In both cases, the source of the male's family-directed violence was probably the same—an overwhelming sense of powerlessness and impotence, which threatened the male's concept of his manhood and fatherhood. Under such pressures, a slave man's attempt to assert dominance and authority, at least in his own family, occasionally took the distorted form of familial abuse. Immediately after emancipation, wives frequently reported abusive husbands to the provost marshal's office, but couples rarely reported on each other to the master during slavery. This was in part because they resented their owners' paternalistic meddling in their marriages and parenting functions. They feared as well that their spouses would receive excessive punishment. Ellen Betts, a slave near Opelousas, recalled the time that Jim, Rachel's husband, "git mad and hit her over de head with de poker. A big knot raise up on Aunt Rachel's head and when Marse 'quire 'bout it, she say she done bump de head. She doesn't tell on Uncle Jim or Marse sho' beat him."[82]

Evidence of marital friction is, however, counterbalanced by more numerous reports and expressions of fidelity, affection, and devotion among slave married couples. Prince, a hired slave who married Little Emmeline, a servant for the family that had hired him, begged his employer to purchase him so that he and Emmeline could remain together.[83] When he later joined the Yankee troops, she loyally followed. Separated spouses often ran away to search for their wives or husbands, and married runaways frequently risked recapture by returning to the plantation to see their mates. As was demonstrated earlier, husbands sometimes risked serious punishment and even death in defense of their wives. Planters' correspondence and journals frequently mentioned the tender nursing that slave wives provided their sick and dying spouses. Owners also described the lengths to which couples would go to avoid even temporary separations. For example, in 1863 a refugee planter wrote his mother on the home plantation that the men, whom he had hired out to the Confederate saltworks, walked sixteen miles each way to be with their wives on Saturdays.[84]

Age Differences between Spouses An additional topic of interest to historians of slave families is the age difference between married slaves. Family historians assume that individuals tend to marry people near their own age in societies in which sufficient and appropriate potential partners are available. My findings concerning age spans between spouses at Oakland, Petite Anse, and Tiger Island were generally confirmed in my larger study of 510 couples residing on nineteen Louisiana plantations between 1840 and 1865.[85] That study showed a mean age difference between spouses of seven years, close to that in the case studies. In cases of older husbands, more than 64 percent were older by less than ten years, but 17 percent of the cases involved marriages in which husbands were more than fifteen years older than their wives. In cases of older wives, 9 percent involved couples with more than a fifteen-year age difference, and wives were more than ten years older than their husbands in more than one-fourth of the cases.

The sample included both large and smallholdings, but most units contained fifty or more slaves. The greatest age differences between spouses appeared in smallholdings or in large holdings with serious gender imbalances. This pattern was also found in the case studies, at Tiger Island, and on other plantations that were not in the sample.[86]

In general, when a community exhibited a pattern of large age differences, other signs of incongruence such as age or gender imbalances were also present. But even on the most stable and mature plantations, a few instances of large age differences were present, indicating that no cultural stigma was attached to matches in which either husbands or wives were older.

Age at First Marriage Age at first marriage differed widely from plantation to plantation, especially according to where individual plantations were in the developmental cycle. The qualitative sources support the idea that the internal code of the slave quarter discouraged early marriages for women, although demographic factors might intercede. One former slave summed up a common attitude: "Dem's moral times. A gal's 21 'fore she marry. They didn't go wanderin' 'round all hours. They mammies knowed where they was."[87]

BIRTH AND PARENTING

Giving birth was hazardous for slave mothers (and white mothers) in nineteenth-century Louisiana. Slave women whispered among themselves that "when a 'omen was a bornin' a chile . . . death wen' roun' her bed seven times a studyin' whether he'd take her or not." Infant mortality was shockingly high, even more so among slaves than whites. Because of the dangers and because reproduction greatly benefited owners, women were usually given better than usual care during pregnancy, birth, and nursing. There are notable exceptions. One former slave recalled that when an overseer wanted to whip a pregnant woman, "he had a hold dug . . . an' made her lay acrost it an' her han's and foots were tied so she had to submit quiet like to the beatin'."[88] Nineteenth-century planters claimed that this common practice of burying the belly of a pregnant slave in the ground to protect the fetus while she was lashed originated with the French colonists.[89] Even slaves in the late stages of pregnancy were sometimes severely beaten, as a former slave related. She told of witnessing a woman "about to give birth" who was sold. She was instructed to follow her new master but was unable or unwilling to do so. The former slave observed, "For that she was given 150 lashes."[90]

Despite the hazards, slaves looked forward to having children and viewed them as a source of pride and pleasure. Charges of parental indifference, neglect, abuse, and even infanticide were occasionally made against Louisiana slave mothers and fathers, but the vast majority appear to be groundless assertions reflecting the owners' prejudice or medical ignorance.[91]

Naming Slave parents first demonstrated pride in their children in the names they chose. Naming was of great significance in African societies, and African Americans also sought to choose names for their infants. Herbert Gutman, Cheryll Cody, John Boles, and others have determined that naming was one way that slaves expressed their respect for kinship ties and cultural continuity. As in so many other areas of their lives, bondage sometimes prevented slaves from exercising this cultural proclivity, and a variety of persons other than parents often named slave infants. Owners of small to medium-sized holdings often took a personal interest in individual births and named the infants. Andrew Durnford noted in his journal at St. Rosalie the births of two infants on 17 July 1862. Hanah's child, he wrote, was "born this day at 1 o'clock in the morning and named by me Alexis." Three hours later, Maria gave birth. Perhaps to reward himself for staying up all night for the deliveries, Durnford named that child Andrew.[92] Overseers, too, named slave infants, though less frequently than owners.

One wrote that "Grace Nott has twins last night. I call them Peter and Grace after their mother and father."[93] In naming them for their parents, he was probably acceding to the parents' expressed wishes, however, for slaves often named their children for family members.

Although difficult to prove, it is likely that the majority of Louisiana infants were named by their own families. Many were named for parents, grandparents, other kin, valued friends, and occasionally for the state of the parents' birth.[94] Female children were named for relatives almost as often as were males. Maria, daughter of Maria, might be called either Little Maria or Maria, Jr. A grandchild namesake was also referred to as junior. To cite just a few examples, on W. P. Welham's Homestead Plantation in 1860, Washington and Lucretia's daughter was named Lucretia, Jr.; among the "orphans of Victoire" was Victor; and Southern and his wife, Maria, named their young son Southern. Nicholas Loisel's 1857 slave community contained Auguste and his son Auguste, as well as Absolom and his son Absolom. And on John Wilkins's plantation in 1853, the youngest of seventy-year-old Dennis's children (by his forty-year-old wife) was two-year-old Dennis. On Calvin Routh's place, the nine-person household headed by sixty-year-old single mother Cynthia included her granddaughter Cynthia Ann.[95] Perhaps as a demonstration of control, some owners forbade slaves to name their own children; this was especially common with house servants, in whose affairs owners took a particular interest. Slaves resented this usurpation of parental prerogative and sometimes gave their children secret, "basket" names.[96]

Mothers' Age at First Birth and Seasonality of Births Two additional areas of interest to students of slavery are ages of mothers at first birth and seasonality of slave births. No systematic study has been made of ages at first birth on Louisiana plantations, although I have collected reliable data to do so. Preliminary examination of those records suggests that the mean age of mothers at first birth on sixteen plantations was nineteen to twenty, higher than Gutman's estimate of eighteen but lower than Steckel's findings; I suspect that the mean ages varied on the same plantation, over time, according to the developmental cycle and the general degree of stability the society had attained.[97]

To study seasonality of births, I compiled a sample of 989 well-documented slave births from fifteen plantations on which births were recorded from 1822 through 1861. The highest number of births occurred, in order, in August, July, and September, the lowest number in November, December, and February. Assuming a nine-month pregnancy, the largest number of conceptions occurred, in order, in December, November, and January. The lowest number of conceptions occurred in March and the second lowest number in June. About the same number of conceptions occurred in the other months. The findings are entirely consistent with what is expected in an agricultural society. End-of-harvest celebrations and work lulls fell between November and mid-January on both cotton and sugar plantations. Slaves not only had more opportunity for socializing and intimacy during these periods, they were more rested and relaxed, better fed, and less subject to debilitating fevers. November was a labor-intensive period in the sugar parishes, but the long night watches involved considerable socializing and were eagerly anticipated by the younger slaves as opportunities for courting. March and June were very busy months in cotton and sugar cultivation, and August was also busy, exhausting, and often unhealthy for workers. It is logical that rates of conception were low in these months.[98] Some historians of the family allege that markedly seasonal patterns in conceptions indicate a low degree of affection in marriage, that seasonal sex was unspontaneous and primarily for procreation rather than for pleasure or as an expression of love. This theory seems a bit simplistic and does not take into consideration fertility problems, work patterns, health, and numerous other variables.[99]

Parental Functions As was true of marriage among slaves, many classical functions of parenting were preempted by owners. Parental functions such as the providing of food, shelter, and clothing of children were generally fulfilled by owners. These preemptions, however, usually did not lessen slave children's respect for their parents. The children knew no other system, and they observed their parents growing the crops that might feed or clothe them, spinning and weaving cloth, and preparing at least part of the meals they consumed. The fact was not lost on slaves that their own labor, directly or indirectly, supplied the means for their own support as well as that of their owners.

The real sense of family among Louisiana slaves did not come from owners, law, the church, or other external sources. Families and households gained their legitimacy from the slave community's recognition of them as units of mutual affection and assistance. If parents—single or married—conducted themselves in accordance with the values of the slave community regarding the understood privileges and responsibilities of parenthood, they, with their children, were respected as a family. As such, they were entitled to community support in their parenting, as expressed by Tennessee Johnson, former slave of the Golden Grove Plantation in eastern Louisiana: "Dey do all dey can to keep de young people out o' trouble, but if dey get into trouble, dere's a place in de quarter de meet an' dey talk it over. One say 'yo' boy do dis, or yo' girl do dat',' and dey help to get dem out o' trouble fo' dey is agreeable famblies an' dey is restrict. . . . Dey would whip each other's children too. I sure wish I was a man when ole Aunt Jane, she ketch me doin' wrong!"[100]

Slave parents attempted to instill their society's values in their children. As Gracie Stafford, slave on Myrtle Grove Plantation in St. James Parish, observed, "When I was a growin' up, we wus taught jus' lak' white folks to keep our knees together an' our dresses down an' never to cross our legs. An' we wore long dresses, too, but folks had raisin's then."[101] Another former slave reiterated the seriousness with which parents took their responsibilities. He said that young courting couples were often chaperoned by the father. "He sit . . . de boy in one corner an' de girl she sit in dis corner, fo' de paw don' want her thrown back on de fambly."[102] Some students of the black family believe that these characteristics are African in origin and have continued in the modern era.[103]

Their dependent status limited the degree of protection that slave parents could provide their offspring. Nevertheless, they defended them as best they could, often at great risk to themselves. One former slave recalled that as a child she had reacted angrily when slapped by her young mistress. The owner ordered that the child be whipped for not quietly submitting to punishment. But as Agatha Babino stated, "My ma say for her not to beat me, she take de beating. So dey beat my ma."[104] Another former slave related that, as she, her sister, and their parents returned from an un-authorized prayer meeting in the woods, they encountered a patrol with dogs. The parents hid the trembling girls and put themselves at risk by luring the patrol after them.[105] Court records tell the story of Luben, a young slave boy who was maliciously shot by a white man. The seriously wounded boy somehow made it to his father, who personally confronted his son's assailant. A major tragedy was averted, the boy recovered, and the white man was brought up on charges for the unprovoked assault—all unusual outcomes in such incidents. It is significant that neither the injured boy nor the father went first to the owner for redress. Without thinking, they automatically took actions consistent with being a family, responsible for each other.[106]

Whites often commented on the depth of parental love among slaves. One owner wrote that he did not sell a young runaway only because the youth's "father & mother are both excellent creatures & so on his whole family—his being sold would . . . give them great trouble."[107] Owners tended to comment on their slaves' familial affections and loyalties only when they were observed in crises so many of the references are to slaves' responses to the illness or death of a family member. Owner Ellen Mc-Collam wrote that she "felt very sorry for Davy and Maria," who were deeply mourning the death of a son who had drowned in a drainage ditch in the quarters.[108] Another owner's sight of a mother tenderly nursing her dying infant caused her to "sincerely Lament its poor Mothers distress."[109] Kate Stone, in northeastern Louisiana, commented on the death of the little daughter of slave woman Malona, "This is the third child the mother has lost since Mama bought her, and she seems devotedly attached to her babies. This is her last child."[110] Not surprisingly, owners cast slave familial concern in their own white mold. Bennet Barrow, lamenting the death of one of his slaves, called him "one of the best negroes I ever saw or knew, to his family as a white person."[111]

Whites not only recognized the depth of slaves' loyalties and affection to family members, they were willing to use them as a means of control. Often the mere threat of harm to a mate, parent, or child was sufficient to ensure obedience. Frederick Law Olmsted talked to a slaveowner on the way from Bayou Sara, Louisiana, to Woodville, Mississippi. The planter, tired of his worn-out cotton land, wanted to relocate in Texas, but he was concerned about the security of slave property so close to Mexico. He mused to Olmsted, "Only way is, to have young ones there and keep their mothers here, eh? Negroes have such attachments you know . . . don't you think that would fix 'em, eh?"[112]

Two other exchanges reveal the depth of slave familial attachment and loyalties, especially between parents and children. Both took place in the context of the Federal invasion of the Teche country in 1863. An officer recalled that as the Union troops passed through, slaves "crowded the highway to see us," and he noticed in particular a very old man among the clapping, praying, singing group. "Uncle," the officer said, "freedom will do you no good; for you are just on the edge of the grave." The elderly slave agreed that he would not live to enjoy much of freedom, but he rejoiced nevertheless because "I've got my boys; and I bless you all, kase you give 'em free." The final illustration is from the same period. The Federal troops, badly in need of fresh mounts, sought to confiscate the horses that hastily retreating planters had hidden in the woods and canebrakes under the care of their most trusted slaves. Forty-five-year-old Jean was one of these trusted slaves. He admitted that he had been well treated by his owners and was considered entirely loyal and trustworthy by them. Yet he readily revealed the horses' whereabouts. A curious officer asked Jean why he was so willing to betray his owners' trust. Jean explained that "in these hard times" he "trembled lest some day he should go home, and find one of his little ones gone or his wife sold."[113] His first and foremost loyalty was to his family, not his owner, no matter how beneficent. And Jean believed his family's best interest was served by allying himself with the Federal troops, whom he viewed as liberators.

The mutual devotion displayed within the slave parent-child relationship has been most often noted in the literature of slavery, but ties among siblings were also very close. In Louisiana, these ties may have been intensified because of the unusually high mortality rates, which characteristically robbed slave children of at least one parent and resulted in older siblings often raising the youngest children. One former slave recalled that after her mother's death, an older sister breast-fed her as an infant and reared her to adulthood.[114] The affection and mutual dependency of slave siblings was not confined to the years of childhood. The most common form of non-nuclear households among Louisiana slaves was those composed of siblings living together, and the most common form of extended family households was that of families having in their households a brother or sister of one of the spouses, an indication of the close ties between siblings in need. There are many examples of sibling devotion among grown slaves. A Louisiana slave who had escaped and joined the Union army made his way to Texas to get his widowed sister and her children away from their master.[115] And a young man separated from his siblings by his owner's migration to Louisiana sent a pathetic message to his young master in school in the town of the former habitation, pleading for word of his siblings: "[Brooks] wishes you to see his brother and say to him that he almost thinks of him as a stranger as it has been almost eight years and he has never written to him to let him know where and how his brothers or sisters are."[116] Sometimes sibling devotion was sorely tested, as when Hector, a rebellious slave on the Grand Cote Plantation, convinced his sister to hide a gourd of powder for the gun he had stolen under her bed, implicating them both.[117]

KINSHIP

The question of kinship among slaves is a thorny one. Almost all who are familiar with slave sources suspect that kinship exerted a powerful influence within the slave community during the mature stages in which it was well developed. But concrete proof is extremely difficult to obtain. In this book I have traced kin groups, and I have argued that extensive kinship was one indicator of stability in slave communities. The case studies demonstrated the high regard in which kin were held by Oakland, Petite Anse, and Tiger Island slaves, and I have indicated that this is an area of great importance for future students of slavery. Beyond that, it is hard to tread with sureness. Of all the various domestic organizations, kinship is the most difficult to delineate, for kinship ties beyond the family are almost never systematically recorded and defined in slave documents. Kinship must be painstakingly and often incompletely retrieved from reconstituted or traced families. This is rarely possible for entire communities over substantial periods. Perhaps the best efforts have been those of Cheryll Cody in her reconstructions for the Ball Plantation and of Stirling slaves in Herbert Gutman's *Black Family*.[118]

Despite the problems in describing kinship in slave societies, one senses that it was critical in providing slaves with support, security, and a sense of belonging during life-course transitions, at crucial turning points, and in periods of crisis. These characteristics are well documented for the decades after emancipation. But during slavery, precisely how this aid was rendered is unplotted. How much did slaves depend on kin rather than friends for assistance—and which kin? Did gender make much difference in the kin slaves identified with or the degree to which kinship mattered on a day-to-day basis? Was there a tendency for male slaves to identify only or more strongly with male kin or with the father's kinship line? Was lineal kinship more important than lateral kinship?

Kinship among slaves is not systematically studied in this book, nor is it adequately studied in any work on slavery of which I am aware, although important beginnings have been made by Gutman, Cody, and others. It is a fruitful, promising area, and much remains to be done, especially regarding the functions rather than the forms of slave kinship over time. For example, it is possible that black kinship was more important after the Civil War because former slaves were free to create their own domestic forms, their basic physical needs were no longer supplied by owners and they were therefore more dependent on each other, they no longer had a geographic focus for their community and kin interaction and therefore had to find other means to assure its continuance, and they encountered virulent race prejudice that encouraged them to bind together in supportive units.

The task of retrieving and defining slave kinship is formidable because slaves, lacking the ability to hold and bequeath property, have not left the most useful quantifiable records for determining close ties with kin outside the immediate family. John Crowley's significant work on southern Anglo-American kinship, however, does have some applications to slaves as well. Nineteenth-century African-American kinship, like Anglo-American kinship, is cognatic—that is, kinship is determined by descent from both males and females. Descent is therefore bilateral, as opposed to unilineal. As Crowley explains, "Kinship is a type of ascribed status; principles of descent and marriage establish obligations. The parent through whom descent is traced determines whether kinship is *patrilineal* or *matrilineal*; in a matrilineal system the ancestors of one's father are not kin but those of one's mother, and hence her mother's and so forth, are."[119] African societies often had such unilineal kinship systems (either matrilineal or patrilineal), but enslavement of Africans and their wide dispersal in the New World erased most unilineal features. One wonders, however, if the strong fictive kin concept in slave society might be an African vestige. One of the advantages of unilineal kinship is that it establishes a coherent, exclusive group defined by descent, allowing the kin group to function despite the death of individual members. Did the community acting as a fictive kinship group provide that corporate body for slaves on long-established plantations? There is some evidence, including the tendency of nonrelated age-group peers to address each other as brother and sister and the custom of addressing all respected elders in kinship terms (aunt and uncle). It is even remotely possible that the figure of the "overlooker," a male slave of outstanding strength and vigor, who was allowed to have several wives, had some connection to the African practice of polygamy and was not simply an owner-directed breeding device.[120]

By the nineteenth century, slave kinship was cognatic, as in the dominant white culture. People in a cognatic kinship system are not easily organized into groups or easily recognized as kin as in unilineal systems. The relationship of an individual with his kin is less structured; obligations are not as clearly understood. In a cognatic system, relationships developed through marriage are more important than in unilineal systems. Members have greater freedom in a cognatic system to choose who is important to them, and nonkin often have as much status as kin other than the immediate family. Were slaves' relationships to kin beyond the immediate family very different from their relations to nonrelated friends? It is difficult to know. Their unfree status often made it virtually impossible to rely on membership in a large kinship group for protection or identification of interests. Certainly slaves valued kinship and strove to further kinship development, but how functional it was is another matter.

Naming patterns are useful but not conclusive in determining how important kin group identification was for slaves. Slaves named their children for esteemed nonrelated members of the community nearly as often as they did for relatives. Co-residence with kin beyond the immediate family cannot provide much evidence because one rarely encounters households containing kin outside the family, other than sons-in-law or daughters-in-law, and, occasionally, single siblings of heads of households. The reason for this has little or nothing to do with kinship; the cabins were too small to accommodate extended and multiple families.[121]

What can be said with assurance, then, about kinship among Louisiana slaves? (1) Basic kin support was found in the immediate family, consisting of parents, children, and siblings. (2) In order, slaves had the next greatest emotional attachment to and identification with grandparents, then aunts and uncles, then cousins. (3) The status of stepfamily members was ambiguous, but half-siblings seemed to be common and were accepted as full siblings. (4) Kinship was cognatic. (5) There is no firm evidence of matrilineal kin-reckoning, even on plantations where female-headed households were unusually common. (6) There is evidence of a serious taboo among slaves against intermarriage with kin, including cousins, even though in the Louisiana planter class the practice of cousin marriage and marriage between former sisters-in-law and brothers-in-law was common.

Intricate, supportive kinship networks were not present on many Louisiana plantations and farms until the 1850s, but the importance of kinship to the state's slaves is apparent throughout the antebellum period. Migration slaves and those brought to the state through the interstate trade provided their children with a sense of belonging to a kinship group by telling stories about their grandparents and other kin in the East. Former Louisiana slaves interviewed in old age not only recalled the names of their parents and siblings but also grandparents, aunts, uncles, and even cousins, some of whom they had never met. In the decade before the Civil War, kinship was quite advanced on larger plantations that had been left relatively undisturbed, and owners or overseers were hard-pressed to unravel their slaves' complicated kinship patterns, often relying on copious notes.[122]

In many new communities, grandparents were not present. When the communities did achieve enough generational depth to produce grandparents, they became highly honored members. They were respected partly because of their age and experience and partly because they were the primary transmitters of history and culture. Perhaps most respected were those born in Africa. Not only did grandparents and other elders serve as links to the past, but their opinions on contemporary problems and events were respected, and they were routinely consulted on community matters. Perhaps it is an indication of their status that, in the Louisiana sample, more grandparents headed households containing other kin than were dependent members of their children's households. That strong, supportive, courageous elders made unforgettable impressions on their grandchildren is apparent in many narratives of Louisiana slaves.[123] One of these grandchildren was Amos Lincoln, who recalled that his African grandfather had not only fascinated him, but after the war, when Amos's father was shot in the back and killed, his grandfather, nearly a century old, provided the family with a home.[124]

Close ties also developed during slavery between aunts and uncles and their nieces and nephews. A letter from slaveowner John Perkins, Sr., to his son speaks of the affection between slaves Robert and his nephew William. They were so close that the elder Perkins offered to buy William or trade for him two younger and stronger slaves with "no blood relatives" to prevent separating the uncle and nephew.[125] Another slave recalled an aunt who taught her how to say her prayers during slavery and lived with her family after emancipation.[126] Orphaned children were frequently absorbed into the households of aunts and uncles, as was Mary Island, a slave in Union Parish.[127]

Most slaves also considered cousins close family. For example, Fred Brown, a slave in Baton Rouge, told his interviewer that "in our family am pappy, mammy, and three brudders and one sister, Julia, and six cousins."[128] The closeness of slaves even to remote cousins was difficult for some whites to understand. Shortly after emancipation, one owner was exasperated when his former slave, who now was able to establish his own priorities more freely, often left work to attend the funeral of an infant who was a third or fourth cousin.[129]

RELIGION

Few would dispute that religion was central to the lives of nineteenth-century American slaves. In the early eighteenth century, slave religion was occasionally Islam, or a native African belief, or a Caribbean variant, but by the second half of the century, Christianity was widely embraced by slaves in the English, French, and Spanish colonies. In the latter two, of course, Catholicism was far more prevalent than Protestant sects. The importance of religion to American slaves by the nineteenth century is extensively documented in Albert J. Raboteau's *Slave Religion: The "Invisible Institution" in the Antebellum South*, John Blassingame's *Slave Community*, John Boles's *Masters and Slaves in the House of the Lord*, and Eugene Genovese's *Roll, Jordan, Roll*, among others. Perhaps the greatest benefit that slaves derived from their religious faith was an affirmation of their value and dignity as children of God. As Genovese puts it, the "religion practiced in the quarters gave the slaves the one thing they absolutely had to have if they were to resist being transformed into the Sambos they had been programmed to become. It fired them with a sense of their own worth before God and man."[130] It was this aspect of black Christianity that was most helpful in reinforcing slave domestic organizations—the family, the household, the kin group, and the community. Religion helped slaves not only believe in themselves as individuals but also as families, as a people, and as a race.

Religion not only strengthened and comforted slaves, separately and collectively, it provided an opportunity to forge an institution that uniquely reflected their needs and culture, despite its many white-derived elements. According to Genovese, "In entering into Christian fellowship with each other the slaves set themselves apart from the whites by creating a distinctive style, sensibility, and theology."[131] White observers marveled at how black Christianity took on its own special characteristics even under the constraints of slavery, within predominantly white churches, and with white supervision and surveillance.[132] Slaves displayed the same adaptability (or mutability) in their practice of religion that they displayed in their household organization. In both cases, they showed an ability to draw from an African-rooted value system of generations past while adopting serviceable aspects of Anglo-derived institutions. Mixing the clay of both, they molded something distinctively their own. Raboteau describes this creative, syncretic ability:

> It was not possible to maintain the rites of worship, the priesthood, or the "national" identities which were the vehicles and supports for African theology and cult organization. Nevertheless, even as the gods of Africa gave way to the God of Christianity, the African heritage of singing, dancing, spirit possession, and magic continued to influence Afro-American spirituals, ring shouts, and folk beliefs. That this was so is evidence of the slaves' ability not only to adapt to new contexts but to do so creatively.[133]

Furthermore, religion provided slaves with social opportunities, emotional release, and an orally transmitted biblical education that served as a training ground for their own ministers and deacons. It gave them status in their families and communities. For many slaves, religion provided a dignified, ritual recognition of important points in their life cycle, marked with appropriate baptismal, marriage, and funeral observances.[134] Most important, black religion in a variety of forms provided many slaves with comfort, solace, and even joy.

Slaves practiced their religion in a variety of settings, both private and public. Devout slaves often eagerly partook of any religious activities open to them. These might include individual prayer and hymn-singing throughout the day's activities (many slave children recalled their mothers' praying and singing); daily or weekly Bible readings with the master, if he were a religious sort; biracial church services on Sunday; clandestine, all-black prayer meetings; and occasional biracial camp meetings.[135]

Historians have long recognized the primacy of religion to slaves, and considerable attention has been given to the religious expressions slaves developed among themselves. Raboteau, Blassingame, Genovese, Sterling Stuckey, Lawrence W. Levine, and George P. Rawick have written extensively about slaves' religious activities.[136] Recent historians of race and of southern religion have extended our understanding of slave religious practices by pointing out their wide participation in biracial church services. Among these historians are John Boles, Blake Touchstone, Robert L. Hall, Larry M. James, Randall M. Miller, and Clarence L. Mohr, to name a few.[137]

Slaves in Louisiana and elsewhere in the South were sometimes members of biracial churches and therefore were baptized, received mass or communion, were confirmed, made confession, gave "experience" or conversion testimony, served as deacons and Sunday school teachers, and were married and buried with appropriate religious rites.[138] Because record-keeping on church membership, baptisms, and marriages was irregular at best, we will probably never know the extent of slave participation in biracial churches. Blassingame, however, has estimated that perhaps as many as a million slaves attended biracial churches on a regular basis in the South on the eve of the Civil War.[139] Over 40 percent of 637 former slaves who mentioned religion in WPA interviews during the 1930s had attended white churches while in bondage. About one-third of the narratives or autobiographies sampled by historian David T. Bailey mentioned attendance at biracial churches, slightly less than the percentage that went to secret black prayer meetings.[140] Some slaves, of course, were opposed or indifferent to religion, but we do not know how many. It seems safe to say that religious slaves tended to be among those workers who enjoyed high status both in the big house and in the quarters.

In the American-dominated parishes of Louisiana, religious slaves attended biracial services in the white churches frequented by their owners. In most cases slaves attended the entire service, sitting in a gallery or in a section at the back of the church and also listened to special words directed at them after the joint service. Or they might be ministered to separately, in a white church, with a white preacher, in an afternoon or evening service. A white woman wrote of such a service: "In the afternoon services for the negroes was held, the church was crowded, there were 5 adults and several children baptized and a large number confirmed. A good many white persons occupied the gallery." Slaves from neighboring plantations came to the afternoon services, and her son-in-law, an Episcopal minister, journeyed to other plantations to hold special services for the slaves, at the request of owners. Interestingly, she mentioned in her diary that in late March 1853, a starving runaway from Mr. Buhler's had broken into the pantry to get food and was later captured in their "little church" (plantation chapel), where he had taken refuge. In June, she wrote that the same Mr. Buhler, while attending a service for slaves in their church, had "remarked that the abolitionists . . . would hardly credit it if told how much interest there is manifested in their [the slaves] behalf and the efforts made to give them good religious instruction."[141]

There is little doubt that most slaves who attended white churches did so because they felt benefited by it. Biracial church attendance provided slaves of small owners with a rare opportunity to interact with other religious blacks and to forge a broader sense of community. Illiterate slaves gained knowledge of the Scriptures through the sermons and Bible readings. Participation provided slaves with an opportunity, however restrained, to pray and sing openly without fear of reprisal. And because, in the church, whites were subject to the same discipline as they, biracial membership allowed slaves to exercise a greater degree of racial equality than in any other area of their lives.[142]

White churches of the South slowly recognized the needs of slave members for greater autonomy, and, according to historian Larry M. James, "Preaching to a separate gathering of black baptists became common practice among the churches toward the end of the antebellum period."[143] Following the leadership of the evangelical sects, the more staid Episcopalian and Presbyterian denominations soon adopted the practice. In some cases, blacks were allowed to hold their own services with a slave preacher, though whites were always present, as observers if not co-worshipers. Former slave in Bossier Parish Chris Franklin related that "dey had a li'l church house for de niggers and preachin' in de afternoon, and on into de night lots of time. Dey have de cullud preacher. He couldn't read. He jes' preach from nat'ral wit and what he larn from white folks. De whole outfit profess to be Baptis'." Owners not only allowed black ministers to conduct services but occasionally hired them. For example, a "black priest" was engaged to perform a series of slave marriages on the plantation of an Episcopalian minister in January 1853.[144]

Church membership or attendance at biracial services was usually voluntary, but some owners encouraged and even compelled their slaves to attend white-controlled services, for a variety of reasons. Many saw it as their Christian duty and moral obligation to minister to their slaves' spiritual needs. Touchstone quotes Louisiana Bishop Leonidas Polk, himself a large slaveowner, concerning slaveowners' duty to provide religious training and opportunities for their slaves: "You may not save him [the slave], but you will save yourself." Others encouraged their slaves to attend church because they believed it would inculcate higher moral standards in them. A few embarked upon converting their slaves with missionary zeal, to save what they considered doomed, heathen souls. And very many encouraged white-orchestrated religious services for their slaves as a means of social control, a way to render their servants more obedient, orderly, and content. In her diary, Clarissa Leavitt wrote that the Reverend A. H. Lamon "had a large congregation of Negroes in the afternoon. They are much interested in the subject of religion at this time. I rejoice at it for it makes them happier here, and a promise of bliss hereafter. And it makes them much better servants and more easily managed."[145]

Slaves were aware of their owners' mixed motives, and some saw white-sponsored services as meaningless or simply another form of indoctrination and control. Former slave William Mathews of Franklin Parish resented the coercion involved: "Sometime, dey make de slaves go to church. De white folks sot up fine in dere carriage and drive up to de door and git de slaves out of one cabin, den git de slaves out of de nex' cabin, and keep it up till dey gits dem all. Den all de slaves walks front de carriage till dey gits to church. De slaves sot outside under de shade trees."[146]

On some plantations, participation was optional, but slaves resented the segregated seating and the constant surveillance by whites.[147] Even when special services were held for them, they often found the white minister's message indoctrinary. A former slave complained that even the slave preachers were instructed as to what they could preach. "If a cullud man take de notion to preach, he couldn't preach 'bout de Gospel. Dey didn't low him to do dat. All he could preach 'bout was obey de massa, obey de overseer, obey dis, obey dat."[148]

Whereas the Episcopal church was frequented by wealthier American planters, the Methodist and Baptist churches, popular among the smaller planters, were more to the liking of slaves, primarily because of their more emotional tenor and evangelical zeal. The emotionalism of evangelical religion appealed to slaves because it was compatible with remaining vestiges of their traditional African beliefs and practices and because it allowed them to vent repressed emotions. The emotional fervor of slaves' prayers and preachings impressed and moved white observers. A Bostonian observing a Louisiana slave service later wrote that it "was a very interesting and affecting sight and when an old slave led in prayer I was affected to tears at the sincerity and earnestness with which he poured forth his heart in broken english, suplicating for blessings upon Africa, upon their pastor, and the missionary. I was very much benefited by the exercise."[149]

The writer of an 1863 article in *Harper's Monthly* described a biracial church meeting in New Orleans attended primarily by slaves but having both a white and a black minister. He was struck by the black preacher's "descriptive eloquence," "pathos," and "simple imagery," adding that "we were all in tears." In contrast, he found the white preacher "didactic, dry, and powerless." He contended that whites could not effectively preach to blacks: "No one can move the negro but a negro. He alone understands the avenue to their emotions and sympathies, because they are identical with his own." The preacher, recently a slave, whose freedom was purchased by his congregation, spoke as one who had experienced their tribulations and knew the language of their hearts. "They believed the promises and assurances of the [black] preacher without caviling; and they shouted over their certain salvation."[150]

The need to sway, clap, call responses, and shout in ecstasy was deeply rooted in the African religious experience and remained strong among Louisiana slaves. The desire to shout was irrepressible, and slave believers, even those who were Catholics, in no way perceived the practice as undignified or inappropriate. An eclectic, mutable aspect was especially characteristic of slave religion in Louisiana, where French Catholic as well as Anglo-American influences were strong. Orelia Franks was a slave of a

French Acadian master near Opelousas, Louisiana. A French-speaking Catholic, baptized at St. John's Catholic Church, she also regularly attended services led by a black Methodist preacher and participated in secret, all-black prayer meetings that the slaves held for themselves. In those secret meetings, did she shout? "Shout? Yes, Lawd!," she responded to an inquiry of her interviewer, sounding very much like a Baptist slave.[151] Such sectarian contradictions did not bother slaves, but they upset some white lay people as well as church leaders. At one point, a Catholic priest attempted to forbid his slave parishioners from shouting. One slave protested that "the angels shout in heaven. The Lawd said you gotta shout if you want to be saved."[152] In extreme cases, slaves were severely punished for spontaneously shouting within a biracial religious gathering. Sol Walton recalled that "I seed my mammy whipped for shoutin' at white folks' meetin'. Old massa stripped her to the waist and whipped her with a bullwhip."[153]

Even though many Louisiana churches and churchmen felt a religious mission to the slaves, most slaveowners were probably indifferent to their chattels' spiritual needs. Catholic masters in Louisiana were more concerned about baptizing their slaves than were Protestant owners, but they too largely neglected any further responsibilities for their slaves' spiritual well-being. The neglect occurred in part because priests were scarce in rural areas, but many owners resented the church's interference in their internal plantation affairs. Even priests bold enough to urge Catholic masters to attend to the religious needs of their slaves (as the church required) did not dare venture into the quarters without permission. A Lafayette Parish slave related: "De priest he never come 'round de quarters, but he go to de big house and tell old Mistus to teach de older ones dere prayers. I ax my aunt and she teach me. But we didn't go to church in slavery."[154] It could be dangerous for a priest to attend to his duties in a biracial setting, as Priscilla Bond reported in her diary. She noted that a drunken Leon Landry had shot at the priest on at least three occasions because the priest was "confessing black and white together."[155]

A few devout Catholic masters regularly took their personal servants to mass. Pauline Johnson recalled, "Us goes to Mass every Sunday mornin' and church holiday, and when the cullud folks sick massa send for the priests same's for the white folks." Oliver Blanchard remembered that "my old missus was good Catholic and she have us christened and make the first communion." But many south Louisiana Catholic slaveholders believed that providing for their slaves' baptism was the extent of their obligation. Peter Ryas recalled, "Us not go to church, but all chillen christen . . . in St. Martinville Catholic Church."[156]

The sacraments, especially that of marriage, were as sacred to Catholic slaves as to any other Louisiana Catholics. Sisters Pauline Johnson and Felice Boudreaux recalled that when their father became gravely ill and expected to die, he incessantly called for a priest. The master allowed his dying request. Although he had long been married "by de massa's word," his marriage was finally solemnized by a priest just before the old man died.[157]

At no time was religion of more importance to slaves than at their own or their loved ones' deaths. Louisiana owners usually allowed their slaves to bury their dead with prayers, hymn-singing, and a eulogy. Wakes were also customary. Former slave Agatha Babino recalled that slaves on her plantation were buried with the blessing of a priest in a separate section of the Catholic cemetery at Grand Coteau. Others recalled burials in slave cemeteries on the plantation, and personal servants were sometimes buried near the white family they served. Slaves often held their own observance before burial. "Dey didn't do no work den. De slaves would gather 'round in a crowd and spend de night sitting up with de corpse. Dey had prayers and sung Baptist songs."[158] In Bossier Parish, a similar custom prevailed. "De night de pusson die dey has de wake and sing and pray all night long. Dey all very 'ligious in dere profession. Dey knock off all work so de slaves can go to de buryin'."[159] Clara Brim's master employed a preacher to bury his slaves with "Bible readin' and prayin'." But, she noted, "mostest de massas didn't do dat-a-way."[160] A former slave of Catholics, and herself a Catholic during her enslavement, recalled that funeral sermons were preached at the slave graveyard by a Methodist preacher.[161] He might have been what slaves called a "funeral preacher," widely known for his talents on such an occasion. If he was unavailable at the time of death, a funeral preacher might be engaged as much as a year later to deliver a sermon in honor of the deceased.[162]

Some owners forbade funeral observances. One former slave in Louisiana bitterly recounted that "when a Nigger died they let his folks come out'n the field to see him. . . . They would take a big plank and bust it with an ax in the middle enough to bend it back and put the dead Nigger in betwixt it. They 'ud cart them down to the graveyard and they wouldn't bury them deep nuf that the buzzards wouldn't come circlin' roun. Niggers mourn now but in them days there wan't no time for mournin."[163]

Biracial worship and white-sponsored religious observances were meaningful to many slaves, but the heart of slave communal religion was probably the private, secret prayer meetings held in remote cabins, woods, canebrakes, or hollows, where slave worshipers could escape the eyes and ears of whites. These secret meetings were especially critical for slaves for whom religious activities had been forbidden. One recalled that "Massa never 'lowed us to go to church but they have big holes in the fields they gits down in and prays. They done that way 'cause the white folks didn't want them to pray. They used to pray for freedom."[164] This theme was often repeated in ex-slave interviews from Louisiana. Adeline White, for example, said, "In the night we would creep out in the woods and have the prayer meetin', prayin' for freedom to come quick. We has to be careful for if massa find out he whip all of us, sho. We stays nearly all night and sleeps and prays and sleeps and prays."[165]

On A. R. Kilpatrick's Black River Plantation, the slaves were not given an opportunity to go to church, but they compensated by having their own "prayin's and singings" in their cabins. The Christian slaves sat on the floor, heads bowed, quietly praying and singing. Despite precautions, they often caught the attention of Solomon, the black driver, who would beat on the cabin wall with his whip's stock, shouting, "You can't pray all night and work tomorrow. I'll come in there and tear the hide off you backs." Mary Reynolds's narrative reveals how private worship allowed slaves to express their spiritual and temporal concerns to their God—concerns they could never express openly in a biracial service. The elders instructed them to pray that "God don't think no different of the blacks and the whites," that in his eyes they were equal. One of the old ones prayed "that a day would come when Niggers only be slaves of God." She remembered that they prayed for the "end of tribulation and beatings," for "all that we wanted to eat" and "fresh meat . . . and shoes that fit our feet."[166]

Secret prayer meetings were just as prevalent among slaves who were allowed to attend church. Even Catholic slaves cherished the secret, separate prayer meetings. "Sometimes Massa Jim 'low us to go to de Catholic Church. . . . Dey wouldn't 'low us to pray by ourself. But we sneaks off and have a pot prayin'. Two men carry de great big hog pot dey uses to scald hogs and take it out in de woods and us stick de head in it and pray. All de noise go in de pot and you couldn't hear it outside."[167] Former slaves told of many variations of pot praying. A Louisiana slave mentioned that each individual brought a pot to prayer meeting "and put dere head in it to keep de echoes from gittin back. Den dey pray in de pot."[168]

Even though religion was a pervasive part of slave community life, some slaves were so alienated and brutalized by slavery that even religion seemed remote. J. W. Terrill, the slave who spent his childhood with a bell cage welded on his shoulders, told his interviewer that his white father "didn't 'lieve in church. . . . My missy 'lieved there was a Lord, but I wouldn't have 'lieved her if she try to larn me 'bout 'ligion, 'cause my family [his white father and aunt] tell me I wasn't any more than a damn mule."[169] For most slaves, religion, along with a sense of belonging to a family and to a community with its own values and culture, could counter such devastating dehumanization. Family and religious values reinforced each other. A body of believers formed a cell of mutual support within a slave community, but they also comforted and counseled members of the larger slave community. Religion buttressed marital and parental duties and obligations. Religion bred forbearance and patience in their trials, but, perhaps most important, it gave them hope.

CHAPTER EIGHT

Findings and Conclusions

Slaves of African descent had been present in Louisiana since its earliest European settlement, but the vast majority of nineteenth-century chattels were transported into the region with migrating owners and professional dealers after 1810 or were descendants of such slaves. Earlier chapters described the dramatic growth in both white and slave populations between 1810 and 1865, resulting from natural increases, the westward movement, expansion of the cotton kingdom, and development of the sugarcane industry in lower Louisiana. Thus the family, household, and community construction of nineteenth-century Louisiana slaves developed in a volatile setting of expansion and change. Nevertheless, the family (and its extensions, the household and community) is perhaps the most conservative of all human institutions, altering its most basic forms at an exceedingly slow pace—over centuries, not decades. In nineteenth-century Louisiana, this conservative institution, confronted with dynamic economic and demographic pressures, survived as a social unit primarily because it made accommodations and adaptations within its traditional, basic forms to counter forces threatening its vital functions.

In *Sweet Chariot* I have sought to discover the perimeters

of domestic organization among slaves living in Louisiana during the first sixty years or so of the nineteenth century. I do not claim that the fundamental forms of the black family were significantly altered within that relatively short period. Peter Laslett reminds us that the "family consists in a systematic normative structure, and normative change is usually a deliberate, inch by inch operation . . . belonging to . . . *l'histoire immobile* rather than *l'historie conjectural.*" The basic structure of slave household composition changed relatively little from the colonial period through emancipation; it was always dominated by simple families but had a considerable number of solitaires and often a small number of complex family households, usually of the multiple family type, with downward disposition of the secondary unit. Within the dominant simple family, most were full nuclear units (or standard nuclear families), but many were truncated, consisting of married couples alone or female-headed single-parent family households. This was the normative configuration, but slave communities, over time, showed remarkable mutability within the general structure, changing naturally and rhythmically, depleting through deaths and young adults moving out of the household to form their own families and regenerating through births and the formation of new families, and also changing cyclically in response to internal and external crises. Laslett provides an excellent description of how mutability is possible (and functional) precisely because of the slow rate of change in the family's fundamental structure, asserting that "the familial normative structure is container-like, since one of its purposes is to outlast emergencies and vicissitudes, economic ups and downs, ideological turnabouts, and religious transformations."[1]

And so it was in nineteenth-century Louisiana. Components of slave family-household structure shifted and stretched, contracted, and expanded to accommodate changing circumstances, but the normative framework was altered very slowly. This book does not attempt to demonstrate changes in the black family from the African past to the urban, northern United States present. But it does chart characteristics of mutability and constancy within a relatively unchanging overall structure that are informative about life under slavery and might also shed light on the black family's capacity for survival and adaptation in the modern era.

The statistical study (when reduced by intervals and related to major economic and demographic trends within the smaller time segments) and the case studies showed that slave household composition was vulnerable to the influence of a wide range of external forces. Those that produced the greatest change in the everyday lives of the slaves themselves had the greatest impact on internal slave family organization. The change need not be catastrophic; it could be precipitated by a brisk but highly speculative market in slaves or agricultural products—perhaps good for owners but disruptive and frequently destructive for their slaves. Although broad economic and political forces influenced Louisiana slave household composition, the personal and business decisions of owners and the results of estate divisions probably affected slaves more.

More difficult to measure were the internal factors that influenced slave household composition during all developmental phases. Exerting subtle influences on household composition were the community's health, the quality of its internal leadership, its morale, and the degree of consensus it achieved through kinship, religion, other shared cultural values, and common work experiences. This area needs further study, for the *mentalité* approach has not been thoroughly applied to the slave family and community, although the works of Genovese, Blassingame, Levine, Stuckey, Charles Joyner, Leslie Owens, and Thomas Webber have made strong contributions toward such a cultural synthesis.[2]

The statistical model also showed that when viewed over time, certain representative family household types consistently acted as barometers of change within slave community organization. These types were the standard nuclear family, the female-headed single-parent family household, the solitaire household, and the multiple family household. The importance of these types was echoed in the case studies as well. Other types and categories were significant in that they demonstrated the diversity and flexibility of slave domestic organization, but they did not vary much in response to factors other than the natural developmental cycle. The statistical study and the various models it produced, the case studies, and Louisiana slavery records in general all indicate that although Louisiana slave domestic organization displayed a remarkable capacity for adaptation, it also reflected a broadly held concept of what constituted the construction of an ideal community. This societal ideal led slaves to move persistently toward a more family- and kin-centered composition despite cyclical setbacks.

Most of the areas just mentioned were extensively treated in earlier chapters, but a few warrant additional comment, either because they depart from current scholarship or because they have methodological features that need explication.

STANDARD NUCLEAR FAMILY HOUSEHOLDS

Throughout the surveyed period, most Louisiana slaves lived in simple families, as did most other Americans of the period. When the simple family is broken down further, however, interesting patterns emerge that in some respects counter implications of recent scholarship.

My findings, for example, indicate that slightly fewer than half of the sampled Louisiana slaves of all ages in the period 1810 to 1864 were members of two-parent nuclear families, as parents or children. In stable phases of development, more slaves were part of such units; in periods of instability, fewer were. Revisionist literature of the 1970s and 1980s on the slave family projected the supposition now frequently reflected in college textbooks that most slaves in the United States lived in families consisting of both parents with their children. This idea developed in part from a misreading of slave family-household studies that analyzed only the composition of simple families rather than that of the entire community. If one looks solely at simple families instead of the households making up the entire social body, then a majority of those slaves in families did live in two-parent nuclear units under normal circumstances. But such an approach obscures the fact that at many points in their lives slaves were not part of a standard nuclear family but functioned as solitaires or as members of other household types. It also fails to perceive the holistic nature of slave society. Part of the confusion results from variations in findings, depending on whether the familial composition being discussed was only that which included children or that of all community members. Generalizations for all slaves have been drawn from studies of only the families slaves recalled being part of as small children, rather than their memories of the entire community structure. Further, generalizations have been drawn from studies of one, or at most a few, individual plantations whose inventories accurately reflected a majority of slaves living in standard nuclear families, but which might not be representative. Finally, the idea was encouraged by the fact that most studies have been of slave communities at a static point in time, which was often a mature point in community development (usually the 1850s) because those records were more thorough and more available.

Historians of the slave family have been more cautious, but many general historians and the popular press, drawing upon their reading (or misreading) of revisionist literature, frequently state or infer that the large majority of American slaves (adults as well as children) lived in the cozy American family unit of mom, dad, and the kids. At least in Louisiana during most phases of the developmental cycle, this conclusion does not reflect historical reality and underestimates the devastating effects of slavery on the stability of the slave family, household, and community.

To put my arguments in perspective, a brief review of the recent historical literature on the subject is in order. Although the notion is often ascribed to them, Fogel and Engerman in *Time on the Cross* do not directly state that the majority of slaves lived in nuclear (meaning two-parent) families. They do correctly assume that the two-parent nuclear family was the preferred form and that among those slaves who lived in simple families, the two-parent nuclear family usually prevailed. They stress that the husband's role within the family was larger and more significant than previously believed. And they infer that slaves played as large a part as did their masters in the adoption of a nuclear family model because "African family forms . . . did not satisfy the needs of blacks who lived and worked under conditions and in a society much different than those which their ancestors experienced."[3] Blassingame also considers the monogamous nuclear family the model for slaves, but he stops short of claiming that most slaves lived in both-parent family units, even if it was the societal ideal. Genovese, in *Roll, Jordan, Roll*, stresses the active role played by many fathers and husbands in their families and assists his revisionist colleagues in burying the myths of the slave matriarchy and the absent family, but he too does not suggest that the normative experience under slavery was to be part of a two-parent family unit. The popular assumption appears to be most directly drawn from the work on black family and kinship done by Herbert Gutman. For example, in his analysis of a Louisiana holding of Lewis Stirling, Gutman discusses the high incidence of female-headed single-parent households but then concludes: "Nevertheless, the two-parent household was the characteristic arrangement at all times, though declining in importance." He is, however, speaking of the experience of slave children in families, not of slaves of all ages within a community. He goes on to state that "most Stirling slave children grew up in two-parent households," admitting that he is describing a "relatively settled" community.[4]

Jacqueline Jones, in *Labor of Love, Labor of Sorrow*, asserts that "out of the father-mother, husband-wife nexus sprang the slaves' beliefs about what men and women should be and do." Almost all historians of slavery agree with her that a family built around a married couple was indeed the societal ideal. But then Jones concludes that the "two-parent, nuclear family was the typical form of slave cohabitation regardless of the location, size, or economy of a plantation, the nature of its ownership, or the age of its slave community."[5] This broad generalization is made with no more evidence than a general reference to Gutman's *Black Family*, citing no specific pages. If Jones had stated that the two-parent nuclear family was the most common unit within the simple family type, perhaps a case could be made, but as the statement stands, it is unconvincing.

A recent synthesis of scholarship on slavery boldly states that "most slaves in the United States . . . lived in 'nuclear' households consisting of two parents and children." The author, Robert Fogel, accompanies the statement with a table comparing percentages of slaves in household types from samples in Trinidad in 1813, Jamaica in 1825, the Bahamas in 1822, and the United States in 1850. According to the table, 64 percent of United States slaves in 1850 lived in two-parent households. A footnote reveals that his data for United States slaves are drawn only from the 1980 dissertation of Stephen C. Crawford, a quantitative study of ex-slave interviews. Fogel's projections concerning slaves in the United States are based on Crawford's analysis of the types of households that interviewees in the 1930s were born into or recalled being part of as young children.[6] Even those who recalled being part of a two-parent family very often mentioned that at least one of the parents died or was otherwise absent for part of the childhood years. Further, Crawford's own table shows only 51 percent of the slaves interviewed as having been born in two-parent, consolidated family households, which seems about right for the 1850s in most parts of the South. The 64 percent figure was arrived at by adding the percentage of slaves in co-resident, two-parent families and the percentage living in households with only one parent, with the other parent presumably residing on a different plantation or farm. In another table, Crawford again includes divided residence households and estimates that 55 to 60 percent of slave children lived in such households. He also asserts that about 47 percent of former slaves from slave-importing states spent at least part of their childhood in such standard nuclear families, very close to my findings. Crawford cannot be faulted for his broad definition of a two-parent nuclear family, but to include divided families as standard nuclear families carries some serious risks and is almost never done in familial studies because co-residency and availability for support are major features of standard nuclear families.

The problems with using Crawford's excellent study as the basis for estimating the percentages of all United States slaves in two-parent nuclear families seem obvious to me. For one, Crawford is dealing only with household composition from the perspective of slave children—that is, the units they were part of during a very restricted period—often not even covering their entire childhood years. Second, his sample is limited, selective, and based on recollection. Third, it is based on a relatively static period, a decade at best. And fourth, Crawford himself cautions that although the Greenwood sample of interviews he used is "an important source of information about slave experiences," it "does not always replicate the proportions in which various attributes existed in the overall slave population."[7]

In some of the most recent county and regional studies of slavery the findings are similar to mine, which were derived from a state study. For example, Alan Kulikoff found in his study of Chesapeake slavery before 1800 that "nearly half of all the Afro-Americans owned by four large planters resided in households that included both parents and at least some of their children." And he found that only "18 percent of the blacks on small units in Prince George's County in 1776 lived in two-parent households."[8] By contrast, in his careful examination of nineteenth-century slaves in Edgefield County, South Carolina, Orville Vernon Burton discovered that a "great majority of plantation slaves lived in families with two parents and permanent marriages."[9]

Neither Deborah White in *Ar'n't I a Woman?* nor Elizabeth Fox-Genovese in *Within the Plantation Household* deals directly with the normative composition of slave domestic organizations. Both works, however, hint at findings that my sample in some ways confirms—that overzealousness in revising earlier misconceptions concerning the composition of the slave family and community has led some recent historians or their popularizers to exaggerate the stability of the slave family, to overemphasize the supposed patriarchal features, and to overestimate the incidence of two-parent family households. Fox-Genovese persuasively argues that "historians of the slave community have minimized the consequences of enslavement for the relationships between slave women and men, and, in defending the strength and vitality of Afro-American culture, have too easily assumed that the slaves developed their own strong attachment to a 'normal' nuclear family life—a remarkably egalitarian form of conjugal domesticity and companionship."[10]

Despite these differences, historians have reached a consensus concerning many aspects of the topic. All recent historians of slavery, including myself, agree that the two-parent nuclear family was the societal ideal; that the dominant household type was the simple family; and that within the simple family category, the two-parent nuclear family usually prevailed. I am convinced that the parents (or parent) and child unit was the vital core of the slave community—the model for other relationships within the larger corporate body. But to overemphasize the numbers of individuals encompassed in two-parent units detracts from the fact that the real strength of the slave community was its multiplicity of forms, its tolerance for a variety of families and households, its adaptability, and its acceptance of all types of families and households as functional and contributing. My study of Louisiana household composition inclines me to urge historians of the slave community to test at the local and regional levels the widespread assumption that a great majority of slaves were part of co-resident families consisting of mothers, fathers, and their children.

FEMALE-HEADED SINGLE-PARENT HOUSEHOLDS: MYTH OF THE MATRIARCHY

The United States slave family household appears not to have been matriarchal in its internal governance, although it was not clearly patriarchal either. In those Louisiana slave families having both husband and wife present, wives had equal or near-equal status with their husbands, probably more so than in the postbellum nineteenth century and early twentieth century. In many respects, slave standard nuclear families actually were double-headed, despite owners' or overseers' penchant for issuing rations under the name of the husband as head of household. The same owners or overseers often identified only women and their dependent children as "families" because women were often viewed as a biological unit with their offspring but not with their husbands. It is only through record linkage that such women's husbands and fathers are identified. But how a family household functioned is not determined by who is listed as head of household by an owner. When individual communities are closely scrutinized, it appears that in Louisiana at least, under normal circumstances, neither husband nor wife totally dominated the family unit.

If the Louisiana slave family household was not matriarchal, neither was slave kinship matrilineal, with privileges, obligations, and family identification following only the female line of descent. It was matrilineal only in the very limited and externally imposed sense that slave status derived from the status of the mother (in other words, a child born to a slave mother was a slave regardless of whether the father was enslaved).

Was the slave family in any sense matrifocal, then? In some stages and under some circumstances, more slave families were matrifocal than were contemporary white families because, under slavery, husbands, fathers, and adult males in general were sold, transferred, hired out, or otherwise removed from constituted family units more often than were females. The female presence in the household was generally more durable and permanent in times of stress than was that of males; a prime example is the removal of countless numbers of young men from their families during the Civil War years, conscripted for service by the Confederacy for labor or by the Union for either labor or military service.

If slave family households were not generally matriarchal or matrifocal, and slave kinship was not matrilineal, then how did the so-called myth of the matriarchy arise, and why has it disappeared so completely? Most historians believe that the myth of the matriarchy originated with abolitionist literature, which argued that slavery destroyed traditional family structure and corrupted morals. Late nineteenth-century historians and other social commentators reinforced the erroneous images of the weak black family, irresponsible fathers, and dominant mothers from an entirely different point of view. They saw racial characteristics rather than slavery as the cause, insisting that weakness and lack of moral fiber in the black character were responsible for the matriarchal structure and inherent instability of the black family. In the 1950s and 1960s (but anticipated by the positions taken by W. E. B. Du Bois and E. Franklin Frazier decades earlier) historians, sociologists, political analysts, and reformers rejected its racial basis but still accepted the myths of matriarchal dominance, absent fathers and husbands, and chronic instability as features of the African-American family. They understood that societal factors such as poverty and race discrimination helped create these features in black families in modern industrial cities. But they also saw a weak black family structure as a historical legacy from slavery.[11]

Revisionist historians of the 1970s and 1980s have demolished the concept of a matriarchal structure in slave society, but the myth has had amazing staying power nonetheless—enough to convince even some notable black scholars of its validity. As Eugene Genovese points out, "Enough men and women fell into [the] pattern to give rise to the legends of the matriarchy, the emasculated but brutal male, and the fatherless children. These legends did not merely arise from contemporary proslavery propagandistic fantasies or from the ethnocentricity of later historians and social scientists; they rest on unquestionable evidence, which, being partial, has misled its interpreters."[12] Much of that partial evidence of a matriarchy was the remembered or observed presence on most plantations of a large number of independent, strong, self-sufficient-appearing women who headed their own households. Some of them did so for their entire adult lives, apparently by choice.

Although it did not dominate, the female-headed single-parent household was an important and normal part of slave household composition, found in all stages of development and among communities of varying degrees of stability. As can be seen in figure 8.1, the general trend was for the percentages of slaves in female-headed single-parent households to decrease over time as the community matured and progressed toward greater stability.[13] Tiger Island is an apt example. In 1842 matrifocal households had a slight edge over two-parent households within the simple family category. But by 1860, the proportion of slaves in such households had declined from 33 percent in 1842 to only 13 percent. In eighteen years the type went from a position of major importance to a relatively minor one.

The single women who headed their own households during slavery have received scant attention as a group, although studies have been undertaken

FIGURE 8.1.

Slaves in Female-Headed Single-Parent Households at Oakland, Petite Anse, and Tiger Island Plantations, by Percentage

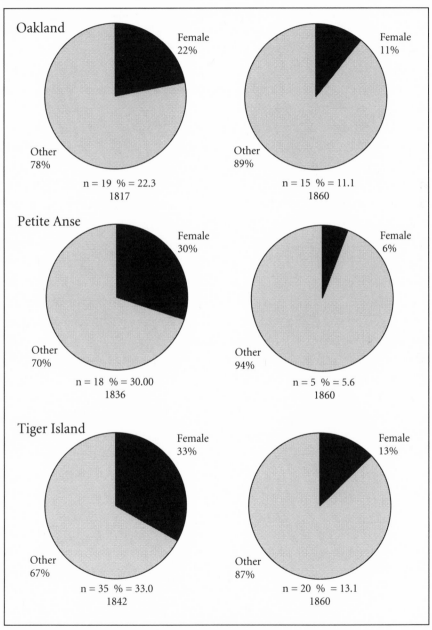

Source: Oakland, Petite Anse, and Tiger Island Data Bases.

of household structure in the late nineteenth and early twentieth centuries that deal extensively with the female-headed single-parent family category. In general works, chapters on the slave family focus almost exclusively on married slave woman in their various roles as wives, mothers, and workers. This is partially the case even in the several very perceptive works primarily or extensively dealing with female slaves, such as those by Jacqueline Jones, Deborah White, and Elizabeth Fox-Genovese.[14] Single as well as married women were members of families and functioned as parents, workers, and heads of households. Yet we know little about this sizable and often powerful group within the slave community. Who fathered their children? Who provided them with emotional support? Was there a single female network? How much emotional support was rendered by kin, especially female kin, or were friends more important? White does include an informative chapter on the female slave network. She states that the "female network and its emotional sustenance was always there—there between an 'abroad' husband's visits, there when a husband or son was sent or sold off or ran away."[15] Did that network also serve women who, through choice or circumstances, spent most of their years as single parents? We know something about their residential patterns in Louisiana. Very young unmarried women with a child or children were usually and temporarily absorbed into their parents' households. But older single females with children often shared cabins.[16] Did these women blend their households, or was it simply a convenient or assigned residential arrangement? Was a family headed by a single female considered any less a family in the typical slave community? In Louisiana, there appears to have been little or no stigma attached to these families. Since there was little internal stigma, why have female-headed single-parent households been regarded by historians as automatic symptoms of instability and weakness in black societies, even when they occur in reasonable and historical proportions?

In comparison with the evidence that I have found, the number of "abroad" or off-plantation or divided-residence marriages appears to be exaggerated in current historical literature, perhaps out of an overabsorption with correcting the myth of the matriarchy and heralding the standard nuclear family. My evidence has been cited elsewhere in this book. On plantations that operated under rules forbidding abroad marriages, female-headed single-parent households appear with about the same regularity as on those that had no such proscription. Therefore, one should not assume that in communities in which 15 percent of the slaves live in female-headed single-parent households, husbands and fathers were ensconced on nearby plantations. Many, perhaps the majority, of such households did not, but they were still able to fulfill their familial functions.

SOLITAIRE HOUSEHOLDS

Another significant segment of slave society that has received scant historical attention is that of the solitaire. Solitaires formed an omnipresent group in Louisiana slave communities. In the early stages of community development, they consisted primarily of young, unattached males, often new purchases, a common and volatile group in any work society. In the later developmental stages of slave communities, many of the solitaires were not young and single, nor were they predominantly male outsiders but respected widows and widowers over age fifty with considerable status in the community.

Not only did the composition of the solitaire group change over time, but their percentages in slave communities tended to decrease. In Louisiana slave societies, this trend indicated increased maturation and stability as families formed from the solitaire pool and kinship advanced. As demonstrated in figure 8.2, the decrease was especially dramatic at Oakland, where, in addition to indicating an increasingly mature stage, the precipitous decline in solitaires also reflects John N. Evans's relinquishing of young solitaires to other heirs to keep families intact during the 1852 estate division. A similar trend was present, however, in all maturing communities under normal circumstances.

A second trend is for age and sex distribution within the solitaire group to progress toward greater balance over time as part of the maturing, stabilizing process. The slave community of Petite Anse is a case in point. It appears that 82 percent of its slaves in 1826 were solitaires. Because of gender-sensitive buying, the proportion of slaves who were solitaires had decreased to 27 percent in 1836, with only one of these under the age of fifteen.[17] By 1839 the proportion of solitaires in the slave population had dropped to 14 percent. In the three years since the previous inventory most of the prime-age men had found wives from among the new purchases.[18] In 1860 solitaires still constituted only 15 percent of the slave community,

FIGURE 8.2.

Solitaires in the Slave Communities of Oakland, Petite Anse, and Tiger Island Plantations

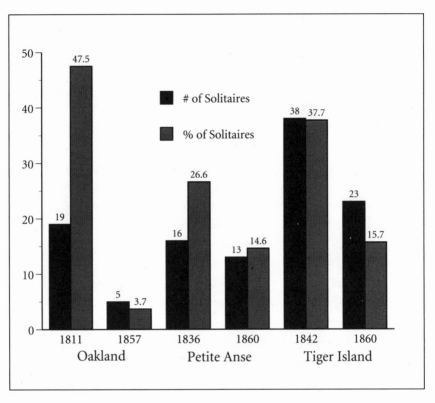

Source: Oakland, Petite Anse, and Tiger Island Data Bases.

and even this relatively small proportion is deceptive.[19] Many were older slaves who had strong kinship ties to existing Petite Anse families.

The reduction in the number of solitaires and the changing composition of the group to one less dominated by males, the young, and the never married were part of a natural progression toward a more balanced, mature society. Most slave societies made such progress. Of the plantations in the case study, Tiger Island was the least successful, although its percentages of solitaires decreased and its gender imbalance improved over time. In 1842 solitaires composed 38 percent of Tiger Island's population. The percentages slowly declined until in 1860 solitaires composed 15.7 percent of the slaves, about the same as were part of multiple family households.

The community was less successful, however, in reducing the gender imbalance within the solitaire group.

Tiger Island provides a cogent example of the connections between demographic factors and social realities in the lives of ordinary slave men and women. On Tiger Island Plantation, the combination of the generally imbalanced sex ratio and the high percentage of one-gender solitaires had concrete repercussions for its slaves. It was a major reason why 72 percent of the single males of 1842 did not marry during the next thirteen years and more than half would still be without wives in 1860.[20] Such severe shortages of potential wives for single males had many social effects at Tiger Island. Young males without families were likely to search elsewhere for sexual and companionate relationships. Without wives, they had less to lose and were more prone to disciplinary problems than were married family men. Tiger Island had its share of such difficulties. Walter Brashear wrote his daughter in 1838 about a slave who was assuming dangerous authority and influence over other island slaves. He was quickly removed from the island and later sold. Reflecting upon the incident, Brashear wrote that his son Robert had thought that the rebellious slave "would do better if we indulged him in taking Maria for his wife but I always doubted."[21] Although marrying Maria did not cure the man, Jim Roy, of his insubordination, it is significant that Robert Brashear thought it might.

MULTIPLE FAMILY HOUSEHOLDS:
NURTURING TENDENCIES

The multiple family unit was the great umbrella form in slave societies, enveloping and shielding vulnerable family and community members until they could survive and venture out on their own. As can be seen in figure 8.3, multiple family households encompassed many slaves on each of the case study plantations at the time of their most mature inventory. It is a form associated primarily with mature stages or periods of crisis. The importance of this complex family form should be recognized, especially as a nurturing body, but its presence in no way diminishes the centrality of the standard nuclear family or the simple family model for slave society. The simple family—and most often the standard nuclear family—provided the foundation for the multiple family group and remained the basic

FIGURE 8.3.

Slaves in Multiple Family Households at Oakland, Petite Anse, and Tiger Island Plantations

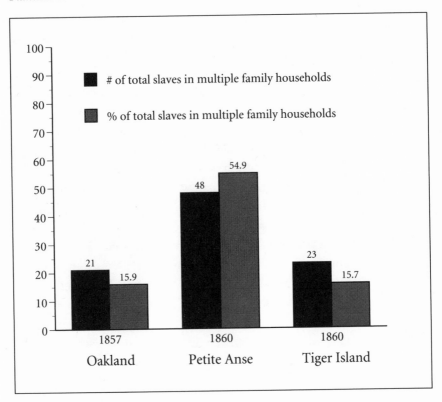

Source: Oakland, Petite Anse, and Tiger Island Data Bases.

organizational unit for slave households in Louisiana throughout its history. B. W. Higman's assertion regarding West Indian slave families applies to Louisiana slaves as well: "The nuclear family, as a unit of residence, was a constant model. It could be stunted or extended by the process of birth, death, and mating. It could be used as the basic element in larger spatial groups of kin. It also suffered directly from the institution, especially through the separation of mates, the demographic selectivity of the slave trade, and the interposition of white men. Yet it remained the model."[22]

Social responses to demographic changes can be seen in the reactions of slave household organization to premarital births, to deaths, to chronic illness, to dislocations, and to separations. The multiple family household was perhaps the most effective in dealing with such emergencies, but a nurturing tendency was found among most household types, both in the case studies and on plantations not included in the sample.

NURTURING TENDENCY

A nurturing tendency was present to some degree in all phases of slave community development and appears to have been a general characteristic. Yet stable and mature communities with well-developed kinship networks and generational depth were most likely to have the human resources to support members in crisis. The nurturing tendency is most obvious in periods of externally precipitated crises such as the Civil War. But if one delves deep enough into the inner structure of almost any slave community at any time, some individual examples of nurturing are revealed.

At Petite Anse, the most common nurturing tendency was for established family households to absorb unmarried daughters, grandchildren, and very young married couples until they were able to cope as separate units. Nurturing might also consist of a family taking in an ill, handicapped, abandoned, or elderly member of the community (either related or nonrelated) on a temporary or permanent basis. The nurturing tendency was especially strong and broad-based at Oakland. Not only were young unmarried females with children absorbed into their parents' households, but orphans were frequently reared by kin or nonrelatives. There were also a few cases of grandparents living with a grandchild. In one example, a grandfather provided care and protection for his orphaned grandchildren. In another case a newly married couple took in a much esteemed grandfather.[23]

Many instances of nurturing are found at Tiger Island in the later inventories but not during its early years. In 1842, shortly after the plantation was established, young unmarried mothers were unassociated with other households because most had no parents or close kin on the plantation. Likewise, orphans and adolescent solitaires lacked permanent household identifications. These hapless individuals faced their crises with little support. But by the 1859–60 period, young unmarried mothers were sheltered in the households of their parents; orphans lived permanently with kin or friends; and young or otherwise dependent siblings were cared for in households of older siblings, whether these were married or unmarried. To illustrate further, Ed Davis, his wife, Jenny, and their children included in their 1860 household Washington, aged twenty, Ara Ann, seventeen, and Ara Ann's baby. Washington and Ara Ann were children of Ed Davis's sister Violetta. They were assimilated into the Davis household and listed as their children, although they were actually a nephew and niece, identified as Violetta's children on earlier inventories. Another example is that of Sandis and Maria, who in 1859 included within their large family their unmarried seventeen-year-old daughter and her infant. The baby died by 1860, but Charlotte, the daughter, continued to take refuge in her parents' household. When marriages of grown children were broken by divorce or death, the remaining partner and children frequently were reabsorbed into their parents' households. One of many possible examples at Tiger Island is that of Amanda and her young son Jeff, who moved back into the household of her parents after the death of her husband. Usually it was the mature and well-established families who took on the additional responsibility of needy family and kin, but not always. A young married couple, Leven, aged twenty-four, and Louisa, eighteen, made Louisa's fourteen-year-old sister a part of their family in 1859 and also took care of the six-year-old daughter of an elderly widower. Peter, twenty-five, had his "afflicted" brother Clifton in his household in 1859. Peter married the next year, but he and his wife, Fanny, continued to care for Clifton in their household.[24]

SLAVE FAMILY HOUSEHOLD COMPOSITION
AND SIZE OF HOLDING

Analysis of the data by variables revealed that patterns in family and household organization did not vary dramatically from the overall model according to size of holding and type of agriculture practiced. Nevertheless, findings relating to the influence of size of holding on slave domestic organization are of considerable historical significance and need to be placed in the perspective of slavery scholarship. Early studies of the black family, such as that of E. Franklin Frazier, projected the view that impersonally run, large plantations were most destructive of slave family life and values.[25] A more "normal" and stable familial structure prevailed in the intimate setting of smallholdings, where slaves were more likely to labor along with their owners and to develop close ties with fellow workers. Recent studies agree that the size of holding created substantial differences in the quality of life for slaves, but they have reversed the earlier stance. In most respects, my study supports the latter view—that family and household organization was generally more stable on larger units. The major points on the subject from my study can be quickly summarized. Generally, smallholdings (those having fewer than twenty slaves) had proportionately more members in female-headed single-parent households than did larger units and the model, and more slaves were in such households than would be considered normative for a stable community structure. A greater percentage of the population on the smallholdings were solitaires, and the solitaire ranks contained a higher percentage of males. Fewer slaves on the smaller units were part of two-parent nuclear families, and fewer were part of complex forms. Although variations occurred within the various size-of-holding categories, the differential between the smallholding and the large holding increased as the size of the holding increased. These factors, as interpreted in earlier chapters, suggest that in general the larger the community, the greater stability it exhibited in its domestic organization.

Others have reached similar conclusions, from different sets of data. Crawford's analysis of the Greenwood collection of ex-slave interviews revealed that female-headed single-parent households were 50 percent more common on holdings of fifteen and fewer slaves than on larger units. And he found that on the smallholdings only one of every three children was socialized in a household containing both parents.[26] Small units allowed fewer choices for mates, and off-plantation marriages were therefore much more common than they were on large holdings.[27] Such marriages were more vulnerable to separation. If a small owner did not allow socializing and intermarriage with slaves of neighboring owners, competition was intense, resulting in earlier marriages for women, earlier and more frequent pregnancies, postponement or inability to marry for some men, and—in general—fewer familial choices for slaves.[28] The family unit of a smallholding was more likely to be divided through estate division or sheriff's sale. Recent scholarship also suggests that slaves were able to exercise more autonomy and forge more effective communities on larger holdings.[29]

My study provides additional evidence for these conclusions except that I do not perceive the differences as being as marked as do some of my colleagues.[30] For example, in the communities in my sample having 1 to 19 slaves, 21 percent of the population were solitaires, 48 percent were part of standard nuclear families, and 21 percent resided in female-headed single-parent households. Plantations having a population from 100 to 199 had 18 percent of the slaves as solitaires, 51 percent in standard nuclear families, and 12 percent in female-headed households. The differences became much greater, however, when the slave population was over 200.

DEVELOPMENTAL CYCLE

The developmental cycle is a key to understanding slave household composition. In this study two types of developmental cycles were shown to influence household composition over time—one related to collective family cycles, another to crisis and adaptation. Both of these were partially quantitatively derived but were also observed in qualitative sources.

A developmental approach has become a mainstay in familial history. Anticipated by a few pioneering works in the late 1940s, such as those of anthropologist Meyer Fortes, social scientists of the late 1960s and 1970s were widely applying a dynamic rather than a static approach to the study of domestic groups, especially in life cycle studies of the family.[31] By the early 1970s family historians were successfully applying the international typology developed by Peter Laslett and Eugene Hammel to classify households. But Lutz Berkner and others warned that typological analysis of a single census was of limited use. Increasingly, then, the developmental dimension was added to household analysis, and a cyclical or life course approach has now become commonplace. As Robert Wheaton observed in 1987, "The use of the nominative household census, informed and modified by the concept of the household developmental cycle, has joined the Family Reconstitution Method as one of the twin foundation piers of kinship history."[32] Historians of United States slavery have not extensively applied these methods, but there are some notable practitioners. Herbert Gutman briefly introduced a crisis-related cycle in his study of the Cohoon plantation, and more recently, Cheryll Cody applied a similar model very successfully in her study of the Ball plantation. Deborah White devoted an entire chapter to the life cycle of the female slave in *Ar'n't I a Woman?*, and Alan Kulikoff skillfully analyzed the effects of the life cycle on both black and white populations in the eighteenth-century Chesapeake in *Tobacco and Slaves*.[33]

One of the earliest scholars to apply the developmental cycle to the study of black populations was Crandall A. Shiflett. In a 1975 study, he observed that as the family cycle progressed among the rural black families in Louisa County, Virginia, in the postbellum period, at "certain points the standard nuclear family becomes a minority type," then regenerates. "Why," he asked, "is the simple nuclear family more prevalent in some stages of life than in others?" As I have, he searched for demographic, economic, and social factors that influenced these cyclical changes in family and household structure. Shiflett points out the strengths as well as the limitations of the life cycle approach, but he convincingly demonstrates what "may be gained by developing a dynamic picture keyed to changes that occur within the family between formation and maturation." Although he is observing Virginia black families in 1880, the following statement speaks to my own study of Louisiana slaves over more than half a century of change:

> What we have done is to show the relationship between economic factors . . . operating within a social order of a specific variety . . . and family structure. One picture that emerges after passing families through this filter is that of families in bondage to forces over which they have no control. In this case it is nonsensical to speak of family structure as a reflection of indigenous cultural choices. And yet another, more hopeful picture has emerged that testifies to the remarkable vitality and adaptability of three-fourths of all black families, and to the institution of the family in general.[34]

This book has been primarily concerned with one major aspect of slavery in Louisiana—slave domestic organization. In describing and analyzing slave family, household, and community organization, I discovered that Louisiana slaves had a well-defined and collective vision of the structure that would serve them best and an iron determination to attain it. But along with this constancy in vision and perseverance was flexibility. Slave domestic forms in Louisiana bent like willows in the wind to keep from shattering. The suppleness of their forms prevented domestic chaos and enabled most slave communities to recover from even serious crises. The chariot of their domestic organizations conveyed most Louisiana chattels through the dangerous, enfeebling circumstances of enslavement with their humanity intact. Along with their religious belief and folk culture, Louisiana slaves' families, households, and communities provided them with respite, comfort, love, support, and encouragement when the pain of bondage grew too great. Their domestic organizations embraced and buffered them even when, as recounted in one of the many slave versions of "Sweet Chariot," they "don't want to stay here no longer."

> Swing low, sweet chariot,
> Freely let me into rest
> 'cause I don't want to stay here no longer.
> Swing low, sweet chariot,
> When Gabriel make his last alarm,
> I want to be rolling in Jesus' arm,
> 'cause I don't want to stay here no longer.

Appendix A: Developmental Patterns in Louisiana Slave Communities

Phase I: Crisis phase (unstable, disorganized)

1. Generally associated with communities recently created by in-migration from another state or region, those newly established in another part of the state, or those whose membership had been greatly altered by massive sales or estate division.
2. Generally associated with first decade in operation, first generation in new surroundings, or first decade after major crisis.
3. In Louisiana, this phase most closely associated with 1810 to early 1830s.
4. Few children present under the age of eleven.
5. Few slaves present over the age of forty.
6. Few married couples present.
7. Relatively high incidence of female-headed households.
8. Very uncomplicated household organization, mainly only solitaires and simple family types.
9. Small incidence of or no complex family types.
10. Relatively large numbers of solitaires.
11. Proportionately more males than females in solitaire category.
12. Solitaires primarily young, under twenty-five.
13. Little apparent kinship beyond nuclear unit.
14. Though most adults are young, the community's average age is higher than in the next phase because of the paucity of children in community.
15. Little apparent social organization.
16. Frequent changes in membership as a result of external circumstances, usually owners' choices.

Phase II: Building or rebuilding phase (expansive, transitional, volatile)

1. Associated with second and third decades in operation or new location, two-generation depth.
2. In Louisiana, generally prevailed in late 1830s and 1840s.

3. Many children under age eleven in the community. Labor force rapidly expanding through reproduction; many infants and children under age five.
4. Few slaves over forty.
5. Many marriages taking place; married couples tend to be young, in their twenties and thirties.
6. Relatively high percentage of female-headed households, containing more children than before.
7. Simple household organization, primarily consisting still of only simple families and solitaires, but with more variety within the simple family category.
8. Few members in complex forms, especially extended families.
9. Numerical increases most apparent in all simple family classifications, particularly those of standard nuclear families (both parents plus children) and female-headed single-parent households (mother plus children).
10. Percentage of solitaires in community remains high, may even increase as the result of slave force expansions by owner.
11. Rapid expansion of slave community both through births and purchases.
12. Younger average age in community because of the presence of large numbers of children.
13. Many changes in community imposed by owners, particularly in the second decade.

Phase III: Consolidation phase (relatively stable, balanced)

1. Associated with third and fourth decades in operation, new location, or after major crisis. Three-generation depth.
2. Fewer young children in the third decade than previous period, rise again in number of children present in fourth decade as the second generation in place begins to reproduce.
3. Greater proportion of the community over age forty; some over fifty.
4. Decrease in number of married couples without children present in the third decade. In fourth decade, married couples without children increase again because of young, newly married second-generation members who have not yet had children and also the increased presence of older couples whose children have left the household to form their own.
5. Dramatic decrease in solitaires.
6. Dramatic change in constituency of solitaire group. More single, middle-aged, and elderly individuals of both genders whose families have died or formed their own households.

7. Solitaire category still displays a male-favored gender imbalance but less so than in earlier phases of development.

8. Decrease in female-headed single-parent households.

9. Though still small in incidence, more of the single-parent households are headed by widowed or divorced males than in earlier phases.

10. Household structure increasingly diverse and complex—some incidence of nonrelated slaves forming households, more co-resident siblings, and some examples of couples bringing siblings into their households.

11. More multiple family households present and more members within these units. Most conform to this pattern: mature couple or single head of household bring into household (in addition to other children) a young married offspring and spouse or unmarried offspring with her own infant or young child.

12. Greater balance in age and sex distribution.

13. Rise in average age in third decade, possible slight drop in fourth decade as third-generation births lower it.

14. Intricately developed kinship systems.

15. Relatively stable and complex social organization.

16. Common in Louisiana during the 1850s, probably would have prevailed in the 1860s as well if war had not intervened.

17. Under normal conditions, sales and transfers infrequent.

18. Highest total population of any phase.

Appendix B: Households and Housefuls in Oakland's Slave Quarter

Actual living arrangements of selected Oakland slaves, 1817	Family household composition designation of Oakland slaves, 1817
1. Solitaires living alone None of the cabins contained a solitaire living alone	1. None of the solitaires lived alone
2. Solitaires living with other solitaires of no known relationship *Cabin 8* Davy Stepney Little Gunny Phill	2. Davy—designated as a solitaire in household analysis Stepney—designated as a solitaire Little Gunny—designated as a solitaire Phill—designated as a solitaire
3. Solitaires living with other solitaires known to be related None of the cabins contained related solitaires living together	3. None of the solitaires are known to have lived with related solitaires
4. Married couple living alone *Cabin 11* Andy Phyllis *Cabin 13* John Sarah	4. John and Sarah—designated as a married couple alone Andrew and Phyllis—designated as a married couple alone
5. Two or more married couples without children present living together *Cabin 9* Jem Stack Maria Big Harry Susan	5. Jem Stack—designated in household analysis as a solitaire because Maria was not present on 1 June 1817 roll. She was on cabin list and later lists. Big Harry and Susan—designated as a married couple alone

6. Two or more married couples with children living together

None

7. Married couple with children living alone

Cabin 4
Isaac
Anarky
  Squire
  Sally

8. Married couple without children plus family solitaire who may or may not be related

Cabin 1
Ben
Peggy
+
Vicy

Cabin 2
Little Harry
Lydia
+
Y. Milly

Cabin 14
Alex
Nancy
+
Tenah

9. Married couple with children plus unmarried female and her children

Cabin 3
Randolph
Harriet
  Fanny
+
Grace
  Mary
  Martha

6. None

7. Nine married couples with children were present on the cabin lists, but only one, that of Isaac, Anarky, and their two children, occupied a cabin by themselves

8. Ben and Peggy—designated as a married couple alone in household composition
Vicy—listed as a solitaire
Little Harry, Lydia, and Y. Milly—designated as an extended family, with lateral extension. Lydia (Harry's wife) was Y. Milly's sister.
Alex and Nancy—designated as a married couple alone
Tenah—identified as a solitaire

9. Randolph, Harriet, and Fanny—designated as a married couple with children
Grace and her children Mary and Martha—identified as a female-headed single-parent household
Jack, Milly, and John—designated as a married couple with children
Jenny and her children Phyllis, Hetty, and Herbert—identified as female-headed single-parent household

Cabin 5
Jack
Milly
  John
  +
  Jenny
    Phyllis
    Hetty
    Herbert
    —— (an unidentified child who
        died)

10. Married couple with children plus
solitaire of no known relationship

Cabin 10
Jerry
Nancy
  Charity
  Ellen
  +
Gundy

Cabin 15
Alex Carpenter
Nancy James
  Jenny
  +
Jem Gillum

Cabin 6
Will
Winney
  Peter
  Phyllis
Dorcas (who would shortly have
an infant daughter, Cely)

Cabin 12
Peter
Rhoda
  Booker
  Carlos
  +
Bess (Betsy)

10. Jerry, Nancy, and their children,
Charity and Ellen, identified as
married couple with children
Gundy—identified as a solitaire
Alex Carpenter, Nancy James, and
their daughter, Jenny, designated as
married couple with child
Jem Gillum—identified as a solitaire
Will, Winney, and their children,
Peter and Phyllis identified as
married couple with children
Dorcas and her baby Cely—identified
as female-headed single-parent
household
Peter, Rhoda, and their sons Booker
and Carlos—designated as a married
couple with children
Bess (Betsy)—designated as a solitaire

11. Unmarried females with children
    residing alone

    None

12. Unmarried females (or females with
    absent husband) with children plus
    other unmarried female with children

    Cabin 7
    Hannah—(married to Jacob, not
       Henry on cabin list)
    Nick
    Sirus (Cyrus)
    Thornton
       +
    Tall Jenny
    Anthony
    Susan

11. At least four units of female-headed
    single-parent households appear on
    cabin lists, but none resided as a unit
    alone

12. See above
    Jacob, Hannah, and their children
    Nick, Sirus (Cyrus), and Thornton—
    designated as married couple with
    children
    Tall Jenny and her children Susan and
    Anthony identified as a female-
    headed single-parent household

❧ NOTES ❧

Note: Wherever possible, the original spelling of place-names and personal names and the punctuation of quoted material have been retained throughout the book.

INTRODUCTION

1. Bill of Sale, Rachel O'Connor to David Weeks, 5 June 1829; Notification of Writ of Seizure, Case of William D. Flowers v. Rachel O'Connor, District Court no. 445, West Feliciana Parish, 2 Oct. 1832; Rachel O'Connor to David Weeks, 6 Oct. 1832, box 4, folders 28 and 30, David Weeks Papers, Louisiana State University. Amended Answer of Mary C. Conrad Moore to Petitions of Frances M. Magill and Augustin S. Magill for Partition of the Estate of David Weeks, 26 Jan. 1846, box 61, portfolio 75, ibid.

2. Among those who were removed with Sam by January 1831 were John and Young Sampson. John had been raised in the house with his parents, Patience (Rachel's cook) and old John. Young Sampson's father, old Sampson, grieved deeply for his son. In 1833 another contingent was sent away, hired out by Weeks to his brother-in-law, who was reputed to be a harsher master. In 1834, Rachel, in acceding to having a group sent to Weeks, recalled the trauma caused by the earlier piecemeal removals: "The old women would grieve so much to part with their boys." She recalled that when the first group left, "the old ones made such long sorrowful faces that I made up my mind to let all go at once rather than see them as they were" (Rachel O'Connor to David Weeks, 5 Apr. 1832, 25 Apr. 1834, box 4, folder 27, box 5, folder 36, ibid.).

3. In the group sent in 1833 were Dave, Eben, Harry, Littleton, and Frank. Harry, Eben, and Littleton ran away in November in an attempt to return home but were caught in Baton Rouge and returned to Conrad. Harry and Frank ran away again and made it home in early December but were soon sent to Weeks's Grand Cote Plantation in the Attakapas. Old Sampson died in December 1833 without seeing his son again. By January 1834, all except Eben, who was sick, had escaped and returned to Rachel O'Connor's plantation, "without leave from Mr. Conrad." She eventually recovered Eben temporarily and nursed him back to health (Rachel O'Connor to David Weeks, 17 Mar. 1831, box 3, folder 25; 3, 16, 20 Nov. 1833, box 4, folder 35; 2 Jan. 1834, box 5, folder 36, ibid.).

4. Rachel O'Connor to Mary C. Weeks, 4 Sept. 1840, to Frances Weeks, 2 Oct. 1840, box 8, folder 62, ibid.

5. Rachel O'Connor to Harriet Weeks, 12 Apr. 1841, box 9, folder 64, ibid.

6. "Note Regarding Slaves Who Had Died or Were Sold since 1835," box 61, folder 75, ibid.

7. The literature on the debate is too lengthy to be cited in its entirety here, but the

following works are essential: Phillips, *American Negro Slavery*; Frazier, *Negro Family in the United States*; Stampp, *Peculiar Institution*; Elkins, *Slavery*; Rawick, *From Sundown to Sunup*; Blassingame, *Slave Community*; Genovese, *Roll, Jordan, Roll*; Fogel and Engerman, *Time on the Cross*; Gutman, "Persistent Myths about the Afro-American Family"; Engerman, Fogel, and Genovese, "New Directions in Black History"; Fogel, *Without Consent or Contract*; Gutman, *Black Family*; David et al., *Reckoning with Slavery*; Engerman, "Studying the Black Family"; David and Temin, "Capitalist Masters, Bourgeois Slaves"; Davis, *Problem of Slavery in Western Culture*; Davis, "Slavery and the Post–World War II Historians"; Davis, *Problem of Slavery in the Age of Revolution*; Davis, *Slavery and Human Progress*; Boles, *Black Southerners*; Escott, *Slavery Remembered*; Crawford, "Quantified Memory"; Stuckey, *Slave Culture*; Levine, *Black Culture and Black Consciousness*; Fox-Genovese, *Within the Plantation Household*; Jones, *Labor of Love*; Krech, "Black Family Organization in the Nineteenth Century"; Moynihan, *Negro Family*; Smith, "Nuclear Family in Afro-American Kinship"; Tanner, "Matrifocality in Indonesia and Africa among Black Americans"; Manfra and Dykstra, "Serial Marriage and the Origins of the Black Step-family"; Herskovits, *Myth of the Negro Past*; Kolchin, "American Historians and Antebellum Southern Slavery."

8. British demographic historian, pioneer in the field of family history, and co-founder of the Cambridge Group for the History of Population and Social Structure, Peter Laslett applied his methodology to the study of seven plantations, all but one apparently associated with the Stephen Duncan family of Adams County, Mississippi. Three of these plantations were located in Louisiana: L'Argent of Terrebonne Parish and adjacent holdings in St. Mary Parish, Oxford, and Camperdown. Laslett analyzes total numbers of households rather than of slaves and percentages of household units in each type rather than of individuals in each type (*Family Life*, pp. 233–60). Also see "Negroes on Oxford Plantation, Attakapas, 1851," "Negroes on Camperdown Plantation, Attakapas, 1851," "List of Slaves on Carlisle Plantation, 1856," 1 Jan. 1860, Vol. 3, pp. 1–3, 20–26, Duncan Papers; Re-Conveyance of Slaves and Land at Oxford and Camperdown Plantations, 12 Apr. 1859, A. McWilliams to Stephen Duncan, Conveyance Vol. O, pp. 242–47, St. Mary Parish Conveyance Records; McLemore, *History of Mississippi*, vol. 1, Table 6, n.p.; Inventory, 7 Mar. 1851, of Land and Slaves of L'Argent Plantation in "Estate of William Cochran, Adams County, Mississippi," and sale of same Tensas property to Stephen Duncan, Succession Book B, pp. 382–84, Tensas Parish Probate Records; Donation of Land and Slaves, 1 Jan. 1852, Conveyance, Stephen Duncan, Sr., to Stephen P. Duncan, L'Argent Plantation, Wills and Donation Book A, pp. 68–69, Tensas Parish Conveyance Records.

9. A partial listing of the best of these works must include Dunn, "Tale of Two Plantations"; Dunn, "Servants and Slaves"; Higman, "Household Structure and Fertility on Jamaican Slave Plantations"; Higman, "African and Creole Slave Family Patterns in Trinidad"; Higman, "Slave Family"; Higman, *Slave Populations of the British Caribbean*; Craton, "Changing Patterns of Slave Families in the British West Indies"; and Handler and Corruccini, "Plantation Slave Life in Barbados." Also see Friedman, "Demography of Trinidad Slavery"; John, "Demography of Slavery in Nineteenth Century Trinidad"; Kulikoff, *To-*

bacco and Slaves; Webber, *Deep Like the Rivers*; Rosengarten, *Tombee*; Malone, "Searching for the Family and Household Structure of Rural Louisiana Slaves"; Creel, *"A Peculiar People"*; Burton, *In My Father's House*; Joyner, *Down by the Riverside*; Cody, "Slave Demography and Family Formation"; Morrissey, "Women's Work."

10. Dew, "David Ross and the Oxford Iron Works"; Kulikoff, "Beginnings of the Afro-American Family in Maryland"; Trussell and Steckel, "Age of Slaves at Menarche and Their First Births"; Steckel, "Miscegenation and the American Slave Schedules"; Steckel, "Peculiar Population"; Steckel, "Birth Weights and Infant Mortality among American Slaves"; Steckel, "Slave Height Profiles from Coastwise Manifests"; Steckel, *Economics of U.S. Slave and Southern White Fertility*; Campbell, "Work, Pregnancy, and Infant Mortality among Southern Slaves"; Cody, "Slave Demography and Family Formation"; Cody, "Naming, Kinship, and Estate Dispersal"; Miller, "Mortality in the Atlantic Slave Trade"; Diedrich, " 'My Love Is Black as Yours Is Fair' "; Hutchinson, "Age-Sex Structure of the Slave Population in Harris County, Texas"; Fine, Schwebel, and James-Myers, "Family Stability in Black Families"; Sudarkasa, "African and Afro-American Structure"; King, "African Survivals in the Black American Family"; McGowan, "Creation of a Slave Society"; Olsen and Angel, "Life Stresses of Slavery"; Owsley, Owsley, and Mann, "Demography and Pathology of an Urban Slave Population from New Orleans"; Menard, "Maryland Slave Population"; Rutman, Wetherell, and Rutman, "Rhythms of Life"; Kiple and Kiple, "Slave Child Mortality"; Inscoe, "Carolina Slave Names"; Johnson, "Smothered Slave Infants"; Savitt, "Smothering and Overlaying of Virginia Slave Children"; Eblen, "New Estimates of the Vital Rates of the United States Black Population"; White, "Female Slaves"; Labinjoh, "Sexual Life of the Oppressed"; Faust, "Culture, Conflict, and Community"; Johnson, "Runaway Slaves and the Slave Community in South Carolina"; Berlin, "Time, Space, and the Evolution of Afro-American Society."

11. Taylor, *Negro Slavery in Louisiana*; Ripley, "Black Family in Transition"; Ripley, *Slaves and Freedmen in Civil War Louisiana*.

12. Estate records provided the greatest number of inventories showing familial groups or allowing their reconstitution. Parish records were drawn from Ascension, Assumption, Avoyelles, Catahoula, Concordia, De Soto, East Baton Rouge, East Feliciana, Franklin, Iberville, Lafourche, Natchitoches, Pointe Coupee, Rapides, St. Bernard, St. James, St. Landry, St. Martin, St. Mary, Tensas, Terrebonne, Union, West Baton Rouge, and West Feliciana parishes, although in some cases the records relating to these parishes were located elsewhere. Most useful were inventories and appraisements, sales bills, and partitions, but also important were mortgages of land and slaves, conveyances of land and slaves, and inventories associated with divorces and separations from bed and board. Many planter collections were used, with lists of slaves, ration lists, and cabin lists often collated with parish records in reconstitution procedures. Verbatim transcriptions of all inventories are in my files. Various methods were used by the nineteenth-century enumerators of Louisiana slaves to designate groups of slaves belonging to a household or family. Households were often separated by drawn lines or by spaces. Frequently, the family or household was bracketed or indicated by a wavy line, and sometimes they were designated as a "family" or

"belonging to the same family." Other times they were appraised or valued as a unit and inventoried in a systematic sequence: father, mother, children was the usual order. Within household groups, familial relationships were generally described in words: "his wife," "their children," "grandchild," in the slave communities used in this study. In some cases slaves of a family shared a surname. In a few cases households and families were reconstituted by combining information from several original documents.

An attempt was made to confine the cases for this study to those in which household structure and familial relationships were clearly discernible. Several inventories were located in which kinship groupings rather than households were used to identify slaves. In these, grown children were often assigned to the maternal line whether the adult offspring were married or not. And some attempts were made in these inventories to keep up with offspring of deceased members of a kinship line. For example, on Jean Ursin Jarreau's plantation in Pointe Coupee Parish, Judy, 23, was identified as the "daughtere of Hanny, deceased," Hippolite, 23, was the "son of Lucie." Hannah, 38, the "daughter of Sarah deceased," was listed with Frederick, 19, "son of Hannah." And one multiple family household was identified in this manner:

Jenny, 53

Frank, 33 "child of Jenny"

    Francoise, 16 "child of Lize, deceased" and "grandchild of Jenny"

    Eugenie, 15 "sister of Francoise"

    Rose, 13, "sister of Francoise"

    Emm, 10, "sister of Francoise"

Baptiste, 26, "child of Jenny"

Esther, —, "child of Jenny"

    Charles, 2, "Esther's child"

Rosette, 21, "child of Jenny"

    Josephine, 11 months, "child of Rosette"

(Inventory and Appraisement, 8 May 1855, in "Estate of Jean Ursin Jarreau," Inventory Vol. 1854–55, pp. 445–57, Pointe Coupee Parish Probate Records). If households were obvious in addition to kinship groupings, the cases were included in the sample, but if the listing by kin obscured all other household designations, they were deleted from the study.

13. *Household and Family in Past Time*, ed. Laslett and Wall, pp. 28–31, 86–89. Laslett's rules concerning presumption are followed when necessary, but almost without exception household designations and some familial relationships were provided in the original documents used in this study.

14. Ibid., pp. 28, 29.

15. Ibid., pp. 29, 61. In Laslett's typology, he describes the possible forms of the simple family as married couple, married couple with offspring, and a widowed person with offspring. In my adaptation of his typology, the third form includes all unmarried parents with children in their households whether the parent(s) was widowed, divorced, or had never been married. Slaves could not legally marry in Louisiana or in any southern state, but

they are presumed to have been married when they were recognized as a married couple by their own community and owners. The same is true of divorce.

16. Higman, "Slave Family and Household in the British West Indies," p. 271.

17. *Household and Family in Past Time*, ed. Laslett and Wall, pp. 28, 29.

18. Ibid.

19. Ibid., p. 31.

20. Ibid., p. 29.

21. Ibid., p. 30.

CHAPTER 1

1. Laslett, *The World We Have Lost*, p. 237.

2. The most useful recent synthesis of historical opinion on the "myth of the matriarchy" controversy is Fogel, *Without Consent or Contract*, pp. 163–65.

CHAPTER 2

1. The decennial increase, 1810–20, of the whole population was 100.39 percent (De Bow, *Statistical View of the United States*, p. 105).

2. *Reports of the Superintendent of the Census*, p. 65.

3. Ibid., pp. 80–81.

4. Eaton, *History of the Old South*, p. 221.

5. Ibid., pp. 212–13; Sydnor, *Slavery in Mississippi*, p. 183.

6. Phillips, *American Negro Slavery*, p. 166; Sydnor, *Slavery in Mississippi*, p. 183.

7. Taylor, *Negro Slavery in Louisiana*, pp. 59–91, 37–38; Fogel and Engerman, *Time on the Cross*, 1:194; Stampp, *Peculiar Institution*, pp. 54–55. The decennial increase, 1810–20, was 99.26 percent. Louisiana's slave population in 1810 was 34,660; in 1820, it had nearly doubled to 69,064 (De Bow, *Statistical View of the United States*, pp. 82, 84; Phillips, *American Negro Slavery*, p. 371).

8. Taylor, *Negro Slavery in Louisiana*, p. 37.

9. Inventory, 17 Nov. 1814, "Estate of John O'Connor," Succession File, drawer 70, West Feliciana Parish Probate Records.

10. The entire population in the decade increased by 40.63 percent (De Bow, *Statistical View of the United States*, p. 105; *Reports of the Superintendent of the Census*, p. 151).

11. The slave population's increase in the decade was 58.67 percent. Louisiana had 69,064 slaves in 1820 and 109,588 in 1830 (De Bow, *Statistical View of the United States*, pp. 82, 84, 105).

12. Sydnor, *Slavery in Mississippi*, p. 183.

13. Quoted in Phillips, *American Negro Slavery*, p. 213, from the *Georgia Courier* (Augusta), 11 Oct. 1827.

14. Phillips, *American Negro Slavery*, p. 166; Sydnor, *Slavery in Mississippi*, p. 183; Sitterson, *Sugar Country*, p. 28.

15. Inventory, 7 Aug. 1827, "Estate of John M. Williams," Succession Vol. E, pp. 229–30, Concordia Parish Probate Records; Inventory, 11 Oct. 1822, "Estate of Rebecca Smith," Inventory, 27 July 1821, "Estate of Sylvia Young," Inventory Vol. C, pp. 294–95, 170–72, West Feliciana Parish Probate Records.

16. The decennial increase among the entire population was 63.35 percent; that among slaves was 53.7 percent. Louisiana had 109,588 slaves in 1830 and 168,452 in 1840 (De Bow, *Statistical View of the United States*, pp. 82, 84, 105).

17. Taylor, *Negro Slavery in Louisiana*, pp. 41–45; Phillips, *American Negro Slavery*, p. 190. Phillips stated, "The heydey of the trade fell in the piping times of peace and migration from 1815 to 1860. Its greatest activity was just prior to the panic of 1837, for thereafter the flow was held somewhat in check, first by the hard times and then by an agricultural renaissance in Virginia." The volume of the interstate slave trade has been vigorously debated by historians of the South with particular reference to separations it caused among slave families. See especially David et al., *Reckoning with Slavery*, pp. 94–133; Eaton, *History of the Old South*, pp. 231–33; Stampp, *Peculiar Institution*, p. 239; Fogel and Engerman, *Time on the Cross*, 1:44–58; Tadman, "Slave Trading in the Antebellum South."

18. De Bow, *Statistical View of the United States*, pp. 82, 84, 105.

19. *Reports of the Superintendent of the Census*, p. 81.

20. Phillips, *American Negro Slavery*, p. 167; Sitterson, *Sugar Country*, p. 30.

21. Sydnor, *Slavery in Mississippi*, p. 183.

22. The precise percentage increase was 46.92 (De Bow, *Statistical View of the United States*, p. 105). Louisiana's slave population in 1840 was 168,452; in 1830, it had been 109,588 (ibid., pp. 82, 84).

23. Eaton, *History of the Old South*, p. 213; Phillips, *American Negro Slavery*, p. 167.

24. Thomas Butler to Hon. Luefroy Barras, 3 May 1842, box 8, folder 47, Thomas Butler Papers, Louisiana State University.

25. A recovery was evident, however, in the 1849 and 1850 prices for middling cotton. See price chart in Sydnor, *Slavery in Mississippi*, p. 183.

26. *Reports of the Superintendent of the Census*, p. 91.

27. Sitterson, *Sugar Country*, pp. 27, 30; Eaton, *History of the Old South*, pp. 221–23.

28. In 1849 Louisiana produced 226,001 hogsheads of sugar, by far the highest of any state (*Reports of the Superintendent of the Census*, p. 96; Phillips, *American Negro Slavery*, p. 167; Sitterson, *Sugar Country*, p. 30).

29. See Solomon Northup, *Twelve Years a Slave*, pp. 145, 147; Taylor, *Negro Slavery in Louisiana*, pp. 34–35.

30. Taylor estimates that the growth rate by natural increase was about 25 percent per decade (*Negro Slavery in Louisiana*, p. 101). The decennial increase of the entire population, 1850–60, was 36.74 percent; that of slaves was 35.50 percent (Kennedy, *Preliminary Report of the Eighth Census, 1860*, p. 131; De Bow, *Statistical View of the United States*, p. 82).

31. Taylor, *Negro Slavery in Louisiana*, p. 102.

32. Olmsted, *Slave States*, p. 75.

33. A good example is that of Stephen Duncan and his son. Stephen Duncan of Adams County, Mississippi, owned cotton plantations in Mississippi (Duncan Reserve, Oakley, Carlisle, and Holly Ridge). After the Panic of 1837 he bought plantations in the less-depleted cotton lands of northern Louisiana, among them L'Argent in Concordia and Tensas parishes, purchased in 1849. In 1850 he acquired two sugar plantations in the Attakapas, Oxford and Camperdown, both in St. Mary Parish. They netted more than $50,000 annually in the 1850–60 decade. See McLemore, *History of Mississippi*, 1:348. Notation that Stephen Duncan acquired these sugar plantations in 1850 is found in an 1859 partnership agreement in which a partner sells Duncan most of his one-half interest (Sale of Interest in Land and Slaves of Oxford and Camperdown Plantations, A. McWilliams to Dr. Stephen Duncan, 12 Apr. 1859, Conveyance Vol. O, pp. 242–57. Also see Wills and Donations, 31 Dec. 1853, Stephen Duncan to Stephen Duncan, Jr., Donation Book A, Tensas Parish, pp. 68–69).

34. Sydnor, *Slavery in Mississippi*, pp. 183–84; Kennedy, *Preliminary Report of the Eighth Census, 1860*, pp. 200–201.

35. Eaton, *History of the Old South*, p. 239; Phillips, *American Negro Slavery*, pp. 211, 226. Phillips commented that "in 1859 Joseph Bond of Georgia had marketed 2199 bales of his produce, [and] that numerous Louisiana planters particularly about Concordia Parish commonly exceeded that output."

36. Phillips, *American Negro Slavery*, pp. 211, 226; Sitterson, *Sugar Country*, pp. 29, 30, 65; Eaton, *History of the Old South*, pp. 224–25.

37. Eaton, *History of the Old South*, p. 234; Phillips, *American Negro Slavery*, pp. 273–75. Joe Gray Taylor defines the "economic sin" of "Negro Fever" as a tendency among southwestern planters to "continually . . . buy more land and slaves with which to grow more sugar or cotton in order to buy more land and slaves." He asserts that the criticism was unjustified. The contractions in slave population increases and mean sizes of slave communities during hard times encourage me to agree with Taylor (*Negro Slavery in Louisiana*, p. 165).

38. Taylor, *Negro Slavery in Louisiana*, p. 56.

39. Inventory and Estate Partition, 30 Dec. 1858, "Estate of Robert Perry," Partitions and Family Meetings Vol. B, pp. 383–91, East Feliciana Parish Probate Records; Inventory, 27 Apr. 1859, "Estate of Enos Mackey," Probate Vol. D, p. 77, Franklin Parish Probate Records; Inventory, 1 Dec. 1857, "Estate of Gilbert T. Nelson," Inventory Vol. D, pp. 125–26, and Probate Sales Vol. B, pp. 218–22, Avoyelles Parish Probate Records; Inventory and Probate Sale, 12 Jan. 1857, "Estate of Nicholas Loisel," Conveyance Vol. L, pp. 642–45, and Inventory for Probate Sale, 25 Feb. 1859, "Estate of Modest Guidry, widow of Dorsine L. Rentrop, both deceased," Conveyance Vol. N, pp. 91–95, St. Mary Parish Probate Records.

40. Inventory, 21 Apr. 1851, "Estate of Alexis Blanchard," Inventory Vol. 1849–52, pp. 425–26, Assumption Parish Probate Records.

41. The three older sons were all sold to different owners. See Inventory, 31 Oct. 1850,

"Estate of Martha C. Hargroves," Inventory Vol. C, pp. 2−4, and Probate Sale, 1855, Martha C. Hargroves, Sale of Probates, Vol. A, pp. 282−94, Avoyelles Parish Probate Records.

42. Taylor, *Negro Slavery in Louisiana*, p. 52.

43. In a total population of 708,002, 331,726 were slaves, 18,647 were free blacks, and the remaining 357,629 were whites (Kennedy, *Preliminary Report of the Eighth Census*, pp. 22, 131, 200−203).

44. Sitterson, *Sugar Country*, p. 207.

45. Prices for the crops were very favorable at the start of the new decade. The average export price in 1860 was 11.1 cents per pound; the highest price for middling cotton in New Orleans that year was 13.0 cents. Louisiana's 1861 sugar crop was record-breaking—459,410 hogsheads—but planters received only 2 ¼ cents to 3 ¾ cents for fair quality sugar. This was from 1 to 1 ½ cents less than received in 1860 (Sydnor, *Slavery in Mississippi*, p. 184; Sitterson, *Sugar Country*, pp. 180−81, 208−9, 226).

46. Quoted in Sitterson, *Sugar Country*, p. 209.

47. Ripley, "The Black Family in Transition"; Ripley, *Slaves and Freedmen in Civil War Louisiana*, pp. 146−59.

48. On the D. W. Magill list of 1865, four males were noted to have "ran away and joined the enemy in April, 1863, one died at the Battle of Mansfield in April 1864, one was accidentally shot, six were killed in an 1863 insurrection near St. Martinsville," and several others were in the service of the Confederacy in various capacities both in Texas and Louisiana ("List of Slaves Belonging to the Estate of D. W. Magill, deceased," St. Martin and De Soto parishes, 16 Mar. 1865, Weeks Papers, Tulane University).

49. William J. Minor's diary entries for 28, 29 September 1863. Fourteen men were taken by Union soldiers on 29 September (Plantation Diary 32, Minor Papers, Louisiana State University).

50. "Liste par 1854 Familles," Alexandre de Clouet Memorandum Book, 1853−58; "Liste de Negroes," 15 Nov. 1865, Lists, 1860−62, in Memorandum Book, 1848−65, in de Clouet Papers, ibid.

51. "Petition of Mary Clara Conrad, late widow of David Weeks, deceased, and now wife of John Moore, St. Martin," 23 Aug. 1856, "Estate of Frances Weeks, widow of A. S. Magill, deceased, late wife of Buford A. Prewitt," estate folder 1540; see also "Estate of Augustin S. Magill," 24 Dec. 1851, estate folder 1314, all in St. Martin Parish Probate Records.

52. An 1858 inventory of the same slaves was useful in reconstitutions ("Annual Record of D. W. Magill's Slaves, St. Martin Parish, Close of the Year 1858," in Weeks Papers, Tulane University).

53. Petition, Mary Clara Conrad (Moore), 7 Sept. 1863, in "Estate of David Weeks Magill," Probate File 1811, St. Martin Parish Probate Records.

54. "Ex-Slave Stories (Texas), Susan Smith, former Slave of Charles Weeks, New Iberia, Louisiana," in Rawick, ed., *American Slave*, Supp. Ser. 2, vol. 9, pt. 8, pp. 3663−70. This former slave's recollections concerning her own family and that of her owner were confirmed in the Weeks Papers, Tulane University. Her parents, "Dennis Joe" and "Sabry Joe,"

were located on several lists, including the lot drawn for Charles Weeks in the "Estate Division, David Weeks," 23 Apr. 1846, Original Records Vol. 13, pp. 358–62, St. Martin Parish Probate Records; "1846 Memo Regarding Partition," box 61, folder 75, Weeks Papers, Louisiana State University.

55. "Deposition, Dr. John Smith, St. Martin Parish," 17 Feb. 1866, "Estate of David Weeks Magill," Succession 1811, 6192 B, n.p., St. Martin Parish Probate Records. Dr. Smith confirmed that Mary Conrad Weeks (Moore) died 29 December 1863. He stated that David Magill died in May rather than June 1863.

56. "Petition of Mary Clair Conrad (Moore)," 7 Sept. 1863, "Estate of David Weeks Magill," Probate File 1811, St. Martin Parish Probate Records.

57. "List of Slaves Belonging to the Estate of D. W. Magill, deceased, March 26, 1865" (St. Martin and De Soto parishes), Weeks Papers, Tulane University. Interestingly, one of Magill's slaves, A. C. Pruitt, was interviewed in Texas by WPA workers. He, too, left an extremely informative and documentable account of his life with the Weeks-Magill family. He, his mother, Rachel Smith, and sister Clementine were all identified in the overseer's lists. His family was among those taken to Texas. See Rawick, ed., *American Slave*, 4:218–21. Pruitt is a spelling variation of Prewitt, taken from Buford Prewitt. The WPA interviewer probably misunderstood the name when given by the informant, a common occurrence, and spelled it wrong.

58. "List of Slaves of Prescott and Moore, April 17, 1864, De Soto Parish," box 61, folder 76, Weeks Papers, Louisiana State University. To identify family groups I also used an inventory of the same slaves, 26 June 1865, ibid.

59. van der Walle, "Household Dynamics in a Belgian Village," esp. p. 90; *Household and Family in Past Time*, ed. Laslett and Wall, p. 32; Wheaton, "Family and Kinship in Western Europe"; Hareven, "Cycles, Cohorts"; Segalen, "Family Cycle and Household Structure," pp. 223–25, 228–29, 235; Berkner, "The Stem Family and the Developmental Cycle of the Peasant Household," esp. p. 406; Berkner, "Household Arithmetic"; Seider and Mitterauer, "Reconstruction of the Family Life Course."

60. Kertzer, "Anthropology and Family History"; Stone, "Family History in the 1980s"; Krech, "Black Family Organization in the Nineteenth Century," esp. pp. 431–35. In discussing the dangers of analyzing household structure apart from kinship systems, Robert Wheaton warns that "for all their precision, the statistics on mean household size and distribution of household types are only the beginning of an understanding which must recognize the fluidity of structure, the impermanence of boundaries, and the existence of kin relations which continues behind it" ("Family and Kinship in Western Europe," pp. 601, 605, 623–24).

CHAPTER 3

1. Menn, *Large Slaveholders*, pp. 3, 5–6.

2. Phillips, *American Negro Slavery*, pp. 382–86. It is easy to see how many contemporaries

and historians have assumed that sugar producers were more concerned than other planters with obtaining the short-term benefits accruing from a slave force dominated by male prime-age slaves with no familial obligations. Such a pattern was present on enough sugar plantations to feed the myth. For example, Louis Landry's slave community displayed a radical skewing in its household composition. Only 30 percent of his slaves lived in standard nuclear families, and over half were solitaires, most of them young males. That estate was sold in 1832, and the sale reflected a lack of regard for family organization. Children over the age of ten were appraised separately from their parents and frequently sold to different purchasers. The separation of a married couple was openly stated: "Alexis, a negro man, aged twenty-eight years, and his wife Victoire, aged sixteen, offered together in one lot not having attained the price they were estimated at . . . were sold separately." On the sugar-producing unit of Charles Breaux, 42 percent of the slaves were solitaires, and half were residents of female-headed single-parent households. Only two married couples lived on the Breaux place, and they were childless. Although not as often noticed by contemporary observers, similar patterns of disorganization and skewing toward single male workers also were common among sugar producers in the Mississippi River regions. For example, 32 percent of the workers were solitaires on William Disharoone's cotton plantation. Similarly, nearly half of the 132 slaves on the Grove Plantation on Bayou Vidal were solitaires, and only one-fourth of its chattels lived in two-parent households. Males dominated the solitaire contingents at both plantations. See Inventory for Sale, "Estate of Louis Landry," 29 July 1831, Inventory and Sales Vol. 1831–32, pp. 67–75, Ascension Parish Probate Records; Inventory, "Estate of Charles Breaux," 8 July 1839, Probate File 644, n.p., Iberville Parish Probate Records; Inventory, "Estate of William Disharoone," 3 Aug. 1839, Succession Vol. 1, pp. 298–99, and Inventory, "Estate of Rachel Grove," 27 Oct. 1837, ibid., 73–81, Concordia Parish Probate Records.

3. Katz, *Eyewitness*, pp. 123–24; G. W. Featherstonhaugh quoted in Phillips, *American Negro Slavery*, p. 198.

4. Weld, comp., *American Slavery as It Is*, p. 162.

5. Douglass, *Life and Times of Frederick Douglass*, p. 174.

6. Clarke and Clarke, *Narrative of the Sufferings of Lewis and Milton Clarke*, p. 121.

7. Stroyer, *Sketches of My Life in the South*, pp. 29–31.

8. Rice, *Rise and Fall of Black Slavery*, pp. 286–87.

9. Ibid.; Weld, comp., *American Slavery as It Is*, pp. 35–39.

10. Last Will and Testament of J. William Provan, 8 Dec. 1832, Will Book A, Iberville Parish Probate Records.

11. Francis Du Bose Richardson, "The Teche Country Fifty Years," pp. 3–5, Caffery Papers, Louisiana State University.

12. Olmsted, *Slave States*, p. 122.

13. Sugar plantations required a larger work force, at least during the sugarmaking months, than cotton did. Consolidation resulting from mechanization of some of the rolling processes cut down on manpower requirements by the late 1840s, but there still were

frequent labor shortages in the sugar parishes, resulting in a frenzy of hiring in the fall months. Even in the late 1850s, the sugar parishes and the Mississippi River cotton parishes had the "greatest concentration of slaves in the hands of the large planters" (Menn, *Large Slaveholders*, p. 9).

14. On the William Duprey sugar estate, the cooper was sixty and the engineer was a thirty-year-old husband and father. On the plantation of William N. Ivy, Stephen, fifty, a "good cooper, carpenter, & sugar boiler," was also married and the father of two children. See Inventory and Estate Partition, 8 July 1859, in "Estate of Desire Carlin," Conveyance Vol. N, pp. 272–74, 282, St. Mary Parish Probate Records; Conveyance of Land and Slaves, Antoine Duprey to George Reagan Price, 2 Jan. 1855, Conveyance Vol. 3, no. 553, n.p., Iberville Parish Conveyance Records; Conveyance, Modest Guidry to William N. Ivy, 24 Feb. 1859, Conveyance Vol. N, pp. 91–95, Assumption Parish Probate Records; Inventory and Appraisement, "Estate of Henry Doyal," 5 Feb. 1859, Succession Vol. 3, pp. 195–205, Ascension Parish Probate Records; and Inventory and Appraisement, "Estate of William Pugh," 24 Dec. 1836, Inventory Vol. 1836, pp. 47–51, Assumption Parish Probate Records.

15. "List of Vienna Plantation Slaves of A. LeComte, Cote Joyeuse, 1852," in Plantation Vol. 3, Prudhomme Papers.

16. Small slaveowners were encouraged to believe that they could prosper in Louisiana during the 1815–37 period. For example, a Maryland farmer who had moved to Louisiana wrote a letter back home which was printed in *Niles' Register* in 1817: "In your states a planter with ten negroes with difficulty supports a family genteely; here well managed they would be a fortune to him. With you the seasons are so irregular your crops often fail; here the crops are certain, and want of the necessities of life never for a moment causes the heart to ache—abundance spreads the table of the poor man, and contentment smiles on every countenance" (Phillips, *American Negro Slavery*, p. 174, quoting from *Niles' Register*, p. 38); see also Taylor, *Negro Slavery in Louisiana*, pp. 66–67; De Bow, *Statistical View of the United States*, p. 96.

17. Fogel cogently reviews and presents historical opinion on the influence of size of holding on slave life and culture in *Without Consent or Contract*, pp. 169–71; 178–86. Also see Kulikoff, *Tobacco and Slaves*, p. 30.

18. Webber, *Deep Like the Rivers*, pp. xiii, 3; Owens, *This Species of Property*, p. 137.

19. Northup, *Twelve Years a Slave*.

20. Probate Sale of Land and Slaves, "Estate of Louis Breau," 5 Dec. 1821, Docket Vol. G, Notarial Acts, 304/541, Iberville Parish Probate Records.

21. Inventory of Land and Slaves, "Separation from Bed and Board," Ursin Carlin (St. Martin Parish) and Celeste Colette Prevost (St. Mary Parish), 18 Oct. 1843, Vol. F, p. 173, St. Mary Parish Probate Records.

22. Inventory, "Estate of Jane Lewis," 12 June 1828, Succession Vol. E, pp. 289–90, Concordia Parish Probate Records.

23. Inventory, "Estate of James Garvis," 4 Oct. 1847, Inventories Vol., 1846–49, pp. 98–99, Pointe Coupee Parish Probate Records.

24. Inventory and Sale, "Estate of John B. Evans," 4 Aug. 1863, Probate Sale Vol., pp. 396–99, in Avoyelles Parish Probate Records.

25. Stampp, *Peculiar Institution*, pp. 30–31, 34–38, 52–54, 330–31; Gutman, *Black Family*, p. 568 n. 20; Genovese, *Roll, Jordan, Roll*, pp. 7–11, 13; Fogel and Engerman, *Time on the Cross*, 1:194.

26. Menn, *Large Slaveholders*, pp. 1–2; Stampp, *Peculiar Institution*, p. 31; Fogel and Engerman, *Time on the Cross*, 2:148–49; Hilliard, *Atlas of Antebellum Southern Agriculture*, pp. 35–38.

27. Menn, *Large Slaveholders*, p. 2.

28. Stampp, *Peculiar Institution*, pp. 42–43.

29. One example of a large plantation having a very stable structure at the point of inventory was the Donaldson-Clark place (part of Houmas Plantation) in Ascension Parish. In 1858, only 9 percent of its 346 slaves were solitaires, and 74 percent lived in simple families. Over half resided in two-parent nuclear units. In Rapides Parish, on one of William Clark's plantations an astonishing 92 percent of its 219 slaves lived in simple families, only 5 percent were solitaires, and 75 percent formed part of standard nuclear units. The same pattern prevailed at William J. Minor's Southdown Plantation, where in 1852 some 86 percent of his 233 slaves were residents of simple families and 72 percent were members of two-parent families (only 4 percent were solitaires). An exception to this pattern was found on one of the large plantations of the sample, the Hynes plantation in Iberville Parish in 1854. Of 235 slaves, 21 percent were solitaires, and 66 percent lived in simple families. But only 32 percent of the Hynes slaves were members of standard nuclear families, and 29 percent formed part of female-headed single-parent households. See Sale of Houmas Plantation Land and Slaves—Donaldson-Clark Place, Ascension Parish, 15 Apr. 1858, Caroline Preston to John Burnside, in Gaudet Papers; "List of Negroes at Southdown," Terrebonne Parish, 1 Jan. 1852, in Minor Papers; Inventory of Slaves, Bayou Boeuf Upper Plantation, "Estate of William Clark," 16 May 1850, Rapides Parish, in Thompson Papers; Inventory in Conjunction with Conveyance, Mary Jane Hynes to Edward Gay, 2 Mar. 1854, Conveyance Vol. 3, n.p., Iberville Parish Conveyance Records.

PART II: INTRODUCTION

1. Johnson, *British West Florida*, p. 146; Arthur, *Story of the West Florida Rebellion*, p. 10.

2. British control of West Florida, including the western part containing Feliciana, was brief, ending in 1783, but nevertheless significant. As historian Cecil Johnson states, during the British period backcountry people began using the Mississippi River as a "highway of commerce; and the inhabitants of the older colonies learned the value of land in West Florida" (*British West Florida*, pp. 144–46, 234).

3. Robinson, *Early Feliciana Politics*, pp. 76–77, 80–81; Abernathy, *The South in the New Nation*, pp. 10–25, 211, 353. Arthur, *Story of the West Florida Rebellion*, pp. 10–25; Davis, *Louisiana*, p. 173.

4. Abernathy, *The South in the New Nation*, p. 211.

5. For example, Thomas Butler was born in Pennsylvania but by 1809 practiced law in the Mississippi Territory, representing many members of the merchant-planter class, including Nathaniel Evans, Abijah Hunt, and Daniel Clark. By 1813 he was a planter in West Feliciana Parish (Inventory and Correspondence, 1800–1809, 1810–14, 1815–19, Thomas Butler Papers).

6. Flint, *Recollections of the Last Ten Years*, p. 28.

7. Bergerie, *They Tasted Bayou Water*, pp. 13–14, 16; Glenn R. Conrad to Ann Patton Malone, 30 July 1990. Also see Conrad, *Land Records of the Attakapas District*, vol. 1.

8. Conrad to Malone, 30 July 1990; Moody, "Slavery on Louisiana Sugar Plantations," pp. 189–93; Flint, *Recollections of the Last Ten Years*, pp. 316–17; Richardson, "The Teche Country Fifty Years Ago," pp. 1–3.

9. Conrad to Malone, 30 July 1990.

10. Even in the late 1820s, the Attakapas region, and especially St. Mary, was known for its remoteness. In a letter to his brother-in-law, who was a St. Mary planter, A. T. Conrad warned that a fellow planter's object in offering a slave for sale in the Attakapas was to rid himself of a habitual runaway. "[It] being a remote corner of the Globe he [the slave] would find . . . difficulty in getting out." In 1810, J. P. Palfrey writes of the "extreme fatigue of a journey to New Orleans and back which at this season . . . would be very great on horse back." Travel from St. Mary to New Orleans by boat in the 1820s would take only several days, but by barge it would take six weeks (A. T. Conrad, New Orleans, to David Weeks, Attakapas, 16 Dec. 1827, box 2, folder 18, Weeks Papers, Louisiana State University; John Palfrey, Attakapas to David Weeks, 6 Aug. 1810, box 11, folder 3, ibid.; Bergerie, *They Tasted Bayou Water*, p. 16).

11. Dormon, "Aspects of Acadiana Plantation Life," p. 361; Raphael, *Battle in the Bayou Country*, p. 54.

12. Gertrude Taylor recounts the tradition that the Attakapas Indians shunned the island because they believed it to have been the location of a catastrophic event. The island contains numerous archaeological fragments from early Indian habitation. Taylor also meticulously disentangled the various early transactions regarding property on Petite Anse. John Hayes, depressed after the death of his son, sold his remaining land on Petite Anse to Daniel D. Avery in 1868, six months before his own death. Taylor drew upon Guy Soniat's *Synopsis of the History of Louisiana from the Founding of the Colony to the End of the Year 1791* in "Saga of Petite Anse Island," p. 161; Dormon, "Aspects of Acadiana Plantation Life," p. 361; Wood, "Hayes Family," pp. 165–67.

13. Conveyance, Jesse McCall to William Stone and John C. Marsh, 8 Feb. 1818, Conveyance Vol. A-B, p. 267, St. Mary Parish Conveyance Records. In 1821 and 1825 Stone and Marsh bought additional tracts on the island (Taylor, "Saga of Petite Anse Island," p. 161).

14. As late as the 1860s the plank road could not accommodate the passage of two wagons approaching from opposite ends of the causeway, and the road was often covered by water at high tides. Consequently, signs at each end provided the days and times of safe passage

(Statement by Samuel Hoatling, 1863, quoted in Raphael, *Battle in the Bayou Country*, p. 138).

15. *Morgan City Review*, 29 Dec. 1950; Peltier and Lehman, comps. and eds. *History of Morgan City*, pp. 9–13; Mortgage (Tiger Island), Walter Brashear and Wife to the New Orleans Canal and Banking Company, 3 June 1833, St. Mary Parish Mortgage Records.

16. Brashear purchased the island upon which he operated the Belle Isle sugar plantation from Henry Johnson on 5 August 1809, although it had been previously owned by François Gonsoulin. See Mortgage of Land and Slaves (Belle Isle), Walter and Margaret Brashear to the Bank of Louisiana, 13 July 1833, Vol. A-B, pp. 54–55, St. Mary Parish Mortgage Records; Deposition of Robert B. Lawrence, Athens, Georgia, 3 July 1901, in Heirs of Gonsoulin v. The Gulf Company, Brashear Papers, Morgan City Library and Archives, Morgan City, La. Items from the Morgan City Archives were provided by archivist Lela Lehman whose assistance is gratefully acknowledged. See also *Planter's Banner* (Franklin, La.), 13 Mar. 1853.

CHAPTER 4

1. Abernathy, *The South in the New Nation*, pp. 246–57; Robinson, *Early Feliciana Politics*, p. 89.

2. Although Nathaniel Evans was born in Springfield, Galway, Ireland, his parents, Francis and Jane Richardson Evans, were born in Wales. See Transcription of note written by Evans's grandson Albert Sidney Johnston Evans in back of Volume 2 of *Louisiana Biographical and Historical Memoirs*, in the possession of Evans's descendant, Helen R. Dietrich, St. Francisville, Louisiana; also see "Family Notes," box 7, folder 47, Evans Papers, Louisiana State University; Chronology of the Nathaniel Evans Family, Evans Papers, West Feliciana Parish Historical Society, St. Francisville, Louisiana, kindly provided by archivist Elizabeth Dart. John N. Evans and Sarah Bloomfield Spencer were married on 11 March 1800, according to her tombstone inscription in the Oakland Family Cemetery, West Feliciana Parish. The first Spencer, a member of a distinguished English family, arrived in the colonies in 1631, settling in Massachusetts. Eventually, Sarah's father, Oliver Spencer, moved to Elizabeth Town, New Jersey, marrying Anna Ogden (whose brother Aaron Ogden became governor of New Jersey). Oliver Spencer served in the Continental Army and was honored for his gallantry. After the Revolution, Colonel Oliver Spencer moved to an area outside of Cincinnati, Ohio, and became prominent there. The Ogdens and Spencers of New Jersey, New York, and Ohio kept in close touch and maintained a keen interest in the developing West. Dr. Oliver Spencer, one of Sarah's relatives and probably a brother, was a respected merchant and physician in New Orleans; another was a partner in the firm of Harrod and Ogden, New Orleans factors. See Inventory, Evans Papers, Louisiana State University; Chronology, Evans Papers, West Feliciana Parish Historical Society. Evans's appointment was made in July 1801.

3. A store Evans built with a short-term partner, Abijah Hunt, at Fort Adams served as a dwelling for Evans, although he also maintained a house for his family at Pinckneyville. In

an insurance document of 1806, the store was described as frame and two-storied, with a brick-floored store on the front, double chimneys, and a rear kitchen. In 1806 the building was valued at $3,000; merchandise was valued at $10,000 (Partnership Agreement, Abijah Hunt, Natchez, and Nathaniel Evans, Fort Adams, Oct. 1802; Insurance Policy on Hunt-Evans Store, 9 Aug. 1806, Evans Papers, Louisiana State University; Chronology, Evans Papers, West Feliciana Parish Historical Society).

4. These connections, especially for the 1805–11 period, are confirmed in dozens of invoices and correspondence in the Evans Papers, Louisiana State University, especially for the years 1805–11.

5. Lieutenant (later General) James Wilkinson, in charge of the United States armies in the western regions, had expensive tastes. His accounts with Evans show frequent orders of fine Irish linen, striped silk, Spanish cigars, French wine, and London port (Account of Lt. James Wilkinson, Fort Adams, with Nathaniel Evans, Esq., June 1807–Jan. 1808, Evans Papers, Louisiana State University).

6. Voucher, Nathaniel Evans, for services rendered in conjunction with an Indian treaty of 20 November 1804, reproduced in Wilkinson, *Memoirs of My Own Times*, 2:n.p., but Appendix CXXI.

7. Nathaniel Evans, Fort Adams, to Thomas Butler, 5 Jan. 1811, in Correspondence, 1810–19, Thomas Butler Papers. Also see various accounts and invoices in Evans Papers, Louisiana State University; Clark, *New Orleans*, pp. 306–7.

8. Nathaniel Evans, Fort Adams, Mississippi Territory, to Captain Francis Johnson, Feb. 1802, in Correspondence, 1800–1809, Thomas Butler Papers.

9. Oliver H. Spencer, New Orleans, to Nathaniel Evans, Fort Adams, 19 Dec. 1806, Evans Papers, Louisiana State University; Thomas Gemmell to Daniel Clark, 22 Mar. 1808, in Wilkinson, *Memoirs of My Own Time*, 2:Appendix X; Deposition of Colonel T. H. Cushing, 15 Nov. 1806, ibid., Appendix XCII; Captain James Sterrett to Nathaniel Evans, 19 Dec. 1806, Evans Papers, Louisiana State University; Note of Albert Sidney Johnston Evans, Evans Papers, West Feliciana Parish Historical Society.

10. Abernathy, *The South in the New Nation*, pp. 279–80.

11. One claimed that "the Banking sistem [*sic*] in this place will most unquestionably blow some of our merchants up" (ibid., pp. 321–22; Clark, *New Orleans*, pp. 311–12).

12. Evans maintained his equanimity and his stores through the crisis and in 1808 was appointed to the board of the branch Bank of Louisiana (Clark, *New Orleans*, pp. 326–28, 347).

13. Plantation Record Book 36, 1811–17, entries for 8–12 Nov. 1811, Evans Papers, Louisiana State University. Evans bought land in Wilkinson County on Bayou Sarah in February 1808, planning to establish a cotton operation. By May 1809, he had moved his family to Feliciana, first to a house in St. Francisville and later to the plantation near the Mississippi line in western Feliciana. On 20 September 1809, he bought eight hundred arpents in Feliciana and on 21 June 1811, he acquired an additional eight hundred arpents adjoining the Oakland land (Chronology, Evans Papers, West Feliciana Parish Historical Society).

14. Samuel Swartwout, New York, to Nathaniel Evans, Fort Adams, Mississippi Territory, 28 Mar. 1807, Evans Papers, Louisiana State University.

15. Micajah Davis served as overseer for Nathaniel Evans from 1809 until at least 1816. He could not be located in the federal census for Feliciana in 1820.

16. The cotton picking daily work record is complete for 1811 and 1812 and partially so for the years through 1817 (Plantation Record Book 36, Evans Papers, Louisiana State University). Evans's 1811 record is the earliest I located. Covering a comparable period but not providing individual picking totals is William Weeks's "Negro Book for the Years 1811–1814, Thompson's Creek and Bayou Sarah," box 1, folder 4, Weeks Papers, Louisiana State University.

17. Nathaniel Evans to Micajah Davis, 14 Oct. 1816, box 3, folder 20, Roll, 1814, Plantation Record Book, 1811–17, all in Evans Papers, Louisiana State University.

18. In November 1811, Alex spent four days "hauling to Fort Adams," probably transporting ginned cotton from Oakland. Another Oakland slave, Andrew, spent four days in the week following 8 September 1811 "sawing at F. Adams." Evans hired six slaves from a Captain Mulford in 1811, and he hired out to other planters in the parish his own workers, including Andrew and Jacob. See especially the notations for September and October 1811, in Plantation Record Book 36, Evans Papers, Louisiana State University; Davis, ed., *Plantation Life*, p. 149.

19. For example, see the owner's rule in Davis, ed., *Plantation Life*, p. 409, and a typed transcript accompanying the original diary, pp. 41–51, box 11, folder 1, Barrow Diary and Papers.

20. Entries for 5 Apr., 31 Dec. 1836, 1 Jan. 1837, p. 6, box 11, folder 1, Barrow Diary and Papers; Cotton-picking record for week starting 14 Oct. 1811, Plantation Record Book 36, Evans Papers, Louisiana State University. An 1814 notation read "Gundy ranaway June 14, returned home about 31 or so, in the stocks through July 28, off and on" (ibid.). Micajah Davis, Oakland, to Nathaniel Evans, Pinckneyville, Mississippi, 14 Feb. 1819, box 3, folder 20, ibid.

21. On 2 June 1811, Evans entered into a purchase agreement with Samuel Hutchinson to buy an eight-hundred-acre tract joining Oakland, and he bought several lots in St. Francisville in 1818 (Chronology, Evans Family, West Feliciana Parish Historical Society; Inventory and Appraisement, "Estate of Nathaniel Evans," 23 Oct. 1819, file drawer 2, West Feliciana Parish Probate Records).

22. Inventory of Slaves, 1 June 1817, Rolls, 1811, 1814, all in Plantation Record Book 36, and Francis Evans, Bardstown, Kentucky, to Nathaniel Evans, 1816, in Inventory of Papers, p. 9, Evans Papers, Louisiana State University.

23. The child who was born in 1803 and died in infancy was Louisiana Evans. Margaret Emma Butler Evans, born in 1806, died 11 November 1811 (Entry for 12 Nov. 1811, Plantation Record Book 36, 1811–1817, Evans Papers, Louisiana State University; Chronology, Evans Papers, West Feliciana Parish Historical Society).

24. Dr. O. H. Spencer, New Orleans, to Nathaniel Evans, Fort Adams, 1808; Richard Butler

to Nathaniel Evans, Feb. 1809. The letter from Butler stated that Francis was placed with a Church of England minister, "the Rev. Mr. Chase," who was "under the necessity of opening a school for a few children of the first class." Peter Ogden wrote in 1809 that "the only danger [to Francis] is that Mr. Chase will make him too honest for this part of the world." Also see Francis A. Evans, Morris Town, New Jersey, to Nathaniel Evans, 1814; Cornelia Evans, Elizabeth Town, New Jersey, to Nathaniel Evans, 1817; O. H. Spencer, Elizabeth Town, New Jersey, to Nathaniel Evans, 1817; Nathaniel Evans to Cornelia Evans, 1819, all in Correspondence, 1813, 1814, 1815, 1817–19, as described in the annotated Inventory, Evans Papers, Louisiana State University, and the Chronology, Evans Papers, West Feliciana Parish Historical Society.

25. Inventory, "Estate of Nathaniel Evans," 23 Oct. 1819; Rogers, "Oakland," p. 4.

26. Rogers, "Oakland," p. 4; U.S. Census, 1820, Feliciana Parish, Louisiana, p. 48.

27. Mortgage, in conjunction with "Estate of Nathaniel Evans," 3 Apr. 1822, probate file 32, West Feliciana Parish Probate Records. Not all of the slaves of the estate were mortgaged in this effort to secure funds to "pay the inheritance [as] result of a family meeting." The forty-four mortgaged slaves were drawn from the portions of J. N. Evans and the DeHart children; familial relationships were designated on the inventory of mortgaged slaves. These slaves were primarily mortgaged to settle Francis Evans's portion of the inheritance because he had reached his majority.

28. Inventory, "Estate of Nathaniel Evans," 23 Oct. 1819. Francis Allison Evans was still in his mother's household in 1820, but by 1830 he had his own plantation in West Feliciana Parish and owned sixty-nine slaves (U.S. Census, 1820, Feliciana Parish, p. 48; U.S. Census, 1830, West Feliciana Parish, p. 232).

29. Orange Grove was described in 1833 as a "sugar plantation situated in the Indian Bend" area of St. Mary Parish. It had a depth of forty arpents and extended eight hundred arpents on the eastern side of Bayou Teche. Its appraised value was $12,000 (Inventory and Appraisement, "Estate of Cornelia DeHart," 17 Mar. 1833, Original Estates Vol. 10, pp. 136–37, St. Mary Parish Probate Records; Biographical and Historical Memoirs, 1:404).

30. U.S. Census, 1830, West Feliciana Parish, p. 232.

31. List of Taxable Property, 1834–41, Sarah B. Evans and John N. Evans, Plantation Record Book 37, Evans Papers, Louisiana State University.

32. John Briton (John Evans's slave) married Mima (Sarah Evans's slave); Big George (John Evans's slave) wed Barbara (Sarah Evans's slave); Robin (John Evans's slave) married Patsy (Sarah Evans's slave); Jem Gillum (Sarah Evans's slave) married Mary (John Evans's slave); and Squire (John Evans's slave) married Ellen (Sarah Evans's slave). Several of these matches produced large families. Family reconstitutions were done by the author from Evans Papers, Louisiana State University and West Feliciana Parish Historical Society.

33. List of Taxable Property, 1834–41, Evans Papers, Louisiana State University.

34. Rogers, "Oakland," p. 5.

35. Cornelia Evans DeHart was born 28 July 1805. Her birth and death dates were obtained from inscriptions on her tombstone. She is buried at Oakland rather than at Orange Grove,

perhaps attended in her last illness by her mother, Sarah Evans. Despite family tradition that the marriage was an unhappy one and the fact that she was buried at Oakland, her inscription identifies her as the "wife of Capt. J. DeHart and daughter of Nathaniel and Sarah B. Evans." Transcription of the Oakland cemetery records is courtesy of Elizabeth Dart, St. Francisville, Louisiana.

36. Inventory, "Estate of Cornelia DeHart," 1 Feb. 1833, Vol. 10, pp. 134–36, St. Mary Parish Probate Records. In 1822 Phyllis was identified as the wife of Armstead on a mortgage document; Simon and Sally were also identified as a couple. In 1830 Captain DeHart reported to census enumerators that he owned forty slaves in St. Mary Parish. Most were the separate property of his wife, Cornelia, inherited from her father (Mortgage, "Estate of Nathaniel Evans," loose document in Probate File 32, 3 Apr. 1822, n.p., West Feliciana Parish Probate Records; U.S. Census, 1830, St. Mary Parish, n.p., but western district).

37. Rolls, 1811, 1814, Plantation Record Book 36, Evans Papers, Louisiana State University; Inventory, "Estate of Cornelia DeHart," 1 Feb. 1833, Petition of John DeHart for Family Meeting, 20 Feb. 1833, Probate Sale, 25 Feb. 1833, "Estate of Cornelia DeHart," Vol. 10, pp. 136–39, 141–42, St. Mary Parish Probate Records. For familial designations used in reconstituting the families mentioned see Quarter Bill for 1817, Oakland Plantation, Roll, 1811; Record of Work, 1811–12, Plantation Record Book 36, Evans Papers, Louisiana State University.

38. No reason was given for not selling Jim's wife and children at the same time. DeHart received court authorization to sell the entire family, and he may have been dissatisfied with the bids for the group. Jim brought a good price, however. He was sold for $400 to John B. Bemis (Probate Sale, 25 Feb. 1833, "Estate of Cornelia DeHart," Vol. 10, pp. 141–42, St. Mary Parish Probate Records).

39. Mrs. A. C. Griffin, Elmslie, Woodville, Mississippi, to Bethia Richardson, Bayside, St. Mary Parish, 24 Oct. 1841, Caffery Papers, Southern Historical Collection; W. F. Weeks, University of Virginia, to Mrs. F. M. Magill, St. Martinsville, Louisiana, 12 Dec. 1841, box 9, folder 7, Weeks Papers, Louisiana State University; *New Orleans Daily Picayune*, 24, 26 Oct., 3 Nov. 1841.

40. It is possible that the children already lived with their grandmother, for the 1840 census records John DeHart as the sole member of his household (U.S. Census, 1840, St. Mary Parish, p. 324). See also Succession of John DeHart, 30 Jan. 1842, folio 949, St. Martin Parish Probate Records. For an undetermined reason, DeHart's estate was not probated in St. Mary Parish where Orange Grove was located. Also see "Renunciation of claim against the estate of John DeHart," 1 Feb. 1842, Conveyance Vol. I, pp. 357–59, St. Mary Parish Probate Records; "Last Will and Testament," Sarah Bloomfield Spencer Evans, 1 Oct. 1851, Probate File drawer 31, and Inventories Vol. F, pp. 597–99, 607, West Feliciana Parish Probate Records.

41. Rogers, "Oakland," pp. 4–5.

42. The 1860 census provides a means of comparison. John N. Evans's worth was reported as $164,000 in real and personal property; M. C. Stirling's reported wealth was $590,000,

and Daniel Turnbull's was estimated at $700,000 (U.S. Census, 1860, West Feliciana Parish, pp. 25–26, 43).

43. Inventory and Appraisement, "Estate of Mary A. B. Evans," 7 July 1849, Inventories Vol. F, pp. 405–11, West Feliciana Parish Probate Records. In addition to her husband, her heirs were her four minor children: Mary Cornelia, John Eugene, Corinne, and Frank Evans (Partition of Slaves and Personal Property Bequeathed to Stephen Windham and Mary Chandler Evans, deceased, 12 Oct. 1852, in Record Book P, pp. 563–67, West Feliciana Parish Probate Records). The Hazlewood property had been left equally to Windham and Mary Chandler Evans by Mary Ann Windham. This inheritance and Evans's purchase of Stephen Windham's one-half interest in Hazlewood greatly increased Evans's holdings and stature. Evans wrote in his journal that he purchased the one-half interest in December 1852 (Plantation Journal 12, 1849–52, Evans Papers, Louisiana State University).

44. U.S. Census, 1850, West Feliciana Parish, p. 277. The household included Sarah B. Evans, seventy-three, John N. Evans, forty-one, Cornelia M. Evans, thirteen, John E. Evans, nine, Corinne Evans, six, Frank Evans, five, Margaret E. DeHart, twenty-two, Sarah A. DeHart, twenty, and Louisa C. DeHart, seventeen (U.S. Census, 1850, Free Populations, West Feliciana Parish, p. 276; U.S. Census, 1850, Slave Schedules, St. Mary Parish, p. 57).

45. Conveyance of Land and Slaves, 4 Apr. 1850, Conveyance Book I, pp. 357–59, St. Mary Parish Conveyance Records.

46. The charge was made that Dr. DeHart on 15 June 1849 "cruelly mutilated, punished, and ill treated" his slave John, having "subjected" him to "diverse bruises, burns, lacerations, and mutilations." Four planters, including J. B. Birdshaw and J. N. Baldridge (an inkspot obliterates the other two names) certified that they "examined a bright mulatto boy named John, a slave of Dr. J. N. DeHart of St. Mary, found 3 distinct brands on the left side of his buttock, two on the opposite side, of the shape of a heart with a letter D in the center thereof." They swore that they found a "slit cut from each ear . . . a new scar over the left testical, one inch and a half long and we find many distinct scars, as from the whip" (State of Louisiana v. John DeHart, Judgment Passed 30 July 1850, in Criminal Records of the Fourteenth District Court, 1850–71, St. Mary Parish Courthouse, Franklin, Louisiana).

47. U.S. Census, 1850, Slave Schedules, St. Mary Parish, p. 251. John DeHart does not appear either in the population schedules for St. Mary or St. Martin parishes in 1850, nor does he appear in any census for those parishes in 1860.

48. "Last Will and Testament," Sarah Bloomfield Spencer Evans, 1 Oct. 1850 (probated 26 Mar. 1851), Probate File drawer 31, Inventories Vol. F, pp. 597–99, 609, West Feliciana Parish Probate Records.

49. The name of Marcus, appearing on an inventory for 1834, was marked through, with a notation, "sold, 1841." He was a slave of Sarah Evans. John Robinson, appearing on a list of J. N. Evans's slaves, was also noted, "sold N. Orleans, Apl. 1845." Another slave, Dennis, was sold in 1850–51. A claim was made against the estate of Sarah Evans for his value by the buyer, Henry Johnson, who asserted that Dennis died of a disease "supposed to have existed unperceived at the time of sale" ("List of slaves of Mrs. S. B. Evans, August, 1834," "List of

Negroes Belonging to J. N. Evans, November 20, 1847," Plantation Record Book 37, Debit Statement, 12 June 1851, box 7, folder 49, Evans Papers, Louisiana State University).

50. Plantation Record Book 37, ibid.

51. Ibid.; Plantation Record Book 38, ibid.

52. Inventory and Appraisement, "Estate of Sarah B. Evans," 14 Apr. 1851, Probate File drawer 31, West Feliciana Parish Probate Records.

53. "Memoranda, Property Received by Heirs of Mrs. C. L. DeHart from the Estate of Mrs. S. B. Evans, 1852," "Partition of Estate of S. B. Evans [partially torn. 1851?]," "Property of the Heirs of Mrs. C. L. DeHart from Estate of Mrs. S. B. Evans, January 20, 1852—Personal Property" in box 7, folders 47 and 48, Evans Papers, Louisiana State University.

54. "List of J. N. Evans' Negroes at Oakland, July 15, 1852," Plantation Record Book 38, Plantation Journal 12, 1849–65, Evans Papers, Louisiana State University.

55. "Succession of John N. Evans, deceased," filed 13 Mar. 1891, drawer 32, case 351, West Feliciana Parish Probate Records; Rogers, "Oakland," p. 5.

56. Roland, *Louisiana Sugar Plantations during the Civil War*, p. 74.

57. E. E. McCollam to Andrew McCollam, 26 Mar. 1863, folder 16, McCollam Papers; Josephine Nicholls Pugh, "Dark Days," ca. 1865, pp. 9–11; Wadley Diary, 1859–86, p. 49.

58. Roland, *Louisiana Sugar Plantations during the Civil War*, p. 74.

59. Davis, *Louisiana*, p. 256.

60. Power Diary, pp. 75, 86.

61. Davis, *Louisiana*, pp. 257–58; Power Diary, p. 89; Taylor, *Louisiana*, pp. 92–93.

62. "List of Negroes on Hazlewood, 1861," Plantation Record Book 38, p. 154. On the bottom of the page it was noted that "the Hazlewood negroes all ran off to the Yankees on the ninth day of July 1863." Also see "Negroes from Hazlewood Reported Dead at Port Hudson," ibid., p. 161, Evans Papers, Louisiana State University. See also E. E. McCollam to Andrew McCollam, 26 Mar. 1863, folder 16, McCollam Papers; "Rosedown List of Slaves Who Fled to Port Hudson," Bowman Papers. Identification of the ages of these slaves was made through Inventory and Appraisement, "Estate of Daniel Turnbull," 16 Jan. 1862, file drawer 106, West Feliciana Parish Probate Records.

63. Pugh specifically mentions the deaths of contraband slaves from disease and exposure, but numerous other sources also attest to the unhealthy conditions of the camps and recount the high incidence of disease and demise among the contraband slaves. See Pugh, "Dark Days," p. 11; Taylor, *Louisiana*, pp. 94–95.

64. List entitled "All of These ran off at the siege of Port Hudson" and "List of those who went to the Yankees," Diary of Martha Turnbull, pp. 59, 69, 83, Bowman Papers.

65. "Roll of Negroes at Oakland, 1864," Plantation Record Book 38, p. 161, Evans Papers, Louisiana State University.

66. "Roll, 1811," Plantation Record Book 36, ibid.

67. John Marsh was the son of Jonathan Alston Marsh (1765–1832) and Sarah Craig Marsh (1767–1826) of Cherry Bank Farm, Rahway, New Jersey. His brother Stewart accompanied him to Louisiana for a while, and another brother, Jonas Marsh, migrated to St.

Martin Parish and became a large planter there (Sanders, comp., *Selected Annotated Abstracts of Marriages*, pp. 112–13). The daughters were Margaret H., Eliza Ann, and Helen McKay Marsh. The infant son was John Craig Marsh, Jr.

68. "Family Notes," folder 1, Avery Papers.

69. U.S. Census, 1820, St. Mary Parish, p. 148.

70. See notes on the succession of Eliza Ann Marsh of St. Martin Parish under Succession 179, St. Mary Probate Records, in Sanders, comp., *Annotated Abstracts of the Successions of St. Mary Parish*, pp. 90–91. In a petition of 29 July 1829, John C. Marsh stated that his wife, Eliza Ann Baldwin Marsh, had died in New York City in August 1826.

71. Inventory and Appraisement, "Estate of William Stone," 13 Oct. 1826, 20 July 1827, Succession Record 151, pp. 11–16, St. Mary Parish Probate Records. At the time of his death, Stone's heirs were his widow, Euphemia Craig Stone, and their son David (sometimes written as "Davis"), a minor, both residing in St. Mary Parish, as well as two sons by his first marriage to Mary Baldwin Stone (some believe her to have been the sister of John Marsh's wife, Eliza Baldwin Marsh). The sons were Samuel, "a minor above the age of puberty," and William, "a minor below the age of puberty," both living in the Northeast. By 1827, young Samuel Stone had moved to St. Mary Parish, where he soon married Mary McCall (the daughter of Jesse McCall, who had sold land on Petite Anse to his father and John Marsh). By 1829 he lived in Lafayette Parish (Sanders, comp., *Selected Annotated Abstracts of Marriages*, p. 111).

72. Marsh had a prior residence in New Iberia, but in 1828 he bought the old François Maingonnet place, Mingana, on Bayou Teche in New Iberia, next to the David Weeks's property. Maingonnet, reputedly a confederate of the pirate Jean Lafitte, had sold the property in 1813 to Elizabeth Norwood, a free woman of color (Bergerie, *They Tasted Bayou Water*, p. 32; U.S. Census, 1830, St. Martin Parish, p. 112; "Necrological of William F. Weeks," p. 6, Weeks File, Iberia Parish Library).

73. "Family Notes," folder 1, Avery Papers; Inventory, "Estate of Euphemia Craig Marsh," 14 Mar. 1836, Original Estates Vol. 15, pp. 170–73, St. Mary Parish Probate Records.

74. "Conveyance of Land and Slaves, John C. Marsh to George C. Marsh," 1 Jan. 1839, Conveyance Vol. G, pp. 66–69, St. Mary Parish Probate Records. In this conveyance, the elder Marsh sold his undivided one-third of a "sugar plantation on Petite Anse Island in St. Mary Parish containing 1,319 arpents." John C. Marsh had bought out the heirs of his partner and his second wife in 1835 (Agreement, William A. Stone and John C. Marsh, 11 May 1835, Conveyance Vol. 9, p. 297, ibid.).

75. George Marsh, New Iberia, to Sarah Avery, Baton Rouge, 1 Feb. 1840, folder 5, Avery Papers; U.S. Census, 1840, St. Mary Parish, p. 325.

76. U.S. Census, 1840, St. Martin Parish, p. 314.

77. "Conveyance of Land and Slaves, John C. Marsh to George C. Marsh," 1 Jan. 1839.

78. John C. Marsh, Baltimore, to George Avery, New Iberia, 4 Aug. 1850, George Marsh, Petite Anse Isle, to John Craig Marsh, New York City, 14 June 1845, folder 5, Avery Papers.

79. U.S. Census, 1850, St. Martin Parish, p. 183.

80. Daniel D. Avery to Ashbal B. Henshaw, 17 Sept. 1849, folder 5, Avery Papers. Apparently, the conveyance was private because it was not recorded in either St. Mary or St. Martin Parish conveyance records, but it must have taken place between 17 September and December of 1849.

81. U.S. Census, 1840, East Baton Rouge Parish, p. 186; U.S. Census, 1850, St. Mary Parish, p. 220; U.S. Census, 1850, Slave Schedules, St. Mary Parish, p. 187.

82. Marsh's residence in New Jersey is documented in several documents. In a handwritten document manumitting slaves Vina, John Henry, and Ben, Marsh refers to himself as being "formerly of the Parish of St. Martin, State of Louisiana, but now of the County of Essex Township of Rahway and State of New Jersey" (Manumission Document, 5 May 1856; "Family Notes," folder 1; John C. Marsh to Margaret Henshaw, 21 June 1853, John C. Marsh to George C. Marsh, 7 May 1856, folder 6, all in Avery Papers).

83. Conveyance of Land and Slaves, Ashbal B. Henshaw of St. Martin Parish to Daniel D. Avery, East Baton Rouge Parish, 19 Apr. 1854, in Conveyance Vol. O, pp. 382–85, St. Mary Parish Probate Records; Last Will and Testament of George Marsh, 15 July 1858, pp. 1–2; "Estate of George Marsh," Succession 1042, St. Mary Parish Probate Records; First Registry of the Episcopal Church of the Epiphany, New Iberia, Louisiana, Burial Record, 21 Dec. 1859, quoted in Sanders, comp., *Selected Annotated Abstracts of Marriages*, p. 112; Inventory and Appraisement, "Estate of George Marsh," 22 Feb. 1860, Succession 1042, pp. 31–35, St. Mary Parish Probate Records.

84. U.S. Census, 1860, Slave Schedules, St. Mary Parish, p. 39.

85. The island was referred to as Avery Island by the early 1870s ("Family Notes," folder 1, Avery Papers; Bergerie, *They Tasted Bayou Water*, p. 64).

86. Young John Hayes reportedly was the first Anglo to discover the salt springs, in about 1791. By 1810, Jesse McCall had purchased the portion of the island containing the saline springs, and by 1812 he was evaporating salt from the springs and transporting it by schooners for sale (Notes from Historical Marker, Avery Island, 1985; Taylor, "Saga of Petite Anse Island," p. 160; Wood, "Hayes Family," p. 166). A "saline establishment" and "seven hundred and fifty barrels of salt" are among the items inventoried at the death of William Stone (Inventory, 13 Oct. 1826, "Estate of William Stone," pp. 11–16). Also see the 1836 inventory, which mentions "the saline apparatus for making Salt" (Inventory, 4 Mar. 1836, "Estate of Euphemia Craig Marsh," pp. 170–73).

87. Raphael, *Battle in the Bayou Country*, pp. 55, 19.

88. The weak rationale offered by Union General Nathaniel Banks for the thorough destruction of the saltworks was that Colonel William B. Kimball's troops of the Twelfth Maine Infantry were fired on by enemy guns loaded with salt. In a correspondence criticizing an earlier unsuccessful attempt to eliminate the Petite Anse saltworks, another Union officer, Colonel McMillan, called the action ill-advised. The solid rock deposits were not easily destroyed. Moreover, he advised, the saltworks, kept intact, would have been of invaluable use to the United States. He was correct in that the salt deposits were not easily obliterated. The Avery correspondence of the 1866–67 period is filled with expressions of

interest in the reestablishment of profitable salt-mining operations, a potential developed by the late 1870s (ibid., pp. 62, 137–39).

89. Plantation Account Book 4, 1866–67, Avery Papers.

90. Inventory and Appraisement, 13 Oct. 1826, 10 July 1827, "Estate of William Stone," pp. 11–16; Inventory and Appraisement, 4 Mar. 1836, "Estate of Euphemia Craig Marsh," pp. 170–73; Sale, 26 Apr. 1836, ibid., pp. 181–83; Inventory and Sale, 1 Jan. 1839, "Conveyance of John C. Marsh to George Marsh," pp. 66–69; Inventory and Appraisement, 20 Feb. 1860, "Estate of George Marsh," pp. 24–35; Sale of Interest in Land and Slaves, 19 Apr. 1854, "Conveyance, A. B. Henshaw to Daniel D. Avery," Conveyance Vol. O, pp. 382–85, St. Mary Parish Conveyance Records.

91. Zilversmit, *First Emancipation*, pp. 193–99, 214; Litwack, *North of Slavery*, pp. 1, 3; *N.J. 28 Assembly 2*, pp. 91, 94, 99, 111, 113–18; *N.J. 28 Council 2*, pp. 280–88; *N.J. 28 Laws 2*, pp. 251–52. Zilversmit's treatment of the passage of gradual emancipation legislation in New Jersey and New York is excellent.

92. Zilversmit, *First Emancipation*, p. 214; Field, *Politics of Race*, pp. 31–33.

93. Zilversmit, *First Emancipation*, p. 214.

94. Ibid., p. 216; Price, comp. and ed., *Freedom Not Far Distant*, pp. 84–85.

95. See *New Jersey Journal* (Elizabeth Town), Mar. 1816–Dec. 1818, esp. 30 Jan., 6 Feb., 26 Mar., 16 Apr., 4 June, 2 July, 17, 24 Sept. 1816, 7 Jan. 1817, 13 Jan., 31 Mar., 7 Apr. 1818.

96. Ibid., 20 Jan., 16 June 1818.

97. Ibid., 16 June 1818; Catterall, ed., *Judicial Cases*, 3:471–72.

98. *True American* (Trenton), 22 June 1818; *Fredonian* (New Brunswick), 4 June 1818; *General Advertiser* (New Brunswick), 28 May 1818, as cited in Zilversmit, *First Emancipation*, p. 216.

99. *New Jersey Journal*, 2 June 1818, p. 3.

100. Ibid., 16 June 1818, p. 3.

101. Zilversmit, *First Emancipation*, pp. 216–17; *N.J. 43 Assembly 1*, pp. 7–15, 41–42; *N.J. 43 Council*, pp. 11–12; *N.J. 43 Laws*, pp. 3–5; William Stone, New York, to John C. Marsh, Nova Iberia, 1 Dec. 1818, folder 2, Avery Papers. Stone mentions a 24 October 1818 deadline.

102. *New Jersey Journal*, 17 Nov., 2 June 1818; *True American* (Trenton, N.J.), 10, 23, 24 June 1818.

103. The twelve were as follows: George, sixteen, a "limited slave" to be emancipated at the age of twenty-eight, sold by Martha Phillips of Sussex, New Jersey, to John C. Marsh, New York City, 18 July 1818; Hannah, a slave of Abraham VanCleat, Hunterdon, New Jersey, to William Rayburg (consent form); Han, twenty-one, a slave sold by John Pettit of Sussex, New Jersey, to Lewis Compton, Perth Amboy, 29 July 1818; Will, twenty-one, a slave sold by John Pettit of Sussex, New Jersey, to Lewis Compton, 29 July 1818; Samuel Jackson, eighteen, a slave of Josiah Hornblower, Bergen County, New Jersey, to William Stone, 28 July 1818; Cain, a slave sold by John G. Smock, Middlesex County, New Jersey, to Lewis Compton, 1 Oct. 1818 (title transferred to William Stone on 16 Oct. 1818); Frank, twenty-one, a slave of Middlesex County, New Jersey, mentioned in consent form, 6 Oct. 1818, to serve William

Stone in Louisiana "for Life as a Slave"; Lewis, twenty-two, a slave of Daniel P. Polhemus, Middlesex, New Jersey, to Lewis Compton, 12 Oct. 1818 (title transferred to William Stone on 22 Oct. 1818); Jack, twenty-two, a slave sold by Joseph Scott of Essex County, New Jersey, to Lewis Compton, Perth Amboy, 15 Oct. 1818 (title transferred to William Stone on 22 Oct. 1818); Jane, a slave sold by Lewis Abrams, Middlesex, New Jersey, to William Stone (consent form signed 21 Oct. 1818); Susan, a slave sold by Lewis Abrams, Middlesex County, New Jersey, to William Stone, 16 Oct. 1818; Peter, a slave of Middlesex County, New Jersey (consent form), sold to William Stone in New Iberia, Louisiana, to serve as a slave for life, all in folder 2, Avery Papers.

104. Among the indentured servants were Ann Moore, indentured in New York, 28 Aug. 1818; Susan Jackson, New York, 28 Aug. 1818; Eliza Thompson, New York, 28 Aug. 1818; Betsy Carpenter, New York, 28 Aug. 1818; Mary Harris, New York, 28 Aug. 1818; Margaret Boss, New York, 22 Sept. 1818; and Joseph Hendrickson, (New Jersey ?; place not stated), 23 Oct. 1818. Though William McClane's indenture is not present, his indentured status is confirmed in a Bill of Sale of the indenture of William McClane, 28 Feb. 1819. Likewise, information in the Release of Indenture, 2 Jan. 1838, confirms that Robert Cook was indentured in New York in 1818. Two additional indentures were for Sally Cross, 26 Dec. 1822 (place of indenture not given) and Hannah Jones, 26 Dec. 1822 (place not given). In all, fifteen indentures are documented in folders 2 and 3, Avery Papers.

105. Consent forms were required for removal of indentured servants from New York. Despite New York's passage in 1799 of a gradual emancipation act, and although the western sections of the state were outspokenly antislavery, the inhabitants of some regions, especially New York City and the Hudson Valley, were proslavery and continued to discriminate against blacks. Zilversmit calls the abandonment programs "thinly disguised schemes for compensated abolition," just as the indenture system was another form of social and economic control (Field, *Politics of Race*, pp. 32–33; Zilversmit, *First Emancipation*, p. 199).

106. Englishman Isaac Holmes, visiting New Jersey shortly before the 1818 prohibition went into effect, stated that slaves selling for $300 in New Jersey could be sold in New Orleans for $700 to $800 (*Account of the United States of America*, p. 324). Louisiana did have an acute shortage of skilled slaves, and this could well have been a reason for Stone and Marsh's actions in regard to some of the indentures of trained servants. Most of the New Jersey slaves, however, were young and had no stated skills.

107. A comparison of prices paid in Louisiana for both local slaves and those from the trade differ from the prices Stone and Marsh paid for New Jersey slaves, but the costs involved in paying agents and transportation probably made the differences insignificant. The partnership paid from $225 to $400 for New Jersey males and females in their teens and early twenties. Prices in Louisiana from 1816 to 1820 varied widely. In 1816, David Weeks bought a twenty-five-year-old woman and a nine-year-old boy for a total of $800, a sixteen-year-old male for $1,000, and five prime-age male and female slaves for an average of $440 each. Alexander Stirling's estate sale in 1818 indicates that when families were bought as a lot, prices were comparable to those for New Jersey slaves of similar ages, but male solitaires

sold for more. Tom, sixteen, sold for $900. Because of the considerable expenses incurred by Marsh and Stone in transporting the New Jersey slaves, they probably did not save much by buying northeastern workers. See Bills of Sale, box 1, folder 4, Weeks Papers, Louisiana State University; Estate Sale, "Estate of Alexander Stirling," 7 May 1818, Original Estates Vol. 1, pp. 251–53, St. Mary Parish Probate Records.

108. A consent form for removal of a Middlesex, New Jersey, slave named Hany, to "remove and go out of this State to Pointe Coupee in the State of Louisiana" to serve Nicholas Van Wickle and his partner Colonel Charles Morgan was signed 22 April 1818. One of the two judges signing the form was Jacob Van Wickle (Special Collections, Alexander Library, Rutgers University, reproduced in Price, comp. and ed., *Freedom Not Far Distant*, pp. 85–86). Numerous other consent forms for Louisiana slaves involving the Van Wickles and Morgan are found in Slave Manumissions Volume, Middlesex, Record Group 2171, Special Collections and Archives (Jersey Room), Rutgers University. Some were signed as early as 10 February 1818. Judge Jacob Charles Van Wickle was married to Charles Morgan's sister Sarah. In the buying scheme, Nicholas Van Wickle (the judge's son) claimed that he was moving to Pointe Coupee, Louisiana, to become Morgan's partner. He never moved to Louisiana, and it is extremely doubtful that he was ever Morgan's partner. Two other sons of Judge Van Wickle did move to Pointe Coupee Parish—Stephen and Jacob Charles, Jr. Stephen married Adele Morgan, his cousin and the daughter of Charles Morgan ("Descendants of the Morgan and Van Wickle Families," pp. 5–7, Morgan Fly History 1368, Louisiana State University).

109. Zilversmit, *First Emancipation*, quoting contemporary newspapers of New Jersey, p. 217.

110. *Augusta Chronicle*, 22 Aug. 1818, quoting *New Orleans Chronicle*, 14 July 1818.

111. William Stone, New York, to John C. Marsh, Nova Iberia, 1 Dec. 1818, folder 2, Avery Papers. "Amboy" was Perth Amboy, New Jersey. "Compton" refers to Lewis Compton, a Perth Amboy resident who acted as William Stone's agent and purchased slaves in behalf of the Stone-Marsh partnership. "George" was one of the slaves bought by the partnership (Bill of Sale, 18 July 1818, for George, a slave sold by Martha Phillips, Sussex County, New Jersey, to John C. Marsh, New York, folder 2, Avery Papers). "Rayburg" was William Rayburg, also a New Jersey resident, who was hired by the partnership to assist in the buying and transporting of slaves to Louisiana. "DeHart" might have been Captain John DeHart, who lived in the general area where the partners would locate; he might have been hired to assist in the transportation of the slaves to Louisiana. "Sumervil" was Somerville, New Jersey, a town on the route south. "Reding" was Reading, Pennsylvania, and "Lebonen" was Lebanon, Pennsylvania.

112. Stone to Marsh, 1 Dec. 1818. "Phoebe" does not appear on the Louisiana lists, nor is she mentioned in subsequent family correspondence. She probably remained in New York. "Betsy" was the house servant later referred to as Old Betsy, who usually resided at the Marsh town residence in New Iberia ("Note regarding Betsy, April 20, 1836," Inventory, "Estate of Euphemia Craig Marsh," 14 Mar. 1836, p. 177). Less likely, she could have been the

indentured servant Betsy Carpenter, who agreed in 1818 to serve out a contract of three years and nine months in Louisiana for $30 per year. Betsy apparently regretted the arrangement. A note attached to her indenture agreement stated that she ran away at least twice while in Louisiana, in March and June of 1821. She was recovered both times (Indenture between Betsy Carpenter, New York City, and William Stone and John C. Marsh, New York City, 28 Aug. 1828, folder 2, Avery Papers).

113. According to a carefully researched family history, Benjamin (Benoit) Brashear moved from the colony of Virginia to Calvert County, colony of Maryland, in 1658 and died there in late 1662 or 1663. The tradition of slaveholding started early in the Brashear family for the first American progenitor owned at least one slave, according to his succession, and his grandson Samuel had five slaves in his estate. Samuel Brashear's grandson Ignatius or Nacy Brashear, born 17 April 1734, was the first of his direct line to leave the Chesapeake Bay area, migrating in 1784 to an area of Kentucky on the Salt River. He and his wife, Frances Pamela Edmonston, were the parents of Walter Brashear. See Back and Brashear, *Brashear Story*, pp. 5, 8–9, 37–38, 51–52.

114. McDowell, "Bullitt's Lick," pp. 252–53; Clift, *Second Census of Kentucky*, p. 31. Ignatius Brashear, Sr., died in 1807, and records concerning his slaves are unavailable. In 1810 Walter Brashear had twenty-two slaves, his brother Robert Brashear had six, and Levi Brashear had six, all in Nelson County. In Bullitt County, another brother, Ignatius, Jr., had four slaves. Two other brothers owned no slaves in 1810 (U.S. Census, 1810, Nelson County, Kentucky, pp. 10–11; U.S. Census, 1810, Bullitt County, Kentucky, pp. 173–74).

115. Although some of the information concerning Brashear's short military career appears legendary, most of the salient aspects are well documented and other "romantic" aspects are plausible in view of the family's involvement in trade with the Orient, documented in family correspondence (see Brashear Papers Inventory, Southern Historical Collection). One story is that in 1799 Dr. Brashear served as ship's surgeon on one of his uncle's trading vessels. While in port at Canton, he was required to remove a tumor from the breast of the wife of a high-ranking Chinese dignitary, then was held for three days to await the outcome of his surgery. She lived, and he was rewarded, according to Louisiana Governor Robert Wickliffe, Brashear's nephew. See M. F. Coomes, "Doctor Walter Brashear," *Kentucky Medical Journal*, 1 Nov. 1917, pp. 1–2; Back and Brashear, *Brashear Story*, p. 52; Jillson, "Flamma Clara Maturae Medicinae Kentuckiensis," pp. 155–56; Robert Barr Lawrence to the Collector of the United States Customs House, Philadelphia, 11 Feb. 1922, incompletely identified clippings from *Kentucky's Illustrious Doctors*, p. 15, and *Medical Life*, p. 40, all in Brashear Papers, Morgan City Library and Archives.

116. Marriage bond, 5 May 1803, Margaret Barr and Walter Brashear, Lexington, Fayette County, Kentucky, facsimile in Brashear Papers, Morgan City Library and Archives. Margaret Barr's father was Robert Ross Barr, editor of the *Lexington Gazette*. She was related to the Todds, Tiltons, and Barrs, all socially prominent families in the Lexington-Bardstown area. See also Mrs. William T. Ray, Athens, Georgia, to James W. Kennedy, Lexington, Kentucky, 12 Nov. 1947; pamphlet, *Beautiful Historic Bardstown, Kentucky*, given by John

Wakefield Muir; John Wakefield Muir, Bardstown, Kentucky, to Mrs. William Tyler Ray, Athens, Georgia, 27 Feb. 1942, all in Brashear Papers, Morgan City Library and Archives; Collins, *History of Kentucky*, p. 645; Jillson, *Old Kentucky Entries and Deeds*, pp. 473, 558.

117. Gray, "Ephraim McDowell," p. 28; Coomes, "Doctor Walter Brashear," pp. 1–2, quoting address by Professor David W. Yandell in 1890 before the American Medical Association.

118. Mortgage of Land and Slaves (Belle Isle), Walter and Margaret Brashear to the Bank of Louisiana, 13 July 1825, Mortgage Vol. A-B, pp. 54–55, St. Mary Parish Mortgage Records.

119. Walter Brashear, Philadelphia, to Thomas Barr, Lexington, Kentucky, 17 Apr. 1802, folder 1, Brashear Papers, Southern Historical Collection.

120. "Mortgage of slaves, furniture and carpets," Walter Brashear to Thomas Wallace, administrator of the Estate of George Anderson, dec'd, 11 June 1814, Deed Book, pp. 1248–50, and Mortgage of slaves and "a medical shop . . . and all instruments," Walter Brashear, Fayette, Kentucky, to James Darrack, Fayette, Kentucky, 30 Sept. 1814, Deed Book L, pp. 218–20, Fayette County Conveyance Records. Many pieces of real estate were also mortgaged.

121. As late as 1830, Robert Barr was considered a partner in the Belle Isle enterprise (Sale of slaves, M. Payne of Bedford County, Tennessee, to Walter Brashear and Robert Barr, planters of Belle Isle, co-partners, 12 Apr. 1830, Mortgage Record Book B-5, p. 69, St. Mary Parish Mortgage Records).

122. U.S. Census, 1840, Nelson County, Kentucky, pp. 10–11.

123. Mortgage of Land and Slaves (Belle Isle), 13 July 1825, and Fanny B. [Frances] Lawrence to Henry Lawrence, 10 Feb. 1850, folder 17, Brashear Papers, Southern Historical Collection.

124. Among the Kentucky slaves sold in 1819 were Bill, age forty, a "boy" John (age not given), and Clem, eleven (Bill of Sale and Mortgage, Walter Brashear, Kentucky, to W. B. Wilcoxon, St. Mary, 30 Mar. 1819, and Bill of Sale and Mortgage, Walter Brashear, Kentucky, to George Dougherty, St. Mary, 27 Mar. 1819, Mortgage Vol. A-B, pp. 25, 22, St. Mary Parish Mortgage Records).

125. U.S. Census, 1820, St. Mary Parish, p. 145.

126. Walter Brashear, on board steamboat *Fayette*, to Eden Brashear, near Fort Gibson, Mississippi, 10 May 1822, folder 2, Brashear Papers, Southern Historical Collection.

127. Margaret Brashear, Belle Isle, to Caroline Brashear, Lexington, Kentucky, 16 Nov. 1822, 30 Jan. 1823, folder 2, Brashear Papers, Southern Historical Collection.

128. *New Orleans Picayune*, 22 Oct. 1838.

129. Mary Eliza Brashear, St. Mary, to Caroline Brashear, Lexington, Kentucky, 19 Feb. 1823, folder 2, and Margaret Brashear, Belle Isle, to Frances Emily Brashear, Lexington, Kentucky, 10 July 1832, folder 5, Brashear Papers, Southern Historical Collection.

130. Margaret Brashear, her infant son, Mary Eliza, Caroline, and Rebecca Brashear are buried in a family cemetery on Belle Isle (Deposition of Robert Brashear Lawrence, Athens, Georgia, 3 July 1901, in Heirs of Gonsoulin v. The Gulf Company; photograph of graves, Sun Oil Company Pamphlet on Belle Isle, Brashear Papers, Morgan City Library and Archives).

131. In 1833 Margaret Brashear reported that "the cholera has visited this section. . . . After taking off 1 to 2 hundred from St. Martins to Franklin [the outbreak] has entirely ceased, they were principally poor half naked, starved French negroes." Rebecca claimed that in the cholera epidemic, "all the plantations owned by French creoles suffered more than any others" (Margaret Brashear, Belle Isle, to Frances E. Brashear, Lexington, Kentucky, 20 Jan. 1822, and Rebecca T. Brashear, Belle Isle, to Frances E. Brashear, Lexington, 10 Jan. 1833, folder 5, Brashear Papers, Southern Historical Collection).

132. Mortgage, Walter and Margaret Brashear to Bank of Louisiana, 13 July 1825, Bill of Sale, 27 Mar. 1827, Mortgage of Land and Slaves, 7 May 1828, Walter Brashear to Mercantile Firm of Howard and Mary of Boston, Mortgage Vol. A-B, pp. 54–55, 22–25, 88; Sale of Slaves, 12 Apr. 1830, Mortgage Record B-5, p. 69; Mortgage of Land and Slaves, Walter Brashear to W. W. and J. Montgomery, 15 Apr. 1831, Mortgage Vol. A-B, pp. 212–14, St. Mary Parish Mortgage Records; William Tyler Ray, Athens, Georgia, to Rex Laney, Baton Rouge, Louisiana, 6 Dec. 1941, Brashear Papers, Morgan City Library and Archives; Mortgage of Land and Slaves (Tiger Island), Walter Brashear and Wife to the New Orleans Canal and Banking Company, 1 June 1833, Mortgage Vol. C-6, pp. 332–34, St. Mary Parish Conveyance Records; Morgan City Review, 29 Dec. 1950.

133. Walter Brashear, Golden Farm, Louisiana, to Frances E. Brashear, Lexington, Kentucky, 16 Sept. 1838, folder 7, Brashear Papers, Southern Historical Collection. When Brashear bought Golden Farm and Bayou Boeuf plantations around 1838, the properties had suits against them. The land was later put up for auction and repurchased for Brashear by his son-in-law in March 1845, then reconveyed to Brashear. This legal maneuver (the same was done in regard to Belle Isle at one point) was noted in Conveyance of Land and Slaves (Golden Farm), 3 Mar. 1845, Henry E. Lawrence, Orleans Parish, to Walter Brashear, St. Mary Parish, Conveyance Vol. G, pp. 203–4, St. Mary Parish Conveyance Records. The Bayou Boeuf Plantation was purchased at a sheriff's sale on 8 December 1838, according to Brashear's Conveyance (no. 7135) of the plantation and twelve slaves to Frances E. Lawrence, 31 May 1852, Conveyance Vol. I, p. 37, ibid.

134. His grandson recalled that Walter Brashear's home "on magnificent Belle Isle was a noted place with . . . majestic oaks. After losing his wife and several children who are buried at Belle Isle, he moved to his sugar plantations at Berwick [Golden Farm] and Tiger Island" (William Tyler Ray, Athens, to Rex Laney, Baton Rouge, 6 Dec. 1941; also see statement of another grandson, Robert Brashear Lawrence, 3 July 1901, in "Heirs of Gonsoulin vs. the Gulf Company," Brashear Papers, Morgan City Library and Archives; Walter Brashear, Golden Farm, to Frances E. Brashear, Lexington, Kentucky, 16 Sept. 1838, folder 7, Brashear Papers, Southern Historical Collection).

135. Mortgage, Walter Brashear to W. W. Montgomery, 15 Apr. 1833, Conveyance Records, Mortgage Vol. B-5, pp. 212–14; Mortgage (Tiger Island), 19 Nov. 1842, Robert B. Brashear et al. to Walter Brashear; List of Golden Farm Slaves in Conveyance, Robert D. Hockley, Nelson County, Kentucky, to Mrs. Frances Lawrence, St. Mary Parish, Louisiana, 4 Jan. 1861,

Conveyance Vol. Q, pp. 217–21, St. Mary Parish Conveyance Records. The latter inventories were used to determine shifts of slaves between Tiger Island and Golden Farm.

136. Sale of Slaves, M. Payne of Bedford County, Tennessee, to Walter Brashear, St. Mary Parish, 12 Apr. 1830, Mortgage Vol. B-5, St. Mary Parish Conveyance Records.

137. Northup, *Twelve Years a Slave*, passim; *Buhler* v. *McHatton*, 9 La. An. 192, Mar. 1854, *Walker* v. *Hays*, 15 La. An. 640, Dec. 1860, Catterall, *Judicial Cases*, 3:632, 685.

138. Among those early Tiger Island slaves who were able to return to Brashear's home plantation after a short tenure were Queny, Ellen, and Hannah.

139. Walter Brashear, New Orleans, to Robert Brashear, 7 Feb. 1836, folder 6, Brashear Papers, Southern Historical Collection.

140. Walter Brashear, Golden Farm, to Frances E. Brashear, Lexington, Kentucky, 16 Sept. 1838, folder 7, ibid.

141. U.S. Census, 1840, St. Mary Parish.

142. Mortgage (Tiger Island), 19 Nov. 1842, Robert B. Brashear et al. to Walter Brashear. This mortgage accompanied the conveyance of the Tiger Island plantation and slaves to his heirs, Robert B. Brashear, Thomas T. Brashear, and Frances Brashear. The conveyance bore the same date.

143. A St. Mary planter complained in 1842 that "all that is talked of nowadays here is the hard times, hard times. The planters nearly all made bad crops and cannot get much for them—the latest news from New Orleans is that the Sheriff has shut up six banks" (Peltier and Lehman, comps. and eds., *History of Morgan City*, p. 14).

144. Walter Brashear, Golden Farm, to Henry E. Lawrence, New Orleans, 17 June 1844, folder 11, Brashear Papers, Southern Historical Collection.

145. Most of Fanny Lawrence's letters to her husband in the late 1840s and early 1850s were from Belle Isle. See folders 15–18, ibid. She and her four children were enumerated in St. Mary Parish in 1850, but Henry E. Lawrence was not (U.S. Census, 1850, St. Mary Parish, p. 204).

146. U.S. Census, 1850, St. Mary Parish, pp. 204, 208; U.S. Census, 1850, Slave Schedules, St. Mary Parish (no pagination but enumerated 7 Dec. 1850).

147. Conveyance of Land and Slaves, 31 May 1852, Walter Brashear, St. Mary Parish, to Frances E. Lawrence, St. Mary Parish, Conveyance 7135; Conveyance of Slaves, 21 May 1852, Walter Brashear, St. Mary Parish, to Robert B. Brashear and Thomas T. Brashear, St. Mary Parish, Conveyance 7136, Conveyance Vol. I, pp. 39–40, St. Mary Parish Conveyance Records; *Morgan City Review*, 18 Feb. 1925.

148. *Planter's Banner* (Franklin, Louisiana), 15 Nov. 1845, 19 June 1847, 22 June 1848, 3, 25 Jan. 1849, 27 Mar. 1850, 24 Apr., 9 Oct. 1852.

149. *Planter's Banner*, 1 May 1852.

150. Walter Brashear had been impressed with the commercial potential of ports since he had observed the exciting commercial scene at Philadelphia as a young medical student. His interests were also shaped by the involvement of his wife's uncles in shipping and interna-

tional trade. His confidence in the commercial promise of coastal property had influenced his early choices of property in Louisiana. Robert Barr Lawrence's correspondence with the collector of the United States customshouse in Philadelphia relates the activities of Walter Brashear in the importation of rhubarb from Canton and the buying and shipping of ginseng roots to China. Walter Brashear's maternal uncle Captain James Barr of the tea-importing firm of Barr and Stuart was a partner in three ships involved in the China trade before 1801 (Robert Barr Lawrence, Lexington, Kentucky, to the Collector at the United States Customs House, Philadelphia, 14 Feb. 1922, Brashear Papers, Morgan City Library and Archives; *Morgan City Review*, 18 Feb. 1925).

151. *Morgan City Review*, 18 Feb. 1925; "The Gathright Family," typescript manuscript, Apr. 1984, pp. 1–2; Segar Family File, untitled typescript statement on Brashear Family History, by Robert Lawrence Brashear, n.d., p. 3, all in Brashear Papers, Morgan City Library and Archives; Peltier and Lehman, comps. and eds., *History of Morgan City*, p. 15; *Planter's Banner*, 11 Aug. 1853.

152. Robert B. Brashear died between 6 October and 31 December 1856 ("Last Will and Testament," 6 Oct. 1856, Robert B. Brashear, and Inventory and Appraisement, 28 Jan. 1857, "Estate of Robert B. Brashear (no. 947)," Original Estates Vol. 50, pp. 3–4, 8–14; Inventory and Appraisement, 31 May 1859, "Estate of Thomas T. Brashear (no. 1001)," Original Estates Vol. 52, pp. 10–16; Inventory and Partition, 28 May 1860, "Estates of T. T. and Robert Brashear," Inventory and Estate Partition Vol. N, pp. 795–805, St. Mary Parish Probate Records).

153. Brashear's will was dated 17 September 1860. A copy is contained in folder 21, Brashear Papers, Southern Historical Collection. The will was probated and filed 30 October 1860. See Original Estates Vol. 55, pp. 122–26, and Inventory and Appraisement, 16–17 Nov. 1860, "Estate of Walter Brashear, Sr. (no. 1068)," ibid., pp. 130–34, St. Mary Parish Probate Records.

154. U.S. Census, 1860, Slave Schedules, St. Mary Parish, pp. 40, 211.

155. Inventory and Appraisement, "Estate of Walter Brashear, Sr.," 16–17 Nov. 1860.

156. Will, Walter Brashear, Sr., 17 Sept. 1860.

157. Peltier and Lehman, comps. and eds., *History of Morgan City*, pp. 16–17; Raphael, *Battle in the Bayou Country*, p. 49.

158. Quoted in Raphael, *Battle in the Bayou Country*, p. 49. Some of the Union soldiers were very aware of its importance. A New York soldier said, "Well, I just believe that Brashear City is the centre of gravity in this department. If we get away from it a little ways, why the whole d——d concern would lose its balance" (quoted in Finch, "Surprise at Brashear City," p. 408).

159. "Gathright Family," Apr. 1984, p. 4, Morgan City Library and Archives; Raphael, *Battle in the Bayou Country*, p. 72.

160. Unidentified letter of Union soldier in the Civil War Collection, Morgan City Library and Archives, and quoted in "Gathright Family."

161. Raphael, *Battle in the Bayou Country*, pp. 50–51; Hepworth, *Whip, Hoe, and Sword*, pp. 25–26; Taylor, *Louisiana Reconstructed*, p. 9; Diary of Henry E. Lawrence, 1:315–17, Brashear Papers, Southern Historical Collection.

162. Among those sold was Hazzard, sold to a "Texas cattle drover" for $1,400 (Diary of Henry E. Lawrence, 1:317, Brashear Papers, Southern Historical Collection).

163. Rawick, ed., *American Slave*, Ser. 1, vol. 5, pt. 3, p. 154.

164. Raphael, *Battle in the Bayou Country*, pp. 162–65.

165. Quoted from *New York Tribune*, 8 July 1863, in Edmonds, *Yankee Autumn in Acadiana*, pp. 425–27.

166. Lease, 15 Feb. 1866, Henry E. Lawrence to Oliver Richardson, Fanny Richardson, Mary Brient, John Williams, Jack Fowler, Harriet Brown, and Josephine Brown (freed people), Brashear Papers, Morgan City Library and Archives.

167. Although Frances Brashear Lawrence and her children moved to New York by early 1864, she spent some time at Bayou Boeuf in 1865 (Frances Lawrence, Bayou Boeuf, to Bob Lawrence, New York, 2 Apr. 1865; Diary of Henry E. Lawrence, 1:315–17, Brashear Papers, Southern Historical Collection; Letter to the Editor of the *Planter's Banner* from R. B. Lawrence, July 1910, a newspaper clipping with no further identification in the Brashear-Lawrence File, Brashear Papers, Morgan City Library and Archives).

168. *Morgan City Review*, 18 Feb. 1925, 6 Feb. 1976; Peltier and Lehman, comps. and eds., *History of Morgan City*, p. 33.

CHAPTER 5

1. Roll, 1817, Plantation Record Book 36, Evans Papers, Louisiana State University.

2. Work Record, 1811–12, ibid.

3. French demographers categorize a population as "youthful" if more than 35 percent of its population is under twenty. At Tiger Island in 1857, 44 percent of the inhabitants were under seventeen; 34 percent of Petite Anse slaves in 1854 were under seventeen, as were 53 percent of Oakland's slaves in 1857; the trend was present earlier as well. The criteria for establishing "demographic youth" are found in Molen, "Population and Social Patterns in Barbadoes," p. 296.

4. Edward Rosset describes as a characteristic of demographic youth the presence of less than 8 percent of the population in the over-sixty age group (ibid.; Inventory, 23 Oct. 1819, "Estate of Nathaniel Evans").

5. U.S. Census, 1820, Feliciana Parish, p. 48.

6. Ibid.; U.S. Census, 1830, West Feliciana Parish, p. 232; "Taxable Property, 1834, 1835, 1841, Mrs. S. B. Evans and J. N. Evans," Plantation Record Book 37, Evans Papers, Louisiana State University.

7. Reconstituted Roll of Oakland slaves, 1846, combining the slaves of Sarah B. Evans and

John N. Evans, based on the Blanket and Ration Lists of November 1846 and other appropriate inventories in Plantation Record Book 37, Evans Papers, Louisiana State University; Inventory, 14 Apr. 1851, "Estate of Sarah B. Evans."

8. Based on my examination of Louisiana slave communities, 1810–65, as reflected in plantation and court records, including the tracing of many over their societal life course.

9. Inventory, 14 Apr. 1851, "Estate of Sarah B. Evans"; "J. N. Evans' Negroes at Oakland, 15 July 1852," Plantation Record Book 38, Evans Papers, Louisiana State University.

10. Inventory, 1857, reconstituted from "List of Negroes on Oakland, July, 1857," Blanket List, 18 Nov. 1857, and previous inventories, Plantation Record Book 38, Evans Papers, Louisiana State University.

11. Roll, 1811, Plantation Record Book 36, ibid.

12. Roll, 1814, ibid.

13. Roll, 1817, ibid.

14. Inventory, 23 Oct. 1819, "Estate of Nathaniel Evans."

15. Quarter Bill, 1817, Plantation Record Book 36, Evans Papers, Louisiana State University.

16. Higman, "Slave Family and Household in the British West Indies," p. 267.

17. Fogel and Engerman, *Time on the Cross*, 1:28; Genovese, *Roll, Jordan, Roll*, pp. 524–25; Blassingame, *Slave Community*, p. 159.

18. Reconstituted Roll of Oakland Slaves, 1846, Evans Papers, Louisiana State University; Inventory, 14 Apr. 1851, "Estate of Sarah B. Evans."

19. Blanket List, Dec. 1849; "List of Negroes Belonging to J. N. Evans, 1847"; "Rations, 1849"; Blanket List, 1 Jan. 1850; "List of Slaves at Oakland, 1857," in Plantation Record Books 37 and 38, Evans Papers, Louisiana State University.

20. Roll of Oakland Slaves, 1846, Evans Papers, Louisiana State University; Inventory, 14 Apr. 1851, "Estate of Sarah B. Evans."

21. "J. N. Evans' Negroes, Oakland, 15 July 1852," with reconstitution of families from additional previous inventories, Plantation Record Book 38, Evans Papers, Louisiana State University. This inventory represents the community left at Oakland after the removal in January 1852 of slaves drawn by other heirs from the estate of Sarah B. Evans.

22. Ibid.

23. Inventory, 1857, Plantation Record Book 38, Evans Papers, Louisiana State University.

24. Ibid.

25. Comparison of previous rolls with "Roll of Negroes at Oakland, 1864," Plantation Record Book 38, p. 151, Evans Papers, Louisiana State University.

26. Pugh, "Dark Days," p. 11.

27. Inventory, 13 Oct. 1826, "Estate of William Stone," pp. 11–16.

28. Conveyance of Land and Slaves (Tiger Island), 28 Nov. 1842, Walter Brashear to Robert Brashear et al.; Mortgage (Tiger Island), 19 Nov. 1842, Robert Brashear et al. to Walter Brashear, St. Mary Parish Conveyance Records.

29. The oldest woman on the 1826 inventory was forty-year-old Old Hanny, mother of a

young son, Durand. She was not part of the migration from New Jersey but was bought in November 1823. None of the migration females were older than thirty-five (Inventory, 13 Oct. 1826, "Estate of William Stone").

30. Sabry was forty-five, and Old Perry was fifty in 1826, but both were purchased in the 1820s. The oldest of the migration males was younger than thirty-five (ibid.).

31. The only two children were a newborn male infant, John, born to a twenty-year-old new purchase, Sylvia, and a three-year-old boy, Durand (Duval), bought with his parents in the 1820s (Inventory, 13 Oct. 1826, "Estate of William Stone").

32. Inventory, 4 Mar. 1836, "Estate of Euphemia Craig Marsh."

33. At Tiger Island in 1842, males formed 63 percent of the population and females, 36 percent (Mortgage, 28 Nov. 1842, Robert Brashear et al. to Walter Brashear).

34. Conveyance, 1 Jan. 1839, John C. Marsh to George Marsh.

35. Conveyance, 19 Apr. 1854, A. B. Henshaw to Daniel Avery; Inventory, 20 Feb. 1860, "Estate of George Marsh."

36. Conveyance, 19 Apr. 1854, A. B. Henshaw to Daniel Avery; Inventory, 20 Feb. 1860, "Estate of George Marsh."

37. Inventory, 13 Oct. 1826, "Estate of William Stone."

38. Inventory, 4 Mar. 1836, "Estate of Euphemia Craig Marsh."

39. The childless couples were New Frank and Jane, Ned and Grace, Bill and Susy, Tom and Charity, and Dick and Aggy. The marriage between New Frank, a mid-1830s purchase, and Jane, a house servant ten years his senior, was of short duration (Inventory, 4 Mar. 1836, "Estate of Euphemia Craig Marsh"; Conveyance, 1 Jan. 1839, John C. Marsh to George Marsh). The main reason for the reduction in the size of female-headed households was that by 1839 Sylvia had married Edmund. In 1836 she had been the single mother of four children. By 1839 they were part of the household of their stepfather and mother. Also, Mary—in 1836 the single mother of two children—was absent by 1839, and her children were listed as solitaires.

40. Conveyance, 19 Apr. 1854, A. B. Henshaw to Daniel Avery.

41. The childless couple was the cooper, Charles, twenty-eight, and his wife, Jane, twenty-six. They were still childless in 1860 (ibid.; Inventory, 20 Feb. 1860, "Estate of George Marsh").

42. Inventory, 20 Feb. 1860, "Estate of George Marsh."

43. Mortgage (Tiger Island), 1 June 1833, Walter Brashear and Wife to the New Orleans Canal and Banking Company, Mortgage Vol. C-6, pp. 332–34, St. Mary Parish Mortgage Records.

44. Mortgage, 19 Nov. 1842, Robert Brashear et al. to Walter Brashear, Mortgage Vol. II, pp. 117–19, ibid.

45. Dunn, "Tale of Two Plantations," p. 46.

46. Mortgage, 19 Nov. 1842, Robert Brashear et al. to Walter Brashear.

47. Since members of an older generation played important roles in slave society, the separation of Tiger Island's chattels from their progenitive generation no doubt seriously

affected the internal stability of the 1842 community. See Genovese, *Roll, Jordan, Roll*, pp. 522–23; Gutman, *Black Family*, pp. 195–200.

48. U.S. Census, 1850, Slave Schedules, St. Mary Parish, no page numbers but enumerated on 7 December 1850.

49. Inventory and Appraisement, 28 Jan. 1857, "Estate of Robert B. Brashear," Original Estates Vol. 50, pp. 8–14, St. Mary Parish Probate Records.

50. The lower mean age in 1850 may have been related to generational changes, a surge in births since 1842, or—more likely—the 1850 census may have been less exact and accurate in its age designations than the court-related and conveyance inventories.

51. Inventory, 28 Jan. 1857, "Estate of Robert B. Brashear"; Inventory, 31 May 1859, "Estate of Thomas T. Brashear"; Inventory and Partition, 28 May 1860, "Estates of T. T. and Robert Brashear."

52. Dunn, "Tale of Two Plantations," p. 46.

53. Some island planters were concerned that their slave's sex ratio might become too heavily male-dominated. William Palfrey wrote John Moore that "my proportion of men on the plantation is too great already" (Palfrey to Moore, New Iberia, 11 Dec. 1845, box 12, Weeks Papers, Louisiana State University).

54. U.S. Census, 1850, Slave Schedules, St. Mary Parish (no pagination but enumerated 8 Dec. 1850).

55. Menard, "Maryland Slave Population," p. 35.

56. F. D. Richardson, "The Teche Country Fifty Years Ago," pp. 593–99, typescript in Caffery Papers, Louisiana State University.

57. The Stephen Duncan, William J. Minor, David Weeks, Walter Brashear, and John Marsh families are but a few that engaged in the practice.

58. Examples of plantations or farms in the data-base sample whose slave communities exhibited such imbalances are the following, with the dates that each community was inventoried: Zenon Allain, West Baton Rouge, 5 Apr. 1818; Alexander Stirling, St. Mary Parish, 7 May 1818; Josiah Morris, Concordia Parish, 5 Jan. 1825; Louis Landry, Ascension Parish, 29 July 1831; Lydia Lee, Concordia Parish, 2 Nov. 1837; Letitia Hanna Ogden, Avoyelles Parish, 24 July 1841; Charles Aubert, 5 May 1843; Ursin Carlin, St. Martin Parish, 13 Oct. 1843; R. R. Barrow, Terrebonne Parish, 21 Mar. 1841; Charles Morgan, Pointe Coupee Parish, 28 Mar. 1848; Isaac Franklin's Lochlomond and Lonago plantations, West Feliciana Parish, 24 June 1850; Isaac Dunbar, Pointe Coupee, 7 Aug. 1850; Christopher Adams, Iberville Parish, 5 Apr. 1853; Jacob Payne, St. Landry Parish, 30 May 1853; Antoine Duprey, Iberville Parish, 2 Jan. 1855; and Nicholas Loisel, St. Mary Parish, 12 Jan. 1857.

59. Conveyance, 2 Jan. 1855, in "Conveyance, Antoine Duprey and Company to George Reagan," Conveyance Vol. 3, n.p., Iberville Parish Probate Records.

60. Inventory, 21 Dec. 1852, "Estate of Ulgere Baugnon," Conveyance Vol. 2, pp. 21–23, ibid; Inventory, 29 July 1831, in "Estate of Louis Landry," Inventory and Sales, 1831–32, pp. 57–75, Ascension Parish Probate Records; Inventory, 24 Mar. 1848, "Estate of Charles Morgan," Inventories, 1846–49, pp. 192–212, Pointe Coupee Probate Records; Estate Parti-

tion and Sale, 20 June 1860, in "Estate of Parchin A. Young and Conveyance to Olympus Young," Conveyance Vol. O, pp. 24–28, St. Mary Parish Probate Records; Inventory and Sale, 12 Jan. 1857, in "Estate of Nicholas Loisel and Celeste Prevost Loisel," Conveyance Vol. L, pp. 642–45, St. Mary Parish Probate Records.

61. Mortgage, 28 Nov. 1842, Robert Brashear et al. to Walter Brashear; Inventory and Partition, 28 May 1860, "Estates of T. T. and Robert Brashear"; Inventory, 16 Nov. 1860, "Estate of Walter Brashear, Sr."

62. Mortgage, 28 Nov. 1842, Robert Brashear et al. to Walter Brashear. Thirty-eight of the solitaires were male; only two were females.

63. U.S. Census, 1850, Slave Schedules, St. Mary Parish (no pagination but enumerated 8 Dec. 1850).

64. Inventory, 28 Jan. 1857, "Estate of Robert B. Brashear."

65. Inventory, 31 May 1859, "Estate of Thomas Brashear."

66. Inventory and Partition, 28 May 1860, "Estates of T. T. and Robert Brashear."

67. The 1860 population that lived in female-headed single-parent units formed three families, with an average size of 6.6 members. The 1860–65 sample of St. Mary slaveholders had 9 percent of its slaves in female-headed households.

CHAPTER 6

1. Rolls, 1814, 1817, in Plantation Record Book 36, various lists of 1830s and 1840s in Plantation Record Book 37; Inventory, 14 Apr. 1851, "Estate of Sarah B. Evans"; "List of J. N. Evans' Negroes at Oakland," 15 July 1852, Plantation Record Book 38; "List of Oakland Slaves," 15 June 1853, Plantation Record Book 39; Inventory, 1857, reconstituted from "List of Negroes on Oakland, July, 1857," and Blanket List, 18 Nov. 1857, supplemented by previous inventories, Plantation Record Book 38, all in Evans Papers, Louisiana State University. All Evans Papers cited in this chapter are from this depository.

2. Inventory, 4 Mar. 1836, "Estate of Euphemia Craig Marsh"; Conveyance, 1 Jan. 1839, John C. Marsh to George Marsh; Conveyance, 19 Apr. 1854, A. B. Henshaw to Daniel Avery; and Inventory, 20 Feb. 1860, "Estate of George Marsh."

3. Mortgage (Tiger Island), 28 Nov. 1842, Robert Brashear et al. to Walter Brashear; Inventory, 28 Jan. 1857, "Estate of Robert B. Brashear"; Inventory, 31 May 1859, "Estate of Thomas T. Brashear"; Inventory and Partition, 28 May 1860, "Estates of T. T. and Robert Brashear."

4. I have calculated age differences from the previously cited inventories and rolls.

5. Mortgage (Tiger Island), 28 Nov. 1842, Robert Brashear et al. to Walter Brashear; Inventory, 31 May 1859, "Estate of Thomas T. Brashear"; Inventory and Partition, 28 May 1860, "Estates of T. T. and Robert Brashear."

6. The death rate was high for the entire state but was highest in the coastal parishes. Regarding the high incidence of illness on Grand Cote, another St. Mary Parish island

plantation, the owner remarked, "I cannot conceive why they [his slaves] have been more sickly there than elsewhere. Perhaps they were more imprudent having a white person there but rarely" (William F. Weeks, Grand Cote, to Mary C. Moore, Louisville, Kentucky, 1 Sept. 1845, in box 12, folder 90, Weeks Papers, Louisiana State University).

7. Mortgage (Tiger Island), 28 Nov. 1842, Robert Brashear et al. to Walter Brashear; Inventory, 28 Jan. 1857, "Estate of Robert B. Brashear"; Inventory, 31 May 1859, "Estate of Thomas T. Brashear"; Inventory and Partition, 28 May 1860, "Estates of T. T. and Robert Brashear."

8. Data for the marriage analysis were drawn from the sources cited in note 7 and Conveyance, Land and Slaves, 31 May 1852, Walter Brashear to Frances Lawrence; Will, Walter Brashear, 17 Sept. 1860, Brashear Papers in both Southern Historical Collection and Morgan City Library and Archives. In his will Walter Brashear ratified the division that he had made in 1852, including the conveyance of the Bayou Boeuf property to Frances Lawrence and her heirs and Tiger Island to Robert and Thomas Brashear and their heirs.

9. Reconstituted Roll of 1814; Inventory, 23 Oct. 1819, "Estate of Nathaniel Evans"; Reconstituted Roll of Oakland Slaves, 1846, combining the slaves of Sarah B. Evans and John N. Evans, using the Blanket and Ration Lists of November 1846 and other appropriate inventories in Plantation Record Book 37; "J. N. Evans' Negroes, Oakland, 15 July 1852," with reconstitution of families from additional previous inventories; Inventory, 1857; "Roll of Negroes at Oakland, 1864," Plantation Record Book 38, all in Evans Papers.

10. Roll, 1817, Plantation Record Book 36, ibid.

11. Plantation Record Books 37 and 38, ibid.

12. "List of Oakland Slaves," 15 June 1853, Plantation Record Book 39, ibid.

13. Plantation Journal 12, 1849–65, ibid.

14. Inventory, 13 Oct. 1826, "Estate of William Stone"; Inventory, 4 Mar. 1836, "Estate of Euphemia Craig Marsh"; Conveyance, 1 Jan. 1839, John C. Marsh to George Marsh; Conveyance, 19 Apr. 1854, A. B. Henshaw to Daniel Avery; Inventory, 20 Feb. 1860, "Estate of George Marsh."

15. The spouses of Cane, Jim, and Sukey had died, but only Jim had remarried.

16. See Gutman, Black Family, pp. 16–17, 51.

17. Mortgage (Tiger Island), 28 Nov. 1842, Robert Brashear et al. to Walter Brashear; Inventory and Partition, 28 May 1860, "Estates of T. T. and Robert Brashear."

18. Inventory and Partition, 28 May 1860, "Estates of T. T. and Robert Brashear"; Inventory, 28 Jan. 1857, "Estate of Robert B. Brashear"; Inventory, 31 May 1859, "Estate of Thomas T. Brashear." Eliza, wife of Nat Williams in 1857, was by 1859 married to his brother Osborn, and their household contained a two-year-old son (Ned) by Eliza's marriage to Nat. By 1860, their household also included their own infant. Nat had returned to the household of his (and Osborn's) mother and was still there in 1859.

19. "Negroes at Bayou Mallet, June 18, 1863," Diary of Henry E. Lawrence, 1:315, Brashear Papers, Southern Historical Collection.

20. "Register of Births among Slaves, 1843–1865" and periodic diary entries in Plantation Diary 334, Palfrey Papers.

21. Inventory, 23 Oct. 1819, "Estate of Nathaniel Evans"; Mortgage, 3 Apr. 1822, regarding the "Estate of Nathaniel Evans," Probate file 32, West Feliciana Parish Probate Records.

22. List of Taxable Property, 1834–41, Sarah B. Evans and John N. Evans, Plantation Record Book 37, Evans Papers.

23. See "Last Will and Testament," Sarah Bloomfield Spencer Evans, 1 Oct. 1851, Probate Drawer 31 and recorded in Inventories Vol. F, pp. 597–99, 607; Inventory and Appraisement, 14 Apr. 1851, "Estate of Sarah B. Evans," all in West Feliciana Parish Probate Records.

24. See Chapter 4, note 32.

25. "Memoranda, Property Received by Heirs of Mrs. C. L. DeHart from the Estate of Mrs. S. B. Evans, 1852"; "Partition of Estate of S. B. Evans" (partially torn, 1851?); "Property of the Heirs of Mrs. C. L. DeHart from Estate of Mrs. S. B. Evans, 30 Jan. 1852—Personal Property" in box 7, folders 47 and 48, Evans Papers.

26. Rolls, 1811, 1814, 1817, Plantation Record Book 36, ibid.

27. The family for which J. N. Evans traded was that headed by his slave Bob. It consisted of Bob's wife, Louisa, and their three children, Emma, Louis, and Patience. Evans made at least one more trade. On one memo, an "X" is scribbled in pencil with the notation "swapped for Kitty." Apparently he traded Kitty (who would remain with her adopted mother, Nancy) for an old Oakland slave, Alex, who was drawn by the DeHarts and had orphaned grandchildren at Oakland.

28. Roll, 1811, 1811 Work Record, Plantation Record Book 36, Evans Papers; Inventory, 23 Oct. 1819, "Estate of Nathaniel Evans."

29. "Property of Heirs of Mrs. C. DeHart from the Estate of Mrs. S. B. Evans," 30 Jan. 1852, box 7, folder 48, Evans Papers.

30. Estate Partition, 5 Dec. 1854, in "Estate of Cornelia L. Evans on Petition of Heirs of Margaret E. DeHart, deceased," Conveyance Vol. J, pp. 459–65, St. Mary Parish Probate Records.

31. Inventory, 14 Apr. 1851, "Estate of Sarah B. Evans." Both Susannah and her husband, Ben Hill, appeared as unmarried on an 1846 Blanket List of Sarah B. Evans's Negroes, November, Plantation Record Book 37. Ben was bought about 1845. Susannah [Susanne] was born to an unnamed mother at Oakland in 1830. See "List of S. B. E's Negroes, August, 1834," Plantation Record Book 37, Evans Papers.

32. Roll, 1811, Roll, 1814, Plantation Record Book 36, Evans Papers; Inventory, 23 Oct. 1819, "Estate of Nathaniel Evans"; Inventory, 14 Apr. 1851, "Estate of Sarah B. Evans."

33. Inventory, 14 Apr. 1851, "Estate of Sarah B. Evans"; Roll, 1814, Roll, 1817; Quarter Bill, 1817, Plantation Record Book 36. The 1834 roll contained a notation that Mima had a daughter Vicy (born 1843), and all subsequent inventories of Mima's family mention Vicy. See "List of S. B. E's Negroes, August 1834," Plantation Record Book 37, Evans Papers; Inventory, 14 Apr. 1851, "Estate of Sarah B. Evans."

34. Consent Form for slave Peter, 21 Oct. 1818, New Jersey, folder 2, Avery Papers (this consent form did not state the county); Inventory, 4 Mar. 1836; "Estate of Euphemia Craig Marsh"; Bill of Sale, 23 Apr. 1826, for slave Milly, Samuel Woolfolk [New Orleans] to William Stone and John Marsh, St. Mary, folder 3, Avery Papers.

35. Conveyance, 19 Apr. 1854, A. B. Henshaw to Daniel Avery.

36. Inventory, 20 Feb. 1860, "Estate of George Marsh."

37. Bill of Sale, 26 Apr. 1826, for Sylvia, Samuel M. Woolfolk [New Orleans] to William Stone and John C. Marsh, folder 3, Avery Papers; Inventory, 4 Mar. 1836, "Estate of Euphemia Craig Marsh."

38. Conveyance, 1 Jan. 1839, John C. Marsh to George Marsh.

39. Conveyance, 19 Apr. 1854, A. B. Henshaw to Daniel Avery; Inventory, 20 Feb. 1860, "Estate of George Marsh"; Plantation Account Book, Vol. 4, Avery Papers.

40. Bill of Sale for Sawney, Estate of Jesse McCall, deceased, 23 Dec. 1824, to William Stone and John C. Marsh, Register Vol. A, pp. 344–45, St. Martin Parish Probate Records.

41. Among those with freedmen accounts were Sawney McCall (the surname of his first master), Lucy Stephens (Sawney's daughter, who married Peter Stephens, Jr.), Betsy Ann McCall, and Fanny McCall (Plantation Account Book, 4:20–21, 25, 66, 68, Avery Papers).

42. Bill of Sale, 19 May 1827, for slaves Augustus, Arena, and Fanny, Austin Woolfolk and Ira Bowman, Adams County, Mississippi, to John C. Marsh and the heirs of William Stone, New Iberia, Louisiana, folder 3, ibid.

43. Inventory, 4 Mar. 1836, "Estate of Euphemia Craig Marsh"; Conveyance, 1 Jan. 1839, John C. Marsh to George Marsh; Conveyance, 19 Apr. 1854, A. B. Henshaw to Daniel Avery; Inventory, 20 Feb. 1860, "Estate of George Marsh."

44. Bill of Sale, 17 Nov. 1823, for slave Harriet, a "mulatto girl," Raphael Semmes, Charles County, Maryland, to William Stone, Louisiana, folder 3, Avery Papers.

45. "Servants at Petite Anse Homes" in "Ledger and Anecdotes about Family Servants," Vol. 6, ibid.

46. Inventory, 4 Mar. 1836, "Estate of Euphemia Craig Marsh."

47. An 1840 list of slaves on the reverse of a letter shows eighty-two slaves and is divided into two groups, apparently those residing on the two Marsh properties. Ben, Vina, and John Henry are listed together and appear to be at New Iberia (John C. Marsh, Baltimore, to George Avery, New Iberia, 4 Aug. 1840, folder 5, Avery Papers).

48. Conveyance, 1 Jan. 1839, John C. Marsh to George Marsh.

49. "Oleographic Statement," 5 May 1856, and John C. Marsh to George Marsh, 8 May 1856, folder 6, Avery Papers.

50. Conveyance, 19 Apr. 1854, A. B. Henshaw to Daniel Avery; Inventory, 20 Feb. 1860, "Estate of George Marsh."

51. "Oleographic Statement," 5 May 1856; George Marsh, Petite Anse Isle, to John Marsh, 25 Aug. 1845, and John C. Marsh, New Iberia, to George Marsh, Petite Anse Island, 8 May 1856, folder 6, Avery Papers; Plantation Account Book, 4:63, ibid.

52. Margaret Marsh Henshaw, New Iberia, Louisiana, to John C. Marsh, Rahway, New

Jersey, 16 May 1853, and John C. Marsh, Rahway, New Jersey, to Margaret Henshaw, New Iberia, Louisiana, 21 June 1853, folder 6, ibid.

53. "Oleographic Statement," 5 May 1856.

54. Inventory, 20 Feb. 1860, "Estate of George Marsh."

55. "Ledger and Anecdotes about Family Servants."

56. Harriet is inventoried at Petite Anse but made frequent trips to New Iberia with her mistress. See Margaret Marsh Henshaw, New Iberia, to John C. Marsh, Rahway, New Jersey, 16 May 1853.

57. D. D. Avery, New Iberia, to Sarah Avery, East Baton Rouge, 20 May 1854, folder 6, Avery Papers.

58. "Ledger and Anecdotes about Family Servants."

59. U. B. Phillips mentions the brig *Ajax* as one of the ships that "consigned numerous parcels [of slaves] to various New Orleans correspondents." He found ship manifests regarding the *Ajax* and other slave carriers in the Library of Congress collection of ship manifests from the internal trade (*American Negro Slavery*, p. 196).

60. "Recollects by Aunt Maria Houston," in "Ledger and Anecdotes about Family Servants."

61. Inventory, 4 Mar. 1836, "Estate of Euphemia Craig Marsh."

62. John C. Marsh, New Iberia, to George Marsh, Petite Anse Island, 5 May 1856. John C. Marsh states his wishes regarding eventual emancipation of certain slaves, including Vina, in this letter and the accompanying "oleographic statement," both in folder 6, Avery Papers.

63. Conveyance, 19 Apr. 1854, A. B. Henshaw to Daniel Avery; Bill of Sale for John Houston, Bien and Cohen of New Orleans to John C. Marsh of New Iberia, 8 Feb. 1837, folder 4, Avery Papers. Houston's value as a skilled slave is noted in Conveyance, John C. Marsh to George Marsh, 1 Jan. 1839.

64. Inventory, 20 Feb. 1860, "Estate of George Marsh." The child, a light mulatto with a white father, might not have been inventoried, as had been the case of other children for whom emancipation was planned, or she may have been sent to New Iberia to be reared. This child is specifically mentioned in George Marsh's will: "I further desire and request that Mr. Avery's interest in the mulatto girl called Vena (the daughter of yellow Maria and born July 9, 1854) be purchased by my estate, and that my God Daughter Sarah Avery shall take charge of the said Vena after she arrives at the age of eight or ten . . . the said Vena to remain with her until she is twenty-one years old and then to be set free" (Will, George Marsh, 15 July 1858, Succession 1042). Yellow Maria is Little Maria. The baby was named Vena (or Vina) after her sister.

65. Plantation Account Book, 4:11–15, Avery Papers.

66. "Ledger and Anecdotes about Family Servants."

67. Conveyance, 1 Jan. 1839, John C. Marsh to George Marsh.

68. Conveyance, 19 Apr. 1854, A. B. Henshaw to Daniel Avery.

69. Inventory, 20 Feb. 1860, "Estate of George Marsh."

70. George Marsh, Petite Anse, to John Craig Marsh, New York City, 14 June 1845, and

Sarah Marsh Avery, Baton Rouge, to George Marsh, New Iberia, 3 Aug. 1845, folder 5, Avery Papers.

71. Conveyance, 19 Apr. 1854, A. B. Henshaw to Daniel Avery; Inventory, 20 Feb. 1860, "Estate of George Marsh."

72. Olmsted, *Slave States*, p. 121; David Todd, Franklin, Louisiana, to Thomas T. Barr, Lexington, Kentucky, 6 May 1822; Margaret Brashear, Belle Isle, Louisiana, to Caroline Brashear, Lexington, Kentucky, 16 Nov. 1822; Walter Brashear, Lexington, Kentucky, to Margaret Brashear, Belle Isle, 9 Aug. 1827, folders 2 and 3, Brashear Papers, Southern Historical Collection.

73. Gutman, *Black Family*, p. 129.

74. Margaret Brashear, Belle Isle, Louisiana, to Caroline Brashear, Lexington, Kentucky, 16 Nov. 1822; Rebecca T. Brashear, Belle Isle, Louisiana, to Walter Brashear, Jr., Bardstown, Kentucky, 18 Jan. 1830; Walter Brashear, Lexington, Kentucky, to Margaret Brashear, Belle Isle, Louisiana, 9 Aug. 1827, folders 2 and 3, Brashear Papers, Southern Historical Collection.

75. Mortgage of Slaves, 14 June 1824, Walter Brashear, Louisiana, to Robert R. Barr, Fayette, Kentucky, Deed Book V, pp. 33–35, Fayette County, Kentucky, Conveyance Records.

76. Brooks's age was given as sixteen in 1825 (Mortgage of Land and Slaves, Walter and Margaret Brashear to Bank of Louisiana, 13 July 1825, Mortgage Vol. A-B, pp. 54–55, St. Mary Parish Mortgage Records; Mortgage of Slaves, 14 June 1824, Walter Brashear to Robert R. Barr).

77. Rebecca T. Brashear, Belle Isle, Louisiana, to Walter Brashear, Jr., Bardstown, Kentucky, 18 Jan. 1830, and Frances Brashear Lawrence, Belle Isle, to Henry E. Lawrence, New Orleans, 10 Feb. 1849, folders 3 and 15, Brashear Papers, Southern Historical Collection.

78. Mortgage, Walter Brashear to W. W. Montgomery, 15 Apr. 1833, Mortgage Vol. B-5, pp. 212–14, St. Mary Parish Mortgage Records; Fanny [Frances] Lawrence, to Henry E. Lawrence, Jan. 1850, folder 17, Brashear Papers, Southern Historical Collection.

79. David Todd, Franklin, Louisiana, to Thomas T. Barr, Lexington, Kentucky, 6 May 1822, folder 2, Brashear Papers, Southern Historical Collection.

80. Mortgage, Walter Brashear to W. W. Montgomery, 15 Apr. 1833; Conveyance of Land and Slaves, Walter Brashear to Henry E. Lawrence, 11 Apr. 1848, Conveyance Vol. G, pp. 203–4, St. Mary Parish Conveyance Records; Mortgage of Slaves, Walter Brashear to James Darrack, Fayette County, Kentucky, 20 Sept. 1814, Deed Book L, pp. 218–20, Fayette County, Kentucky, Mortgage Records.

81. Mortgage of Slaves, Brashear to Darrack, 20 Sept. 1814.

82. By 1830 Rachel was gravely ill. Rebecca Brashear wrote her brother, "It is probable she will never recover" (Margaret Brashear, Belle Isle, to Caroline Brashear, Lexington, Kentucky, 16 Nov. 1822, Rebecca T. Brashear, Belle Isle, Franklin, Louisiana, to Walter Brashear, Jr., Bardstown, Kentucky, 18 Jan. 1830, folders 2 and 3, Brashear Papers, Southern Historical Collection).

83. Mary Eliza Brashear, St. Mary Parish, to Caroline Brashear, Lexington, Kentucky, 19 Feb. 1823, folder 2, ibid.

84. Conveyance of Land and Slaves (Golden Farm), Henry E. Lawrence to Walter Brashear, 27 Mar. 1848, Conveyance Vol. G, pp. 203–4; Fanny Lawrence to Henry E. Lawrence, Jan. 1850, folder 17, Brashear Papers, Southern Historical Collection.

85. Mortgage, Walter and Margaret Brashear to Bank of Louisiana, 13 July 1825, Mortgage Vol. A-B, pp. 54–55, St. Mary Parish Mortgage Records.

86. Mortgage, Walter Brashear to Robert R. Barr and Thomas T. Barr, 14 June 1824, Deed Book V, pp. 33–35, Fayette County, Kentucky, Mortgage Records.

87. Mortgage (Tiger Island), 1 June 1833, Walter Brashear and Wife to New Orleans Canal and Banking Company; Mortgage (Tiger Island) 19 Nov. 1842, Robert Brashear et al. to Walter Brashear.

88. Margaret Brashear, Belle Isle, to Frances Emily Brashear, Lexington, Kentucky, 14 Apr. 1832, folder 5, Brashear Papers, Southern Historical Collection.

89. Inventory (Golden Farm), 28 Mar. 1848, with Conveyance, Henry E. Lawrence to Walter Brashear.

90. Fanny E. Lawrence to Henry E. Lawrence, Jan. 1850, folder 17, Brashear Papers, Southern Historical Collection; Will, Walter Brashear, 17 Sept. 1860.

91. Inventory of Golden Farm Slaves, 4 Jan. 1861, contained in "Lease of Land and Slaves," Mrs. Frances Lawrence, St. Mary Parish, to Robert D. Hockley, Nelson County, Kentucky, Conveyance Vol. O, pp. 217–21 (original lease dated 13 July 1860), St. Mary Parish Conveyance Records.

92. Mortgage (Tiger Island), 1 June 1833, Walter Brashear and Wife to New Orleans Canal and Banking Company; Mortgage (Tiger Island), 19 Nov. 1842, Robert Brashear et al. to Walter Brashear.

93. Inventory and Partition, 28 May 1860, "Estates of T. T. and Robert Brashear."

94. Margaret Brashear, Belle Isle, to Caroline Brashear, Lexington, Kentucky, 16 Nov. 1822.

95. Will of Robert R. Barr of Fayette County, Kentucky, but written at Belle Isle, Louisiana, 14 Oct. 1831, Will Book M, pp. 315–16, Fayette County, Kentucky, Probate Records. Barr lived with the Brashears for long periods at a time during the 1820s and early 1830s.

96. Robert R. Barr died about 20 February 1836, legally "without issue." His heirs were his three surviving sisters and the children of Walter Brashear (Estate of Robert R. Barr, Succession 203, 6 Apr. 1837, in Sanders, comp., *Selected Annotated Abstracts of St. Mary Parish, Louisiana, Court Records*, 3:78).

97. Walter Brashear, Golden Farm, to Frances Brashear, Lexington, Kentucky, 16 Sept. 1838, folder 7, Brashear Papers, Southern Historical Collection.

98. Inventory (Golden Farm), 11 Apr. 1848, Conveyance, Henry E. Lawrence to Walter Brashear.

99. Inventory and Partition, 28 May 1860, "Estates of T. T. and Robert Brashear."

100. Mortgage (Belle Isle), 13 July 1825, Walter and Margaret Brashear to the Bank of Louisiana; Mortgage (Tiger Island), 1 June 1833, Walter Brashear and Wife to New Orleans Canal and Banking Company.

101. Inventory (Golden Farm), 4 Jan. 1861, in "Lease between Frances Lawrence and Robert D. Hockley"; Will, Walter Brashear, 17 Sept. 1860.

102. Lease, 15 Feb. 1866, Henry E. Lawrence to Oliver Richardson et al., Brashear Papers, Morgan City Library and Archives.

103. Bill of Sale, 12 Apr. 1830, for a lot of seventeen slaves, M. Payne of Bedford County, Tennessee, to Walter Brashear and Robert Barr, co-partners, Belle Isle, Mortgage Vol. B-5, p. 69, St. Mary Parish Mortgage Records.

104. Inventory and Partition, 28 May 1860, "Estates of T. T. and Robert Brashear."

105. Ibid.

106. Bill of Sale, 12 Apr. 1830, M. Payne, Bedford County, Tennessee, to Walter Brashear and Robert Barr, co-partners, Belle Isle, Louisiana.

107. Mortgage (Tiger Island), 28 Nov. 1842, Robert Brashear et al. to Walter Brashear; Inventory and Partition, 28 May 1860, "Estates of T. T. and Robert Brashear." The information in the following two paragraphs is from the same sources.

108. Wheaton, "Family and Kinship in Western Europe," p. 608.

CHAPTER 7

1. "Memoirs of Francis D. Richardson," 1 Dec. 1895, pp. 12–14, Caffery Papers, Louisiana State University.

2. Emily Caroline Douglas Autobiography, 1855–58, p. 91, Douglas Papers.

3. Olmsted, *Slave States*, p. 119.

4. Eaton, *History of the Old South*, pp. 232–33; Phillips, *American Negro Slavery*, pp. 190–96; Eaton, *History of the Old South*, pp. 232–33; Stampp, *Peculiar Institution*, p. 239.

5. Fogel and Engerman, *Time on the Cross*, 1:44–58; Gutman and Sutch, "Slave Family," pp. 99–123; Gutman, *Slavery and the Numbers Game*, pp. 130–38; Genovese, *Roll, Jordan, Roll*, pp. 456–57 (see also Boles, *Black Southerners*, p. 68); Tadman, *Speculators and Slaves*, pp. 124–54.

6. Stampp, *Peculiar Institution*, pp. 257–58; Weld, comp., *American Slavery as It Is*, pp. 166–69.

7. Northup, *Twelve Years a Slave*, pp. 57–58.

8. Olmsted, *Slave States*, p. 119.

9. Ex-Slave Narrative, John W. H. Barnett, slave in East Feliciana Parish, Louisiana, in Rawick, ed., *American Slave*, Ser. 1, vol. 8, pt. 1, p. 107; also see Ex-Slave Narrative, John Williams, a Louisiana slave whose mother was sold apart from her mother and siblings, ibid., vol. 11, pt. 7, p. 173.

10. Ex-Slave Narrative, Virginia Bell, slave in St. Landry Parish, Louisiana, in Rawick, ed., *American Slave*, Supp. Ser. 2, vol. 2, pt. 1, p. 246; also in Yetman, ed., *Voices from Slavery*, pp. 25–27.

11. Stroyer, *Sketches of My Life in the South*, pp. 29–31.

12. Hannah Blair to "My Dear Husband," Jonesboro, Tennessee, 8 Apr. 1861; Bills of Sale, J. W. Wilson, New Orleans, to Richard L. Pugh, 9 Dec., 8 June 1860, box 1, folder 4, Richard L. Pugh Papers.

13. T. D. Jones to Eliza, 7 Sept. 1860, box 14, folder 100, Thomas Butler Papers.

14. Ibid.

15. Jane Dennis, St. James Parish, to Eliza Jones, Bayou Sara, 6 Oct. 1861, box 15, folder 102, ibid.

16. Caramouche Papers and Reminiscences, p. 8.

17. Mary Ann Colvin Mayfield Biography, folder L, Mayfield Papers; Smedes, *Memorials of a Southern Planter*, p. 35.

18. Rachel O'Connor to David Weeks, 3 Nov. 1833, box 4, folder 35, Weeks Papers, Louisiana State University.

19. Carmouche Papers and Reminiscences, pp. 40–50.

20. Rachel O'Connor to "My Dear Brother" (David Weeks), 25 Apr. 1834, box 5, folder 38, Weeks Papers, Louisiana State University.

21. Allie, to her mother, Mary C. Moore, 17 Dec. 1852, box 20, folder 81, ibid.

22. Lewis Stirling, Sr., Wakefield Plantation, to Lewis Stirling, Jr., Arbroath Plantation, West Baton Rouge, 19 Jan. 1843, box 3, folder 31, Stirling Papers.

23. The prospect that slaves might be seized in a lawsuit or foreclosure caused panic in the slave community. For example, Rachel O'Connor received a writ from the West Feliciana Parish sheriff to seize her stored cotton and twenty-six slaves. She wrote a family member that when the sheriff arrived, the slaves "flew to the woods . . . like wild hogs, and carried their little ones with them, and returned after he went away" (Rachel O'Connor to David Weeks, 6 Oct. 1832, and Writ in the Case of William D. Flowers v. Rachel O'Connor, box 4, folder 30, Weeks Papers, Louisiana State University).

24. Sale in Suit of Pierre Flogny v. Pamela Hatch, 18 Apr. 1825, Sheriff's Sale Vol. B, p. 58, Iberville Parish Conveyance Records.

25. Appeal from the Fourth Judicial District to the Louisiana Supreme Court, Christopher Adams v. Ira R. Lewis, Document 1685, Record Book 2A, pp. 69–78; Case 752, Answer of Joseph Erwin, in G. E. Russel v. Durham Tudor Hall, 3 Apr. 1829, Fourth Judicial District, Iberville Parish Court Records; Bills of Sale, Isaac Erwin to Miles Bristow, 29 May 1835, 5 Jan. 1835; Isaac Erwin to Charles Breaux, 18 Feb. 1839, in Conveyance Books S and T, Iberville Parish Conveyance Records.

26. "Last Will and Testament," in Estate of Alexander Stirling, Jan. 1806, Probate Drawer 120, West Feliciana Parish Probate Records.

27. "Inventory and Appraisement," Estate of Alexander Stirling, 5 May 1809, Probate Drawer 120, in West Feliciana Parish Probate Records. The plantation in St. Mary, also owned by the Stirlings, is described in the "Inventory and Appraisement, Estate of Alexander Stirling, 7 May 1818," Original Estates Vol. 1, pp. 251–53, St. Mary Parish Probate Records; Statement of Executor John H. Johnson in regard to the estate of Alexander Stirling, 17 Jan. 1818, Probate Drawer 120, West Feliciana Parish Probate Records; Sales Bill,

Estate of Alexander Stirling of West Feliciana and St. Mary, 1 Feb. 1819, Original Estates Vol. 1, pp. 271–74, 359; Sales Bill, Estate of Dennis Carlen [Carlin], 24 Jan. 1828, Original Estates Vol. 2, pp. 209–10, 216; "Inventory and Appraisement," Estate of Pierre Etie, 6 Dec. 1821; Sales Bill, 14 Jan. 1822, Original Estates Vol. 2, p. 291, St. Mary Parish Probate Records.

28. "Inventory and Appraisement," Estate of Mrs. (Mary Simmons) Stephen Read, 27 Aug. 1842, Inventory Vol. A, pp. 83–84; "Inventory and Appraisement," Estate of Stephen Read, 5 Apr. 1848, Inventory Vol. B, pp. 172–74; Sales Bill, Estate of Stephen Read, 14 Jan. 1855, Partition Vol. A, pp. 335–39, Avoyelles Parish Probate Records.

29. "Inventory and Appraisement," Estate of Lydia Bass, 2 Mar. 1829, Succession Book E, pp. 343–45; "Inventory," Estate of Lydia Bass, 14 Oct. 1830, Succession Book E, pp. 415–16; Partition, Estate of Lydia Bass, 4 Mar. 1831, Succession Book E, pp. 432–34, Concordia Parish Probate Records.

30. "Inventory and Appraisement," Estate of Philemon Nicholas Prevost, 11 Sept. 1850, and Sales Bill, Philemon Nicholas Prevost, 1 Feb. 1851, Inventory Vol. A, pp. 52–64, 191–93, St. Mary Parish Probate Records.

31. Rachel O'Connor to Mrs. M. C. Moore, ca. Apr. 1844, box 61, portfolio 75, Weeks Papers, Tulane University.

32. "Last Will and Testament," Catherine Turnbull, 14 May 1832, recorded 18 Aug. 1834, box 1, folder 9, Stirling Papers.

33. "Last Will and Testament," John Palfrey, 15 May 1842, recorded 1 Nov. 1843, in "Estate of John Palfrey," no. 995, St. Martin Parish Probate Records.

34. "Exchange of Slaves," 14 Sept. 1857, folder 2, Moore Papers, Michael Wynne Collection.

35. Anderson, ed., Brokenburn, pp. 84, 86.

36. Ex-Slave Interview, Dinah Watson, slave in Orleans Parish, Louisiana, in Rawick, ed., American Slave, Ser. 1, vol. 5, pt. 4, p. 1/144; Ex-Slave Interview, J. W. Terrill, slave in De Soto Parish, Louisiana, ibid., pp. 1–3/80–82.

37. Carmouche Papers and Reminiscences, p. 49.

38. Boles, Black Southerners, pp. 51, 104–5.

39. One example of miscegenation involving black men and white women can be found in Frances Lawrence to Henry Lawrence, Brashear Papers, Southern Historical Collection.

40. Fogel and Engerman, Time on the Cross, 1:132–33. General treatments of the topic of miscegenation can be found in Taylor, Negro Slavery in Louisiana, pp. 233–34; White, Ar'n't I a Woman?, pp. 34–43, 61; Jones, Labor of Love, pp. 20, 28, 37–38; Clinton, Plantation Mistress, pp. 210–11, 220–21; Scott, Southern Lady, pp. 19, 52–53; Genovese, Roll, Jordan, Roll, pp. 413–31; David et al., Reckoning with Slavery, pp. 21, 136, 149–53; Steckel, "Miscegenation and the American Slave Schedules"; Fox-Genovese, Within the Plantation Household, pp. 188–89; Blassingame, Slave Community, pp. 154–57, 172–73.

41. Gutman and Sutch, "Victorians All," pp. 149–53, esp. 152; Olmsted, Cotton Kingdom, p. 240; Moody, "Slavery on Louisiana Sugar Plantations," p. 284; Genovese, Roll, Jordan, Roll, p. 414.

42. Fogel, *Without Consent or Contract*, pp. 181–82; Steckel, "Miscegenation and the American Slave Schedules," pp. 251–63; Crawford, "Quantified Memory," pp. 159–63.

43. Ex-Slave Interview of Chris Franklin, slave in Bossier Parish, Louisiana, in Rawick, ed., *American Slave*, Supp. Ser. 2, vol. 4, pt. 3, p. 1408; Ex-Slave Interview of Gabriel Gilbert, in Rawick, ed., *American Slave*, Ser. 1, vol. 4, pt. 2, p. 2/69.

44. Barrow Diary and Papers, 1833–38 (transcription), entries for 1 Jan. 1838, 4 Sept. 1837.

45. Ex-Slave Interview of Victor Duhon, slave in Lafayette Parish, Louisiana, in Rawick, ed., *American Slave*, Ser. 1, vol. 4, pt. 1, p. 1/307.

46. Ex-Slave Interview of Gabriel Gilbert, slave in Iberia Parish, ibid., pt. 2, p. 2/69; Ex-Slave Interview of Alexander Kenner, slave in Louisiana and Kentucky, in Blassingame, *Slave Testimony*, pp. 392–93.

47. Transcriptions of Rosedown Papers, item dated 21 May 1841, no. 2199, box 1, Flint Transcriptions.

48. Rachel O'Connor to "Dear Brother" (David Weeks), 20 Nov. 1833, box 4, folder 35, Weeks Papers, Louisiana State University.

49. Regarding problems with overseers and miscegenation see Rachel O'Connor's letters to David or Mary Weeks of 8 July 1832, 19 Jan., 6 May, 23, 31 Oct. 1833, box 4, folders 29–35, ibid. See also Fox-Genovese, *Within the Plantation Household*, p. 325; Scarborough, *The Overseer*, p. 77.

50. Ex-Slave Interview of Jacob Aldrich, slave in St. Mary and Terrebonne parishes, in Rawick, ed., *American Slave*, Supp. Ser. 2, vol. 2, pt. 1, p. 24.

51. Ex-Slave Interview of Isaac Throgmorton (Canada, 1863), in Blassingame, *Slave Testimony*, pp. 432–34.

52. Blassingame, *Slave Community*, p. 164.

53. Northup, *Twelve Years a Slave*, pp. 42–43.

54. Ibid., pp. 42–43, 151–52, 196–99; also see Jones, *Labor of Love*, pp. 37–38; Fox-Genovese, *Within the Plantation Household*, pp. 325–26; Clinton, *Plantation Mistress*, pp. 211–12.

55. Ex-Slave Interview of Henrietta Evelina Smith, slave in East Feliciana Parish, in Rawick, ed., *American Slave*, Ser. 1, vol. 10, pt. 6, p. 195.

56. Ex-Slave Interview of J. W. Terrill, slave in De Soto Parish, Louisiana, ibid., vol. 5, pt. 4, pp. 1–2/80–81.

57. Ex-Slave Interview of Anna Osborne, slave near Mansfield, Louisiana, in Rawick, ed., *American Slave*, Supp. Ser. 2, vol. 8, pt. 7, pp. 2990–91.

58. Ex-Slave Interview of Agatha Babino, slave in Lafayette Parish, WPA Slave Interviews for Texas, original typescript (unedited), p. 2, Barker Texas History Center.

59. Ex-Slave Interview of Mary Reynolds, slave in Concordia Parish, Louisiana, original typescript (unedited), pp. 1–13, ibid.

60. "Last Will and Testament," Alexander H. Harrington, 15 June 1853, filed 23 Oct. 1854, Record of Wills A-A, no. 4, pp. 4–5, and "Last Will and Testament," Seville Marionneaux, 2 Nov. 1855, filed 2 Jan. 1856, ibid., no. 11, pp. 13–14, Iberville Parish Probate Records;

Document "Freeing and Legitimizing Mulatto Children" of Stephen Cokafor, Miscellaneous Record Vol. A, p. 27, Rapides Parish Probate Records; Inventory and Appraisement of Anton Nolasco, 24 Feb. 1817, Inventory Record Vol. 1815–19, West Feliciana Parish Probate Records; Oleographic Statement, 5 May 1856, and John C. Marsh to George Marsh, 8 May 1856, folder 6, Avery Papers.

61. "Last Will and Testament," William Boyce, 8 Nov. 1825, filed same day, Original Estates Vol., pp. 131–50, St. Mary Parish Probate Records.

62. "Last Will and Testament," William Weeks, 30 May 1816, Inventory and Appraisement, William Weeks, 29 Dec. 1819, Probate Drawer 113, West Feliciana Parish Probate Records; Letter and Accounts, Joseph Hodgson to David Weeks, 2 Mar. 1820, box 1, folder 7, and Joseph Hodgson to David Weeks, 2 June 1825, box 2, folder 16, Weeks Papers, Louisiana State University; Proceedings in Succession 344, Helen O'Hara, admr. v. Mary C. Conrad et al., Vol. 6, St. Martin Parish Probate Records; Henry Flower to David Weeks, 24 Nov. 1827, box 2, folder 18, and Document dated 1 Apr. 1834, box 22, folder 90, Weeks Papers, Louisiana State University.

63. "Last Will and Testament," John Turnbull, 27 June 1855, filed 19 Dec. 1856; Lewis E. Turner v. C. D. Smith, executor, re. Estate of John Turnbull, filed 3 Sept. 1856, in Succession of John Turnbull, Drawer 107, West Feliciana Probate Records.

64. A good description of a rather elaborate Scripture wedding is found in Bond Diary, entry for 4 Jan. 1862, p. 123, Journal 1, box 2. Also see Ex-Slave Interview of Virginia Bell, slave in Opelousas, Louisiana, in Rawick, ed., *American Slave*, Supp. Ser. 2, vol. 2, pt. 1, p. 246. Broom ceremonies are noted in Ex-Slave Interview of Agatha Babino, slave in Lafayette Parish, WPA Slave Narratives for Texas, original typescript (unedited), pp. 2–3, Barker Texas History Center; Fred Brown, slave in Baton Rouge, in Rawick, ed., *American Slave*, Supp. Ser. 2, vol. 2, pt. 1, p. 468; Aaron Russell, slave in Ouachita Parish, ibid., vol. 8, pt. 7, p. 3390; Donaville Broussard, slave in Lafayette Parish, ibid., vol. 2, pt. 1, p. 455; Mary Reynolds, slave in Concordia Parish, ibid., pp. 272–73.

65. Ex-Slave Interview of Agatha Babino, slave in Lafayette Parish, WPA Slave Narratives for Texas, original typescript (unedited), pp. 2–3, Barker Texas History Center; Ex-Slave Interview of Aaron Russell, slave in Ouachita Parish, in Rawick, ed., *American Slave*, Supp. Ser. 2, vol. 8, pt. 7, p. 3390; Donaville Broussard, slave in Lafayette Parish, ibid., vol. 2, pt. 1, pp. 455–56.

66. Ex-Slave Interview of Ellen Betts, slave in St. Mary Parish, in Rawick, ed., *American Slave*, Supp. Ser. 2, vol. 2, pt. 1, p. 272; Ex-Slave Interview of Chris Franklin, slave in Bossier Parish, ibid., vol. 4, pt. 3, p. 1407.

67. "Rules and Regulations," in Plantation Diary 34, Minor Papers.

68. Ex-Slave Interview of Willie Williams, slave in Vermilion Parish, in Rawick, ed., *American Slave*, Supp. Ser. 2, vol. 10, pt. 9, p. 4158; Ex-Slave Interview of Fred Brown, slave in Baton Rouge, ibid., vol. 2, pt. 1, p. 468.

69. "Mother" to Sarah [Flint family], 23 Oct. 1853, Seip Papers.

70. L. S. Tibbetts to Sophie Tibbetts, 23 Jan. 1853, folder 2, Tibbetts Correspondence.

71. Ex-Slave Interview of Willie Williams, slave in Vermilion Parish, in Rawick, ed., *American Slave*, Supp. Ser. 2, vol. 10, pt. 9, p. 4158.

72. Town Diary, entry for 13 Feb. 1853, p. 44.

73. Ex-Slave Interview of Chris Franklin, slave in Bossier, Louisiana, in Rawick, ed., *American Slave*, Supp. Ser. 2, vol. 4, pt. 3, p. 1407; Ex-Slave Interview of Sylvester Wickliffe, free black in St. Mary Parish, ibid., vol. 10, pt. 9, p. 4039; Ex-Slave Interview of Donaville Broussard, slave in Lafayette Parish, ibid., vol. 2, pt. 1, p. 455.

74. Some slave marriages were recorded in Catholic church records, such as the St. Landry Church Records, Register of Blacks no. 8, Vol. 2. Also see Ex-Slave Interview of Pauline Johnson and Felice Boudreaux, slaves near Opelousas, Louisiana, in Rawick, ed., *American Slave*, Supp. Ser. 2, vol. 6, pt. 5, p. 2037. Slave weddings were frequently noted in F. D. Richardson's Bayside Plantation Journal, Vols. 1 and 2 (see 28 Mar. 1846, 25 Dec. 1849, 23 Aug. 1862), Bayside Plantation Records; see also "Cotton Book for 1860," Bermuda Plantation, Vol. 2, box 2, Prudhomme Papers.

75. Ex-Slave Interviews of La Sin Mire, slave near Abbeville, Louisiana, in Rawick, ed., *American Slave*, Supp. Ser. 2, vol. 7, pt. 6, p. 2708; Fred Brown, slave in Baton Rouge, ibid., vol. 2, pt. 1, p. 468; Virginia Newman, slave in St. Mary Parish, ibid., vol. 7, pt. 6, p. 2905. Also see entry for 18 Mar. 1860, "Cotton Book for 1860," Bermuda Plantation, Vol. 2, box 2, Prudhomme Papers.

76. Walter Brashear to Frances Brashear, 16 Sept. 1838, Brashear Papers, Southern Historical Collection. On divorce, see Northup, *Twelve Years a Slave*, pp. 140–41, 169. On separation by the master, see Ex-Slave Interview of William Mathews, slave in Franklin Parish, in Rawick, ed., *American Slave*, Supp. Ser. 2, vol. 7, pt. 6, p. 2616; Blassingame, *Slave Community*, pp. 176–77, 341.

77. Crawford, "Quantified Memory," pp. 151–54, 170, 191–93; Escott, *Slavery Remembered*, pp. 50–52; Blassingame, *Slave Community*, pp. 164–65.

78. For example, Bennet Barrow devoted a long passage in his diary to the problems of off-plantation matches in his rules for Highland; among his six reasons why they were inadvisable, he mentions that "they are liable to be separated from each other, as well as their children, either by the caprice of either of the parties [owners], or when their is a sale of property" (Barrow Diary and Papers [transcription], p. 55).

79. Northup, *Twelve Years a Slave*, p. 169; Bond Diary, entry for 10 Feb. 1865; Alfred Dusperier v. Bernard Dautrieve and Joseph Boutte et al., Appeal from the District Court of St. Martin to the Supreme Court of Louisiana, Western District, Opelousas, 25 Aug. 1856, St. Martin Parish Court Records.

80. Blassingame, *Slave Community*, pp. 175–77, 361; Fogel, *Without Consent or Contract*, pp. 149–52; Fogel and Engerman, *Time on the Cross*, 1:129.

81. Transcription of Plantation Journals for 1862, Airlie Papers; Barrow Diary and Papers, entries for 30 Dec. 1838, 1 Dec. 1836.

82. Ex-Slave Interview of Ellen Betts, slave in St. Mary Parish, in Rawick, ed., *American Slave*, Supp. Ser. 2, vol. 2, pt. 1, p. 266. Paternalism is reflected in one of William J. Minor's

rules: "Men must not be allowed to beat their wives, nor parents or other relations to punish the children severely" ("Rules and Regulations," Plantation Diary 34, Minor Papers).

83. Wadley Diary, entry for 27 Aug. 1863.

84. Weld, comp., *American Slavery as It Is*, pp. 153–66; Rachel O'Connor to Mary C. Weeks, 1 Sept. 1833, box 4, folder 34, Weeks Papers, Louisiana State University; Henry Winborne Drake to "My Dear Mother" (Susanna Margruder Drake), 13 Oct. 1863, Boundurant Papers. A particularly vivid example of a man risking injury or death in defense of his wife is reported in William Jacobs (overseer) to Mary C. Weeks, 29 Nov. 1837, box 7, folder 56, Weeks Papers, Louisiana State University.

85. The plantations used in the survey of age differences between spouses were Grand Cote (1840), thirteen couples; Grand Caillou (1843), thirteen couples; Waterloo (1848), fifty-eight couples; China Grove (1848), twenty-four couples; Bayou Boeuf (1850), twenty-eight couples; Upper Plantation (1850), thirty-three couples; Killarney (1850), twenty-one couples; Bellevue (1850), twenty-nine couples; Lochlomond (1850), nineteen couples; Angola (1850), twenty-seven couples; Loango (1850), twelve couples; Camperdown (1851), twenty-one couples; Oxford (1851), seventeen couples; Southdown (1852), forty-nine couples; W. B. Prescott Plantation (1855), twenty-two couples; Donaldson Place, Houmas (1858), fifty-eight couples; Conway Place, Houmas, twenty-eight couples; Homestead (1860), twenty-one couples; and David McGill Plantation (1864), seventeen couples. Fogel and Engerman contend that well over 40 percent of slave spouses had an age difference of only one to three years (*Time on the Cross*, 1:140–41). Their evidence is challenged in Gutman and Sutch, "Victorians All," pp. 146–48. I find abundant evidence that, although it was not the norm, slave women were frequently older than their husbands and sometimes the age differences were considerable. Suthia, forty-seven, was married a man who was thirty. Harriet, seventy, was married to Bug, fifty, and both couples were on the same plantation ("Inventory of China Grove Plantation," 6 Dec. 1848, Snyder Papers).

86. Inventory and Appraisement of Samuel Rembert, 23 Mar. 1848, Succession Vol. A, pp. 336–37, Tensas Parish Probate Records; Application for Partition of Slaves, Estate of Truman S. Phelps, 21 Feb. 1851, Succession Vol. B2, p. 411, Catahoula Parish Probate Records; Inventory and Appraisement, Estate of John D. Smith, M.D., 26 Nov. 1838, Succession Vol. I, Concordia Parish Probate Records. Also see Inventory and Appraisement, Enos Mackey, 27 Apr. 1859, in Probate Vol. D, p. 77, Franklin Parish Probate Records; Inventory and Appraisement of William Routh, 19 July 1847, Succession Vol. A, p. 49, Catahoula Parish Probate Records; Inventory and Appraisement, Calvin Routh, 10 Apr. 1851, Succession Vol. A, pp. 421–25, Tensas Parish Probate Records; Inventory and Appraisement of John Wilkins, 18 Feb. 1853, Conveyance Vol. I, pp. 237–38, St. Mary Parish Probate Records. A striking example is China Grove in 1848. There, Ishmael was forty-eight, his wife, Binah, twenty-eight; Big Charles was forty-nine, his wife, Katy, twenty-seven; Billy was seventy-four, his wife, Huldah, forty; Stephen was thirty-eight, his wife, Patience, twenty-nine; John Kentuck was thirty-eight, his wife, Sophia, twenty-nine; Old Stephen was seventy, his wife, Jenn, forty-five ("Inventory of China Grove Plantation," 6 Dec. 1848, Snyder Papers).

87. Ex-Slave Interview of Amos Lincoln, slave in Orleans Parish, in Rawick, ed., *American Slave*, Supp. Ser. 2, vol. 6, pt. 5, p. 2371.

88. Ex-Slave Interview of Rebecca Fletcher, 21 Mar. 1940, WPA Slave Interviews for Louisiana, microfilm, Louisiana State University Archives.

89. Former slave William J. Anderson, interviewed in Canada, recalled that "female slave enciente were . . . formerly tied up for punishment, but to avoid the pecuniary loss . . . the masters adopted the *humane* method said to have been first practiced by the French of Louisiana [woman attached to four stakes, with abdomen in dug-out area]" (quoted in Drew, *North-Side View of Slavery*, p. 256).

90. Ex-Slave Interview of Hinton Love, 8 Jan. 1941, WPA Slave Interviews for Louisiana, microfilm, Louisiana State University Archives; Ex-Slave Interview of Fannie Clemons, slave in Farmerville, Louisiana, in Rawick, ed., *American Slave*, Arkansas Narratives, 2:28.

91. See Wadley Diary, entry for 15 Apr. 1864, p. 202; Barrow Diary and Papers, "List of Deaths, 1844–1845," folder 4, also p. 419 of transcription; "Memorandum on the Birth of Negro Children," Kleinpeter Record Book, Kleinpeter Papers. Kleinpeter attributes the deaths of several infants to being smothered by their mothers.

92. St. Rosalie Plantation Book, B-90, Durnford Papers.

93. Seale Diary, 1853, notation for 27 May 1853.

94. Rachel O'Connor to Mary Weeks, 15 Sept. 1828, box 3, folder 28, Weeks Papers, Louisiana State University; Inventory, William B. Barrow, Loose Box, 27 May 1845, La-fourche Parish Probate Records; Inventory and Appraisement of James G. Hoover, 13 Dec. 1855, Succession Record F, pp. 534–36, Concordia Parish Probate Records; Estate of Robert Perry, 30 Dec. 1858, in Partition Book B, pp. 383–91, East Feliciana Parish Probate Records; Conveyance of Slaves and Land, Parchin Young to Olympus Young, 20 June 1860, Con-veyance Vol. O, pp. 24–28, St. Mary Parish Probate Records. Boles convincingly argues that "in a society where slave marriages were not legally recognized and families could be separated at the whim of a master, genealogically significant names gave permanence to otherwise fragile family arrangements" (*Black Southerners*, pp. 42–43).

95. "List of Women and Their Children, 1858," in Homestead Plantation Record Book of Reine S. Welham, Welham Papers; Estate Sale, John Wilkins, 8 Feb. 1853, Conveyance Vol. I, St. Mary Parish Probate Records; Inventory of Calvin Routh, 10 Apr. 1851, Succession Vol. A, pp. 441–42, Tensas Parish Probate Records; Inventory and Sale, Estate of Philemon Nicholas Prevost, 11 Sept. 1850, 1 Feb. 1851, Inventory Vol. A, pp. 52–64, 191–93, St. Mary Parish Probate Records.

96. Although not from Louisiana, ex-slave Sarah Wilson's interview points up the "secret name" (or in Louisiana folklore, the "basket name") dilemma: "[Old mistress] would call me, 'Come here Annie.' And I wouldn't know what to do. If I went when she called me 'Annie' my mammy would beat me for answering to that name, and if I didn't go old Mistress would beat me for that" (Ex-Slave Interview of Sarah Wilson, in Rawick, ed., *American Slave*, Ser. 1, vol. 7, pt. 1, p. 347. Also see Weld, comp., *American Slavery as It Is*, p. 44).

97. Trussell and Steckel, "Age of Slaves at Menarche and Their First Births," esp. p. 492; Steckel, *Economics of U.S. Slave and Southern White Fertility*; Gutman, *Black Family*, pp. 50, 114, 124, 160; Fogel and Engerman, *Time on the Cross*, 1:137; Gutman and Sutch, "Victorians All," pp. 142–44; Cody, "Slave Demography and Family Formation," pp. 168–69.

98. The fifteen plantations used in the seasonality study were Roseland Plantation, Charles Oxley, Kenner Papers; Airlie Plantation, Airlie Papers; Bayou Goula Plantation, Hudson Diary; St. Rosalie Plantation, Durnford Papers; Hazlewood Plantation, Evans Papers, Louisiana State University; Palfrey Plantation, Palfrey Papers; Kleinpeter Plantation, Kleinpeter Papers; Ledoux Plantation, A. Ledoux and Company Record Book; Le Carpe Plantation, Richard Butler Papers; Waterloo Plantation and Southdown Plantation, Minor Papers; Highland Plantation, Barrow Diary and Papers; Bermuda Plantation, Shallow Lake Plantation, and Magnolia Plantation, Prudhomme Papers. See Cody, "Slave Demography and Family Formation," p. 178. She found for the years 1800–1829 that the months having the highest number of conceptions were October, November, and December, and she attributed disease as well as heavy work duties as contributing factors to lower conceptions in the earlier months. My findings are very close to hers, except that January had more conceptions than did October. This is no doubt because in Louisiana's sugar parishes, sugarmaking could extend into December, and January was often a holiday period when the harvest was late. Ironically, in today's nonagricultural society, the largest number of conceptions still occur in December, according to analysis of U.S. births from 1942 to 1981 made by University of Michigan researchers Lam and Miron, *Psychology Today*, Dec. 1989. A pioneering article in this area is Rutman, Wetherell, and Rutman, "Rhythms of Life."

99. Shorter, *The Making of the Modern American Family*, pp. 158–59.

100. Ex-Slave Interview of Tennessee Johnson, slave in eastern Louisiana, 13 May 1940, WPA Slave Interviews for Louisiana, microfilm, Louisiana State University Archives.

101. Ex-Slave Interview of Gracie Stafford, slave in St. James Parish, 23 Oct. 1940, ibid. Another Louisiana slave said much the same thing. "My papa and ma had 19 chil'ren—all by the same Pa and Ma—an' we was raised right" (Ex-Slave Interview of Ellen Broomfield, 20 Feb. 1941, ibid.).

102. Ex-Slave Interview of Tennessee Johnson, 13 May 1940, ibid.

103. Fine, Schwebel, and James-Myers, "Family Stability in Black Families," pp. 12–15.

104. Ex-Slave Interview of Agatha Babino, WPA Slave Narratives for Texas, original typescript (unedited), p. 2, Barker Texas History Center.

105. Ex-Slave Interview of Mary Reynolds, ibid.

106. State of Louisiana v. William Read, 25 Mar. 1855, Criminal Records, 1850–71, St. Mary Parish Court Records.

107. W. F. Weeks to "Mother," Mary C. Weeks, 28 Apr. 1852, box 21, folder 85, Weeks Papers, Louisiana State University.

108. Ellen McCollam, Bayou Black, to Andrew McCollam, Terrebonne, 5 Oct. 1860, folder 6, McCollam Papers.

109. Rachel O'Connor to Mary C. Weeks, 23 Jan. 1826, box 2, folder 17, Weeks Papers,

Louisiana State University. Also see W. F. Weeks to Mrs. Mary C. Moore, 1850, box 17, folder 57, ibid.

110. Anderson, ed., *Brokenburn*, p. 87.

111. Barrow Diary and Papers, entry for 7 Oct. 1837.

112. Olmsted, *Slave States*, p. 182.

113. Hepworth, *Whip, Hoe, and Sword*, pp. 140–41, 145–47.

114. Ex-Slave Interview of Elizabeth Hines, slave in Baton Rouge, in Rawick, ed., *American Slavery*, Ser. 2, vol. 9, pt. 3, p. 273. Another example of deep affection between sisters and mothers and daughters is related in Interview of John Williams, ibid., vol. 11, pt. 7, p. 173. Ellen Butler tells of her sister sneaking her siblings food and of her brother being beaten severely for running off in search of food (Ex-Slave Interview of Ellen Butler, slave in Calcasieu Parish, in Rawick, ed., *American Slave*, Supp. Ser. 2, vol. 3, pt. 2, p. 546).

115. See Conveyance, Parchin A. Young to Olympus Young in Case of Olympus Young v. Appoline Patout, Tutor, 20 June 1860, Conveyance Vol. O, pp. 24–28, St. Mary Parish Probate Records; Inventory and Appraisement, 1 May 1832, Estate of Catherine Turnbull, Vol. C, pp. 189–203, West Feliciana Parish Probate Records; "List of Negroes of James Miller, offered for Sale," 13 Mar. 1841, Boundurant Papers.

116. Rebecca T. Brashear to Walter Brashear, Jr., 18 Jan. 1830, folder 3, Brashear Papers, Southern Historical Collection.

117. Boyd Smith, Grand Cote, to David Weeks, New Iberia, 20 Aug. 1834, box 5, folder 42, Weeks Papers, Louisiana State University.

118. Gutman, *Black Family*, pp. 113–18, 122–23, 181, and passim; Cody, "Slave Demography and Family Formation," pp. 313–64.

119. Crowley, "Importance of Kinship," pp. 559–60, 563. Other family historians use the term *kinship* more loosely. Wheaton uses kinship to "refer to a social relationship arising from a tie based on either descent or alliance or both, and to the groups created by such ties" ("Observations on the Development of Kinship History," p. 297, n. 1; also see Kertzer, "Anthropology and Family History," p. 206). A good analysis of how kinship continued to function in African-American slavery is in Boles, *Black Southerners*, pp. 41–42.

120. The term *overlooker* refers, in slave lore, to a male slave who served as the exclusive mate for several women. He fathered children by all of them, and they were not allowed to have other husbands. It is generally viewed by historians as a breeding mechanism insti-gated by the owners, but it may also be a carryover from African custom. See Ex-Slave Interview of Fred Brown, in Rawick, ed., *American Slave*, Supp. Ser. 2, vol. 2, pt. 1, p. 468, and Ex-Slave Interview of Willie Williams, ibid., vol. 10, pt. 9, p. 4158.

121. Katz, speaking of a different population, but one with limited housing, writes that "the presence of boarders or relatives in individual households was more a matter of circumstances or chance than of systematic relationships" (Katz, Doucet, and Stern, *Social Organization of Early Industrial Capitalism*, p. 300).

122. Inventory and Appraisement, Jean Ursin Jarreau, 8 May 1855, Inventory Vol. 1854–55, pp. 445–77, Point Coupee Parish Probate Records; Rachel O'Connor to "My dear Sister"

(Mary C. Moore), Apr. 1844, box 61, portfolio 75, Weeks Papers, Tulane University; Barrow Diary and Papers (typescript), box 1, folder 5. Siblings Pauline Johnson and Felice Boudreaux still lived together in their old age and remembered well the names and fates of their various family members, including uncles (Ex-Slave Interview of Pauline Johnson and Felice Boudreaux, slaves in Lafayette Parish, in Rawick, ed., *American Slave*, Supp. Ser. 2, vol. 6, pt. 5, p. 2035).

123. Ex-Slave Interview of Rebecca Fletcher, 21 Sept. 1940, WPA Slave Interviews for Louisiana, microfilm, Louisiana State University Archives (Fletcher's interview stresses cultural transmission by grandparents and parents); Ex-Slave Interview of Louis Love, slave in St. Mary Parish, in Rawick, ed., *American Slave*, Supp. Ser. 2, vol. 7, pt. 6, p. 2445; Ex-Slave Interview of Virginia Newman, slave in St. Mary Parish, ibid., pp. 2903–4; Ex-Slave Interview of Victor Duhon, slave in Lafayette Parish, ibid., vol. 4, pt. 3, p. 1239; Ex-Slave Narrative of Evelina Smith, slave in East Feliciana Parish, in Rawick, ed., *American Slave*, Ser. 2, vol. 10, pt. 6, pp. 193–94; Ex-Slave Interview of A. C. Pruitt, slave in St. Martin Parish, in Rawick, ed., *American Slave*, Supp. Ser. 2, vol. 8, pt. 7, p. 3204; Ex-Slave Interview of John Williams, slave in Baton Rouge, in Rawick, ed., *American Slave*, Ser. 2, vol. 11, pt. 7, p. 173.

124. Ex-Slave Narrative of Amos Lincoln, in Rawick, ed., *American Slave*, Supp. Ser. 2, vol. 6, pt. 5, p. 2370.

125. John Perkins, Sr., The Oaks (Lowndes County, Mississippi) to John Perkins, Jr. (Somerset, Tensas Parish, Louisiana), 11 Dec. 1858, Perkins Papers.

126. Ex-Slave Interview of Agatha Babino, WPA Slave Narratives for Texas, original typescript (unedited), p. 3, Barker Texas History Center.

127. Ex-Slave Interview of Mary Island, slave in Union Parish, in Rawick, ed., *American Slave*, Ser. 2, vol. 9, pt. 3, p. 389.

128. Ex-Slave Interview of Fred Brown, slave in Baton Rouge, in Rawick, ed., *American Slave*, Supp. Ser. 2, vol. 2, pt. 1, p. 465.

129. "List of Field Laborers Accounts and Notes, 1866," Gillespie Papers.

130. Genovese, *Roll, Jordan, Roll*, p. 283.

131. Ibid., p. 281.

132. Raboteau, *Slave Religion*, pp. 70–74; Wadley Diary, entry for 14 July 1861.

133. Raboteau, *Slave Religion*, p. 92.

134. Boles, "Introduction," in *Masters and Slaves in the House of the Lord*, ed. Boles, pp. 6, 13–15, 17.

135. Ibid., pp. 2, 6, 10.

136. Raboteau, *Slave Religion*, pp. 95–318; Blassingame, *Slave Community*; Genovese, *Roll, Jordan, Roll*, pp. 183–93, 232–55, 280–84; Levine, *Black Culture and Black Consciousness*, pp. 3–80; Rawick, *From Sundown to Sunup*, pp. 32–38.

137. Boles, *Black Southerners*, pp. 157–69; Boles, "Evangelical Protestantism in the Old South," pp. 13–14; Boles, "Introduction," in *Masters and Slaves in the House of the Lord*, ed. Boles, pp. 1–18; Hall, "Black and White Christians in Florida"; Hall, " 'Yonder Come Day' "; Miller, "Slaves and Southern Catholicism"; Miller, " 'Failed Mission' "; Mohr, "Slaves and

White Churches in Confederate Georgia"; Mathews, "Charles Colcock Jones and the Southern Evangelical Crusade"; Sernett, *Black Religion and American Evangelicalism*; Sobel, *Trabelin' On*; Bailey, *Shadow on the Church*; Touchstone, "Planters and Slave Religion in the Deep South"; and James, "Biracial Fellowship in Antebellum Baptist Churches."

138. Boles, "Introduction," in *Masters and Slaves in the House of the Lord*, ed. Boles, pp. 2, 12.

139. Blassingame, *Slave Community*, pp. 98–99.

140. Bailey, "Divided Prism," p. 392.

141. Town Diary, entries for 27 Mar. 1853, p. 86, 5, 19 June 1853, pp. 156–70, 17 July 1853, p. 198, 30 Mar. 1953, p. 87, 5 June 1853, p. 156.

142. Boles, "Introduction," in *Masters and Slaves in the House of the Lord*, ed. Boles, p. 9.

143. James, "Biracial Fellowship in Antebellum Baptist Churches," p. 55.

144. Ex-Slave Interview of Chris Franklin, in Rawick, ed., *American Slave*, Supp. Ser. 2, vol. 4, pt. 3, p. 1407; L. S. Tibbetts to Mrs. Sophia Tibbetts, 23 Jan. 1853, folder 2, Tibbetts Correspondence.

145. Touchstone, "Planters and Slave Religion in the Deep South," pp. 103, 120–21; Sparks, "Religion in Amite County," p. 64; Transcriptions, Airlie Plantation Account Book, 1862, notation for 6 July 1862, Airlie Papers.

146. Ex-Slave Interview of William Mathews, in Rawick, ed., *American Slave*, Supp. Ser. 2, vol. 7, pt. 6, pp. 2613–14.

147. Ex-Slave Interview of Clara Brim, slave in Branch, Louisiana, ibid., vol. 2, pt. 1, p. 430.

148. Ex-Slave Interview of William Matthews, in Rawick, ed., *American Slave*, Ser. 1, vol. 5, pt. 3, p. 3169.

149. Marsh Scuddeo, New Orleans, to Charles Scuddeo, Boston, 20 Dec. 1846, Miscellaneous Collection 2466. A similar observation was made by young Sarah Wadley concerning the moving piety of her father's slaves (Wadley Diary, 14 July 1861, p. 9).

150. "The Religious Life of the Negro Slave," *Harper's Monthly Magazine*, June–Nov. 1863, pp. 481–83.

151. Ex-Slave Interview of Orelia Franks, slave near Opelousas, Louisiana, in Rawick, ed., *American Slave*, Supp. Ser. 2, vol. 4, p. 1424.

152. Genovese, *Roll, Jordan, Roll*, p. 238.

153. Ex-Slave Interview of Sol Walton, slave in Caddo Parish, Louisiana, in Rawick, ed., *American Slave*, Supp. Ser. 2, vol. 10, pt. 9, p. 3953.

154. Ex-Slave Interview of Agatha Babino, WPA Slave Narratives for Texas, original typescript (unedited), p. 2, Barker Texas History Center.

155. Bond Diary, p. 148.

156. Ex-Slave Interview of Pauline Johnson and Felice Boudreaux, in Rawick, ed., *American Slave*, Ser. 1, vol. 4, pt. 2, p. 2/226; Ex-Slave Interview of Oliver Blanchard, slave in St. Martin Parish, ibid., pt. 1, p. 2/90; Ex-Slave Interview of Peter Ryas, slave in St. Martin Parish, ibid., vol. 5, pt. 3, p. 2/275.

157. Ex-Slave Interview of Pauline Johnson and Felice Boudreaux, ibid., vol. 4, pt. 2, p. 2/226.

158. Ex-Slave Interview of Agatha Babino, WPA Slave Narratives for Texas, original typescript (unedited), pp. 1–2, Barker Texas History Center.

159. Ex-Slave Interview of Chris Franklin, in Rawick, ed., *American Slave*, Supp. Ser. 2, vol. 4, pt. 3, p. 1410.

160. Ex-Slave Interview of Clara Brim, in Rawick, ed., *American Slave*, Ser. 1, vol. 4, pt. 1, p. 2/148.

161. Ex-Slave Interview of Orelia Franks, in Rawick, ed., *American Slave*, Supp. Ser. 2, vol. 4, pt. 3, p. 1425.

162. "Religious Life of the Negro Slave," pp. 678–79.

163. Ex-Slave Interview of Mary Reynolds, WPA Slave Narratives for Texas, p. 331, Barker Texas History Center.

164. Ex-Slave Interview of Ellen Butler, slave at Whiskey Chitto, Louisiana, in Rawick, ed., *American Slave*, Supp. Ser. 2, vol. 3, pt. 2, p. 546.

165. Ex-Slave Interview of Adeline White, slave in St. Landry Parish, in Rawick, ed., *American Slave*, Ser. 1, vol. 5, pt. 4, p. 2/154.

166. Ex-Slave Interview of Mary Reynolds, WPA Slave Narratives for Texas, Barker Texas History Center.

167. Ex-Slave Interview of Ella Washington, slave in St. Mary Parish, in Rawick, ed., *American Slave*, Ser. 1, vol. 5, pt. 4, p. 2/132.

168. Ex-Slave Interview of William Mathews, ibid., pt. 3, p. 2/68.

169. Ex-Slave Interview of J. W. Terrill, slave in De Soto Parish, Louisiana, ibid., pt. 1, pp. 1–2/80–81.

CHAPTER 8

1. Laslett, "Character of Familial History," p. 275.

2. For an assessment of the mentalité approach, see Wheaton, "Observations on the Development of Kinship History," pp. 296–97; Kertzer, "Anthropology and Family History," pp. 204–5; Kertzer, "Future Directions in Historical Household Studies," p. 105; Tilly, "Family History, Social History, and Social Change," p. 324; and Smith, "Study of the Family in Early America," pp. 10–11. Current slavery scholarship generally combines approaches. As Hareven states, "The recurring issues running through all historical research on the family concern linking quantitative behavioral data with qualitative analysis of perceptions (mentalité), and constructing longitudinal patterns from cross-sectional data. Initially, some critics of the new social history and of family history posed false dichotomies between quantitative behavioral and qualitative data. These are not mutually exclusive or conflicting approaches. Ideally, family history should integrate the two" ("Family History at the Crossroads," p. xx). Successful examples of the mentalité or combined approach include

Genovese, *Roll, Jordan, Roll*; Blassingame, *Slave Community*; Levine, *Black Culture and Black Consciousness*; Stuckey, "Through the Prism of Folklore"; Stuckey, *Slave Culture*; Joyner, *Down by the Riverside*; Webber, *Deep Like the Rivers*; and Owens, *This Species of Property*.

3. Fogel and Engerman, *Time on the Cross*, 1:142. I do not see the adoption of the nuclear model so much as a choice than as a necessity. Because of constant dispersions and limits on choices and actions, slaves were unable to sustain the African forms in an unfree and alien society. Regarding the transition period see Kulikoff, *Tobacco and Slaves*, pp. 353–58.

4. Blassingame, *Slave Community*, p. 149; Genovese, *Roll, Jordan, Roll*, pp. 450–58, 483–501; Gutman, *Black Family*, pp. 118, 123.

5. Jones, *Labor of Love*, p. 32.

6. Fogel, *Without Consent or Contract*, pp. 150, 178 n. 75, 448; Crawford, "Quantified Memory," pp. 149, 150, 189. A more useful gauge might be to use childhood as a vantage point because it is in early childhood that socialization takes place, but it is debatable. On this point, see Laslett, "The Family Cycle and the Process of Socialization," quoted in and commented upon by Wheaton, "Family and Kinship in Western Europe," p. 610.

7. Crawford, "Quantified Memory," p. 32.

8. Kulikoff, *Tobacco and Slaves*, p. 371. In his excellent synthesis, John Boles states that "while one must be careful not to romanticize the ability of slaves to develop stable families—the two-parents-present household was probably never the most common arrangement—or carve out areas of cultural autonomy, neither should one minimize what slaves achieved" (*Black Southerners*, p. 41).

9. Burton, *In My Father's House*, p. 159.

10. Fox-Genovese, *Within the Plantation Household*, p. 48.

11. Burton, *In My Father's House*, pp. 315–16, 321; Fogel, *Without Consent or Contract*, pp. 164–65.

12. Genovese, *Roll, Jordan, Roll*, p. 491. Burton has made a major contribution to the debate by demonstrating quantitatively that the high incidence of female-headed households in urban areas misled early scholars such as Du Bois and Frazier into assuming that this was the general pattern, whereas just the opposite is true.

13. The sample of female-headed single-parent households no doubt inadvertently includes some women with off-plantation marriages, but I did attempt to determine marital status through record linkage and excluded those known to have a husband close by or temporarily absent.

14. Jones, *Labor of Love*; White, *Ar'n't I a Woman?*; Fox-Genovese, *Within the Plantation Household*. Both Burton and Crawford briefly consider the female-headed single-parent household: Burton, *In My Father's House*, pp. 316–21; Crawford, "Quantified Memory," pp. 190–93, 238.

15. White, *Ar'n't I a Woman?*, p. 132.

16. Cabin Lists, Oakland Plantation, Evans Papers, Louisiana State University.

17. Inventory, 4 Mar. 1836, "Estate of Euphemia Craig Marsh."

18. Conveyance, 1 Jan. 1839, John C. Marsh to George Marsh.

19. Conveyance, 19 Apr. 1854, A. B. Henshaw to Daniel Avery; Inventory, 20 Feb. 1860, "Estate of George Marsh." In 1854 divorced forty-five-year-old Jane was the only female solitaire. Three of the twelve single males were in their fifties or sixties, one was forty-nine, and two were in their late thirties. Men clearly in the market for first wives included two eighteen-year-olds, a nineteen-year-old, two men in their early to mid-twenties, and several young men still in their parents' households. It might appear that these men would have difficulty in finding single women in their age bracket, but some were available. Four single women in the sixteen-to-twenty-eight group still resided in their parents' conjugal units, and there was also the possibility of marriage to five young single women with infants who lived in their parents' households. Some of the male solitaires were fathers of these women's infants. In 1860 solitaires formed 15 percent of the population, and even this relatively small proportion is deceptive. Many were older slaves who had once been members of Petite Anse families and had strong kinship ties to existing families. Four were widowers (Cane, Dick, Bill, and Edmund). Two, John Congo and Roy, were stepchildren of the last-named widower. Another was divorced, having been married for a short time to Jane, a female solitaire, in 1860. In other words, Henry was the only older male solitaire who spent most of his adult life on the plantation without close family associations. Female solitaires in 1860 included Old Jane, Aime (a widow with grown children and grandchildren on the plantation), and twenty-year-old Anna Maria (Little Maria).

20. Mortgage (Tiger Island), 28 Nov. 1842, Robert Brashear et al. to Walter Brashear; Inventory and Partition, 28 May 1860, "Estates of T. T. and Robert Brashear."

21. Walter Brashear, Golden Farm, to Frances Brashear, Lexington, 16 Sept. 1838, folder 7, Brashear Papers, Southern Historical Collection. Concerning social unrest among solitaires of other St. Mary plantations, see William T. Palfrey to Boyd Smith, 23 Aug. 1834, box 5, folder 42, and W. F. Weeks to Mary C. Weeks, 28 Apr. 1852, box 21, folder 85, Weeks Papers, Louisiana State University.

22. Higman, "Slave Family and Household in the British West Indies," pp. 283-84.

23. Inventory, 14 Apr. 1851, "Estate of Sarah B. Evans"; Inventory, 1857, Oakland, in Plantation Record Book 38, Evans Papers.

24. Mortgage, 28 Nov. 1859, Robert Brashear et al. to Walter Brashear; Inventory, 31 May 1859, "Estate of Thomas T. Brashear"; Inventory and Partition, 28 May 1860, "Estates of T. T. and Robert Brashear"; Inventory, 28 Jan. 1857, "Estate of Robert B. Brashear."

25. Gutman, *Black Family*, p. 102; Frazier, *Negro Family*, p. 236.

26. Crawford, "Quantitative Memory," paraphrased in Fogel, *Without Consent or Contract*, p. 179. Also see Crawford, "Quantitative Memory," tables 60 and 61, pp. 189-91.

27. White, *Ar'n't I a Woman?*, p. 65; Burton, *In My Father's House*, p. 169; Kulikoff, *Tobacco and Slaves*, pp. 330-31.

28. Fogel, *Without Consent or Contract*, p. 183; Kulikoff, *Tobacco and Slaves*, p. 331; Richard H. Steckel also found that women on large holdings tended to have higher rates of childlessness than those on small holdings (*Economics of U.S. Slave and Southern White Fertility*, quoted in Fogel, *Without Consent or Contract*, p. 180).

29. Kulikoff, *Tobacco and Slaves*, pp. 331, 339; Stampp, *Peculiar Institution*, pp. 327–31; Webber, *Deep Like the Rivers*, pp. xiii, x, 3; Fogel, *Without Consent or Contract*, pp. 152, 169, 183–85, 452 n. 95.

30. Escott also did not seem to see major variations in the condition of life for slaves on small and large plantations in his analysis of former slave interviews (*Slavery Remembered*, pp. 53–55).

31. Fortes, *Web of Kinship among the Tallensi*.

32. Laslett, "Introduction," in *Household and Family in Past Time*, ed. Laslett and Wall; Wheaton, "Family and Kinship in Western Europe," pp. 606–7; Wheaton, "Observations on the Development of Kinship History," p. 288; Berkner, "The Stem Family and the Developmental Cycle of the Peasant Household"; Berkner, "The Use and Misuse of Census Data for the Historical Analysis of Family Structure"; *Developmental Cycle in Domestic Groups*, ed. Goody; *Transitions*, ed. Hareven; Segalen, "Family Cycle and Household Structure." Laslett answers his critics in a 1987 article. He correctly asserts that no typological system has been devised that allows for the developmental cycles of households, "articulating successive forms as to follow that cycle," while satisfying all "other essential criteria, providing for all relationship possibilities" ("Character of Familial History," p. 280).

33. Gutman, *Black Family*, pp. 129–38; Cody, "Slave Demography and Family Formation," pp. 116–18, 313, 323–54; White, *Ar'n't I a Woman?*, pp. 91–118; Kulikoff, *Tobacco and Slaves*, pp. 184–93, 371–81, 402–5.

34. Shiflett, "Household Composition of Rural Black Families," pp. 244, 258–59.

BIBLIOGRAPHY

MANUSCRIPT SOURCES

Austin, Texas
  Eugene C. Barker Texas History Center, University of Texas
    Airlie Papers
    WPA Slave Interviews for Texas (typescript and manuscript)
  Travis County Collection, Austin Public Library
    WPA Slave Interviews for Texas (typescript and manuscript)
Baton Rouge, Louisiana
  Archives Division, Louisiana State Library
    WPA Slave Interviews for Louisiana (microfilm)
  Department of Archives and Manuscripts, Louisiana State University
    Anonymous Day Books (Oscar Dubreuil?)
    Anonymous Planter Ledger (J. L. Lobdell)
    Anonymous Slave List
    D. D. Arden Letters
    Ashland Plantation Record Book
    Norbert Badin Papers
    Bennet H. Barrow Diary and Papers
    Priscilla Munnikhuysen Bond Diary
    Hubbard S. Bosley Papers
    James P. Bowman Papers
    Rosella Kenner Brent Papers
    Louis Amedee Bringier Papers
    James Bryan Document
    Bruce, Seddon, and Wilkins Plantation Records
    John C. Burruss Papers (George M. Lester Collection)
    Butler Family Papers (Ellis-Farar Papers)
    Richard Butler Papers
    Thomas W. Butler Papers
    Donelson Caffery and Family Papers
    Concordia Parish Inquest Case File
    Alexandre de Clouet Papers
    Eloi Joseph Derouen Notebook
    Emily Caroline Douglas Papers
    Joseph Dunbar Document

Stephen Duncan Account Book

Stephen and Stephen Duncan, Jr., Papers

Isaac Erwin Diary

Nathaniel Evans and Family Papers

Alexander K. Farrar Family Papers

Lewis H. Flint Transcriptions (Rosedown)

Morgan Fly History

Andrew Hynes Gay and Family Papers

Edward J. Gay and Family Papers

James A. Gillespie and Family Papers

Joseph Girod Papers

Good Hope Plantation Papers

Hephzibah Church Record Books

Phillip Hickey and Family Papers

Franklin Hudson Diary (John H. Randolph Papers)

John C. Jenkins and Family Papers

Patrick F. Keary Correspondence

Benjamin Kendrick Papers

Kenner Family Papers

Duncan F. Kenner Memorandum

Joseph Kleinpeter and Family Papers

Elu Landry Plantation Record Book

La Reunion Plantation Document

LeBlanc Family Papers

A. Ledoux and Company Record Book

Moses Liddell Papers

Eliza Ann Marsh Diary

Henry Marston and Family Papers

Charles L. Mathews Family Papers

Mary Ann Colvin Mayfield Papers

William J. Minor Papers

John Moore and Family Papers (Michael Wynne Collection)

Natchitoches Parish Miscellaneous Documents

Robert A. Newall Papers

William T. and George D. Palfrey Papers

Samuel Plaisted Correspondence

Pre Aux Cleres Plantation Record Books

Jean Charles de Pradel and Family Papers

Alexander Franklin Pugh Plantation Diaries

Josephine Nicholls Pugh Civil War Account, "Dark Days: A Woman's Record"

Richard L. Pugh Papers

W. W. Pugh and Family Papers

John H. Randolph Papers

Marsh Scuddeo Letter

H. M. Seale Diary

Slavery Collection

Alonzo Snyder Papers

Lewis Stirling and Family Papers

William Taylor Diary

John C. Tibbetts Correspondence

Benjamin Tureaud and Family Papers

David Weeks Papers (Weeks-Hall Memorial Collection)

William P. Welham Plantation Record Book

WPA Slave Narratives, Louisiana (microfilm)

Chapel Hill, North Carolina

    Southern Historical Collection, University of North Carolina Library

Avery Family Papers

R. R. Barrow Journals

Bayside Plantation Records

Taylor Beatty Diaries

John Boyd Diary

Brashear and Lawrence Family Papers

Caffery Family Papers

Annie Jeter Carmouche Papers and Reminiscences

Paul L. DeClouet Papers

Evan Hall Plantation Account Books

James Amedee Gaudet Papers

Wade Hampton Papers

Charles Howard Family Domestic History

Kean and Prescott Family Papers

Andrew McCollam Papers

Robert Campbell Martin Papers (microfilm of manuscripts in Archives, Francis T. Nichols State College, Thibodaux, Louisiana)

John Perkins Papers

Leonidas Polk Papers

William Polk Papers

Ellen Louise Power Diary

Pierre Phanor Prudhomme Records and Papers

William Page Saunders Papers

Frederic Seip Papers

William A. Shaffer Papers

Lewis Thompson Papers

    Clarissa E. (Leavitt) Town Diary

    Sarah L. Wadley Diary

    Henry Clay Warmouth Papers

    Maunsel White Papers

    Trist Wood Papers

Morgan City, Louisiana

    Morgan City Library and Archives

        Brashear Papers

        Civil War Collection

        Gathright Family Papers

        Segar Family Papers

New Brunswick, New Jersey

    Special Collections and Archives (Jersey Room), Alexander Library,
    Rutgers University

        Slave Manumissions Volume, Middlesex County

New Iberia, Louisiana

    Iberia Parish Library

        Weeks File

New Orleans, Louisiana

    Historic New Orleans Collection, Louisiana State Museum Library

        Valcour Aime Papers (typescript)

Manuscripts, Rare Books, and Archives, Howard-Tilton Memorial Library, Tulane
University

        Burruss Family Papers

        Mrs. Isaac Hilliard Diary

        Plantation Record Book, 1850–61

        David Rees Papers

        St. Rosalie Plantation and Andrew Durnford Papers

        Weeks Family Papers

St. Francisville, Louisiana

    West Feliciana Parish Historical Society Library and Archives

        Evans Papers

Trenton, New Jersey

    New Jersey State Archives

        Newspapers Collection

PRIVATE COLLECTIONS

St. Joseph, Louisiana

Kirk Boundurant Family Papers

PUBLIC RECORDS

Abbeville, Louisiana
  Conveyance Records, Vermilion Parish Courthouse
  Probate Records, Vermilion Parish Courthouse
Alexandria, Louisiana
  Conveyance Records, Rapides Parish Courthouse
  Probate Records, Rapides Parish Courthouse
Baton Rouge, Louisiana
  Conveyance Records, East Baton Rouge Parish Courthouse
  Probate Records, East Baton Rouge Parish Courthouse
Clinton, Louisiana
  Conveyance Records, East Feliciana Parish Courthouse
  Probate Records, East Feliciana Parish Courthouse
Convent, Louisiana
  Conveyance Records, St. James Parish Courthouse
  Probate Records, St. James Parish Courthouse
Donaldsonville, Louisiana
  Conveyance Records, Ascension Parish Courthouse
  Probate Records, Ascension Parish Courthouse
Farmerville, Louisiana
  Probate Records, Union Parish Courthouse
Franklin, Louisiana
  Conveyance Records, St. Mary Parish Courthouse
  Court Records, St. Mary Parish Courthouse
  Mortgage Records, St. Mary Parish Courthouse
  Probate Records, St. Mary Parish Courthouse
Hahnville, Louisiana
  Conveyance Records, St. Charles Parish Courthouse
  Probate Records, St. Charles Parish Courthouse
Harrisonburg, Louisiana
  Conveyance Records, Catahoula Parish Courthouse
  Probate Records, Catahoula Parish Courthouse
Homer, Louisiana
  Probate Records, Claiborne Parish Courthouse
Lafayette, Louisiana
  Probate Records, Lafayette Parish Courthouse
Lake Charles, Louisiana
  Probate Records, Calcasieu Parish Courthouse
Lake Providence, Louisiana
  Conveyance Records, East Carroll Parish Courthouse

Probate Records, East Carroll Parish Courthouse
Lexington, Kentucky
  Conveyance Records, Fayette County Courthouse
  Mortgage Records, Fayette County Courthouse
  Probate Records, Fayette County Courthouse
Mansfield, Louisiana
  Conveyance Records, De Soto Parish Courthouse
  Probate Records, De Soto Parish Courthouse
Marksville, Louisiana
  Conveyance Records, Avoyelles Parish Courthouse
  Probate Records, Avoyelles Parish Courthouse
Napoleonville, Louisiana
  Conveyance Records, Assumption Parish Courthouse
  Probate Records, Assumption Parish Courthouse
Natchitoches, Louisiana
  Conveyance Records, Natchitoches Parish Courthouse
  Probate Records, Natchitoches Parish Courthouse
New Orleans, Louisiana
  Conveyance Records, Orleans Parish Courthouse
  Probate Records, Orleans Parish Courthouse
New Roads, Louisiana
  Conveyance Records, Pointe Coupee Parish Courthouse
  Probate Records, Pointe Coupee Parish Courthouse
Opelousas, Louisiana
  Conveyance Records, St. Landry Parish Courthouse
  Probate Records, St. Landry Parish Courthouse
Plaquemine, Louisiana
  Conveyance Records, Iberville Parish Courthouse
  Court Records, Iberville Parish Courthouse
  Mortgage Records, Iberville Parish Courthouse
  Probate Records, Iberville Parish Courthouse
St. Francisville, Louisiana
  Conveyance Records, West Feliciana Parish Courthouse
  Mortgage Records, West Feliciana Parish Courthouse
  Probate Records, West Feliciana Parish Courthouse
  Tax Records, West Feliciana Parish Courthouse
St. Joseph, Louisiana
  Conveyance Records, Tensas Parish Courthouse
  Probate Records, Tensas Parish Courthouse
St. Martinsville, Louisiana
  Conveyance Records, St. Martin Parish Courthouse

Court Records, St. Martin Parish Courthouse
Probate Records, St. Martin Parish Courthouse
Thibodaux, Louisiana
Conveyance Records, Lafourche Parish Courthouse
Probate Records, Lafourche Parish Courthouse
Vidalia, Louisiana
Conveyance Records, Concordia Parish Courthouse
Mortgage Records, Concordia Parish Courthouse
Probate Records, Concordia Parish Courthouse
Washington, D.C.
National Archives
U.S. Census, 1810, 1820, 1830, 1840, 1850, 1860

NEWSPAPERS

Augusta (Georgia) *Chronicle*
Fredonian (New Brunswick, New Jersey)
General Advertiser (New Brunswick, New Jersey)
Morgan City Review
New Iberia Enterprise
New Jersey Journal (Elizabeth Town, New Jersey)
New Orleans Chronicle
New Orleans Daily Picayune
Planter's Banner (Franklin, Louisiana)
St. Francisville Democrat

BOOKS, ARTICLES, AND DISSERTATIONS

Abernathy, Thomas P. *The South in the New Nation, 1789–1819.* Baton Rouge: Louisiana State University Press and the Littlefield Fund for Southern History, 1961.
Anderson, John Q., ed. *Brokenburn: The Journal of Kate Stone, 1861–1868.* Baton Rouge: Louisiana State University Press, 1955.
Arthur, Stanley Clishy, *The Story of the West Florida Rebellion.* St. Francisville: *St. Francisville Democrat*, 1935.
Back, Troy L., and Brashear, Leon. *The Brashear Story: A Family History.* Arlington, Va., 1963.
Bailey, David T. "A Divided Prism: Two Sources of Black Testimony on Slavery." *Journal of Southern History* 46 (Aug. 1980): 381–404.
———. *Shadow on the Church: Southwestern Evangelical Religion and the Issue of Slavery, 1783–1860.* Ithaca: Cornell University Press, 1985.

Bergerie, Maurine. *They Tasted Bayou Water: A Brief History of Iberia Parish.* New Orleans: Pelican Publishing Company, 1962.

Berkner, Lutz. "Household Arithmetic: A Note." *Journal of Family History* 2 (Summer 1977): 159–62.

———. "The Stem Family and the Developmental Cycle of the Peasant Household: An Eighteenth Century Example." *American Historical Review* 77 (1972): 393–418.

———. "The Use and Misuse of Census Data for the Historical Analysis of Family Structure." *Journal of Interdisciplinary History* 5 (1975): 721–38.

Biographical and Historical Memoirs of Louisiana. Vols. 1 and 2. 1892. Reprint. Baton Rouge: Claitor's, 1975.

Blassingame, John W. *The Slave Community: Plantation Life in the Antebellum South.* New York: Oxford University Press, 1972.

———. *Slave Testimony: Two Centuries of Letters, Speeches, Interviews, and Autobiographies.* Baton Rouge: Louisiana State University Press, 1977.

Boles, John B. *Black Southerners, 1619–1869.* Lexington: University Press of Kentucky, 1983.

———. "Evangelical Protestantism in the Old South: From Religious Dissent to Cultural Dominance." In *Religion in the South*, ed. Charles R. Wilson, pp. 13–34. Jackson: University Press of Mississippi, 1985.

———, ed. *Masters and Slaves in the House of the Lord: Race and Religion in the American South, 1740–1870.* Lexington: University Press of Kentucky, 1988.

Burton, Orville Vernon. *In My Father's House Are Many Mansions: Family and Community in Edgefield, South Carolina.* 1985. Reprint. Chapel Hill: University of North Carolina Press, 1987.

Campbell, John. "Work, Pregnancy, and Infant Mortality among Southern Slaves." *Journal of Interdisciplinary History* 14 (Spring 1984): 793–812.

Catterall, Helen T., ed. *Judicial Cases Concerning American Slavery and the Negro.* Vol. 3 of 5 vols. Washington, D.C.: Carnegie Institution of Washington, 1926. Reprint. New York: Negro Universities Press, 1968.

Clark, John G. *New Orleans, 1718–1812: An Economic History.* Baton Rouge: Louisiana State University Press, 1970.

Clarke, Lewis, and Milton Clarke. *Narrative of the Sufferings of Lewis and Milton Clarke, Sons of a Soldier of the Revolution: During a Captivity of More Than Twenty Years among the Slaveholders of Kentucky.* Boston: Bela Marsh Publishers, 1846.

Clift, G. Glenn. *Second Census of Kentucky, 1800.* 1954. Reprint. Lexington: Genealogical Publishing Company, 1979.

Clinton, Catherine. *The Plantation Mistress: Woman's World in the Old South.* New York: Pantheon Books, 1982.

Cody, Cheryll Ann. "Naming, Kinship, and Estate Dispersal: Notes on Slave Family Life on a South Carolina Plantation, 1786 to 1833." *William and Mary Quarterly* 3d ser., 39 (Jan. 1982): 192–211.

——. "Slave Demography and Family Formation: A Community Study of the Ball Family Plantations, 1720–1896." Ph.D. dissertation, University of Minnesota, 1982.

——. "There Was No 'Absolom' on the Ball Plantations: Slave-Naming Patterns in the South Carolina Low Country, 1720–1865." *American Historical Review* 92 (June 1987): 563–96.

Collins, Richard H. *History of Kentucky.* Louisville: John P. Morton, 1924.

Conrad, Glenn R. *The Attakapas Domesday Book: Land Grants, Claims, and Confirmations in the Attakapas District, 1764–1826.* Lafayette, La.: Center for Louisiana Studies, 1990.

Craton, Michael. "Changing Patterns of Slave Families in the British West Indies." *Journal of Interdisciplinary History* 10 (Summer 1979): 1–35.

Crawford, Stephen C. "Quantified Memory: A Study of the WPA and Fisk University Slave Narrative Collections." Ph.D. dissertation, University of Chicago, 1980.

Creel, Margaret Washington. *"A Peculiar People": Slave Religion and Community Culture among the Gullahs.* New York: New York University Press, 1988.

Crowley, John. "The Importance of Kinship: Testamentary Evidence from South Carolina." *Journal of Interdisciplinary History* 16 (Spring 1986): 559–77.

David, Paul A., et al. *Reckoning with Slavery: A Critical Study in the Quantitative History of American Negro Slavery.* New York: Oxford University Press, 1976.

David, Paul A., and Peter Temin. "Capitalist Masters, Bourgeois Slaves." *Journal of Interdisciplinary History* 5 (Winter 1975): 445–57.

Davis, David Brion. *The Problem of Slavery in the Age of Revolution, 1770–1823.* Ithaca: Cornell University Press, 1975.

——. *The Problem of Slavery in Western Culture.* Ithaca: Cornell University Press, 1966.

——. *Slavery and Human Progress.* New York: Oxford University Press, 1984.

Davis, Edwin Adams. *Louisiana: A Narrative History.* Baton Rouge: Claitor's, 1976.

——. "Slavery and the Post–World War II Historians." *Daedalus* 103 (Spring 1974): 1–16.

——, ed. *Plantation Life in the Florida Parishes of Louisiana, 1836–1846: As Reflected in the Diary of Bennet H. Barrow.* New York: Columbia University Press, 1943.

De Bow, J. D. B. *Statistical View of the United States: A Compendium of the Seventh Census.* Washington, D.C.: Beverly Tucker, Senate Publisher, 1854.

Dew, Charles. "David Ross and the Oxford Iron Works: A Study of Industrial Slavery in the Early American Nineteenth Century South." *William and Mary Quarterly* 3d ser., 31 (July 1974): 189–224.

Diedrich, Maria. " 'My Love Is Black as Yours Is Fair': Premarital Love and Sexuality in the Antebellum Slave Narrative." *Phylon* 47 (Sept. 1986): 238–47.

Dormon, James M. "Aspects of Acadiana Plantation Life in the Mid-Nineteenth Century: A Microcosmic View." *Louisiana History* 16 (Winter 1975): 361–70.

Douglass, Frederick. *Life and Times of Frederick Douglass: His Early Life as a Slave, His Escape from Bondage, and His Complete History.* 1892. Reprint. New York: Bonanza Books, 1962.

Drew, Benjamin. *A North-Side View of Slavery: The Refugees or the Narratives of the Fugitive Slaves in Canada*. 1856. Reprint. New York: Johnson Reprint Company, 1958.

Dunn, Richard S. "Servants and Slaves: The Recruitment and Employment of Labor." In *Colonial British America: Essays in the Early Modern Era*, ed. Jack P. Greene and J. R. Pole, pp. 157–94. Baltimore: Johns Hopkins University Press, 1984.

———. "A Tale of Two Plantations: Slave Life at Mesopotamia in Jamaica and Mount Airy in Virginia, 1789 to 1828." *William and Mary Quarterly* 3d. ser., 34 (Jan. 1977): 32–65.

Eaton, W. Clement. *A History of the Old South*. New York: Macmillan, 1966.

Eblen, Jack E. "New Estimates of the Vital Rates of the United States Black Population in the Nineteenth Century." *Demography* 11 (May 1974): 300–319.

Edmonds, David C. *Yankee Autumn in Acadiana: A Narrative of the Great Overland Expedition through Southwestern Louisiana, October–December, 1863*. Lafayette, La.: N.p., 1979.

Elkins, Stanley M. *Slavery: A Problem in American Institutional and Intellectual Life*. Chicago: University of Chicago Press, 1959.

Engerman, Stanley L. "Studying the Black Family, a Review Essay of *The Black Family* by Herbert G. Gutman." *Journal of Interdisciplinary History* 3 (Mar. 1978): 78–101.

Engerman, Stanley L., Robert W. Fogel, and Eugene Genovese. "New Directions in Black History." *Forum: A Journal of Social Commentary and the Arts* 1 (1972): 22–41.

Escott, Paul D. *Slavery Remembered: A Record of Twentieth-Century Slave Narratives*. Chapel Hill: University of North Carolina Press, 1979.

Faust, Drew Gilpin. "Culture, Conflict, and Community: The Meaning of Power on an Ante-Bellum Plantation." *Journal of Social History* 14 (Fall 1980): 83–98.

Featherstonhaugh, G. W. *Excursion through the Slave States*. 1844. Reprint. New York: Harper, 1968.

Fee, Walter R. *The Transition from Aristocracy to Democracy in New Jersey, 1789–1829*. Somerset, N.J.: Somerset Press, 1933.

Field, Phyllis F. *The Politics of Race in New York: The Struggle for Black Suffrage in the Civil War Era*. Ithaca: Cornell University Press, 1982.

Finch, L. Boyd. "Surprise at Brashear City: Sherod Hunter's Sugar Cooler Cavalry." *Louisiana History* 25 (Fall 1984): 403–34.

Fine, Mark, Andrew I. Schwebel, and Linda James-Myers. "Family Stability in Black Families: Values Underlying Three Different Perspectives." *Journal of Comparative Family Studies* 18 (Spring 1987): 1–23.

Flint, Timothy. *Recollections of the Last Ten Years, Passed in Occasional Residence and Journeys in the Valley of the Mississippi*. 1826. Reprint. New York: Knopf, 1932.

Fogel, Robert William. *Without Consent or Contract: The Rise and Fall of American Slavery*. New York: Norton, 1989.

Fogel, Robert William, and Stanley L. Engerman. *Time on the Cross*. 2 vols. Boston: Little, Brown, 1974.

Fortes, Meyer. *The Web of Kinship among the Tallensi*. Oxford: Oxford University Press, 1949.

Fox-Genovese, Elizabeth. *Within the Plantation Household: Black and White Women of the Old South.* Chapel Hill: University of North Carolina Press, 1988.

Frazier, E. Franklin. *The Negro Family in the United States.* Chicago: University of Chicago Press, 1939.

Friedman, Gerald C. "The Demography of Trinidad Slavery." Paper presented at Workshop in Economic History, Harvard University, 1980.

Genovese, Eugene D. *Roll, Jordan, Roll: The World the Slaves Made.* 1974. Reprint. New York: Vintage Books, 1975.

Genovese, Eugene D., and Elizabeth Fox-Genovese. "The Religious Ideals of Southern Slave Society." *Georgia Historical Quarterly* 70 (Spring 1986): 1–16.

Goody, Jack, ed. *The Developmental Cycle in Domestic Groups.* Cambridge: Cambridge University Press, 1971.

Gray, Laman A. "Ephraim McDowell: Father of Abdominal Surgery, Biographical Data." *Filson Club Historical Quarterly* 43 (1969): 218–26.

Gutman, Herbert G. *The Black Family in Slavery and Freedom, 1750–1925.* New York: Pantheon, 1976.

——. "Persistent Myths about the Afro-American Family." *Journal of Interdisciplinary History* 6 (Autumn 1975): 181–210.

——. *Slavery and the Numbers Game: A Critique of Time on the Cross.* Urbana: University of Illinois Press, 1975.

Gutman, Herbert, and Richard Sutch. "The Slave Family: Protected Agent of Capitalist Masters or Victim of the Slave Trade?" In *Reckoning with Slavery,* ed. Paul A. David et al., pp. 94–133. New York: Oxford University Press, 1976.

——. "Victorians All? The Sexual Mores and Conduct of Slaves and Their Masters." In *Reckoning with Slavery,* ed. Paul A. David et al., pp. 134–62. New York: Oxford University Press, 1976.

Hall, Robert L. "Black and White Christians in Florida, 1822–1860." In *Masters and Slaves in the House of the Lord: Race and Religion in the American South, 1740–1870,* ed. John B. Boles, pp. 81–98. Lexington: University Press of Kentucky, 1988.

——. "'Yonder Come Day': Religious Dimensions of the Transition from Slavery to Freedom in Florida." *Florida Historical Quarterly* 65 (Apr. 1987): 411–32.

Handler, Jerome S., and Robert S. Corruccini. "Plantation Life in Barbados: A Physical and Anthropological Analysis." *Journal of Interdisciplinary History* 14 (Summer 1983): 65–90.

Hareven, Tamara. "Cycles, Cohorts: Reflections on Theoretical and Methodological Approaches to the Historical Study of Family Development." *Journal of Social History* 1 (Fall 1978): 98–109.

——. "Family History at the Crossroads." *Journal of Family History* 12 (1987): ix–xxiii.

——, ed. *Transitions: The Family and Life Course in Historical Perspective.* New York: Academic Press, 1978.

Hepworth, George H. *The Whip, Hoe, and Sword; Or, The Gulf Department in '63.* 1864. Edited by Joe Gray Taylor. Baton Rouge: Louisiana State University Press, 1979.

Higman, B. W. "African and Creole Slave Family Patterns in Trinidad." *Journal of the Family* 3 (Summer 1978): 163–80.

———. "Household Structure and Fertility on Jamaican Slave Plantations: A Nineteenth Century Example." *Population Studies* 27 (1973): 527–50.

———. "The Slave Family and Household in the British West Indies, 1800–1834." *Journal of Interdisciplinary History* 6 (Autumn 1975): 261–87.

———. *Slave Populations of the British Caribbean, 1797–1834.* Baltimore: Johns Hopkins University Press, 1964.

Hilliard, Sam Bowers. *Atlas of Antebellum Southern Agriculture.* Baton Rouge: Louisiana State University Press, 1984.

Holmes, Isaac. *An Account of the United States of America.* London: Caxton Press, 1823.

Hutchinson, Janis. "The Age-Sex Structure of the Slave Population in Harris County, Texas, 1850 and 1860." *American Journal of Physical Anthropology* 74 (Oct. 1987): 231–38.

Inscoe, John S. "Carolina Slave Names: An Index to Acculturation." *Journal of Southern History* 49 (Nov. 1983): 527–54.

James, Larry M. "Biracial Fellowship in Antebellum Baptist Churches." In *Masters and Slaves in the House of the Lord: Race and Religion in the American South, 1740–1870,* ed. John B. Boles, pp. 37–57. Lexington: University Press of Kentucky.

Jillson, Willard Rouse. "Flamma Clara Maturae Medicinae Kentuckiensis." *Filson Club Quarterly* 27 (1953): 152–65.

———. *Old Kentucky Entries and Deeds.* Baltimore: Genealogical Publishing Company, 1979.

John, Ann Meredith. "The Demography of Slavery in the Nineteenth Century Trinidad." Ph.D. dissertation, Princeton University, 1984.

Johnson, Cecil. *British West Florida, 1763–1783.* New Haven: Yale University Press, 1943.

Johnson, Michael P. "Runaway Slaves and the Slave Community in South Carolina, 1799–1830." *William and Mary Quarterly* 3d ser., 38 (July 1981): 418–41.

———. "Smothered Slave Infants: Were Slave Mothers at Fault?" *Journal of Southern History* 47 (Nov. 1981): 493–520.

Jones, Jacqueline. *Labor of Love, Labor of Sorrow: Black Women, Work, and the Family from Slavery to the Present.* 1985. Reprint. New York: Vintage Books, 1986.

Joyner, Charles. *Down by the Riverside: A South Carolina Slave Community.* Urbana: University of Illinois Press, 1984.

Katz, Michael B., Michael J. Doucet, and Mark J. Stern. *The Social Organization of Early Industrial Capitalism.* Cambridge, Mass.: Harvard University Press, 1982.

Katz, William L. *Eyewitness: The Negro in American History.* New York: Pitman, 1967.

Kennedy, Joseph C. G. *Preliminary Report of the Eighth Census, 1860.* Washington, D.C.: Government Printing Office, 1862.

Kertzer, David I. "Anthropology and Family History." *Journal of Family History* 9 (Fall 1984): 201–16.

———. "Future Directions in Historical Household Studies." *Journal of Family History* 10 (Spring 1985): 98–107.

King, J. R. "African Survivals in the Black American Family: Key Factors in Stability." *Journal of Afro-American Issues* 4 (1976): 153–67.

Kiple, Kenneth F., and Virginia Kiple. "Slave Child Mortality: Some Nutritional Answers to a Perennial Puzzle." *Journal of Social History* 10 (Mar. 1977): 284–310.

Klein, Herbert S., and Stanley Engerman. "Fertility Differentials between Slaves in the United States and the British West Indies: A Note on Lactation Practices and Their Possible Implications." *William and Mary Quarterly* 3d ser., 35 (Apr. 1978): 357–74.

Kolchin, Peter. "Reevaluating the Antebellum Slave Community: A Comparative Perspective." *Journal of American History* 70 (Dec. 1983): 579–601.

Krech, Shepard III. "Black Family Organization in the Nineteenth Century: An Ethnological Perspective." *Journal of Interdisciplinary History* 12 (Winter 1982): 429–52.

Kulikoff, Alan. "The Beginnings of the Afro-American Family in Maryland." In *Law, Society, and Politics in Early Maryland*, ed. Aubrey Land, Lois G. Carr, and Edward C. Papenfuse, pp. 171–96. Baltimore: Johns Hopkins University Press, 1977.

———. *Tobacco and Slaves: The Development of Southern Cultures in the Chesapeake, 1680–1800*. Chapel Hill: University of North Carolina Press, 1986.

Labinjoh, Justin. "The Sexual Life of the Oppressed: An Examination of the Family Life of Ante-Bellum Slaves." *Phylon* 35 (1974): 375–97.

Lantz, Herman, and Lewellyn Hendrix. "Black Fertility and the Black Family in the Nineteenth Century: A Re-examination of the Past." *Journal of Family History* 3 (Fall 1978): 251–61.

Laslett, Peter. "The Character of Familial History: Its Limitations and the Conditions for Its Proper Pursuit." *Journal of Family History* 12 (1987): 263–84.

———. "The Family Cycle and the Process of Socialization: Characteristics of the Western Pattern Considered Over Time." Paper for Thirteenth International Sociological Association, Paris, 1973.

———. *Family Life and Illicit Love in Earlier Generations: Essays in Historical Sociology*. Cambridge: Cambridge University Press, 1977.

———. *The World We Have Lost: England before the Industrial Age*. New York: Scribner's, 1965.

Laslett, Peter, and Richard Wall, eds. *Household and Family in Past Time*. Cambridge: Cambridge University Press, 1972.

Levine, Lawrence W. *Black Culture and Black Consciousness: Afro-American Folk Thought from Slavery to Freedom*. New York: Oxford University Press, 1977.

Littlefield, Daniel C. *Rice and Slaves: Ethnicity and the Slave Trade in Colonial South Carolina*. Baton Rouge: Louisiana State University Press, 1981.

Litwack, Leon. *North of Slavery: The Negro in the Free States, 1790–1860*. Chicago: University of Chicago Press, 1961.

McDowell, Robert E. "Bullitt's Lick: The Related Saltworks and Settlements." *Filson Club Quarterly* 30 (1956): 241–69.

McGowan, James Thomas. "Creation of a Slave Society: Louisiana Plantations in the Eighteenth Century." Ph.D. dissertation, University of Rochester, 1976.

McLemore, Richard Aubrey. *A History of Mississippi*, Vol. 1 of 2 vols. Jackson: University and College Press of Mississippi, 1973.

Malone, Ann Patton. "Searching for the Family and Household Structure of Rural Louisiana Slaves, 1810–1864." *Louisiana History* 28 (Fall 1987): 357–79.

Mathews, Donald G. "Charles Colcock Jones and the Southern Evangelical Crusade to Form a Biracial Community." *Journal of Southern History* 41 (Aug. 1975): 299–320.

———. *Religion in the Old South.* Chicago: University of Chicago Press, 1977.

Menard, Russell E. "The Maryland Slave Population, 1658 to 1730: A Demographic Profile of Blacks in Four Counties." *William and Mary Quarterly* 3d ser., 32 (Jan. 1975): 29–54.

Menn, Joseph Karl. *The Large Slaveholders of Louisiana, 1860.* New Orleans: Pelican, 1964.

Miller, Joseph C. "Mortality in the Atlantic Slave Trade: Statistical Evidence on Causality." *Journal of Interdisciplinary History* 11 (Winter 1981): 285–323.

Miller, Randall M. "Black Catholics in the Slave South: Some Needs and Opportunities for Study." *Records of the American Historical Society* 86 (1975): 93–106.

———. "The Failed Mission: The Catholic Church and Black Catholics in the Old South." In *The Southern Common People: Studies in Nineteenth-Century Social History*, ed. Edward Magdol and Jon L. Wakelyn, pp. 37–54. Westport, Conn.: Greenwood Press, 1980.

———. "Slaves and Southern Catholicism." In *Masters and Slaves in the House of the Lord: Race and Religion in the American South, 1740–1870*, ed. John B. Boles, pp. 127–52. Lexington: University Press of Kentucky, 1988.

Mohr, Clarence L. "Slaves and White Churches in Confederate Georgia." In *Masters and Slaves in the House of the Lord: Race and Religion in the American South, 1740–1870*, ed. John B. Boles, pp. 153–72. Lexington: University Press of Kentucky, 1988.

Molen, Patricia A. "Population and Social Patterns in Barbadoes in the Early Eighteenth Century." *William and Mary Quarterly* 3d ser., 28 (Apr. 1971): 287–300.

Moody, V. Alton. "Slavery on Louisiana Sugar Plantations." *Louisiana Historical Quarterly* 7 (Apr. 1924): 190–301.

Morrissey, Marietta. "Women's Work, Family Formation, and Reproduction among Caribbean Slaves." *Review* 9 (Winter 1986): 339–68.

Moynihan, Daniel P. *The Negro Family: The Case for National Action.* Washington, D.C.: Department of Labor, Office of Policy Planning and Research, 1965.

New Jersey 28, 43, *Laws* and *Minutes* of the Assembly and Council.

Northup, Solomon. *Twelve Years a Slave.* Edited by Sue Eakin and Joseph Logsdon. Baton Rouge: Louisiana State University Press, 1968.

Olmsted, Frederic Law. *The Cotton Kingdom.* Edited by Arthur M. Schlesinger. New York: Knopf, 1953.

———. *The Slave States.* Edited by Harvey Wish. New York: G. P. Putnam's Sons, 1959.

Olsen, Jennifer, and J. Lawrence Angel. "Life Stresses of Slavery." *American Journal of Physical Anthropology* 74 (Oct. 1987): 199–211.

Owens, Leslie H. *This Species of Property: Slave Life and Culture in the Old South.* New York: Oxford University Press, 1976.

Owsley, Douglas W., Charles E. Owsley, and Robert W. Mann. "Demography and Pathology of an Urban Slave Population from New Orleans." *American Journal of Physical Anthropology* 74 (Oct. 1987): 185–97.

Peltier, C. J., Jr., and Lela King Lehman, comps. and eds. *A History of Morgan City, Louisiana.* Morgan City: Morgan City Historical Society, 1960.

Phillips, U. B. *American Negro Slavery: A Survey of the Supply, Employment, and Control of Negro Labor as Determined by the Plantation Regime.* 1918. Reprint. Baton Rouge: Louisiana State University Press, 1966.

Price, Clement Alexander, comp. and ed. *Freedom Not Far Distant: A Documentary History of Afro-Americans in New Jersey.* Newark: New Jersey Historical Society, 1980.

Raboteau, Albert J. *Slave Religion: The "Invisible Institution" in the Antebellum South.* Oxford: Oxford University Press, 1978.

Raphael, Morris. *The Battle in the Bayou Country.* Detroit: Harlo Press, 1975.

Rawick, George P. *From Sundown to Sunup: The Making of the Black Community.* New York: Oxford University Press, 1972.

———, ed. *The American Slave: A Composite Autobiography.* Ser. 1 and 2. 19 vols. Westport, Conn.: Greenwood Press, 1972.

———. *The American Slave: A Composite Autobiography.* Supp. Ser. 2. 10 vols. Westport, Conn.: Greenwood Press, 1977.

"The Religious Life of the Negro Slave." *Harper's Monthly Magazine,* June–Nov. 1863.

Reports of the Superintendent of the Census, Seventh Census, December 1, 1851–December 1, 1852. Washington, D.C.: Robert Armstrong, Printer, 1853.

Rice, Duncan. *The Rise and Fall of Black Slavery.* Baton Rouge: Louisiana State University Press, 1975.

Ripley, C. Peter. "The Black Family in Transition: Louisiana, 1860–1865." *Journal of Southern History* 41 (Aug. 1975): 369–81.

———. *Slaves and Freedmen in Civil War Louisiana.* Baton Rouge: Louisiana State University Press, 1976.

Robinson, Elrie. *Early Feliciana Politics.* St. Francisville: *St. Francisville Democrat,* 1936.

Rogers, Marcia Westerfield. "Oakland: Sarah's Dream." *St. Francisville Democrat,* 11 Mar. 1976.

Roland, Charles P. *Louisiana Sugar Plantations during the Civil War.* Leiden: E. J. Brill, 1957.

Rosengarten, Theodore. *Tombee: Portrait of a Cotton Planter.* New York: McGraw-Hill, 1987.

Rutman, Darrett B., Charles Wetherell, and Anita H. Rutman. "Rhythms of Life: Black and White Seasonality in the Early Chesapeake." *Journal of Interdisciplinary History* 11 (Summer 1980): 29–53.

Sanders, Mary Elizabeth, comp. *Selected Annotated Abstracts of Marriages: St. Mary Parish, Louisiana, 1811–1829.* Vol. 1. New Iberia, La.: N.p., 1973.

———. *Annotated Abstracts of the Successions of St. Mary Parish, Louisiana.* New Iberia, La.: N.p., 1972.

———. *Selected Annotated Abstracts of St. Mary Parish, Louisiana, Court Records, 1811–1837.* Vol. 3. New Iberia, La.: N.p., 1978.

Savitt, Todd L. "Smothering and Overlaying of Virginia Slave Children: A Suggested Explanation." *Bulletin of the History of Medicine* 49 (Fall 1975): 400–406.

Scarborough, William K. *The Overseer: Plantation Management in the Old South.* Baton Rouge: Louisiana State University Press, 1966.

Scott, Anne Firor. *The Southern Lady: From Pedestal to Politics, 1830–1930.* Chicago: University of Chicago Press, 1979.

Segalen, Martine. "The Family Cycle and Household Structure: Five Generations in a French Village." *Journal of Family History* 2 (Fall 1977): 223–36.

Seider, Reinhard, and Michael Mitteraurer. "The Reconstruction of the Family Life Course: Theoretical Problems and Empirical Results." In *Family Forms in Historic Europe*, ed. Richard Wall, Jean Robin, and Peter Laslett, pp. 304–45. Cambridge: Cambridge University Press, 1983.

Sernett, Milton C. *Black Religion and American Evangelicalism: White Protestants, Plantation Missions, and the Flowering of Negro Christianity, 1787–1865.* Metuchen, N.J.: Scarecrow Press, 1975.

Shiflett, Crandall A. "The Household Composition of Rural Black Families: Louisia County, Virginia, 1880." *Journal of Interdisciplinary History* 6 (Autumn 1975): 235–60.

Shorter, Edward. *The Making of the Modern Family.* New York: Basic Books, 1977.

Sitterson, J. C. "The McCollams: A Planter Family of the Old and New South." *Journal of Southern History* 6 (Aug. 1940): 347–67.

———. *Sugar Country: The Cane Sugar Industry in the South, 1753–1950.* Lexington: University of Kentucky Press, 1953.

Smedes, Susan Dabney. *Memorials of a Southern Planter.* Edited by Fletcher M. Green. New York: Knopf, 1968.

Smith, Daniel Blake. "The Study of the Family in Early America: Trends, Problems, and Prospects." *William and Mary Quarterly* 3d ser., 39 (Jan. 1982): 3–28.

Smith, Raymond. "The Matrifocal Family." In *The Character of Kinship*, ed. Jack Goody, pp. 121–44. Cambridge: Cambridge University Press, 1973.

———. *The Negro Family in British Guiana: Family Structure and Social Status in the Villages.* London: Routledge & Kegan Paul, 1956.

———. "The Nuclear Family in Afro-American Kinship." *Journal of Comparative Family Studies* 1 (Autumn 1970): 57–70.

Sobel, Mechal. *Trabelin' On: The Slave Journey to an Afro-Baptist Faith*. Westport, Conn.: Greenwood Press, 1979.

Sparks, Randy J. "Religion in Amite County, Mississippi, 1800–1861." In *Masters and Slaves in the House of the Lord: Race and Religion in the American South, 1740–1870*, ed. John B. Boles, pp. 58–80. Lexington: University Press of Kentucky.

Stampp, Kenneth M. *The Peculiar Institution: Slavery in the Ante-Bellum South*. 1956. Reprint. New York: Vintage Books, 1964.

Steckel, Richard H. "Birth Weights and Infant Mortality among American Slaves." *Explorations in Economic History* 23 (Apr. 1986): 173–98.

———. *The Economics of U.S. Slave and Southern White Fertility*. New York: Garland, 1985.

———. "Miscegenation and the American Slave Schedules." *Journal of Interdisciplinary History* 11 (Autumn 1980): 251–63.

———. "A Peculiar Population: The Nutrition, Health, and Mortality of American Slaves from Childhood to Maturity." *Journal of Economic History* 45 (Sept. 1986): 721–41.

———. "Slave Height Profiles from Coastwise Manifests." *Explorations in Economic History* 16 (1971): 363–80.

Stone, Lawrence. "Family History in the 1980s: Past Achievements and Present Trends." *Journal of Southern History* 12 (Summer 1981): 51–82.

Stroyer, Jacob. *Sketches of My Life in the South*. Vol. 1. Salem: Newcomb and Gaves, 1879, 1898.

Stuckey, Sterling. *Slave Culture: Nationalist Theory and the Foundations of Black America*. New York: Oxford University Press, 1987.

———. "Through the Prism of Folklore: The Black Ethos in Slavery." *Massachusetts Review* 9 (1968): 417–37.

Sudarkasa, Niaea. "African and Afro-American Structure: A Comparison." *Black Scholar* 8 (Nov.–Dec. 1980): 37–60.

———. "Interpreting the African Heritage in Afro-American Family Organization." In *Black Families*, ed. Harriette Pipes McAdoo, pp. 37–53. Beverly Hills: Sage, 1981.

Sydnor, Charles S. *Slavery in Mississippi*. Baton Rouge: Louisiana State University Press, 1966.

Tadman, Michael. "Slave Trading in the Antebellum South: An Estimate of the Inter-Regional Slave Trade." *Journal of American Studies* 13 (1979): 195–220.

———. *Speculators and Slaves: Masters, Traders, and Slaves in the Old South*. Madison: University of Wisconsin Press, 1989.

Tanner, Nancy. "Matrifocality in Indonesia and Africa and among Black Americans." In *Woman, Culture, and Society*, ed. Michelle Zimbalist Rosaldo and Louise Lamphere, pp. 129–56. Stanford: Stanford University Press, 1974.

Taylor, Gertrude C. "Saga of Petite Anse Island." *Attakapas Gazette* 19 (Winter 1984): 159–64.

Taylor, Joe Gray. *Louisiana: A Bicentennial History*. New York: Norton, 1976.

———. *Louisiana Reconstructed, 1863–1877*. Baton Rouge: Louisiana State University Press, 1974.

———. *Negro Slavery in Louisiana*. Baton Rouge: Thomas J. Moran's Sons, for Louisiana Historical Association, 1963.

Tilly, Charles. "Family History, Social History, and Social Change." *Journal of Family History* 12 (1987): 319–30.

Touchstone, Blake. "Planters and Slave Religion in the Deep South." In *Masters and Slaves in the House of the Lord: Race and Religion in the American South, 1740–1870*, ed. John B. Boles, pp. 99–126. Lexington: University Press of Kentucky, 1988.

———. "Planters and Slave Religion in the Deep South." Ph.D. dissertation, Tulane University, 1973.

Trussell, James, and Richard Steckel. "The Age of Slaves at Menarche and Their First Births." *Journal of Interdisciplinary History* 8 (Winter 1978): 477–505.

Van Deburg, William L. *The Slave Drivers: Black Agricultural Labor Supervisors in the Antebellum South*. Westport, Conn.: Greenwood Press, 1979.

van der Walle, Etienne. "Household Dynamics in a Belgian Village, 1847–1866." *Journal of Family History* 1 (Autumn 1976): 80–94.

Webber, Thomas L. *Deep Like the Rivers: Education in the Slave Quarter Community, 1831–1865*. New York: Norton, 1978.

Weiner, Marli Frances. "Plantation Mistress/Female Slave: Gender, Race, and South Carolina Women, 1830–1880." Ph.D. dissertation, University of Rochester, 1985.

Weld, Theodore, comp. *American Slavery as It Is*. New York: American Antislavery Society, 1839.

Wetherell, Charles. "Slave Kinship: A Case Study of the South Carolina Good Hope Plantation, 1835–1856." *Journal of Family History* 6 (Fall 1981): 294–308.

Wheaton, Robert. "Family and Kinship in Western Europe: The Problem of the Joint Family Household." *Journal of Interdisciplinary History* 5 (Spring 1975): 606–8.

———. "Observations on the Development of Kinship History." *Journal of Family History* 12 (1987): 285–301.

White, Deborah Gray. *Ar'n't I a Woman? Female Slaves in the Plantation South*. New York: Norton, 1985.

———. "Female Slaves: Sex Roles and Status in the Antebellum South." *Journal of Family History* 8 (Fall 1983): 248–261.

Wilkinson, James. *Memoirs of My Own Times*. Vol. 2 of 3 vols. Philadelphia: Abraham Smalls, 1816.

Wood, Judy Clerc. "The Hayes Family: Pioneers of Petite Anse Island." *Attakapas Gazette* 19 (Winter 1984): 165–73.

Yetman, Norman R., comp. and ed. *Voices from Slavery*. New York: Holt, Rinehart, and Winston, 1970.

Zilversmit, Arthur. *The First Emancipation: The Abolition of Slavery in the North*. Chicago: University of Chicago Press, 1967.